THE EXTERNAL DIMENSION OF THE EU'S POLICY AGAINST TRAFFICKING IN HUMAN BEINGS

This book explores the external dimension of the ambitious EU policy on human trafficking. Through this policy the EU institutions and Member States promote the eradication of human trafficking and support, to that end, cooperation with their partners, being third States or international organisations.

Analysing the unilateral and multilateral mechanisms the EU uses to achieve these aims, the book questions whether the EU's external response to human trafficking addresses it in all its dimensions, and whether it does so in a coherent way. As a case study, the book explores the cooperation of the EU with countries of the Western Balkans, which constitutes a specific unilateral mechanism. The analysis of the multilateral mechanisms covers the cooperation of the EU with key international and regional organisations combating human trafficking, including but not limited to the Council of Europe or the United Nations Office on Drugs and Crime.

The book also examines the impact of the evolution of migration flows and the increasing reliance of military tools on the EU's response to human trafficking.

Volume 15 in the series Hart Studies in European Criminal Law

Hart Studies in European Criminal Law

Series Editors: Professor Katalin Ligeti, University of Luxembourg;
Professor Valsamis Mitsilegas, Queen Mary University of London;
Professor Anne Weyembergh, Brussels Free University

Since the Lisbon Treaty, European criminal law has become an increasingly important field of research and debate. Working with the European Criminal Law Academic Network (ECLAN), the series will publish works of the highest intellectual rigour and cutting edge scholarship which will be required reading for all European criminal lawyers.

The series is happy to consider both edited and single authored titles. The series defines 'European' and 'criminal law' in the broadest sense, so books on European criminal law, justice and policy will be considered. The series also welcomes books which offer different methodological approaches.

Volume 1: *EU Criminal Law after Lisbon: Rights, Trust and the Transformation of Justice in Europe* by Valsamis Mitsilegas

Volume 2: *Challenges in the Field of Economic and Financial Crime in Europe and the US* Edited by Vanessa Franssen and Katalin Ligeti

Volume 3: *Chasing Criminal Money: Challenges and Perspectives On Asset Recovery in the EU* Edited by Katalin Ligeti and Michele Simonato

Volume 4: *Limits to EU Powers: A Case Study of EU Regulatory Criminal Law* by Jacob Öberg

Volume 5: *The Needed Balances in EU Criminal Law: Past, Present and Future* Edited by Chloé Brière and Anne Weyembergh

Volume 6: *Redefining Organised Crime: A Challenge for the European Union?* Edited by Stefania Carnevale, Serena Forlati and Orsetta Giolo

Volume 7: *White Collar Crime: A Comparative Perspective* Edited by Katalin Ligeti and Stanislaw Tosza

Volume 8: *Criminal Liability of Managers in Europe: Punishing Excessive Risk* Stanisław Tosza

Volume 9: *The European Union and Deprivation of Liberty: A Legislative and Judicial Analysis from the Perspective of the Individual* Leandro Mancano

Volume 10: *The Legitimacy of EU Criminal Law* Irene Wieczorek

Volume 11: *The Fight Against Impunity in EU Law* Edited by Luisa Marin and Stefano Montaldo

Volume 12: *Controlling Immigration Through Criminal Law: European and Comparative Perspectives on 'Crimmigration'* Edited by Gian Luigi Gatta, Valsamis Mitsilegas, and Stefano Zirulia

Volume 13: *The Principle of Mutual Trust in EU Criminal Law* Auke Willems

Volume 14: *Surveillance and Privacy in the Digital Age: European, Transatlantic and Global Perspectives* Edited by Valsamis Mitsilegas and Niovi Vavoula

The External Dimension
of the EU's Policy against
Trafficking in Human Beings

Chloé Brière

·HART·
OXFORD · LONDON · NEW YORK · NEW DELHI · SYDNEY

HART PUBLISHING

Bloomsbury Publishing Plc

Kemp House, Chawley Park, Cumnor Hill, Oxford, OX2 9PH, UK

1385 Broadway, New York, NY 10018, USA

29 Earlsfort Terrace, Dublin 2, Ireland

HART PUBLISHING, the Hart/Stag logo, BLOOMSBURY and the Diana logo are
trademarks of Bloomsbury Publishing Plc

First published in Great Britain 2021

A catalogue record for this book is available from the British Library.

Library of Congress Cataloging-in-Publication data

Names: Brière, Chloé, author.

Title: The external dimension of the EU's policy against trafficking in human beings / Chloé Brière.

Description: Oxford, UK ; New York, NY : Hart Publishing, an imprint of Bloomsbury Publishing, 2021. |
Series: Hart studies in European criminal law ; volume 15 | Based on author's thesis
(doctoral – Université Libre de Bruxelles and Université de Genève, 2016) issued under title:
EU policy in the fight against trafficking in human beings : a representative example of the
challenges caused by the externalisation of the Area of Freedom, Security and Justice, |
Includes bibliographical references and index.

Identifiers: LCCN 2020053903 (print) | LCCN 2020053904 (ebook) |
ISBN 9781509932825 (hardback) | ISBN 9781509947218 (paperback) |
ISBN 9781509932849 (pdf) | ISBN 9781509932832 (Epub)

Subjects: LCSH: Human trafficking—Law and legislation—European Union countries. |
European Union countries—Foreign relations—Law and legislation. |
Human trafficking—Law and legislation—Balkan Peninsula.

Classification: LCC KJE8781.H86 B75 2021 (print) | LCC KJE8781.H86 (ebook) |
DDC 345.24/02551—dc23

LC record available at https://lccn.loc.gov/2020053903

LC ebook record available at https://lccn.loc.gov/2020053904

ISBN: HB: 978-1-50993-282-5
        ePDF: 978-1-50993-284-9
        ePub: 978-1-50993-283-2

Typeset by Compuscript Ltd, Shannon

To find out more about our authors and books visit www.hartpublishing.co.uk.
Here you will find extracts, author information, details of forthcoming events
and the option to sign up for our newsletters.

CONTENTS

ABBREVIATIONS

AFSJ	Area of Freedom, Security and Justice
CCPCJ	Commission on Crime Prevention and Criminal Justice
CFSP	Common Foreign and Security Policy
COP	Conference of the Parties to the United Nations Convention against Transnational Organised Crime
CSDP	Common Security and Defence Policy
ECHR	European Convention for the Protection of Human Rights and Fundamental Freedoms
ECJ	Court of Justice of the European Union
ECtHR	European Court of Human Rights
EEAS	European External Action Service
EFTA	European Free Trade Association
ENP	European Neighbourhood Policy
EU	European Union
FRA	European Union Agency for Fundamental Rights
FYROM	Former Yugoslav Republic of Macedonia
GRETA	Group of Experts on Action against Trafficking in Human Beings
HRFASP	High Representative for Foreign Affairs and Security Policy
ICAT	Inter-Agency Coordination Group against Trafficking in Persons
ICMPD	International Centre for Migration Policy Development
ILO	International Labour Organisation
IOM	International Organization for Migration
JHA	Justice and Home Affairs
OJ	Official Journal (European Union)
NGO	Non-governmental Organisation

OHCHR	Office of the High Commissioner for Human Rights
OSCE	Organisation for Security and Cooperation in Europe
PCC – SEE	Police Cooperation Convention for South East Europe
SAA	Stabilisation and Association Agreement
SAARC	South Asian Association for Regional Cooperation
SAP	Stabilisation and Association Process
SEEPAG	Southeast European Prosecutors Advisory Group
SELEC	Southeast European Law Enforcement Centre
SEPCA	Southeast Europe Police Chiefs Association
SOCTA	Serious Organised Crime Threat Assessment
SR/CTHB	Special Representative and Co-ordinator for Combating Trafficking in Human Beings
TEU	Treaty on the European Union
TFEU	Treaty on the Functioning of the European Union
THB	Trafficking in Human Beings
UN	United Nations
UNHCR	United Nations High Commissioner for Refugees
UNODC	United Nations Office on Drugs and Crime
UNICEF	United Nations Children's Emergency Fund
UNSC	United Nations Security Council

Introduction: Setting the Scene

Trafficking in human beings is far from being a neglected and under-researched issue. It is considered as a particularly serious criminal activity, ranking in the top five of the criminal activities generating the most illegal profits, and it concerns all regions and countries of the world. This serious crime is committed by a variety of criminals, acting on their own, in loose networks or in organised criminal groups, exploiting victims in their own State of origin or transporting them across countries and continents to maximise profits. The gravity of the offence is inextricably linked to the severe violations of fundamental rights it entails for its victims. Not only is their human dignity placed under threat, but other basic fundamental rights are violated, starting with the prohibition of slavery, forced labour and exploitation. For victims of this crime, consequences are felt long after their exploitation, which often goes unnoticed, due to the limited identification of trafficking victims, and traffickers benefiting from the low number of prosecutions and convictions to further engage in this low-risk/high-reward criminal activity.

In response to this phenomenon, States have developed specific legislation and policies, including at international level. Whereas some authors have dated the initial stages of the international response back to the instrument adopted to address white slaves' trafficking in the early 1900s, the issue has been the subject of increasing attention since the early 1990s. The adoption of key international instruments on the matter has been closely intertwined with the development of specific regional initiatives focusing on the same matter. In Europe, various regional organisations have been able to participate in such efforts, including among others the Council of Europe, the Organisation for Security and Cooperation in Europe (OSCE) and the European Union (EU). The latter has benefited from the deepening of European integration to develop and implement activities in policy fields particularly relevant to address trafficking in human beings, among which are migration and criminal law, previously belonging to the core of States' sovereign powers. The EU relied upon its progressively gained competences to define strategic objectives and enact European legislation binding on its Member States. While its activities initially focused on supporting internal cross-border criminal cooperation between Member States, counter-trafficking measures were soon introduced to its external activities, either in the framework of its development policy or in the external dimension of the Area of Freedom, Security and Justice (AFSJ).

This introductory chapter is dedicated to an initial exploration of the subject of this dissertation, namely the external dimension of the policy adopted by the EU to combat trafficking in human beings. The first section will be devoted to highlighting how trafficking in human beings remains a global challenge impacting the EU (I), and the second section will clarify the key concepts that will be used throughout the book, such as the definition of trafficking in human beings and the EU's approach to trafficking (II). The third section will present the theoretical framework in which the research is enshrined, the research questions to be addressed and the delimitations made (III). Finally, the main arguments and structure of the book will be set out (IV).

I. Trafficking in Human Beings: A Global Challenge Impacting the EU

According to the United Nations (UN), there are close to 250 million people on the move today in the world. These people leave their countries for different reasons. Some are fleeing conflict and war while others may be escaping serious human rights violations or poverty or may simply be seeking to improve their future. Regardless of their specific reasons or status, these people often find themselves engaging in a perilous journey during which they are in danger and vulnerable to abuse from criminals. These unprecedented flows of people are generating new criminal opportunities, especially for migrant smugglers and human traffickers. The subsequent sections will present the challenges generated by trafficking in human beings at the global level (A) and at the level of the EU (B).

A. Trafficking in Human Beings as a Global Challenge

The crime of trafficking in persons is a global security challenge that concerns all countries, either as a destination, transit or origin country, and all regions of the world. In other words, it affects virtually every country in every region of the world and trafficking flows – imaginary lines that connect the same origin country and destination country of at least five detected victims – criss-cross the world.[1] In addition to being a security threat, trafficking in human beings must also be considered as a human rights issue. Trafficking indeed entails severe violations of the fundamental rights of its victims, protected in international instruments. The provisions protecting against slavery and forced labour are usually interpreted as protecting against trafficking in human beings.[2]

The detection and identification of trafficking situations is essential in order to be able to protect victims and compensate them for the damages they suffer. It is also crucial to prosecute and convict those involved in this criminal activity.

---

[1] UNODC, *Global Report on Trafficking in Persons* (2014) 7.
[2] See in this regard *Rantsev v Cyprus and Russia*, App No 25965/04 (ECtHR, 7 January 2010) and the other cases of the European Court of Human Rights (ECtHR).

However, detection and identification of trafficking in human beings is rendered more difficult because this activity can be conducted by single individuals with a limited organisation in place, especially if the crime involves a few victims who are exploited locally. By comparison, transnational and interregional trafficking flows tend to involve many offenders organised in different types of groups and/or networks.[3] Their typical organisational structure consists of loose, flexible networks linked by kinship or ethnicity with interchangeable roles among members.[4] Their flexibility and adaptability is shown by their presence in several countries and by moving their victims around in different countries. These groups are able to adapt to changing circumstances and quickly respond to new opportunities, shifting their operations to other countries upon detection by law enforcement agencies or if they consider the exploitation to be more profitable elsewhere. Their loose structure thwarts detection, especially of the leaders, even when an operational cell is identified and prosecuted.[5] Despite the diversity in their structures and degrees of organisation, the criminals involved in trafficking in human beings share one characteristic: the belief that it constitutes a highly profitable activity, reported to be among the most lucrative criminal activities in the world, and still perceived as a low-risk/high-reward activity.[6]

The scale of the phenomenon and its frequent transnational dimension together with its consequences for its victims make it a major focus of international attention.

From a historical perspective, concerns about trafficking in human beings started in the early 1900s although the exploitation of human beings was designated at the time by the term 'White Slave Traffic'. The very first international texts dealing with it were conventions adopted in the 1900s seeking to suppress 'White Slavery', understood as the 'criminal traffic' of women and girls for immoral purposes.[7] Later, conventions adopted under the League of Nations decided to address the 'traffic in women' or, in other words, the organised and coerced movement of women and girls abroad for the purposes of prostitution.[8] In 1949, the UN adopted the Convention for the Suppression of Traffic in Persons and the Exploitation of the Prostitution of Others[9] complementing this list of treaties,

---

[3] UNODC, *Global Report* (2014) (n 1) 14.

[4] 'Report on the progress made in the fight against trafficking in human beings', Commission Report to the Council and European Parliament, COM (2016) 267 final, 8.

[5] Europol, *Situation Report, Trafficking in human beings in the EU* (2016) 14.

[6] UNODC, *Global Report* (2014) (n 1) 13. Impunity prevails: 'there are still very few convictions for trafficking in persons. Only 4 in 10 countries reported having 10 or more yearly convictions, with nearly 15 per cent having no convictions at all'.

[7] International Agreement for the Suppression of the 'White Slave Traffic', Paris, 18 May 1904, 1 LNTS 83, entered into force on 18 July 1905, amended by a Protocol approved by the UN General Assembly on 3 December 1948, 30 UNTS 23.

[8] League of Nations, Convention for the Suppression of Traffic in Women and Children, 30 September 1921, 9 LNTS 415; and Convention for the Suppression of the Traffic in Women of Full Age, 11 October 1933, 150 LNTS 431.

[9] UN General Assembly, Convention for the Suppression of the Traffic in Persons and of the Exploitation of the Prostitution of Others, 2 December 1949, A/RES/317, 96 UNTS 271.

requiring States to punish the process of trafficking (procurement, etc.) and the result (exploitation of prostitution). Trafficking in human beings has also been addressed in complementary legal instruments, some focusing on the suppression of crime, others on human rights and protection, belonging to international human rights law, humanitarian law, refugee law, labour law and criminal law. However, despite these numerous instruments, for many years trafficking in human beings only received incidental attention from governments. The 1949 UN Convention became known as a 'single, long-forgotten treaty dating back to 1949' and the other instruments as only containing 'a few vague provisions'.[10]

Changes occurred in the 1990s, when specific debates emerged relating to prostitution and the inadequacies of the current international legal framework to prevent the sexual exploitation of women. Several reports, based on serious and reliable sources, indicated that the phenomenon was getting worse and becoming of high interest for organised criminal groups, linking it with other highly lucrative illegal activities.[11] Such awareness gave rise to the development of new instruments that built on the previous ones and provided a new impetus to the international response to trafficking in human beings.

At international level, a specific UN instrument, attached to the Convention against Transnational Organised Crime,[12] was adopted in 2000: the Protocol to Prevent, Suppress and Punish Trafficking in Persons, especially women and children.[13] This instrument is focused on the repressive dimension of the fight against trafficking in human beings (THB). It contains the first internationally agreed definition of THB[14] and has given new impetus to the transnational action in this field. Regional organisations have also developed their own instruments to address the phenomenon. In Asia, the South Asian Association for Regional Cooperation (SAARC) distinguished itself as the organisation in which the first ever regional treaty on trafficking was developed.[15] The elaboration of a regional convention was called for in 1997, and the text, adopted in 2002,[16] expressed the

---

[10] A Gallagher, 'Recent Legal Developments in the Field of Human Trafficking: A Critical Review of the 2005 European Convention and Related Instruments' (2006) 8 *European Journal of Migration and Law* 163.

[11] See for instance the references mentioned in European Parliament, Working Paper 'Trafficking in Women', Civil Liberties Series, LIBE 109 EN, 5.

[12] UN, Convention against Transnational Organised Crime, 15 November 2000, 2225 UNTS 209.

[13] UN General Assembly, Protocol to Prevent, Suppress and Punish Trafficking in Persons, Especially women and Children, Supplementing the United Nations Convention against Transnational Organized Crime, 15 November 2000, 2237 UNTS 319, Doc A/55/383.

[14] Before 2000, international conventions only addressed parts of the trafficking phenomenon, such as the 1949 UN Convention for the Suppression of Traffic in Persons and the Exploitation of the Prostitution of Others, which refers to 'prostitution and the accompanying evil of the traffic in persons for the purposes of prostitution', or the ILO Convention against Forced Labour, which refers to forced labour.

[15] A Gallagher, *The International Law of Human Trafficking*, 1st edn (Cambridge, Cambridge University Press, 2010) 127.

[16] SAARC, Convention on Preventing and Combating the Trafficking in Women and Children for Prostitution, enacted on 5 January 2002 during the 11th meeting of the Heads of State or Government, and entered into force on 15 November 2005, available at: www.saarc-sec.org/userfiles/conv-trafficking.pdf.

collective resolution of its parties 'to treat trafficking in women and children for commercial exploitation as a criminal offence of a serious nature'.[17] More recently, the Association of Southeast Asian Nations adopted its own Convention against Trafficking in Persons, especially Women and Children.[18] Within Europe, such impetus has taken concrete form thanks to actions undertaken by the Council of Europe and the OSCE. The former prepared and adopted a Convention on Action against trafficking in human beings in 2005,[19] which intends to give more attention to the human rights dimension of the fight against human trafficking. The latter adopted, in 2003, an Action Plan,[20] which has been implemented since then and, under the direction of its Special Representative and Coordinator for combating trafficking in human beings, conducts various activities such as the elaboration of thematic reports,[21] the organisation of training sessions and the monitoring of national policies in selected countries.[22]

The EU has not been absent from these international and regional efforts to prevent and fight against THB given that no less than three legislative instruments, referring expressly to THB, were adopted between 1997 and 2011:[23]

- Joint Action 97/154/JHA of 24 February 1997 concerning action to combat trafficking in human beings and sexual exploitation of children.[24]

- Council Framework Decision 2002/629/JHA of 19 July 2002 on combating trafficking in human beings.[25]

- And more recently, Directive 2011/36/EU of 5 April 2011 on preventing and combating trafficking in human beings and protecting its victims.[26]

---

[17] SAARC Heads of State or Government, Declaration of the Eleventh SAARC Summit, Kathmandu, 2002, SAARC/SUMMIT.11/12, 5–6, available at: www.saarc-sec.org/userfiles/Summit%20Declarations/11-%20Kathmandu%2011th%20Summit%202002.pdf.

[18] Convention signed during the meeting in Kuala Lumpur, Indonesia, on 21 November 2015, available at: agreement.asean.org/media/download/20160303122945.pdf.

[19] Council of Europe, Convention on Action against Trafficking in Human Beings, Warsaw, 16 May 2005, CETS No 197.

[20] OSCE, Permanent Council, 'Action Plan to Combat Trafficking in Human Beings', Doc PC.DEC/557, 24 July 2003.

[21] These actions notably include regular publications of thematic reports, such as a paper on 'Following the money: compendium of resources and step-by-step guide to financial investigations into trafficking in human beings' (2019).

[22] See, eg, OSCE, 2018–19 'Report of the SR/CTHB' (2019).

[23] A fourth instrument, Directive 2004/81/EC ([2004] OJ L261/19) must also be mentioned, as it organises the deliverance of residence permits to third-country nationals who are victims of THB and who collaborate with law enforcement authorities.

[24] Council Joint Action 97/154/JHA of 24 February 1997 adopted by the Council on the basis of Article K.3 of the TEU concerning action to combat trafficking in human beings and sexual exploitation of children [1997] OJ L63/2.

[25] Council Framework Decision 2002/629/JHA of 19 July 2002 on combating trafficking in human beings [2002] OJ L203/1.

[26] Directive 2011/36/EU of the European Parliament and of the Council of 5 April 2011 on preventing and combating trafficking in human beings and protecting its victims, and replacing Council Framework Decision 2002/629/JHA [2011] OJ L101/1.

The adoption of numerous instruments, at different levels of governance, has been complemented by diverse activities: research about the trends and factors relating to trafficking in human beings; training for the public authorities in charge of prosecuting this crime and detecting its victims; financial support for civil society organisations that operate shelters for victims etc. The long-term efforts to combat this crime constitute probably one of the characteristics that set it apart from other fields of international action against criminal activities, such as piracy[27] or trafficking in fraudulent medicine,[28] for which the reaction of the international community has been more recent. However, despite the counter-trafficking efforts carried out, the phenomenon remains a subject of concern, as the number of its potential victims remains high. In 2017, the International Labour Organization (ILO) estimated that globally 40 million people were victims of modern slavery, defined as situations of exploitation that they cannot refuse or leave because of threats, violence, coercion, deception and/or abuse of powers.[29]

B. Trafficking in Human Beings as a Challenge for the EU

Although the phenomenon concerns all regions in the world, this section will focus on the situation of trafficking within Europe, and more particularly within the EU. Rather than analysing directly the content of the EU's policy, this section serves a different purpose and seeks to explain why the fight against trafficking in human beings constitutes a challenge for European actors and States. To that end the following elements will be presented: why is the EU vulnerable to such form of crime (i); the trafficking flows from, within and to the EU (ii); and finally the forms of exploitation and profile of the victims (iii).

i. *When Traffickers Abuse EU Integration*

Trafficking in human beings is not a novelty in Europe. In the aftermath of the Second World War, during the negotiations and ratification of the UN Convention for the Suppression of the Traffic in Persons and of the Exploitation of the Prostitution of Other,[30] European States expressed their concerns with trafficking in persons that was taking place on their territories. Despite such concerns, the phenomenon of trafficking in persons was considered to be a purely national

---

[27] UN General Assembly, Convention on the Law of the Sea (UNCLOS), 10 December 1982, 1833 UNTS 3, Arts 100–07 and 110.

[28] CCPCJ, Resolution 20/6, 'Countering fraudulent medicine, in particular their trafficking', April 2011.

[29] ILO (with Walk Free Foundation and IOM), *Global Estimates of Modern Slavery: Forced labour and forced marriage* (2017) 9.

[30] UN General Assembly, Convention for the Suppression of the Traffic in Persons and of the Exploitation of the Prostitution of Others (n 9). The Convention prescribes procedures for combating international trafficking for prostitution, including expulsion of offenders. It also prohibits the running of brothels and renting accommodation for prostitution purposes.

matter and actions, if taken, were adopted and implemented at national level. The need to find a European response to this phenomenon arose in the mid-1990s and resulted from a combination of several factors: a growing awareness about the exploitation of non-EU nationals within Europe together with the deepening of European integration and its risk of abuse by criminals.

The establishment of an AFSJ, in which internal border controls have been abolished and free movement of persons ensured, has the unwanted effect that it makes the EU particularly vulnerable to trafficking in human beings as it offers renewed opportunities to traffickers. The latter are very flexible and adapt quickly to changes in legislation, not hesitating to circumvent EU law to expand their criminal activities.

Differences between the legislation of Member States, for instance concerning prostitution,[31] greatly facilitate the activities of the criminals involved in THB. In Member States where prostitution is legal, traffickers circumvent the legal environment in order to exploit their victims. Criminals also abuse legislative loopholes. For instance, sham and/or forced marriages between EU victims and non-EU nationals are arranged in order to legalise their stay or to obtain social and work benefits and criminals sometimes arrange marriages between EU citizens – who have exercised their right to free movement – and non-EU nationals in order to benefit from more favourable rules.[32] The Common European Asylum System is also abused as traffickers make their victims apply in order to move them freely within the Schengen area during the assessment period.[33]

More generally, regardless of the status of the victims, traffickers abuse the abolition of internal border controls in order to integrate the movement across borders of their victims into their 'business model'. Such a form of abuse is particularly noticeable for the victims of sexual exploitation who have been moved into and around the EU, both across borders and internally. The active rotation of women 'is aimed not only at maximising profits by supplying new "faces" to clients and by exploring new markets, but also at preventing victims from establishing relationships and consequently, avoiding law enforcement detection'.[34] Rotation of victims also occurs in trafficking for the purpose of forced begging. Mobility is a significant feature in such cases, as minors are frequently moved from one country to another in small groups once social services or the police have approached them.[35] Rotation occurs to a lesser extent in other forms of

---

[31] C Brière and A Weatherburn, 'Regulating Desire: The Impact of Law and Policy on Demand for Sexual Exploitation in Europe' (2017) 1 *Ex-Ante* 56.

[32] Commission, 'Helping national authorities to fight abused of the right to free movement: Handbook on addressing the issue of alleged marriages of convenience between EU citizens and non-EU nationals in the context of EU law on free movement of EU Citizens', COM (2014) 604 final. See also Case C-218/14, *Kuldip Singh, Denzel Njume, Khaled Aly against Minister for Justice and Equality (Ireland)* [2015] EU:C:2015:476.

[33] Europol, *Situation Report* (n 5) 12.

[34] Europol, *Trafficking in Human Beings in the EU* (2011) 7.

[35] Europol, *Situation Report* (n 5) 26.

exploitation, such as trafficking for the purpose of labour exploitation, mainly because the exploitation is limited in time and victims usually return to their countries of origin or start a new life at the end of the exploitation.[36]

ii. Trafficking Flows from, within and to the EU

Although this form of trafficking is not the best known, domestic trafficking, ie, trafficking occurring within the same country, is prevalent in many European countries.[37] By 2009, the United Nations Office on Drugs and Crime (UNODC) had already singled out the Netherlands, France, Italy and Romania as the countries in which national victims accounted for a large part of the trafficking victim population.[38] Statistics gathered between 2015 and 2016 in the 28 EU Member States reveals that this form of trafficking remains strong. Nearly one quarter of registered victims were citizens of the reporting country.[39] In addition, whereas victims from certain countries (Slovakia or Bulgaria) are more likely to be registered outside their own country, victims who are nationals of France, Germany or the United Kingdom represent, in absolute numbers, the largest groups of victims identified within their own country.[40] The citizens of the Netherlands, France, the United Kingdom, Germany, Austria and Greece who are victims of trafficking are almost exclusively registered in their country.[41] Domestic trafficking is also particularly noticeable in countries neighbouring the EU.[42]

In addition to these domestic flows, the EU is the destination of intra-EU flows and international flows of trafficking in human beings, which are, if not increasing, remaining stable. Intra-EU trafficking flows cover situations in which EU citizens are trafficked to and exploited in another EU Member State. Again, nearly one quarter of registered victims of trafficking in the EU were citizens of other EU Member States.[43] Such situations are more and more frequent,[44] to the point where Bulgaria and Romania were for some time the first States of origin of victims of trafficking in the EU.[45] In 2018, the Commission stressed how these two countries

---

[36] ibid 28.

[37] UNODC, *Global Report on Trafficking in Persons – Europe* (2009) 9.

[38] ibid 10.

[39] Commission, 'Data collection on trafficking in human beings in the EU' (2018) 80, available at: ec.europa.eu/home-affairs/sites/homeaffairs/files/what-we-do/policies/european-agenda-security/20181204_data-collection-study.pdf.

[40] ibid 82, Table 3.8.3.1. Citizenship of EU Victims.

[41] Eurostat, 'Trafficking in Human beings, Statistical Working Papers' (2014) 34. Out of the 1,080 Dutch victims registered between 2010 and 2012, 1,079 victims have been registered in the Netherlands.

[42] ibid 38. Between 2010 and 2012 the importance of domestic victims in Serbia (230 nationals out of 269 victims.

[43] Commission, 'Data collection on trafficking in human beings in the EU' (n 39) 80.

[44] Europol, *Serious Organised Crime Threat Assessment* (2013) 24.

[45] Eurostat, 'Trafficking in Human beings, Statistical Working Papers' (2013) 52 and Eurostat, 'Trafficking in Human beings, Statistical Working Papers' (2014) (n 41) 35. Yet it must be stressed that the majority of victims are detected within the country, testifying for the importance of internal trafficking, ie, trafficking taking place within the country of origin of the victim.

were with Hungary in the top five countries of citizenship of registered victims, in both statistical reports analysing data for 2010–12 and 2015–16.[46] These statistics confirm that the sub-regional nature of the trafficking flows is the main feature for Western and Central Europe,[47] which is also confirmed by the presence of victims from the near neighbourhood of the EU, with victims from Albania being the second group of registered victims from outside the EU.[48] Finally International flows refer to the situation of third-country nationals being trafficked to and exploited in the EU's territory. Europe remains a privileged destination for these international flows, as is clear from the detection of victims from more than 130 different citizenships and from all regions of the world (Africa, the Middle East, the Americas, South and East Asia and the Pacific).[49] West African victims, including but not limited to Nigerians,[50] are the first group of foreign victims registered in Europe, and account for about 16 per cent of victims detected in Europe in 2016.[51] Nigeria is appearing together with China and Vietnam in the top five countries of citizenship of registered trafficking between 2010 and 2016.[52] If wealthy areas in other regions of the world, like North America or the Middle East, receive cross-border trafficking coming from other countries, Europe must be singled out as the region to detect the highest number of citizenships among trafficking victims.[53]

iii. *Forms of Exploitation and Profile of the Victims*

The available data has identified and continues to identify trafficking for the purpose of sexual exploitation as the most common type of exploitation. It concerned 59 per cent of detected victims in 2016 globally,[54] and the overwhelming majority of these victims of sexual exploitation (83 per cent) were adult women and girls.[55] Such a trend is even stronger within the EU, where 95 per cent of the victims of trafficking for sexual exploitation are female.[56] Although increasing efforts are made to tackle sexual exploitation, there is a high demand for sexual services within all EU Member States, which are considered as markets for sexual services. This constant demand for sexual services and persistent socio-economic inequalities between developed and developing countries drive human trafficking for sexual exploitation.[57]

---

[46] Commission, 'Data collection on trafficking in human beings in the EU' (n 39) 81.
[47] UNODC, *Global Report on Trafficking in Persons* (2018) 53.
[48] ibid 86.
[49] UNODC, *Global Report* (2014) (n 1) 62.
[50] Commission, 'Data collection on trafficking in human beings in the EU' (n 39) 85.
[51] UNODC, *Global Report* (2018) (n 47) 54.
[52] Commission, 'Data collection on trafficking in human beings in the EU' (n 39) 86.
[53] UNODC, *Global Report* (2018) (n 47) 44, Fig 44.
[54] ibid 29.
[55] ibid 28.
[56] Commission, 'Data collection on trafficking in human beings in the EU' (n 39) 64.
[57] Europol, *Serious Organised Crime Threat Assessment* (2013) (n 44) 24.

Trafficking for the purposes of labour exploitation is the second form of trafficking in the EU. This form of exploitation concerns mostly male victims, who represent globally 55 per cent of detected victims,[58] and 80 per cent of victims detected within the EU.[59] Labour exploitation is a recurrent and increasing phenomenon. Several factors may explain the expansion of this form of exploitation: the high demand for low-cost services by producers and consumers; the removal of barriers to employment for all EU citizens across Member States; and/or the worsening of the job market in certain countries because of the economic crisis. Some sectors of the economy now rely on trafficking to provide for workers, especially low regulated industries, such as agriculture (especially seasonal harvesting), the construction sector, hotel/catering businesses and the retail sector. Labour exploitation also occurs in the transportation sector, the cleaning industry and textile and manufacturing industries.[60] And last but not least, service and treatment similar to slavery also take place within the domestic environment, where the rights of maids and housekeepers are frequently infringed.[61] Despite the greater attention given to labour exploitation and the increasing numbers of investigations in the EU, victims of this form of exploitation are very difficult to identify because their exploitation is less visible and evident.[62]

Concerning other forms of exploitation, in practice the most recurrent forms of exploitation are those carried out for the purposes of forced criminality, such as forced street begging and forced sham marriages. The same victims, ie, female minors, are often involved in forced criminality and forced begging. Young victims, and/or victims with psychological and/or physical disabilities are often targeted by traffickers willing to exploit them through forced begging.[63] With the exception of one case in Switzerland,[64] cases of trafficking for the purpose of removal of organs have never been identified within Europe.

In conclusion, the EU appears particularly concerned by trafficking in human beings. Traffickers benefit from the progress made in terms of EU integration. For instance, they use the abolition of internal border controls to move their victims around and avoid their detection by law enforcement authorities or they circumvent rules on free movement of workers and exploit the work or services of EU citizens. Moreover, the EU remains an attractive destination for international trafficking flows and victims of trafficking come not only from distant countries, such as Nigeria or China, but also from neighbouring countries, such as Ukraine,

---

[58] UNODC, *Global Report* (2018) (n 47) 33.

[59] Commission, 'Data collection on trafficking in human beings in the EU' (n 39) 64.

[60] Europol, *Situation Report* (n 5) 24.

[61] ibid.

[62] FRA, *Severe labour exploitation: workers moving within or into the European Union* (2015) 39.

[63] Europol, *Situation Report* (n 5) 28.

[64] GRETA, *Report concerning the implementation of the Council of Europe Convention on Action against Trafficking in Human Beings by Switzerland* (2015) 18, 32, para 119.

Albania or Morocco. In such a context, the study of the EU's policy against trafficking in human beings appears relevant as it allows us to analyse how the EU institutions and Member States have answered the challenge that it constitutes. The answers do not only reflect the use they have made of the competences conferred on the EU to develop its own policy to combat trafficking in human beings. The answers also show how their decisions, especially the decision to develop the external dimension of the EU's counter-trafficking policy, are influenced by the situation of trafficking in human beings in the region.

II. Definition of Key Concepts

Certain notions and concepts used in this book are frequently subject to confusion and incorrect use. The following sections will thus be devoted to clarifying these key notions and concepts, starting with the definition of 'trafficking in human beings' (A). The evolution of the EU's approach to counter trafficking in human beings will then be presented (B) as well as the development of its external dimension (C).

A. Definition of Trafficking in Human Beings

Before examining the EU's policy in the fight against trafficking in human beings in detail, it is important to define the term 'trafficking in human beings'. Whereas in other legal frameworks, other expressions, such as trafficking in persons, forced labour etc, are used, the expression 'trafficking in human beings' is considered as the preferred expression within the EU. It will thus be the expression used in this study. The following paragraphs will be devoted to the legal definition given to this phenomenon within the EU legal order.

As we will analyse in detail in the context of this research, the EU did not develop its definition of the phenomenon in isolation from developments occurring in other legal frameworks, especially within the UN. Yet the EU distinguishes itself thanks to its ambition to apply a modern definition of trafficking in human beings.

The adoption in 2000 of the UN Convention against Transnational Organised Crime[65] and its additional Protocol against Trafficking in Persons, especially against women and children, brought the long-standing impasse on this issue to a close and produced an internationally agreed definition of trafficking in human

---

[65] UN General Assembly, United Nations Convention against Transnational Organized Crime: Resolution adopted by the General Assembly, 8 January 2001, A/RES/55/25.

beings for the first time.[66] The definition contained in Article 3(a) of the Protocol soon became widely accepted and reads as follows:

> 'Trafficking in persons' shall mean the recruitment, transportation, transfer, harbouring or receipt of persons, by means of the threat or use of force or other forms of coercion, of abduction, of fraud, of deception, of the abuse of power or of a position of vulnerability or of the giving or receiving of payments or benefits to achieve the consent of a person having control over another person, for the purpose of exploitation.

A close reading of the definition reveals that it is composed of three separate elements, which also constitute the three constitutive elements of the offence of trafficking in human beings, which are:

- An action, one part of the *actus reus* of trafficking, which would be fulfilled by a variety of activities including, but not limited to, the undefined practices of recruitment, transportation, transfer, harbouring or receipt of persons.[67] Its breadth has the effect of bringing within reach of the definition not just recruiters, brokers and transporters, but also owners, managers, supervisors and controllers of any place of exploitation. It results in extending the concept of trafficking in human beings to situations of exploitation in which there is no previous process.[68]

- The use of certain means against that person,[69] which constitutes the second part of the *actus reus* of trafficking. It applies only to trafficking in adults, and not to trafficking in children where this element has been waived.[70]

- The pursuit of a purpose of exploitation, a *mens rea* element in the definition of trafficking. Trafficking will occur only if the implicated individual or entity intended that the action would lead to exploitation of the victims, but the achievement of the intended aim is not required.[71] The drafters opted for no definition of exploitation and an open-ended list of forms of exploitation, allowing States to elaborate on other forms of exploitation when defining trafficking in human beings in national laws.[72] The Protocol still provides that exploitation shall include at a minimum 'the exploitation of the prostitution of

---

[66] C Rijken, *Trafficking in Persons, Prosecution from a European Perspective* (The Hague, TMC Asser Press, 2003) 66–71; or Gallagher, *The International Law of Human Trafficking* (n 15) 13–25.

[67] Gallagher, *The International Law of Human Trafficking* (n 15) 29.

[68] No previous recruitment or movement is required.

[69] The means are defined as follows: 'by means of the threat or use of force or other forms of coercion, of abduction, of fraud, of deception, of the abuse of power or of a position of vulnerability or of the giving or receiving of payments or benefits to achieve the consent of a person having control over another person'.

[70] Art 3(c) and (d) UN Trafficking Protocol.

[71] Gallagher, *The International Law of Human Trafficking* (n 15) 34: 'The persons concerned can be a recruiter or a broker but also a final exploiter. The purpose or the intent element is not limited to the initial stage of the trafficking cycle. Trafficking could take place even if the first acts (recruitment or movement) were not motivated by an intention to exploit'.

[72] Inter-Agency Coordination Group against Trafficking in Persons (ICAT), 'The International Legal Frameworks concerning Trafficking in Persons' (2012) ICAT Paper series – Issue 1, 3.

others or other forms of sexual exploitation, forced labour or services, slavery or practices similar to slavery, servitude or the removal of organs'.[73]

To avoid turning it into a catch-all notion, it has been constantly stressed that the accumulation of these three elements must be present for certain actions or conduct to qualify as being trafficking in human beings.

The adoption of the international definition of trafficking in 2000 brought clarity within the EU legal order, in which various texts contained definitions of trafficking in human beings. The Commission proposed a first definition of trafficking in a Communication of 1996.[74] Trafficking was defined as 'the transportation of women from third countries to the European Union (including perhaps subsequent movements between the Member States) for the purposes of sexual exploitation'. Trafficking for the purpose of sexual exploitation covers the situation of women who work as prostitutes and who have suffered intimidation and/or violence through the trafficking process, ie, their transport from a third country to the EU. Their initial consent may not be relevant, as even those who knew that they would work as prostitutes can be deprived of their basic human rights.[75] The European Parliament also proposed its own definition of trafficking. Although it identified a clear link between trafficking and exploitation of female prostitution,[76] it also began to view trafficking as something broader and identified coercion and deception as hallmarks of trafficking.[77] The uncertainty ceased when the Council of the European Union adopted Joint Action 97/154/JHA, the first legislative EU instrument on trafficking in human beings.[78] The text contained a definition of trafficking, which reads as follows: 'any behaviour which facilitates the entry into, transit through, residence in or exit from territory of a Member State, for gainful purposes, where use is made is coercion, in particular violence or threats, deceit is used, or there is abuse of authority or other pressure'.[79] Sexual exploitation was the only type of exploitation mentioned and it included at least exploitative use of adults and children in prostitution. The adoption of the UN Trafficking Protocol prompted a raft of regional and national reforms. The 2002 Council Framework Decision on the fight against trafficking in human beings[80]

---

[73] Art 3(a) UN Trafficking Protocol.

[74] Commission, 'Communication on trafficking in women for the purpose of sexual exploitation', COM (1996) 567 final.

[75] ibid 4.

[76] European Parliament, Resolution on the exploitation of prostitution and trade in human beings, Resolution A2-52/89 of 14 April 1989 [1989] OJ C120/352. See also European Parliament, Resolution on trade in women, Resolution B3-1264, 1283 and 1309/93 of 16 September 1993 [1993] OJ C268/141.

[77] The definition proposed read as follows: 'the illegal action of someone who, directly or indirectly, encourages a citizen from a third country to enter or stay in another country in order to exploit that person by using deceit or any other form of coercion or by abusing that person's vulnerable situation or administrative status' (para 1). European Parliament, Resolution on trafficking in human beings, Resolution A4-0326/95 of 18 January 1996 [1996] OJ C032/88.

[78] Council Joint Action 97/154/JHA (n 24) Title I, A and B.

[79] ibid Title I.

[80] Framework Decision 2002/629/JHA (n 25).

was the first text adopted within the framework of the EU after the entry into force of the Protocol.[81] Its Article 1 does not directly provide for a common definition of trafficking in human beings to be applied by all EU Member States, but requires them to take measures to ensure that certain acts are punishable.[82] The text considerably narrowed down the definition of the offence of trafficking in human beings. It has been both clearly distinguished from the smuggling of migrants on the one hand and sexual exploitation and child pornography on the other, as these types of behaviour are subject to other EU instruments.[83] The definition of trafficking it provided was nevertheless largely in line with the one contained in the UN Protocol, as it also confirmed the 'three-way definition' of trafficking in human beings, constituting three cumulative elements. Concerning the action element, the 2002 Framework Decision provided for an extended definition of the action.[84] It referred to the recruitment, transportation, transfer, harbouring and subsequent reception of persons, which were elements listed in the UN Protocol. It further extended the definition by adding two specific elements: 'the exchange or transfer of control over those persons', reflecting modern forms of trafficking. Concerning the use of coercive means, the definition of the means contained in the UN Protocol remained the main point of reference, and under its influence, the Framework Decision introduced two new means in the EU's legal order, namely the abuse of authority or of a position of vulnerability and on the giving or receiving of payments or benefits to achieve the consent of a person having control over another person. Concerning the purposes of exploitation, by comparison with the Joint Action, the Framework Decision extends the definition of sexual exploitation, which includes the exploitation of the prostitution of others and other forms of sexual exploitation, including pornography. Trafficking for the purposes of exploiting the work or services of people[85] reflects the insertion of this area

[81] The EU not only participated in the negotiations of the Protocol, but it also became a party to this Protocol (for aspects covered by Community competences, ie, measures to be taken at borders or concerning travel documents, see 2001/87/EC: Council Decision of 8 December 2000 on the signing, on behalf of the European Community, of the United Nations Convention against transnational organised crime and its Protocols on combating trafficking in persons, especially women and children, and the smuggling of migrants by land, air and sea [2001] OJ L30/44).

[82] Framework Decision 2002/629/JHA (n 25) Art 1, para 1.

[83] For smuggling of migrants, see Council Directive 2002/90/EC of 28 November 2002 defining the facilitation of unauthorised entry, transit and residence [2002] OJ L328/17; and Council Framework Decision 2002/946/JHA of 28 November 2002 on the strengthening of the penal framework to prevent the facilitation of unauthorised entry, transit and residence [2002] OJ L328/1. Concerning sexual exploitation of children and child pornography, see first Council Framework Decision 2004/68/JHA of 22 December 2003 on combating the sexual exploitation of children and child pornography [2004] OJ L13/44; then Directive 2011/92/EU of the European Parliament and of the Council of 13 December 2011 on combating the sexual abuse and sexual exploitation of children and child pornography [2011] OJ L335/1.

[84] 'The recruitment, transportation, transfer, harbouring, subsequent reception of a person, including exchange or transfer of control over that person'.

[85] Framework Decision 2002/629/JHA (n 25) Art, 1 para 1: 'these forms of exploitation include at least forced or compulsory labour or services, slavery and practices similar to slavery or servitude'.

of exploitation into the text of the UN Protocol. The purposes of the exploitation covered slightly differed from the UN Protocol, as the removal of organs is omitted. Furthermore, the Framework Decision deals with the issue of consent in the same way as in the Trafficking Protocol[86] and makes the same distinction between trafficking in children and trafficking in adults.[87] All these elements make it possible to discern 'a distinct, if fragile, international consensus on the critical elements of trafficking'.[88]

The most recent EU instrument, the 2011 Directive on preventing and combating trafficking in human beings,[89] pursues the trend towards strengthening the international consensus while maintaining and introducing certain EU specificities. The Directive changes the definition contained in Council 2002 Framework Decision to largely correspond with the definition contained in international instruments in all its elements.[90] Nonetheless, a few minor differences continue to exist. First, the Directive's definition goes a step further by defining the position of vulnerability,[91] but this definition corresponds to the definition mentioned in the *Travaux préparatoires* of the Protocol[92] and also reflects an international consensus. Second, the Directive extends the objectives of exploitation in order to reflect evolutions of the phenomenon observed in practice and to adopt the most modern possible definition of the phenomenon. Forced begging is explicitly mentioned as an example of forced services and the exploitation of the criminal activities of others has been introduced.[93] This form of exploitation covers situations in which people are forced to commit crimes as a result of their exploitation.[94] The Directive can also potentially cover situations of illegal adoption or forced marriage.[95] It has therefore been observed that 'the definition under the Directive is more

[86] See in parallel Art 3 (b) UN Trafficking Protocol, and Art 1, para 2 Framework Decision 2002/629/JHA.

[87] Framework Decision 2002/629/JHA (n 25) Art 1, paras 3–4.

[88] Gallagher, *The International Law of Human Trafficking* (n 15) 46. On this point, it is interesting to note that Tom Obokata does not consider that the Framework Decision adopts a definition different from the Trafficking Protocol's definition. In his article, he declares that 'this definition is similar to the one adopted under the Protocol' (see T Obokata, 'EU Council Framework Decision on combating trafficking in human beings: a critical appraisal' (2003) 40 *Common Market Law Review* 917, 923). And more recently he repeated his view (see T Obokata and B Payne, 'Implementing Action against trafficking of Human Beings under the TFEU: A Preliminary Analysis' (2012) 3 *New Journal of European Criminal Law* 298, 303).

[89] Directive 2011/36/EU (n 26) Art 1, paras 1 and 3.

[90] The definition now complies exactly with the definition of the UN Protocol and by extension, with the definition contained in the Council of Europe Convention (Art 4(a).

[91] Directive 2011/36/EU (n 26) Art, 2 para 2.

[92] UNODC, *Travaux préparatoires for the Organized Crime Convention and its Protocols* (United Nations Publications, 2006) 347.

[93] It must be noted that these two purposes of exploitation (forced begging and exploitation of criminal activities) are not mentioned; neither are they mentioned in the UN Palermo Protocol or in the Council of Europe Convention.

[94] Anti-Slavery, 'Trafficking for Forced Criminal Activities and Begging in Europe' (2014), available at: www.antislavery.org/wp-content/uploads/2017/01/trafficking_for_forced_criminal_activities_and_begging_in_europe.pdf.

[95] Directive 2011/36/EU (n 26) Recital 11, Preamble.

comprehensive than what is provided for under the Trafficking Protocol …, and is a welcome step forward'.[96]

In conclusion, the definition of trafficking in human beings developed within the EU reflects the international consensus on the issue. As the definition contained in the UN Protocol, the EU legislator preferred to retain a broad definition of the offence, whose broadness is balanced by a three-step test to qualify facts as trafficking in human beings. However, the EU's definition also builds on the internationally agreed definition and goes further. The existence of an internationally agreed definition of trafficking in human beings does not mean that this definition is set in stone. States have a certain margin of discretion when they transpose it into their legal order and have often extended its scope.[97] Moreover, in recent years, different initiatives have led to a certain 'exploitation creep', reshaping anti-trafficking discourse and States' legal conceptualisation of trafficking in terms of modern slavery and forced labour.[98] Whereas the goal of such initiatives is to capture more forms of exploitation, it leads to fundamental shifts under which all forced labour is recast as trafficking and all trafficking is labelled as slavery,[99] which undermines the efforts made previously to bring clarity to the legal definition of trafficking in human beings.

B. The EU's Approach to Combating Trafficking in Human Beings

The EU started to develop a policy to fight against trafficking in human beings in the mid-1990s, a period during which the phenomenon was mainly envisaged as a criminal security threat and/or an immigration issue.

Public concern about and international awareness of the phenomena started in the early 1990s and was followed by the adoption of the first texts at EU level. The Council of the European Union agreed a set of recommendations addressed to EU Member States to counter trafficking in November 1993.[100] The European Parliament adopted a report and a resolution on trafficking in human beings in December 1995.[101] The Commission organised, in June 1996, an international

---

[96] Obokata and Payne (n 88) 305.

[97] A Weyembergh and V Santamaria, 'Conclusions' in A Weyembergh and V Santamaria (eds), *The Evaluation of European Criminal Law: The Example of the Framework Decision on Combating Trafficking in Human Beings* (Brussels, Editions de l'Université de Bruxelles, 2009) 382–84; or C-E Clesse, *La traite des êtres humains: un cadre légal perfectible pour une meilleure protection des victimes? Etude de la législation belge, éclairée des normes internationales et de législations française, luxembourgeoise et suisse* (Brussels, Larcier, 2014) 68.

[98] JA Chuang, 'Exploitation Creep and the Unmaking of Human Trafficking Law' (2014) 108 *American Journal of International Law* 609, 611.

[99] ibid.

[100] Council, 'Recommendations on Trade in human beings', Press release 10550/93 of 29–30 November 1993, Annex 2.

[101] European Parliament, Resolution on trafficking in human beings [1996] OJ C32/88.

conference in Vienna, bringing together experts, civil society organisations, academics, national officials etc. A communication focusing on trafficking in women for sexual exploitation was published few months later.[102] Although the text mentioned the importance of a multidisciplinary and coordinated approach to tackle trafficking in women and addressed diverse policy areas,[103] the adoption of an EU legislative instrument was only evoked in the field of judicial cooperation, in order to improve national criminal legislation.[104] The instruments adopted afterwards, such as Joint Action 97/154/JHA adopted under Title VI of the Treaty on European Union (TEU), aimed primarily at improving operational cooperation between national law enforcement and judicial authorities.[105] However, due to the imprecise legal nature of the joint actions, their impact on national laws was limited and, as a result, the beginnings of the EU policy in this field remained modest.[106]

With the entry into force of the Treaty of Amsterdam, the EU received extended powers to adopt measures to approximate national laws, including on trafficking in human beings. The EU institutions therefore had at their disposal the tools to realise the commitments that they signed up to in the international sphere with the ratification of the UN Protocol as a mixed agreement.[107] The EU institutions also recognised that seeking functional cooperation between the Member States was not sufficient to deal with trafficking in human beings.[108] The Framework Decision thus pursued the objectives of addressing the continuing divergence of legal approaches in the Member States and of promoting a common EU approach

---

[102] Commission, 'Communication on trafficking in women for the purpose of sexual exploitation' (n 74).

[103] See for instance, European Parliament, Resolution on trafficking in human beings (n 101) para 7: 'a common policy on trafficking in human beings must be aimed at prevention, deterrence, prosecution and rehabilitation'. See also Commission, 'Communication on trafficking in women for the purpose of sexual exploitation' (n 74) 6: 'trafficking cannot be tackled effectively without a multidisciplinary and coordinated approach, which involves all concerned players – NGOs and social authorities, judicial, law enforcement and migration authorities – and which involves both national and international cooperation.

[104] Commission, 'Communication on trafficking in women for the purpose of sexual exploitation' (n 74) 13.

[105] See in particular Council Joint Action 97/154/JHA of 24 February 1997 adopted by the Council on the basis of Article K.3 of the TEU concerning action to combat trafficking in human beings and sexual exploitation of children [1997] OJ L63/2; Convention based on Article K.3 of the TEU on the establishment of a European Police Office (Europol Convention) [1995] OJ C316/2; or Council Joint Action 96/700/JHA of 29 November 1996 adopted by the Council pursuant to Article K.3 of the TEU establishing an incentive and exchange programme for persons responsible for combating trade in human beings and the sexual exploitation of children [1996] OJ L322/7.

[106] T Obokata, 'EU Action against Trafficking of Human Beings: Past, Present and the Future' in E Guild and P Minderhoud (eds), *Immigration and Criminal Law in the European Union: The Legal Measures and Social Consequences of Criminal Law in Member States on Human Trafficking and Smuggling in Human Beings* (Leiden, Martinus Nijhoff Publishers, 2006) 394–95.

[107] Council Decision 2006/618/EC of 24 July 2006 [2006] OJ L262/44. The conclusion of the UNTOC Convention was approved on behalf of the Community by Council Decision 2004/579/EC of 29 April 2004 [2004] OJ L261/69.

[108] Obokata, 'EU Action against Trafficking of Human Beings' (n 106) 390.

to trafficking. The text contained three key elements: a common definition of trafficking in human beings;[109] a uniform threshold for minimum penalties to be imposed for trafficking with aggravating circumstances;[110] and a provision on the protection and assistance to the victims.[111] The latter aimed at rectifying the inconsistencies in the protection granted to victims depending on the country in which they are trafficked and identified.[112] The provision on victims' protection only provided that criminal investigations and prosecutions shall not be dependent on the report or accusation made by a person subjected to the offence and referred to other instruments applicable to child victims.[113] The Framework Decision failed to achieve the aim of brining national legislation closer. Because of the broadness of its provisions, national measures might still be in compliance with EU law even if they diverge significantly and create a comparatively inconsistent and unequal system throughout the EU.[114] Furthermore, the text had been criticised for retaining and significantly expanding the Protocol's criminal justice focus.[115] The protection seemed to be reserved to victims who cooperate with law enforcement authorities.[116] No provision referred to the prevention of trafficking.[117] The Framework Decision thus proved influential only in ensuring maximum uniformity between Member States with respect to their criminal approaches.[118] The text had been qualified as representing 'a substantial retreat from previous commitments of the EU',[119] and testifying that the protection of victims was 'not a priority for the EU and Member States'.[120] The Proposal by the Commission in February 2002[121] and the adoption in 2004[122] of a Directive concerning the question of short-term stays or residency permits for victims of trafficking did not change the criminal justice focus of the measures adopted by the EU in the early 2000s. The declared aim of this instrument, which is still

---

[109] Framework Decision 2002/629/JHA (n 25) Arts 1 and 2.

[110] ibid Art 3. This provision was complemented with articles providing for the liability of legal persons and the sanctions to be imposed on them (Arts 4 and 5) and for jurisidiction and prosecution (Art 6).

[111] Framework Decision 2002/629/JHA (n 25) Art 7.

[112] Obokata, 'EU Action against Trafficking of Human Beings' (n 106) 392.

[113] Framework Decision 2002/629/JHA (n 25) Art 7. Reference to the Council Framework Decision 2001/220/JHA of 15 March 2001 on the standing of victims in criminal proceedings [2001] OJ L82/1.

[114] Obokata, 'EU Action against Trafficking of Human Beings' (n 106) 397; or F Calderoni, 'A definition that does not work: the impact of the EU Framework Decision on the Fight against Organized Crime' (2012) 49 *Common Market Law Review* 1365, 1379.

[115] Gallagher, 'Recent Legal Developments in the Field of Human Trafficking' (n 10) 167.

[116] Obokata, 'EU Action against Trafficking of Human Beings' (n 106) 392.

[117] Prevention is just mentioned in para 9 of the Preamble, and there is no provision dealing with this matter.

[118] Gallagher, 'Recent Legal Developments in the Field of Human Trafficking' (n 10) 167.

[119] ibid.

[120] Obokata, 'EU Action against Trafficking of Human Beings' (n 106) 401.

[121] Commission, 'Proposal for a Council Directive on the short-term residence permit issued to victims of action to facilitate illegal immigration or trafficking in human beings who cooperate with the competent authorities', COM (2002) 71 final.

[122] Directive 2004/81/EC (n 23).

in force today, is to strengthen the instruments for combating illegal immigration by introducing a residence permit for third-country nationals who have been victims of trafficking in human beings or who have been the subject of an action to facilitate illegal immigration. The delivery of a residence permit is subject to strict conditions in order to offer safeguards against abuse[123] but it does not circumvent the danger of victims being merely used as a tool to achieve the EU's main objective, the enhancement of law enforcement against trafficking and irregular migration.[124] Moreover, the Framework Decision aimed at the approximation of criminal laws[125] inserted itself among other criminal justice measures, which were not necessarily specific to the fight against trafficking in human beings. Other instruments aimed at the creation of cooperation mechanisms, such as Joint Investigation Teams,[126] a useful tool in trafficking cases,[127] or instruments based on the principle of mutual recognition, such as the European Arrest Warrant,[128] facilitating cross-border criminal proceedings. European agencies, such as Europol and Eurojust, were also set up and designed to support and strengthen criminal cross-border cooperation including in trafficking cases. The first instruments adopted within the EU thus illustrate the focus on criminal justice measures and the priority granted to the reinforcement of prosecution and convictions of traffickers. The limited provisions on victims' protection and the prevention of trafficking, which are present in policy documents, were not translated into obligations binding the Member States.

In the mid-2000s, the EU institutions adopted a series of instruments and carried out a series of actions in the field of the fight against trafficking in human beings, which contributed to a change in the approach in this field. First, the political agenda changed in 2005 with the adoption by the Council of an EU Action Plan on best practices, standards and procedures for combating and preventing trafficking in human beings.[129] Human rights-based measures, such as prevention of trafficking, reduction of demand and protection and support to victims of trafficking, were the subject of detailed discussions in an EU policy document.[130] The Commission also established a consultative group, known as the Experts

---

[123] ibid Preamble, para 9 Directive 2004/81/EC.

[124] Obokata, 'EU Action against Trafficking of Human Beings' (n 106) 403.

[125] Directive 2011/36/EU (n 26).

[126] These teams can be based on either the Framework Decision 2002/465/JAI on Joint Investigation Teams [2002] OJ L16/1, or on Article 13 of the Convention of 29 May 2000 on Mutual Assistance in Criminal Matters between the Member States of the European Union [2000] OJ C197/3.

[127] Eurojust, *Strategic meeting on trafficking in human beings, Outcome report* (2015) 11–12.

[128] Council Framework Decision 2002/584/JHA of 13 June 2002 on the European arrest warrant and the surrender procedures between Member States – Statements made by certain Member States on the adoption of the Framework Decision [2002] OJ L190/1.

[129] Council, 'EU Plan on best practices, standards and procedures for combating and preventing trafficking in human beings' [2005] OJ C311/1.

[130] The Action Plan mentioned that Member States should consolidate the cooperation of public authorities with civil society organisations related to the protection of victims, prevention of and the fight against trafficking in human beings (2, para 5(i)), and detailed measures were envisaged for preventing trafficking (6–7), reducing demand (8) and protecting victims (11).

Group on Trafficking in Human Beings,[131] in applying the Brussels Declaration.[132] This group received an explicit mandate to issue opinions or reports to the Commission at the latter's request or on its own initiative. Second, a series of evaluations conducted in 2008 questioned the efficiency of a purely criminal justice approach. In a review of the EU Action Plan,[133] the Commission pointed out that, despite the upward trend in figures relating to investigations and prosecutions, the number of criminal proceedings was still not high enough to reflect the presumed scale of the problem.[134] Furthermore, although the majority of EU Member States had adopted legislative measures for the protection of victims, the lack of relevant figures proved that there was a 'gap between the situation with respect to legislation and implementation in practice'.[135] In countries where there are a significant number of assisted victims, statistics on criminal proceedings were higher and the Commission highlighted that a human rights-based approach was needed not only to protect victims' rights but also in the interests of justice. Third, the need to revise the Framework Decision was made clear by the Experts Group on Trafficking in Human Beings.[136] Its members highlighted the inadequacy of the EU's definition compared with the one contained in the UN Protocol,[137] as well as the relevance of its extension to increasingly identified forms of exploitation (organised begging, committing petty crimes, drug crimes etc). In relation to victims' protection, the Experts Group stressed that Member States should grant unconditional assistance to trafficked persons and not treat them exclusively as an instrument for the prosecution.[138] The Commission itself identified in its own evaluation report,

---

[131] Commission, Decision 2003/209/EC of 25 March 2003 setting up a consultative group, to be known as the 'Experts Group on Trafficking in Human Beings' [2003] OJ L79/25, amended by Commission Decision 2007/675/EC of 17 October 2007 setting up the Group of Experts on Trafficking in Human Beings [2007] OJ L277/29, and by Commission Decision 2011/502/EU of 10 August 2011 on setting up the Group of Experts on Trafficking in Human Beings [2011] OJ L207/14. This group is composed of national, EU and international practitioners, together with representatives of civil society organisations and academics, with recognised experience and competence to consider matters relating to trafficking in human beings.

[132] European Union, 'Brussels Declaration on Preventing and Combating Trafficking in Human Beings', 29 November 2002 [2003] OJ C137/2.

[133] Commission, 'Evaluation and monitoring of the implementation of the EU Plan on best practices, standards and procedures for combating and preventing trafficking in human beings', (Communication) COM (2008) 657 final.

[134] ibid 3, para 1.3.

[135] H Cullen, 'The EU and Human Trafficking: Framing a Regional Response to a Global Emergency' in A Antoniadis, R Schütze and E Spaventa (eds), *The European Union and Global Emergencies: A Law and Policy Analysis* (Oxford, Hart Publishing, 2011) 238.

[136] Experts Group on Human Trafficking, Opinion No 1/2008 on the revision of the Council Framework Decision of 19 July 2002 on combating Trafficking in human beings, 17 October 2008.

[137] ibid 4.

[138] ibid 3. In this field, the Experts Group also conducted a review of the Residence Permit Directive, in which they criticised the Directive for insufficiently addressing the legitimate needs and rights of victims to support and assistance. Experts Group on Human Trafficking, Opinion No 4/2009 on a possible revision of Council Directive 2004/81/EC on the residence permit issued to third-country nationals who are victims of trafficking in human beings or who have been the subject of an action to facilitate illegal immigration, who cooperate with the competent authorities, 16 June 2009, 2.

published in 2006, some weaknesses in the national measures implementing the Framework Decision[139] and academics pointed out other gaps in the Framework Decision, such as the drafting of Article 6(2) on jurisdiction or the inclusion of sexual exploitation under aggravating circumstances.[140] The EU legal framework was therefore subject to criticisms and pleas were made to transform it into a new system more respectful of victims' rights.

Although at international and regional level, advocacy efforts have paved the way for support for a human rights-based approach, within the EU the inclusion of human rights considerations within the EU's counter-trafficking policy came notably through the work of the Experts Group tasked with the translation of the Brussels Declaration into practice.[141] The Experts Group highlighted first the complex nature of trafficking in human beings, a problem related to different fields and interests: migration, organised crime, labour, prostitution, human rights, unequal international economic relationships, gender issues, violence against women etc. All those aspects were reflected in the necessarily multifaceted strategies developed by different actors, ie, the non-governmental, intergovernmental and governmental actors. The approach that they proposed in order to effectively address trafficking in human beings contained various aspects. It required the EU to integrate a human rights perspective, redressing the imbalance in favour of measures in the area of crime control and migration policies through the adoption of measures in relation to protection and assistance for trafficked persons and the prevention of trafficking. The need for multidisciplinary cooperation and coordination between all agencies and stakeholders involved was further stressed. This meant that not only repressive public authorities, such as law enforcement, border officials and prosecutors, should be involved in counter-trafficking efforts, but also local authorities, labour unions, labour inspections, employers, employees, self-organisations, civil society organisations and international organisations should be involved. Finally, they recommended integrated action, covering the different levels of governance – local, national, regional, European and international – and fields – criminal law, administrative law, aliens' law, migration law, social and labour law, social policies and development policies. Its implementation requires well-structured capacities and procedures, specific institutions, such as National Referral Systems, or national coordination structures.[142] Such an approach received various qualifications, and was for instance referred to as a comprehensive and multidisciplinary approach, a holistic approach or an integrated approach etc. It can be summarised as the idea according to which addressing trafficking meant addressing equally prevention, protection of victims and prosecution of

---

[139] Commission, 'Report based on Article 10 of the Council Framework Decision of 19 July 2002 on combating trafficking in human beings', COM (2006) 187 final, 9.

[140] Obokata and Payne (n 88) 304.

[141] Commission, 'Report of the Experts Group on Trafficking in Human Beings', 22 December 2004, available at: www.institut-fuer-menschenrechte.de/fileadmin/user_upload/PDF-Dateien/EU-Dokumente/report_of_the_experts_group_on_trafficking_in_human_beings_2004.pdf.

[142] ibid 62–64.

traffickers, and also meant involving all of the actors concerned to develop and implement in a coordinated manner counter-trafficking strategies.[143] From 2004, references to this approach appear more and more in policy papers issued by all the EU institutions, referring to the need to develop an EU policy against trafficking in human beings, going beyond the AFSJ, and including external relations, development cooperation, social affairs and employment, education and health, gender equality and non-discrimination.[144] Their shared commitment in favour of such an approach was made clear once more after the adoption of the EU Strategy towards the Eradication of Trafficking in Human Beings.[145]

The commitment of the EU institutions and Member States in favour of a renewed approach was then converted into deeds. In 2009, the Commission proposed a comprehensive reform of the EU's policy against trafficking in human beings. A Proposal for a Framework Decision, was presented in particular in order to bring EU policy into line with new human rights instruments.[146] Negotiations on this Framework Decision were frozen because of the entry into force of the Lisbon Treaty. The Commission proposed a new text,[147] based on Article 83(1) TFEU, which was identical to the previous Proposal for a Framework Decision. The text was adopted only after a few months of negotiations and it became the first Directive adopted under the new regime offered by the Lisbon Treaty.[148] From a criminal justice perspective, the Directive extends the definition of trafficking in human beings.[149] Minimum rules concerning sanctions are introduced, providing

---

[143] C Rijken and E de Volder, 'The EU's Struggle to Realize a Human Rights-Based Approach to Trafficking in Human Beings. A Call on the EU to take THB-Sensitive Action in the Relevant Areas of Law' (2009) 45 *Connecticut Journal of International Law* 49, 54.

[144] Council, 'EU Plan on best practices' (n 129) 1; and Council, 'Presidency Conclusions, Conference Towards a multidisciplinary approach to prevention of trafficking in human beings, prosecution of traffickers and protection of victims', 27 January 2011, Council Doc No 5725/11. Commission, 'Fighting trafficking in human beings: an integrated approach and proposals for an action plan' (Communication), COM (2005) 514 final, Introduction; and Commission, 'Delivering an area of freedom, security and justice for Europe's citizens, Action Plan Implementing the Stockholm Programme' (Communication), COM (2010) 171 final, 35. Council, 'The Stockholm Programme – An open and secure Europe serving and protecting citizens' [2010] OJ C115/1, s 4.4.2. European Parliament, Recommendation to the Council on fighting trafficking in human beings – an integrated approach and proposals for an action plan [2006] OJ C314E/355; or European Parliament, Resolution on preventing trafficking in human beings [2010] OJ C341/18.

[145] Commission, 'The EU Strategy towards the Eradication of Trafficking in Human Beings 2012–2016' (Communication), COM (2012) 286 final. Council, 'Conclusions on the new EU Strategy towards the Eradication of Trafficking in Human Beings 2012–2016', Council Doc No 11838/6/12. European Parliament, Resolution on the situation of fundamental rights in the European Union (2010–2011) [2015] OJ C434/64, para 139.

[146] Commission, 'Proposal for a Council Framework Decision on preventing and combating trafficking in human beings, and protecting victims, repealing Framework Decision 2002/629/JHA', COM (2009) 136 final.

[147] Commission, 'Proposal for a Directive of the European Parliament and of the Council on preventing and combating trafficking in human beings, and protecting victims, repealing Framework Decision 2002/629/JHA', COM (2010) 95 final.

[148] Directive 2011/36/EU (n 26).

[149] *cf* above, A 'Definition of Trafficking in Human Beings', n 89 ff.

for a minimum of five years as a standard penalty, and increasing the penalty for aggravating circumstances from eight years to 10 years' imprisonment, together with minimum rules on aggravating circumstances.[150] The text also extends the scope of the exercise of criminal jurisdiction,[151] and requires Member States to ensure that investigation into or prosecution of human trafficking offences 'is not dependent on reporting or accusation by a victim, and that criminal proceedings may continue even if the victim withdraws his or her statement'.[152] The main innovation of the text resides in the presence of detailed measures to protect victims, and to prevent trafficking. The Directive requires States to provide support and assistance to victims 'before, during and for an appropriate period of time after the conclusion of criminal proceedings', and the Member States are invited to pay attention to victims with special needs (pregnant, health condition, mental or psychological disorder).[153] Other relevant provisions deal with their non-prosecution for the crimes they have been forced to commit (Article 8); measures linked to the Framework Decision on the Standings of Victims (Article 12);[154] access to compensation (Article 17);[155] or special measures for child victims.[156] Moreover, the Member States are required to adopt a multifaceted prevention policy, including measures to discourage and reduce demand, to raise awareness through information campaigns, or to promote regular training for officials.[157] The Directive also invites the Member States to consider taking measures to establish as a criminal offence the use of services, which are the objects of exploitation, with the knowledge that the person is a victim of trafficking.[158]

Even though the Directive's emphasis on assistance during the criminal justice process is still evident,[159] the EU explicitly aims at taking a human rights-based approach.[160]

The EU thus modified its approach to address trafficking in human beings and its commitment in favour of a comprehensive approach has become stronger and more explicit. The explicit prohibition of this change in its approach has had an impact on its policy and legislation. It led to the adoption of a new directive, containing more ambitious provisions in the fields of victims' protection and prevention of trafficking, which is completed by other instruments referring

---

[150] Directive 2011/36/EU (n 26) Art 4.
[151] ibid Art 10.
[152] ibid Art 9.
[153] ibid Art 11.
[154] Framework Decision 2001/220/JHA (n 113).
[155] Access to existing schemes of compensations to victims of violent crimes of intent, as provided in Council Directive 2004/80/EC of 29 April 2004 relating to compensation to crime victims [2004] OJ L261/15.
[156] Directive 2011/36/EU (n 26) Arts 13–16.
[157] ibid Art 18.
[158] ibid Art 18, para 4.
[159] Obokata and Payne (n 88) 318.
[160] A Bosma and C Rijken, 'Key Challenges in the Combat of Human Trafficking' (2016) 7 *New Journal of European Criminal Law* 315, 317.

explicitly to trafficking in human beings and/or aimed at addressing other issues, such as cooperation in criminal matters, common migration policy, border management, labour and social law etc. The change in the EU's approach also had an impact on the extension of counter-trafficking activities in the field of the EU's external relations.

C. The External Dimension of the EU's Policy against Trafficking

Since the 'EU policy on combating trafficking in human beings cannot be limited to internal instruments and must utilise all relevant opportunities, including those in the external dimension,'[161] the EU has also developed the external dimension of its policy to combat trafficking in human beings. Relying on its external competences and with the support of the EU Member States, the EU is promoting the transposition and the implementation of its policy in third countries. Whereas cooperation among Member States enables national authorities to trace the movement of trafficking victims and traffickers within the EU territory, cooperation with third countries is crucial. A mere reinforcement of border controls cannot be considered as a sufficient answer since 'traffickers, with their sophisticated organisations and logistical structures, (are) unlikely to be barred by border controls designed to regulate the flow of legitimate travellers.'[162] The existence of borders with regard to cooperation in criminal matters, migration and the protection of victims allows traffickers to benefit from safe havens. In countries where national counter-trafficking legislation and policy is not developed and implemented sufficiently, traffickers can hide themselves and their criminal assets from investigations and prosecutions. They can also use retaliatory measures against the victims and/or their close relatives to ensure the silence of their victims.

In order to avoid such a situation, which prevents the long-term eradication of trafficking in human beings, more ambitious cooperation must thus be developed. For instance, cross-border cooperation between law enforcement and judicial authorities allows them to have a better knowledge of the criminal threat they have to address and to build up stronger investigation and prosecution files that may potentially lead to the dismantling of trafficking networks. Cooperation between national referral mechanisms and equivalent mechanisms can also be important, as it allows the exchange of best practices, notably in the protection and assistance

---

[161] C Rijken, 'The External Dimension of EU Policy on Trafficking in Human Beings' in M Cremona, J Monar and S Poli (eds), *The External Dimension of the European Union's Area of Freedom, Security and Justice* (Brussels, Peter Lang, 2011) 209.

[162] W Rees, 'Inside Out: The External Face of EU Internal Security Policy' (2008) 30 *Journal of European Integration* 97, 103.

of victims of trafficking, and can lead to the establishment of transnational referral mechanisms. These examples of cooperation initiatives are decisive when they are undertaken within the same country, leading to a coherent national counter-trafficking response, but cooperation efforts necessarily encompass an important cross-border dimension, justified by the frequent transnational character of trafficking cases.

The interdependence between combating trafficking in human beings in third countries and combating trafficking within the EU was soon acknowledged by the relevant stakeholders, ie, the EU institutions and the EU Member States. This interdependence became one of the main arguments for developing the external dimension of the EU policy against trafficking in human beings and for cooperation with countries outside the Union in this field.[163]

The Council in 2005 extended the need for a comprehensive approach in the external dimension of the fight against trafficking in human beings.[164] This political stance was reiterated in the Strategy for the external dimension of Justice and Home Affairs,[165] in which the interdependence between the internal and external dimension of the fight against trafficking in human beings was highlighted. This Strategy also stressed the need for a coherent and coordinated approach in the EU's external relations, leading to the integration of trafficking-related measures in all relevant external policies.[166] Pursuant to the Strategy, the Council issued, in 2009, an Action-Oriented Paper focusing specifically on the external dimension of the fight against trafficking in human beings.[167] The document highlighted that 'trafficking in human beings is … an important area of cooperation within the EU and of partnership between the EU and third countries',[168] and emphasises the importance of 'regional and national investigations'[169] for the prosecution of traffickers.

The development of the external dimension of the EU's counter-trafficking policy was undertaken through several measures. First, the EU integrated the fight against trafficking in human beings into the fight against irregular migration, as reflected in the Global Approach on Migration and Mobility.[170] A broad

---

[163] Council, Conclusions, 'A Strategy for the External Dimension of JHA: Global Freedom, Security and Justice', Council Doc No 14366/3/05, 2.

[164] Council, 'Implementing the Strategy for the External Dimension of Justice and Home Affairs: Global Freedom, Security and Justice – Action-Oriented Paper on Strengthening the EU External Dimension on Action against Trafficking in Human Beings: Towards Global EU Action against Trafficking in Human Beings', Council Doc No 6865/10.

[165] Council, 'A Strategy for the External Dimension of JHA' (n 163).

[166] For instance, in the framework of development cooperation, actions aimed at reducing the poverty and vulnerability of certain groups are conducted and are part of the wish to eradicate the root causes of trafficking.

[167] Council, 'Action-Oriented Paper on strengthening the EU external dimension on Action against trafficking in human beings – Towards Global EU action against THB', Council Doc No 11450/5/09.

[168] ibid 2.

[169] ibid 21.

[170] Commission, 'The Global Approach to Migration and Mobility' (Communication), COM (2011) 743.

understanding of security implies considering irregular migration, not only as a migration issue, but also as an issue connected with organised crime.[171] Migration instruments are thus used to address security threats, and trafficking in human beings is addressed in all relevant agreements, strategic partnerships and political dialogues on migration and mobility with third countries.[172] Second, the EU institutions, with the support of the Member States, externally promoted the policy that they designed to address trafficking in human beings within the EU. To that end, the EU decided to make full use of its external competences. Provisions relating to trafficking in human beings and related issues are inserted into the multitude of existing cooperation instruments, and will be included in any future or revised articles of cooperation and association agreements.[173] Counter-trafficking measures have also been introduced into the broad range of policy instruments at the disposal of the EU, being partnerships, dialogue etc. The abundance of instruments available allows the EU to tailor its external coop-eration in the counter-trafficking field to the situation of each third country.[174] Third, the Union takes part in the global fight against trafficking in human beings. This is meant to enhance its cooperation and coordination with other international and regional intergovernmental organisations active in this field. Cooperation and coordination is also developed with other relevant stakeholders, such as civil society organisations, private actors etc. In all these fields, the promo-tion of a comprehensive approach thus became a clear objective to be pursued in the EU's external actions. Its efforts target not only governmental authorities in third countries, identified as essential partners in the fight against trafficking in human beings, but the EU's efforts also target other intergovernmental and non-governmental actors that are active in this field. These actors are also bound to develop and implement a multidisciplinary, holistic and integrated approach in their relationships. Yet the first evaluations of the EU's efforts[175] were not very positive. The main criticisms were a lack of coordination and coherence caused by the multiplication of both actors (EU, Member States, European agencies, etc) and initiatives at international level.[176] This lack of coordination was also pinpointed with regard to the impact of other external policies (migration law, external border control, development policy) on the fight against trafficking in

---

[171] ibid 15.

[172] ibid 16.

[173] Council, 'Action-Oriented Paper on strengthening the EU external dimension on action against trafficking in human beings' (n 167) 14.

[174] Commission, 'A Strategy on the External Dimension of the Area of Freedom, Security and Justice' (Communication), COM (2005) 491 final, 7.

[175] Council, 'Action-Oriented Paper on strengthening the EU external dimension on action against trafficking in human beings – First implementation report/update of information on Member States' external action', 31 May 2011, Council Doc No 9501/3/11.

[176] C Kaddous, 'Un nouveau cadre pour la dimension externe de l'espace de liberté, de sécurité et de justice' in C Kaddous and M Dony (eds), *D'Amsterdam à Lisbonne, Dix ans d'espace de liberté, de sécurité et de justice* (Basel, Helbing Lichtenhahn, 2010).

human beings.[177] In recent years, efforts have been made to remedy this situation. The EU Strategy adopted in 2012 explicitly foresees the coordination of the EU's external policy[178] and reported on the actions carried out to implement it.[179]

III. How to Analyse the External Dimension of the EU's Policy against Trafficking

The issue of trafficking in human beings has been the subject of an abundant literature and remains a topical issue in several fields. In legal literature, authors have discussed various aspects of the response to human trafficking, addressing its push and pull factors, analysing specific forms of exploitation,[180] and the various aspects of the response to the phenomenon,[181] at national,[182] regional[183] and international[184] levels. The policy and legislation developed by the EU is also scrutinised, assessed and commented on, notably to determine whether the EU effectively applies the comprehensive approach it proclaims to follow.[185] The external dimension of its policy has already been the object of research, as the main focus of the work,[186] or as a part of broader analyses on the EU's external relations in the field of migration,[187] or in response to global emergencies.[188] Comparative analysis between EU instruments and those set out within the Council of Europe,

---

[177] Rijken, 'The External Dimension of EU Policy on Trafficking in Human Beings' (n 161) 223–34.

[178] Commission, 'The EU Strategy towards the Eradication of Trafficking in Human Beings 2012–2016' (n 145) 11–12.

[179] Commission, 'Mid-Term implementation report of the EU Strategy towards the Eradication of Trafficking in Human Beings', SWD (2014) 318 final, 14–17.

[180] See, eg, C Rijken (ed), *Combating Trafficking in Human Beings for Labour Exploitation* (Nijmegen, Wolf Legal Publishers, 2011); or A Weatherburn, 'Clarifying the scope of labour exploitation in human trafficking law: Towards a legal conceptualisation of exploitation' (PhD thesis, Tilburg University, 2019).

[181] See, eg, on the protection of victims J Muraszkiewicz, *Protecting Victims of Human Trafficking from Liability, The European Approach* (London, Palgrave Macmillan, 2019); or K Plouffe-Malette, *Protection des victimes de traite des êtres humains, Approches internationales et européennes* (Brussels, Larcier, 2013).

[182] See, eg, Clesse (n 97).

[183] See, eg, V Roth, *Defining Human Trafficking and Identifying its Victims: A Study on the Impact and Future Challenges of International, European and Finnish Legal Responses to Prostitution-related Trafficking in Human Beings* (Nijmegen, Martinus Nijhoff Publishers, 2011).

[184] Gallagher, *The International Law of Human Trafficking* (n 15).

[185] See, eg, Obokata, 'EU Council Framework Decision on combating trafficking in human beings' (n 88); or Rijken and de Volder (n 143); or Obokata and Payne (n 88).

[186] Rijken, 'The External Dimension of EU Policy on Trafficking in Human Beings' (n 161); or Rijken and de Volder (n 143).

[187] C Boswell, 'The "external dimension" of EU immigration and asylum policy' (2003) 79 *International Affairs* 619; or S Carrera, J Santos Vara and T Stirk (eds), *Constitutionalising the External Dimensions of EU Migration Policies in Times of Crisis, Legality, Rule of Law and Fundamental Rights Reconsidered* (Cheltenham, Edward Elgar Publishing, 2019).

[188] Cullen (n 135).

or in other regional frameworks, has also been carried out.[189] Our purpose will not be to replicate the work of others, but rather to bring a contribution to the current discussions and debates.

Similarly, various scholars in law, political sciences, or international relations have analysed and conceptualised the means or processes by which interactions between the EU and external partners have resulted in EU legal rules or norms being adopted in legal orders of third countries and/or integrated in international instruments. Their work resulted in coining various concepts such as 'norm-export', 'rule transfer' or 'norm diffusion', but also extraterritorial application of EU law,[190] or the 'Brussels effect',[191] which reflect the possibility for the EU to export specific EU rules. Such 'export' can take place in various policy fields, including but not limited to environmental protection, internal market rules,[192] data protection[193] etc. It may result from more or less constraining processes, ranging from the mandatory transposition of the EU acquis by candidate countries as an essential condition of their progress towards accession, to the voluntary compliance or transposition of EU norms in third countries' national legal orders as part of an economic strategy. Scholars have also analysed how the EU does not only act as a norm setter exporting its own standards to serve its interests, but also acts as a norm taker, using EU instruments to support the adoption and application of international law. In this regard, the EU may adopt EU instruments to ensure that its own Member States comply with international obligations, for instance regarding the blacklisting of persons suspected of financing terrorism. The EU may also rely on EU instruments to ensure the compliance of third countries with international instruments. This is for instance the case in its common commercial policy, where it introduced in its new-generation free trade agreements provisions conditioning their application to respect international instruments. All these interactions shape the role and place of the EU as an actor on the international stage, and results in a multilayered process of unilateral, bilateral and multilateral normative interactions which cannot be categorised simply as either norm-export or norm-import.[194]

The present book integrates itself in both fields of research. It proposes to appraise in a comprehensive way the efforts undertaken by the EU in the course

---

[189] Gallagher, 'Recent Legal Developments in the Field of Human Trafficking' (n 10).

[190] M Cremona and J Scott (eds), *EU Law Beyond Borders: The Extraterritorial Reach of EU Law* (Oxford, Oxford University Press, 2019); or J Scott, 'The new EU "extra-territoriality"' (2014) 51 *Common Market Law Review* 1343.

[191] A Bradford, *The Brussels Effect: How the European Union Rules the World* (Oxford, Oxford University Press, 2020).

[192] M-L Öberg, 'Expanding the EU Internal Market without Enlarging the Union: Constitutional Limitations' (PhD thesis, EUI, 2015).

[193] E Fahey, *The Global Reach of EU Law* (Abingdon, Routledge, 2016) 4.

[194] M Cremona, 'Extending the Reach of EU Law: The EU as an International Legal Actor' in M Cremona and J Scott (eds), *EU Law Beyond Borders: The Extraterritorial Reach of EU Law* (Oxford, Oxford University Press, 2019).

of its external activities to promote and support the eradication of trafficking in human beings. It aims at unpacking the mechanisms through which the EU has been engaged in promoting its own policy against trafficking in human beings towards its external partners, third countries and international organisations alike, relying on unilateral and multilateral mechanisms.

In other fields in which the EU attempts to externally promote its values and norms, such ambition is presented as linked to the objectives assigned to the EU to promote its values of respect for human dignity and human rights, internally and on the international scene (Articles 2 and 21(1) TEU). It also participates in achieving an AFSJ with respect for fundamental rights, in which the Union shall frame a common migration policy and shall endeavour to ensure a high level of security through measures to combat crime (Articles 67 and 79 of the Treaty on the Functioning of the European Union (TFEU)). The field of trafficking in human beings presents certain specificities justifying the conduct of an extensive analysis. The external dimension of the EU's policy against trafficking in human beings is inextricably linked to the external dimension of the EU's AFSJ, and as in other policies developed within this area, the EU is subjected to the heavy influence of external norms, starting with the existence of multiple international law instruments, addressing trafficking from both crime prevention and human rights perspectives. Cross-references to external instruments in EU law renders it difficult to isolate specific EU norms. Nevertheless, the external dimension of the EU's counter-trafficking policy cannot be limited to a specific EU competence, whether belonging or not belonging to the AFSJ. The comprehensive approach advocated and supported by the EU institutions requires integrating counter-trafficking measures in external activities developed and undertaken in other policy fields, such as development cooperation, social law etc. A factor of complexity thus appears, which forces the EU to integrate counter-trafficking considerations in most of its external activities, while dealing with the limits of its external competences in certain fields, such as the external promotion of human rights.[195] The latter links to an additional factor of complexity, which lies in the multidimensional response to trafficking that can be addressed equally from a criminal justice perspective and from a human rights perspective. The external dimension of the EU's policy in this field may thus encounter conflicting objectives and face mixed reactions from partners. Diffusion of EU legal standards and promotion of international criminal justice measures may serve the interests of the EU and its partners, eager to create a legal playing field facilitating cooperation in combating crime. However, such a coincidence of interests may not be present when the EU seeks to uphold a more human rights-based approach to the issue, compromising the possibility of the EU developing an external policy in line with its own values.

---

[195] L Pech and J Grogan, 'EU External Human Rights Policy' in RA Wessel and J Larik (eds), *EU External Relations Law: Text, Cases and Materials*, 2nd edn (Oxford, Hart Publishing, 2020).

At the heart of this book is a legal question concerning the capacity for the EU to deliver its promises on the international scene. Ten years after the entry into force of the Treaty of Lisbon, in a field marked by the porosity between the internal and external dimensions of the EU's policy against trafficking, the purpose of this book is to determine whether the EU succeeds in delivering in its external activities a comprehensive response to trafficking. Such appraisal requires us to unpack the multilayered process of unilateral and multilateral interactions through which the EU promotes its policy externally, itself largely influenced by interactions with external norms and partners. The analysis lies at the crossroads of various fields of EU law, including but not limited to EU external relations law, EU criminal law and EU migration law, which are all mobilised. The method of the 'analytical theory of law'[196] appears to be best suited to studying legal norms and fundamental concepts in a given legal order, and for questioning their interactions and the place of a given rule or concept in a field of law. The analysis marginally includes the national aspects of such interactions, relating to the adoption, transposition and implementation of counter-trafficking measures in national legal orders, as well as the bilateral interactions with third countries, which are mostly addressed within broader regional frameworks of cooperation. The analysis does not intend to be purely descriptive and limited to the presentation of the different external activities undertaken by the EU, and its Member States, to develop the external dimension of its counter-trafficking policy. On the contrary, this research aims to conduct an analytical and critical examination of the EU's efforts.

IV. Structure of the Book

To best analyse the analysis of the external dimension of the EU's policy against trafficking in human beings, the book is structured around four main parts.

The first chapter serves to introduce and frame the issue. Mobilising the concept of the acquis, mostly used in the context of EU enlargement policy, the key characteristics and components of the EU's policy against trafficking in human beings are identified through a detailed overview of the international agreements binding on the EU, the internal legislative instruments adopted on the basis of EU treaties and the soft law documents adopted by the EU institutions. This step allows us to pinpoint how broad and diverse counter-trafficking measures can be, revealing the implementation of a comprehensive approach within the EU's policy, even though an emphasis on criminal justice and migration measures can be seen. The next step brings us to the analysis of the external competences at the disposal of the EU to promote its own policy towards its external partners. Whereas the EU possesses limited explicit competences that may be relevant to promote counter-trafficking

---

[196] O Corten, *Méthodologie du droit international public* (Brussels, Editions de l'Université de Bruxelles, 2009) 24–26.

measures, it can rely on implied external competences, whose identification and definition has evolved through time. The abundance of external competences at its disposal, linked to the comprehensive approach supported by the EU to address human trafficking, as well as the possibility for Member States to retain a capacity to act externally in most fields, leads to a first challenge, namely the risk of confusion. Constitutional principles and duties, such as the principle of coherence or the duty of sincere cooperation, are key to mitigating that risk, and the position of the EU Anti-Trafficking Coordinator offers further guarantees.

The next two chapters aim at analysing how such external competences are relied upon to develop the external dimension of the EU's counter-trafficking policy. Chapter two focuses on the unilateral promotion of such policy, which refers to the situation where the EU attempts to persuade third countries to transpose into their national legal orders the key elements of its own policy. This unilateral promotion is best illustrated through the case study selected, namely the promotion of the EU's policy within the Stabilisation and Association Process which concerns the countries of the Western Balkans. The EU relies here on a vast array of instruments and tools, not only to incite these countries to comply with major international and regional instruments, but also to integrate them into the EU's efforts to counter trafficking. A fine example of such ambition lies in the conclusion of cooperation agreements and/or administrative arrangements with the EU AFSJ agencies, such as Europol, Eurojust and Frontex, which form an integral part of the EU's external activities, and allow third countries to be fully associated with the criminal operational response to trafficking. The role of Member States is also highlighted, as they participate in such promotion, either through the conclusion of bilateral agreements, or through their participation in instruments favouring regional cooperation. Chapter three then moves on to the multilateral promotion of the EU's policy against human trafficking. Building upon the EU's strong commitment on multilateralism in its external relations, this chapter addresses how the EU integrated itself in a multilayered governance system marked by the abundance and diversity of stakeholders, which are briefly described, as well as their contribution to international efforts to counter trafficking. Normative interactions regarding the content of relevant legal provisions in international and regional instruments reveals to what extent the EU is building upon international standards and integrating them within its own legal order, but also supporting and promoting the inclusion of new measures, such as the non-prosecution of victims forced to commit offences as a result of their exploitation, in other frameworks. The EU is also fully integrated in various coordination mechanisms that put into practice its commitment to multilateralism, and appears as a key actor, delegating to some of its external partners the implementation of activities aimed at supporting the implementation of counter-trafficking measures in strategic regions and countries. Throughout these multilateral activities, the EU cooperates equally with criminal justice organisations and human rights organisations, which testifies of its commitment in favour of a comprehensive approach to address trafficking in human beings. Yet all these combined efforts face the same limit: their dependence on the willingness of States to implement not only criminal justice measures to prosecute and convict traffickers, but also to fully engage in the protection of trafficking victims and prevention of the phenomenon.

Chapter four concludes by addressing the most recent developments in the external dimension of the EU's policy against trafficking in human beings, which present further challenges. The emergence of mixed migration flows, in which victims of trafficking may travel together with other categories of migrants and/or may be migrants who were trafficked in the course of their journey, has led to a certain confusion in the EU's response to trafficking in human being and the smuggling of migrants. Although the two phenomena are governed by distinct legal frameworks, they are more and more addressed together, especially in the soft law instruments that the EU seems to favour to develop its cooperation with third countries. Moreover, the response to trafficking in human beings is increasingly militarised. Whereas trafficking in armed conflicts emerges as a new form of trafficking addressed at international level, from the EU's perspective this militarisation results from an increasing reliance on instruments belonging to the Common Foreign and Security Policy. As closing remarks, we answer whether the external dimension of the EU's policy against trafficking in human beings manages to be both coherent and comprehensive, and pinpoint the accountability gaps resulting from the abundance of actors involved in the ever more diverse counter-trafficking measures.

1

Framing the EU's Policy and its External Competences

I. Introduction

The notion of trafficking in human beings covers a wide variety of criminal behaviours. Although trafficking often occurs on a transnational basis and involves two or more States, domestic trafficking (ie, taking place within national borders) is rising in most countries. Criminals involved in this criminal activity do not necessarily belong to transnational organised criminal groups, and petty criminals, exploiting one or two persons, can also commit trafficking on a more limited scale.

In recent decades the European Union (EU) has developed its own policy and legislative framework to fight against trafficking in human beings and to prevent it. Actions at EU level complement those carried out at national level and they are well suited to addressing this phenomenon, which frequently has a transnational dimension. On the one hand, the EU has developed measures designed to support, foster and strengthen actions against trafficking in human beings within the EU Member States as well as to boost cooperation between them in this field. They form part of the internal dimension of the EU's counter-trafficking policy, whose aim is to disrupt the 'trafficking chains' within the EU.[1] These measures rely most often on the competences of the EU in the field of police and judicial cooperation in criminal matters, whose content has evolved in parallel to the evolution of the EU Treaties. On the other hand, the EU has developed other actions pursuing a different aim, namely the development of the external dimension of its policy against trafficking in human beings. Like the whole Area of Freedom, Security and Justice (AFSJ), this policy has a necessary and even vital external dimension, which is required for providing an effective response to security threats,[2] and is

---

[1] The literature on this issue is abundant, see for instance, C Rijken, *Trafficking in Persons: Prosecution from a European Perspective* (The Hague, TMC Asser Press, 2003); C Rijken (ed), *Combating Trafficking in Human Beings for Labour Exploitation* (Nijmegen, Wolf Legal Publishers, 2011); or E Guild and P Minderhoud (eds), *Immigration and Criminal Law in the EU: The Legal Measures and Social Consequences of Criminal Law in Member States on Human Trafficking and Smuggling in Human Beings* (Leiden, Martinus Nijhoff Publishers, 2006).

[2] Council, Conclusions, 'A Strategy for the External Dimension of JHA: Global Freedom, Security and Justice', Council Doc No 14366/3/05, 2.

interdependent with its internal dimension. Its external dimension is crucial as a mere reinforcement of border controls is not considered as a sufficient answer since 'traffickers, with their sophisticated organisations and logistical structures, (are) unlikely to be barred by border controls designed to regulate the flow of legitimate travellers'.[3]

The measures developed by the EU as part of the external dimension of its counter-trafficking policy can be found in a variety of instruments, especially those concerning the fight against irregular migration, as reflected in the Global Approach to Migration and Mobility.[4] Indeed, in a critical way the EU follows a broad understanding of security, which often entails considering irregular migration in connection with organised crime.[5] Trafficking in human beings, as well as the smuggling of migrants, are thus often addressed in all relevant agreements and strategic partnerships with third countries and in all political dialogues on migration and mobility.[6]

The EU intends to promote its counter-trafficking policy towards third countries externally (ie, outside the EU's legal order) in order notably to ensure their cooperation.[7] These countries are considered as key partners, in particular in addressing extra-EU trafficking flows. Even though some trafficking flows do not have EU Member States as their destination, they nevertheless constitute a potential threat. The criminals may decide to expand their activities into EU territory or to use the profits generated by their trafficking activities to finance and develop other criminal activities, such as drug trafficking, for which the destination is the EU Member States. The EU thus pursues the objective of influencing third countries towards adopting and implementing in their national legal orders a policy and legislative framework, which is compatible with, if not similar to, the EU's own policy and legal framework.

The approximation of approaches designed to tackle trafficking in human beings is indeed essential for effective and comprehensive cross-border cooperation in this field. Establishing similar structures and institutions and sharing the same approach and priorities will make it easier to identify foreign partners. The approximation of the definitions of the offence and the penalties make it possible to satisfy the requirement of dual criminality and prevent refusals in matters of police and judicial cooperation. The application of similar standards in the protection of and assistance given to trafficking victims ensures that their human rights

---

[3] W Rees, 'Inside Out: The External Face of EU Internal Security Policy' (2008) 30 *Journal of European Integration* 97, 103.

[4] Commission, 'The Global Approach to Migration and Mobility' (Communication), COM (2011) 743 final.

[5] E Pirjatanniemi, 'Victims of Trafficking in the Migration Discourse' in R Haverkamp, E Herlin-Karnell and C Lernestedt (eds), *What is Wrong with Human Trafficking? Critical Perspectives on the Law* (Oxford, Hart Publishing, 2019) 82.

[6] Commission, 'The Global Approach to Migration and Mobility' (n 4) 16.

[7] S Lavenex, 'Channels of Externalisation of EU Justice and Home Affairs' in M Cremona, J Monar and S Poli (eds), *The External Dimension of the European Union's Area of Freedom, Security and Justice* (Brussels, Peter Lang, 2011) 121.

are respected and that incentives for them to cooperate in criminal investigations and prosecutions are provided.

To achieve this objective of promoting its own counter-trafficking policy externally, the EU makes full use of the multitude of existing cooperation instruments, including association agreements,[8] as well as of the broad range of policy instruments at its disposal, tailoring its efforts of promotion to the situation of each third country.[9]

These efforts by the EU to externalise its policy are at the heart of this research, whose overall objective is to identify how these efforts are implemented and whether they achieve a sufficient balance between security and human rights objectives. To answer this question, a preliminary and essential step is to frame the EU's policy against trafficking in human beings and the competences at its disposal to promote it externally.

Our analysis will start with the definition of the content of the EU's policy against trafficking in human beings and, to this end, we will have recourse to the notion of the EU acquis, well known in EU law, in order to identify the EU acquis in the area of the fight against trafficking in human beings (II).

Given that the EU is strictly bound by the principle of conferral of competences, enshrined in Article 4 of the Treaty on European Union (TEU), the boundaries of the competences at its disposal to promote its counter-trafficking acquis externally will then be carefully delimited as well as the principles guiding their exercise (III).

II. The Identification of the Core Components of the EU's Policy

The EU started to adopt and implement measures to prevent and fight trafficking in human beings in the mid-1990s, which was a time when awareness of this phenomenon was growing fast. Since then, it has never stopped developing new initiatives and instruments. The Union's institutions, together with the Member States, have adapted the measures designed to prevent and combat trafficking in human beings to the evolution of the phenomenon in parallel with the constitutional changes that increased the scope of the competences conferred on the Union. Furthermore, considering the evolution of the Union's approach in terms of how best to address trafficking in human beings, counter-trafficking measures are no longer limited to criminal justice measures that focus on the prosecution of traffickers but also include measures of different natures. As a result, the Union's

---

[8] Council, 'Action-Oriented Paper on strengthening the EU external dimension on action against trafficking in human beings – Towards Global EU action against THB', Council Doc No 11450/5/09, 14.

[9] Commission, 'A Strategy on the External Dimension of the Area of Freedom, Security and Justice' (Communication), COM (2005) 491 final, 7.

policy to prevent and combat trafficking in human beings has been developed through the adoption and implementation of a plethora of instruments.

Considering the objective of this chapter, it appears necessary and essential as a preliminary step to identify the content of the Union's counter-trafficking policy precisely, highlighting its most relevant features and characteristics. In order to achieve this objective, the notion of acquis, although not legally defined, is of crucial importance. Although most often used in the context of the pre-accession policy, the notion finds its interest in our analysis of the EU's policy against trafficking in human beings, as it enables us to review the content of a given policy field in a coherent manner and to go beyond its heterogeneous and diverse components. Furthermore, the definition of the EU's acquis in this field constitutes a necessary preliminary step in our analysis of the external dimension of this policy. Whereas Article 21, paragraph 1 TEU clarifies the values that the Union will promote in its external relations, the provision does not regulate the content of the norms and principles that the Union projects externally.[10] Identifying the acquis will allow us not only to map out the substance of the norms externally promoted, but also to determine the extent, the modalities and the limits of the Union's external action.

In the next sections, the concept of the acquis will be presented, focusing particularly on the acquis developed within the AFSJ (A). The acquis relating to the fight against trafficking in human beings will then be defined (B).

A. What is the Acquis? Presentation of a Concept

According to the Glossary of the European Union, the acquis can be defined as

> the body of common rights and obligations which bind all the Member States together within the European Union. It is constantly evolving and comprises among others the content principles and objectives of the Treaties, the legislation adopted in application of the treaties and the case law of the Court of Justice, declarations and resolutions adopted by the Union, measures relating to justice and home affairs and international agreements concluded by the Union and the Member States in the field of the Union's activities.[11]

Such a definition of the concept has the merit of being easily understandable and setting out the different sources of the acquis. However, it fails to grasp the complexities of a notion which has evolved over time and which may vary from one policy field to another.

As a first step, the evolution of the notion will be discussed, as well as its multiple dimensions (i). After these general considerations on the acquis, our analysis

---

[10] M Benlolo Carabot, 'L'influence extérieure de l'Union Européenne' in M Benlolo-Carabot, U Candas and E Cujo, *Union Européenne et Droit International* (Paris, Editions Pedone, 2013) 62.
[11] Glossary 'Community acquis', available at: europa.eu/legislation_summaries/glossary/community_acquis_en.htm.

will focus on the acquis adopted within the AFSJ, formerly known as Justice and Home Affairs (ii).

i. Evolution of the Notion Over Time

Before entering into considerations relating to the acquis in a broad policy field such as the AFSJ, it is of paramount importance to have a clear understanding of the notion of *acquis*. Such an understanding can be obtained if one considers, on the one hand, the evolution of the references made to it in the Union's constitutional treaties. It allows us to see how certain elements of Union law acquire the qualification of acquis in the view of the treaties' drafters. On the other hand, it is also worth discussing the expressions used to refer to the acquis in order to search for potential differences between acquis *communautaire* and the Union's acquis.

a. References to the Acquis in the Union's Constitutional Treaties

Although the acquis is now considered as one of the key notions of European integration, the original Treaties establishing the European Economic Community (Treaty of Rome) did not mention the notion of acquis, even in their first amendments.[12] The term 'acquis' appeared for the first time in an Opinion of the Commission about the accession of the UK, Ireland and Denmark to the European Economic Community,[13] and became recurrent in the practice of the European institutions, notably in parliamentary questions.[14] However the term was not officially mentioned in a legal instrument until 1985, when it was mentioned in the Act concerning the conditions of accession of the Kingdom of Spain and the Portuguese Republic and the adjustments to the Treaties.[15] The term is mentioned in constitutional treaties only since the adoption of the Maastricht Treaty. References to the term can be classified in three different categories, created by different treaties' amendments.

The first type of reference was introduced by the Maastricht Treaty, which provided, in its Article B TEU, that 'the Union shall set itself (the objective) to maintain in full the "acquis Communautaire"' and build on it'. Its Article C TEU also mentioned that the Union shall be served by a single institutional framework, 'which shall ensure the consistency and the continuity of the activities carried out in order to attain its objectives while respecting and building upon the

---

[12] O Audeoud, 'L'acquis communautaire, du mythe à la pratique' (2002) 33(3) *Revue d'études comparatives Est-Ouest* 67, 68.

[13] Advisory opinion of the Commission to the Council, of 1 October 1969 concerning the accession requests of the UK, Denmark, Ireland and Norway, quoted in C Delcourt, 'The *Acquis Communautaire*: Has the concept had its day?' (2001) 38 *Common Market Law Review* 829, 830.

[14] Audeoud (n 12) 68.

[15] Act concerning the conditions of accession of the Kingdom of Spain and the Portuguese Republic [1985] OJ L302/9. See in particular, Joint declaration on the adjustment of the 'acquis communautaire' in the vegetable oils and fats sector, 481.

"acquis Communautaire". The Treaty of Amsterdam and the Treaty of Nice did not modify the content of these provisions, which became and remained Articles 2 and 3 TEU. These references seem to highlight the crucial importance of the acquis communautaire, developed notably in the framework of the EU's Internal Market and composed of norms at the core of European integration and for which there can be no derogations. The Treaty of Lisbon deleted these explicit references to the acquis in Articles 2 and 3 TEU, but the mention in the very first article of the TEU of the process of creating an ever closer union encompasses the idea that the current level of integration achieved up until now to remain and that going back on it is unlikely to be compatible with the Treaties.

The second type of reference to the acquis was introduced by the Treaty of Amsterdam, which made reference to the acquis developed outside Community fields of action. On the one hand it referred to the 'Schengen acquis', integrated into the framework of the EU.[16] It is important to note that this integration of the Schengen acquis was one of the rare occasions where the acquis was actually defined, as the Annex of the Protocol lists the agreements, conventions, protocols, decisions and declarations belonging to this sectorial acquis.[17] Further references to the acquis can be found in the Protocol on the position of the United Kingdom and Ireland[18] and the Protocol on the position of Denmark,[19] organising the modalities of their opt-outs from the measures adopted in the field of Justice and Home Affairs.[20] Neither the Treaty of Nice nor the Treaty of Lisbon alter the references made to the 'Schengen acquis'[21] and the references to the AFSJ acquis in the Protocols on the position of the United Kingdom (UK), Ireland and Denmark.[22] In addition, the Treaty of Lisbon also refers to the term acquis in Protocol No 36 on transitional provisions,[23] and more particularly in the provisions dealing with the acts adopted in the field of police and judicial cooperation in criminal matters prior to the entry into force of the Treaty of Lisbon.[24] These references

---

[16] Protocol No 2 integrating the Schengen Acquis into the Framework of the European Union, and its Annex, [1997] OJ C340/93.

[17] It is also worth mentioning that at the occasion of the integration of the Schengen Acquis, the United Kingdom and Ireland obtained a specific status, referred to as an opt-out. The countries were not (and are still not) parties to the Schengen system. The Protocol regulates in its Article 4 their possibility to participate in some or all of the provisions of this acquis. Recently the Court of Justice insisted on the importance of maintaining the coherence of the Schengen acquis, and concluded that Member States legitimately refused to authorise the participation of the UK to the Frontex Regulation and the Decision concerning access to VIS. See Case C-77/05, *UK v Council (Frontex Regulation)* [2007] EU:C:2007:803 and Case C- 482/08, *UK v Council (Decision concerning access to VIS)* [2010] EU:C:2010:631.

[18] [1997] OJ C340/99.

[19] [1997] OJ C340/101.

[20] See below II.A.iii.a 'The Internal Dimension of the AFSJ Acquis'.

[21] Protocol No 19 [2010] OJ C83/290.

[22] Protocol No 21 [2010] OJ C83/295 and Protocol No 22 [2010] OJ C83/299.

[23] Protocol No 36 [2010] OJ C83/322.

[24] The UK has indeed obtained the possibility to opt out from these acts before the end of the transitional period (after which the Court of Justice of the European Union (ECJ) shall have full jurisdiction and the Commission can conduct infringement proceedings). The UK can then at any moment decide

to the acquis demonstrate that Treaty drafters recognise the development of the acquis beyond old fields of cooperation directly relating to economic cooperation between Member States. For them, the acquis has also been developing in other fields of deepened European integration, such as free movement of persons, abolition of internal border controls and cross-border cooperation in migration and security matters.

Finally, the Treaty of Amsterdam introduced a third type of reference to the 'acquis communautaire' relating to the introduction of the mechanism of enhanced cooperation between Member States. The TEU as amended by the Amsterdam Treaty provided, in Article 43(e) TEU, as one of the conditions for the establishment of an enhanced cooperation, that the proposed cooperation 'respects the acquis communautaire and the measures adopted under the other provisions of the said Treaties'. The Treaty of Nice did not amend this provision and maintained this condition in Article 43(c) TEU. However, this condition is no longer present in the current provisions on enhanced cooperation, ie, Article 20 TEU and Articles 326–30 of the Treaty on the Functioning of the European Union (TFEU), although it is provided in Article 326 TFEU that 'any enhanced cooperation shall comply with the Treaties and Union law'. Despite the deletion of the reference to the acquis, it can be argued that the condition of respecting existing Union law still applies, and its permanence reinforces the idea that the acquis consists of rules accepted by all Member States as rules to which there can be no derogations. The support of all the EU Member States, granted either through unanimity or through qualified majority voting depending on the legislative procedure applicable for the adoption of a given act, appears essential for the inclusion of an instrument into the acquis. According to the current Article 20, paragraph 4 TEU, the acts adopted in the framework of enhanced cooperation, ie, with the support of a limited number of Member States, 'shall not be regarded as part of the acquis which has to be accepted by candidate countries for accession to the Union'.[25]

Most of the references can be considered as addressed to the current Member States,[26] notably in order to insist on the fact that it is not possible to take steps backwards and/or to indicate their direction for the future qualitative evolution of European integration. Furthermore, even though the term is inseparable from the accession process of new Member States,[27] only one provision refers to that

---

to opt in to participate in these acts, accepting the competences of the Commission and the ECJ. According to Art 10, para 5, Protocol No 36, when the UK decides to re-opt in to the acts adopted prior to the entry into force of the Lisbon Treaty, the Union institutions and the UK shall seek to re-establish the widest possible measure of participation of the UK 'in the acquis of the Union in the AFSJ'.

[25] The formulation was slightly different in the Nice Treaty, as Art 44, para 1 TEU provided that 'the acts and decisions adopted for the implementation of enhanced cooperation shall not form part of the Union acquis'.

[26] See in this regard the provisions on the Schengen acquis or provisions on enhanced cooperation.

[27] The Copenhagen Criteria were established by the European Council in June 1993 and strengthened by the Madrid European Council in 1995. They are: 1. stability of institutions guaranteeing democracy, the rule of law, human rights and respect for and protection of minorities; 2. a functioning market economy and the ability to cope with competitive pressure and market forces within the EU;

element and only to stress that the acquis is composed of norms approved by all Member States. The emphasis in the Union's constitutional texts thus seems to be on the consensus surrounding the norms composing the acquis, meaning that they constitute a core of norms to which there can be no derogations. However, almost none of the Treaty provisions we referred to provide for the definition of the acquis, not even in a general way.[28] Although several mentions of the acquis are present in the EU Treaties, its drafters just refer to the acquis without further precision, probably assuming that the acquis is a notion whose definition is of common knowledge to relevant EU actors. One could thus wonder whether more precise elements can be identified in other sources of Union law.

b. Acquis Communautaire, Acquis of the Union: Different Expressions for the Same Notion?

In practice, whereas the notion of acquis is one of the most frequently applied, it also remains one of the least well defined.[29] The silence of the Treaties can most probably be explained by the dynamic nature of the acquis, inseparable from the dynamism of the EU legal order, which is based on acquired common rules, practices and values evolving constantly under the pressure of various internal and external factors.[30] However, the other sources of Union law, which are binding or non-binding, do not provide additional guidance. On the contrary, the creation of the European Union by the Treaty of Maastricht introduced an additional factor of confusion since it introduced the concept of 'acquis of the Union' or 'Union acquis'. The definition of the notion of acquis became thus even more complicated, in particular because of the simultaneous use of these different expressions, sometimes used in the same document. It was indeed not rare to find the 'acquis communautaire' mentioned in the same text as the 'acquis of the Union',[31] or to see in others texts that, whereas the expression 'Union acquis' seems preferred, it does not exclude references to the 'acquis communautaire'.[32]

The most obvious way to distinguish between these two notions[33] is to consider that the expression 'acquis communautaire' refers to the body of rules whose legal basis may be found in the Community pillar, ie, the provisions contained within the Treaties establishing the three Communities. By contrast, the expression

---

and 3. ability to take on the obligations of membership, including the capacity to effectively implement the rules, standards and policies that make up the body of EU law (the 'acquis'), and adherence to the aims of political, economic and monetary union. Source: eur- lex.europa.eu/summary/glossary/accession_criteria_copenhague.html?locale=en.

[28] Delcourt (n 13) 831.

[29] R Petrov, 'The Dynamic Nature of the acquis communautaire in European Union External Relations' (2006) 18 *European Review of Public Law* 741.

[30] ibid 746.

[31] See for instance the examples quoted in Delcourt (n 13) 832, fn 15.

[32] See for instance the examples quoted in Delcourt (n 13) 833, fns 18, 19 and 20.

[33] For an example of such interpretation, see CC Gialdino, 'Some reflections on the *Acquis Communautaire*' (1995) 32 *Common Market Law Review* 1089, 1096.

'Union acquis' would consist of the whole acquis existing within the EU legal order, comprising not only the body of rules adopted in the Community pillar, but also the body of rules adopted on the basis of the provisions belonging to the Second and Third Pillars.[34]

However, despite these circumstances, the expression 'acquis communautaire' does not become obsolete and may evolve to go beyond the reference to the acquis adopted under the First Pillar, ie, the Community acquis. Authors, such as Carlo Curti Gialdino, Christine Delcourt or Roman Petrov have, for instance, considered that this notion, set down in the TEU, refers to a fundamental acquis, representing the core of the supranational EC legal order,[35] on which the Union could not go back[36] and, expressed in a different way, the genetic code of the Union.[37] This category of acquis includes, in its widest scope, 'a patrimony of binding and non-binding rules, principles and practices'[38] that distinguish the Union legal order from other international and national legal systems. This body of rules is not only formed by provisions of the Treaties, but also by general principles of EU law, established by the case law of the Court of Justice, such as the principles of primacy of Union law over national law or the direct effect of certain provisions of Union law.[39] The draft of the EU Constitutional Treaty seemed to prove them right as its Preamble provided that the new EU would 'continue the work accomplished ... by ensuring the continuity of the Community acquis'. The Treaty enhanced even further the scope of the 'fundamental acquis' 'by erecting a coherent edifice of common principles, objectives, values on which the EU is based'.[40]

Even though the Treaty of Lisbon does not take up these elements as such, their interpretation is confirmed by the presence of Title I TEU, containing common provisions, aimed at proclaiming the values on which the Union is founded, the objectives it pursues and the fundamental principles it applies.[41] Furthermore, the fundamental acquis would be complemented by what Pierre Pescatore referred to as the 'ordinary acquis', corresponding to the body of rules referred to in acts of Accession in order to register what has been achieved by the Union.[42]

---

[34] Title V on a Common and Foreign Security Policy and Title VI Provisions on cooperation in the fields of Justice and Home Affairs.

[35] R Petrov, 'The External Dimension of the Acquis Communautaire', EUI Working Paper 2002/07, available at: cadmus.eui.eu/bitstream/handle/1814/6931/MWP_2007_02.pdf, 4.

[36] K Lenaerts and P Van Nuffel, *European Union Law*, 3rd edn (London, Sweet & Maxwell, 2011) 43, para 3-013. See in this regard, the analysis of Gialdino of Opinion 1/91, in which the Court declared the judicial system proposed in the draft European Economic Area (EEA) Agreement to be incompatible with the Treaty (Gialdino (n 33) 1109–14).

[37] Delcourt (n 13) 840.

[38] Petrov, 'The External Dimension of the Acquis Communautaire' (n 35) 3.

[39] Case 26/62, *Van Gend and Loos* [1963] EU:C:1963:1; and Case 6/64, *Costa v Enel* [1964] EU:C:1964:66.

[40] Petrov, 'The External Dimension of the Acquis Communautaire' (n 35) 4.

[41] See in particular current Arts 2–6 TEU.

[42] P Pescatore, 'Aspects juridiques de l'acquis communautaire' [1981] *Revue Trimestrielle de Droit Européen* 617, 618, quoted in Gialdino (n 33) 1108.

Provisions from international agreements, binding the Union and its Member States, are included in this part of the acquis together with, under certain conditions, principles of customary international law.[43] Rules of secondary Union law are also included in this ordinary acquis as well as certain 'soft law' provisions.[44]

Besides these elements, the abolition of the pillar structure may also influence the definition of the acquis. The EU no longer acts through either measures of Community law or non-community measures, and its actions in each of its fields of competence now give rise to measures of 'Union law'.[45] The expression brings both previous Community law and non-Community law, as well as all provisions, measures and other legal rules and principles applicable to the Member States and the Union institutions under a common denominator of 'Union law'.[46] It is thus possible to consider that, under the new EU legal order, there is only one acquis: the Union acquis. However, this does not mean that the expression 'acquis communautaire' ceases to be used, the EU institutions proving their differences (or rather their indifference) regarding the distinction between the two notions.[47]

In conclusion, the existence of different expressions referring to the body of rules belonging to the EU legal order reflects the fuzziness of the definition of the notion of acquis, which varies depending on the context in which it is invoked. Therefore, the EU legal order does not possess a single, homogeneous and indivisible definition of the acquis, but on the contrary the definition of the acquis seems to be multiple and heterogeneous.

ii. *The Acquis in the Area of Freedom, Security and Justice*

The Area of Freedom, Security and Justice (AFSJ) was mentioned for the first time by the Treaty of Amsterdam, building on the integration achieved in Justice and Home Affairs under the previous Treaty regime. Established under the Lisbon

---

[43] Case C-162/96, *Racke* [1998] EU:C:1998:293.

[44] The legal effect of these provisions is determined on a case-by-case basis by the Court of Justice, on the basis of their contents and the intentions of the drafters (Petrov, 'The External Dimension of the Acquis Communautaire' (n 35) 6). Included in this category are measures such as inter-institutional agreements, conclusions and resolutions of the EU institutions and of the Member States, programmes, communiqués. For further details, see GM Borchardt and KC Wellens, 'Soft Law in European Community Law' (1989) 14 *European Law Review* 267, 285, quoted in Petrov, 'The External Dimension of the Acquis Communautaire' (n 35) 6, fn 16.

[45] Lenaerts and Van Nuffel (n 36) 71.

[46] ibid.

[47] Whereas in some contexts, the expression 'acquis communautaire' is used to refer to human rights issues (see for instance, Question for written answer E-009267/13, of 29 July 2013 about freedom of speech in Turkey, [2014] OJ C 88E/180), it is in other situations used to refer to the trade-related and economic acquis (Opinion of the European Economic and Social Committee on the situation of Ukrainian civil society in the context of European aspirations of Ukraine, 16 October 2014 [2015] OJ C12/51, point 4.2). Similarly, the expression 'EU acquis' may be used *largo sensu*, ie, to refer indistinctly to the rules of Union law (Council Conclusions, 'Training of legal practitioners: an essential tool to consolidate the EU acquis' [2014] OJ C443/7); or *stricto sensu*, ie, to refer to rules relating to a specific policy (Question for written answer E-003499/14 about the safeguarding of the EU acquis in the field of health and environmental protection [2014] OJ C343/62).

Treaty as one of the fundamental objectives of the EU, this Area without internal borders shall encompass the assurance of free movement of persons, accompanied by compensatory measures in external border controls, asylum, immigration and the prevention and combating of crime. Considering the broad scope of the measures required for the achievement of such an ambitious objective, the acquis developed within the AFSJ is most probably composed of a plethora of instruments and acts, inextricably linked to each other, rendering the isolation of the acquis in a given policy field difficult.

In order to define patterns for the identification of the acquis in the field of the prevention of and combating of trafficking in human beings, it is important to highlight certain characteristics that possesses the acquis adopted in the framework of the AFSJ. The acquis adopted in this field differs from the acquis developed in other policy fields, mainly because of the differentiated participation of EU Member States and the existence of a variable geometry in its adoption and implementation. Despite these differences, the acquis adopted within the AFSJ shares with the acquis adopted in other fields the characteristic that the EU is now increasingly promoting its extension beyond the circle of Member States towards its immediate neighbourhood.[48] As a consequence, the acquis adopted within the AFSJ becomes part of the EU's external policy and, as an additional source of complexity, the internal dimension of this acquis must now be distinguished from its external dimension.

a. The Internal Dimension of the AFSJ Acquis

The internal dimension of the acquis is traditionally defined according to the objective pursued, which is to ensure the consistent development of the EU, while preserving the EU patrimony through the adherence of the Member States to the obligations enshrined in the EU founding Treaties, EU general principles, international law acquis, applicable to Member States, and 'soft law' acquis.[49] Whereas such a definition may allow us to have a first vision of the content of the internal AFSJ acquis, it does hide the fact that several factors are sources of complexity, rendering its classification difficult, if not impossible.

Historical Development of the AFSJ

The history of the AFSJ is a long and complex one, to which we will not devote too much attention as others have analysed it in much more detail.[50] It nonetheless deserves to be analysed briefly in order to explain the difficulties in identifying an acquis developed under different pillars and different legal frameworks.

---

[48] S Lavenex, 'EU external governance in "wider Europe"' (2004) 11 *Journal of European Public Policy* 680, 681.

[49] Petrov, 'The Dynamic Nature of the acquis communautaire' (n 29) 747.

[50] See for instance, S Peers, *EU Justice and Home Affairs Law*, 3rd edn (Oxford, Oxford University Press, 2011).

Since its informal beginnings in the 1970s with the TREVI group, this policy has progressively been incorporated into the EU's legal framework. The Treaty of Maastricht contained the first provisions setting up a special legal framework, ie, different from the Communities legal framework,[51] for matters concerning Justice and Home Affairs, known as the Third Pillar.[52] The Treaty of Amsterdam introduced as an objective of the Union the maintenance and the development of an AFSJ.[53] This Treaty revision was also the occasion to transfer part of this policy, ie, its aspects dealing with immigration, asylum and civil law, to the Treaty on the European Economic Community, and to integrate the rules forming the Schengen acquis into the framework of the EU.[54] However, this policy area was not yet exempt of specificities. The rules dealing with police and judicial cooperation in criminal matters, although significantly amended,[55] remained part of the Third Pillar and subject to a regime different from the 'Community regime'.[56] The application of different regimes for texts adopted under the First and Third Pillars has not made identification of the AFSJ's acquis more complicated. These different regimes only required an additional effort to analyse two potential sources of norms. It nevertheless made the path towards ensuring respect of the acquis by the Member States more complicated. Whereas the implementation of the texts adopted under the First Pillar could be ensured through enforcement proceedings brought by the Commission before the Court of Justice, this possibility did not exist for the texts adopted under the Third Pillar. The Court of Justice had jurisdiction only to give preliminary rulings on their validity and interpretation and only when a Member State had adopted a declaration accepting its jurisdiction.[57] The Member States were thus left with a broad margin of discretion both in the acceptance of the Court's jurisdiction and in the implementation of the instruments adopted.

However, thanks to the Treaty of Lisbon, the 'normalisation' of the regime applicable to the AFSJ went further, as the differences within the AFSJ and the differences between the AFSJ and other Union internal policies were abolished. All policies necessary for the development of the AFSJ are now organised by provisions contained in Part Three of the TFEU and are subject to the same legal

[51] The specificities of this legal framework can for instance be found in the right of initiative, shared by the Commission with any Member State, or in the types of acts that can be adopted (joint positions, joint actions or conventions).

[52] See Title VI, Provisions on cooperation in the fields of Justice and Home Affairs, Art K to Art K.9.

[53] Art 2 TEU (Amsterdam Treaty [1997] OJ C340/152).

[54] Protocol No 19 on the Schengen acquis integrated into the framework of the European Union. See above II.A.i.a 'References to the Acquis in the Union's Constitutional Treaties'.

[55] These amendments concerned, for instance, the right of initiative conferred to the Member States (requirement of at least seven Member States) or the types of instruments available (framework decisions replaced by joint actions).

[56] The regime applicable to these policy areas was still largely intergovernmental and differences were found in the voting rules (unanimity); the limited involvement of the European Parliament (consultation only); the limited jurisdiction of the ECJ (Art 35 TEU); and the lack of competences of the Commission for launching infringements proceedings.

[57] Art 35 TEU (1997).

regime, barring a few exceptions.[58] The previous legal regime applicable to police and judicial cooperation in criminal matters was worth considering in the past as many pre-Lisbon measures still remain in force, and their legal regime/effect had been preserved pursuant to the transitional rules set out in Protocol No 36 on Transitional Provisions.[59] However, since 1 December 2014 transitional rules no longer apply and the whole of the AFSJ is subject to the same legal regime. This means that the Commission and the ECJ can fully exercise their powers, including the possibility to launch enforcement proceedings against Member States that do not implement EU instruments. The AFSJ acquis is thus nowadays based on common provisions and it can be subject to enforcement proceedings if any lack of implementation or any incorrect interpretation of a text by a Member State is noticed. That constitutes a significant change as it ensures the uniform and consistent interpretation and implementation of the Union's acquis.

Complexity still remains with the preservation of some specificities applicable to the Common Foreign and Security Policy, which has been mobilised to achieve objectives and implement measures sharing a criminal justice rationale.[60]

Differentiated Integration Among Member States

The complexity and multiplicity of the internal acquis have increased in the last decades because of the increasing differentiation between Member States with regard to their acceptance of Union law. Several possibilities are now offered to Member States to choose European integration 'à la carte', especially in the AFSJ.

In general terms, differentiated integration refers to the differentiation among Member States in the application of EU law. It results from the refusal by some Member States to take part in the development of Union law in specific fields and their preference not to participate in these developments.[61] A first example of this type of refusal appeared in the area of social policy,[62] in which the UK and Ireland obtained, in the early 1990s, the option not to participate in an Agreement on Social Policy. Another more recent example can be found in the field of the Economic and Monetary Union, for which the TFEU explicitly provides in its Article 136 that the measures concerning economic governance would only apply to the Eurozone's Member States.

---

[58] This is true for the types of instruments available (directives and regulations), or the legislative procedure applicable (ordinary legislative procedure). However, for police and judicial cooperation in criminal matters, it is important to stress that Member States retain a right of initiative (Art 76 TFEU).

[59] Art 10, in Title VII – Transitional provisions concerning acts adopted on the basis of Titles V and VI of the Treaty of the European Union prior to the entry into force of the Treaty of Lisbon.

[60] See ch 4, II.A 'The Mobilisation of CFSP Competences'.

[61] S Peers, *Trends in differentiation of EU Law and lessons for the future*, In-Depth Analysis for the AFCO Committee of the European Parliament (2015), available at: www.europarl.europa.eu/RegData/etudes/IDAN/2015/510007/IPOL_IDA(2015)510007_EN.pdf.

[62] See the Protocol on Social Policy attached to the Treaty of Maastricht ([1992] OJ C191/90), according to which 11 Member States concluded an Agreement on social policy, not applicable to the United Kingdom and Ireland, but constituting nevertheless an integral part of the acquis communautaire.

This wish for differentiated integration also found another expression: the creation of the mechanism of enhanced cooperation, envisaged as a way to organise and closely regulate the possibility for some Member States to deepen their integration in specific fields, even though other Member States oppose it. This mechanism of enhanced cooperation is strictly framed and reserved for the instruments that aim 'to further the objectives of the Union, protect its interests and reinforce its integration process'. In practice its impact remains modest as only a few instruments have so far been adopted under this regime.[63] However, in certain cases, the possibility to use this mechanism is even facilitated. This is for instance the case for the establishment of the European Public Prosecutor's Office. Article 86, paragraph 1 TFEU provides for an exceptional procedure under which the authorisation to proceed with enhanced cooperation 'shall be deemed to be granted'.[64] Furthermore differentiated integration has been more recently developed in new frameworks, either within the EU where it is not formally provided for,[65] or outside the EU framework.[66] The latter is not a novelty, as the Schengen agreements providing for the abolition of internal border controls were initially concluded outside the framework for the EU and subject to a regime of public international law. Even though such frameworks have been legally challenged before national courts and the ECJ,[67] they have not been dismissed.

In the AFSJ, differentiated integration between EU Member States has been well known since the Treaty of Amsterdam and particularly with regard to the Schengen rules.[68] The specific regimes applicable to the UK, Ireland and Denmark led to numerous discussions on the variable geometry of the AFSJ.[69]

Beginning with the situation of Denmark, this Member State obtained a *sui generis* status with regard to the application of the instruments adopted within the AFSJ. Its differentiation started in 1992, when after the Danish 'no' vote at the Maastricht referendum in June 1992, Denmark obtained a defence opt-out, excluding its participation in the 'elaboration and the implementation of decisions

---

[63] See for instance Council Regulation (EU) No 1259/2010 of 20 December 2010 implementing enhanced cooperation in the area of the law applicable to divorce and legal separation [2010] OJ L343/10; and Regulation (EU) No 1257/2012 of 17 December 2012 implementing enhanced cooperation in the area of the creation of unitary patent protection [2012] OJ L361/1.

[64] Art 329, para 1 TFEU that applies normally provides that the authorisation to proceed shall be granted by the Council, on a proposal from the Commission and after obtaining the consent of the European Parliament.

[65] See in this regard the 'legislation giving banking supervision powers to the European Central Bank and establishing the EU banking resolution fund (that) applies (only) to Eurozone States, and willing participants among non-Eurozone States'. Peers, *Trends in differentiation of EU Law* (n 61) 63.

[66] ibid. See in this regard the treaty establishing the unified patent linked to the EU's unitary Patent legislation, as well as treaties providing for financial assistance to Member States, the 'fiscal compact' and a bank resolution fund, all adopted by groups of Member States.

[67] See for instance the Pringle case (Case C-370/12, *Thomas Pringle* [2012] EU:C:2012:756), in which the Court considered that EU law does not preclude the conclusion by certain Member States of the Treaty establishing the European Stability Mechanism (para 186).

[68] See above II.A.i.b 'The Acquis in the Area of Freedom, Security and Justice'.

[69] For a more detailed analysis see for instance, Peers, *EU Justice and Home Affairs Law* (n 50) 74–88.

and actions of the Union which have defence implications'.[70] With regard to the AFSJ, the country is bound by the Schengen acquis and has agreed to the elimination of checks on persons at the internal borders and to arrangements regarding checks at the external borders and entry for a short stay. However, when negotiating the Treaty of Amsterdam, Denmark obtained the right not to participate in any measure in the fields transferred to the Community pillar (visas, asylum, immigration and judicial cooperation in civil matters), and consequently it is not bound by the measures adopted in these fields. As a consequence, the part of the Schengen acquis incorporated into Community law is still binding for Denmark, but as rules of international law. Furthermore, when negotiating the Treaty of Lisbon, Denmark obtained an extension of its opt-out, organised by Protocol No 22 on the position of Denmark.[71] Although it continues to participate in the Schengen acquis, it obtained the right not to be bound by the measures adopted under Title V of Part Three of the TFEU[72] (provisions on the AFSJ), meaning that the Danish opt-out now also applies to measures dealing with police and judicial cooperation in criminal matters.[73] Denmark does not have the right to participate in the measures adopted under Title V (AFSJ), but EU law may still apply. On the one hand, the Union can still conclude international agreements concluded with Denmark regarding the application of specific measures.[74] On the other hand, Denmark can decide to implement in national law a measure building upon the Schengen acquis, creating an obligation under international law between Denmark and the other EU Member States. A referendum was held in December 2015 on whether the country would convert its current full opt-out to a regime similar to the one applicable to the UK and Ireland, but the change was rejected by 53 per cent of voters. The voters also rejected the participation of their country in the new Regulation on the police cooperation agency, Europol,[75] which has led to the conclusion of a specific agreement, the first ever concluded between an EU agency and an EU Member State, detailing the modalities of their cooperation.[76]

---

[70] Council, Decision of the Heads of State and Government, meeting within the European Council, concerning certain problems raised by Denmark on the Treaty on European Union, Edinburgh, 12 December 1992. With regard to the Justice and Home Affairs, Section D of the Decision provides explicitly that Denmark will participate fully in cooperation on Justice and Home Affairs (JHA) on the basis of the provisions of title VI of the TEU.

[71] [2008] OJ C115/299.

[72] One exception is provided for in Art 6, Protocol No 22: Denmark participates in the measures determining the third countries whose nationals must be in possession of a visa when crossing the EU external borders and measures on uniform format for visas.

[73] Art 2 of Protocol No 22 nevertheless provides that the measures adopted before the entry into force of the Lisbon Treaty are still applicable.

[74] For examples of measures concerned by such agreements, see Lenaerts and Van Nuffel (n 36) 343, para 10-028.

[75] H Jacobsen, 'Denmark rejects further EU integration in referendum', 4 December 2015, available at: www.euractiv.com/section/justice-home-affairs/news/denmark-rejects-further-eu-integration-in-referendum/.

[76] Agreement on Operational and Strategic Cooperation between the Kingdom of Denmark and Europol, signed 29 April 2017, available at: www.europol.europa.eu/publications-documents/agreement-operational-and-strategic-cooperation-between-kingdom-of-denmark-and-europol.

The legal regimes applicable to the UK and Ireland have to be considered together as they share common characteristics. Unlike Denmark, the UK and Ireland are not bound by the Schengen acquis and, by virtue of a separate Protocol to the Treaties,[77] the UK has the right to carry out checks on persons to verify their right to enter its territory and to determine whether or not to grant other persons permission to enter. Both countries may nevertheless request the Council to take part in measures building on the Schengen acquis.[78] The authorisation of the Council is not granted automatically and the UK was, for instance, denied the right to participate in Regulation 2007/2004 establishing Frontex[79] and in Regulation 767/2008 concerning the Visa Information System.[80] The United Kingdom challenged the refusals of the Council but the Court of Justice did not uphold its arguments. Luxembourg judges insisted on the importance of maintaining the coherence of the Schengen acquis, and the absence of obligation for Member States taking part in the Schengen acquis 'to provide special adaptation measures for the other Member States which have not taken part to the adoption of the measures relating to earlier stages of the acquis' evolution'.[81]

Concerning measures adopted under Title V of Part Three TFEU, by virtue of Protocol No 21 attached to the Lisbon Treaty,[82] the UK and Ireland do not in principle 'take part in the adoption' of measures proposed and adopted pursuant to that Title. Their opt-out extended to the whole AFSJ, which constitutes a change as, before the Lisbon Treaty, their opt-out only applied to the measures adopted in the fields transferred to the Community pillar. Under the current regime, the two countries may however notify the presidency of their wish to take part in the adoption and application of measures proposed under Title V,[83] including the measures amending an existing measure to which they are bound. In the case they decide to 'opt in' for the adoption and application of such measures, the 'normal regime' applies notably regarding the jurisdiction of the Court and the competence of the Commission. Finally, the UK had negotiated specific

---

[77] Protocol No 3 attached to the Treaty of Amsterdam, which became after little amendment Protocol No 20 attached to the Treaty of Lisbon.

[78] Art 4, Protocol No 19 on the Schengen acquis integrated into the framework of the European Union, as attached to the Treaty of Lisbon [2008] OJ C115/290.

[79] Council Regulation (EC) No 2007/2004 of 26 October 2004 establishing a European Agency for the Management of Operational Cooperation at the External Borders of the Member States of the European Union [2004] OJ L349/1.

[80] Regulation (EC) No 767/2008 of the European Parliament and of the Council of 9 July 2008 concerning the Visa Information System (VIS) and the exchange of data between Member States on short-stay visas [2008] OJ L218/60.

[81] Case C-77/05 and Case C-482/08 (n 17). On the importance of maintaining the coherence of the acquis see in particular, Case C-482/08, paras 48–49.

[82] Protocol No 21 on the position of the UK and Ireland in respect of the AFSJ [2008] OJ C115/295, replacing Protocol No 4 attached to the Treaty of Amsterdam.

[83] They may express their wish within three months after a proposal or an initiative has been presented to the Council (Art 3, para 1, Protocol No 21), or at any time after the adoption of a measure (Art 4, Protocol No 21).

transitional measures regarding its participation in instruments adopted in the field of police and judicial cooperation in criminal matters prior to the entry into force of the Lisbon Treaty. According to Article 10, paragraphs 4 and 5 of Protocol No 36 attached to the Lisbon of Treaty, at the latest six months before the expiry of the transitional period, the UK could notify to the Council that 'it does not accept the powers of the institutions' and 'all acts … shall cease to apply to it' as from 1 December 2014. The Protocol also provides that, at any time afterwards, the UK may notify the Council of its wish to participate in acts that have ceased to apply. In practice, whereas the UK's authorities notified their intention not to accept the powers of the institutions,[84] they have also indicated that the UK would seek to opt back into 35 instruments[85] adopted in the field of police and judicial cooperation in criminal matters.[86] After internal parliamentary debate, as well as negotiations with the Commission and the Member States and amendments to national legislation, the EU institutions adopted in December 2014 two decisions[87] authorising the UK to take part in the requested measures. In addition, while this regime remains applicable with regard to Ireland, the decision of the UK to withdraw from the EU, effective as of 1 February 2020, has led to the application of a complex legal regime regarding the participation of this country to AFSJ measures for the duration of the transition period, and great uncertainty regarding the modalities of its future cooperation with the EU in AFSJ-related matters.[88]

Eventually all these mechanisms of differentiated integration lead to the 'personalisation' of the acquis, varying from one Member State to another, and may cause problems in identifying the rules belonging to the AFSJ acquis.[89] This complexity is also reflected in the legal regime applicable to the international AFSJ

---

[84] The UK on 24 July 2013 notified that it does not accept, with respect to the acts in the field of police cooperation and judicial cooperation adopted before the entry into force of the Lisbon Treaty, the powers of the institutions (Commission, Court of Justice). By virtue of Art 10, para 5 of the same Protocol, the UK authorities have then indicated that the UK would seek to opt back into 35 measures. Council Doc No 12750/13, 26 July 2013.

[85] The list of measures is available at: www.parliament.uk/briefing-papers/SN06684/in-brief-the-2014-bloc-optout-and-selective-optbackins.

[86] Council Doc No 12750/13 (n 84). Some of these instruments included some provisions of the Schengen acquis, to which the UK was already part in accordance with two Council Decisions (2000/365/EC and 2004/926/EC).

[87] Council Decision 2014/857/EU of 1 December 2014 concerning the notification of the UK of its wish to take part in some of the provisions of the Schengen acquis which are contained in acts of the Union in the field of police cooperation and judicial cooperation in criminal matters and amending decisions 2000/365/EC and 2004/926/EC [2014] OJ L345/1; and Commission Decision 2014/856/EU of 1 December 2014 concerning the notification of the UK of its wish to take part in some of the provisions of the Schengen acquis which are contained in acts of the Union in the field of police cooperation and judicial cooperation in criminal matters adopted before the entry into force of the Treaty of Lisbon and which are not part of the Schengen acquis [2014] OJ L345/6.

[88] See, inter alia, C Brière, 'The Future of Judicial Cooperation in Criminal Matters between the European Union and the United Kingdom' in J Santos Vara, RA Wessel and PR Pollak (eds), *Routledge Handbook on the International Dimension of Brexit* (London, Routledge, 2021).

[89] Delcourt (n 13) 862, 865.

agreements concluded by the EU.[90] While international agreements concluded by the EU are not binding on the UK and Ireland,[91] separate international agreements may be required to accommodate Denmark's special regime.[92]

However, such an approach is undermined when considering that, regardless of the success of differentiated integration and of the complex legal architectures created to accommodate certain countries' specific demands, common and uniform rules remain predominant in the AFSJ. The case law of the Court demonstrates clearly that these specific legal regimes are derogations and do not prevent the constitution of the 'AFSJ acquis', which is composed of the rules adopted and implemented by all the other Member States. These rules are indeed considered as the AFSJ acquis, which has to be transposed and implemented by candidate countries prior to their accession to the EU. The requirements imposed on the States which have joined the EU since the early 2000s demonstrate that there is no possibility for these new Member States to derogate from the application of the full acquis.

Differences in the Scope of the Union's Competences

Another factor of complexity is due to the differences in the scope of the Union's competences from one of the AFSJ's policies to another, reflecting the reluctance of the Member States to relinquish parcels of their sovereignty on certain sensitive topics. Although it is clear from Article 4, paragraph 2(j) TFEU that the AFSJ is an area of shared competence between the Union and the Member States, a closer look at the provisions organising each of the policies necessary for the establishment of the AFSJ reveals some differences, which can be illustrated as follows.

On the one hand, the most extensive competences can be found in the provisions conferring on the EU the mandate to frame a common policy, which implies the adoption of common and even uniform rules. Such a competence is, for instance, foreseen in Article 67, paragraph 2 TFEU, which provided that the Union shall 'frame a common policy on asylum, immigration and external border control'. To attain such an objective, the Union can adopt uniform rules, as for instance in the fields of visa policy or border controls in which the Union has fully harmonised the internal laws of the Member States.[93] The Union also has the power to harmonise national asylum law as fully as it wishes, through the adoption of common and uniform standards, subject to the respect of the principles of subsidiarity and proportionality.[94] In that field, Member States may

---

[90] C Matera, 'The External Dimension of the Area of Freedom, Security and Justice' in RA Wessel and J Larik (eds), *EU External Relations Law: Text, Cases and Materials*, 2nd edn (Oxford, Hart Publishing, 2020) 422.

[91] Protocol 21, Art 2.

[92] Protocol 22, Art 2.

[93] See for more details, Peers, *EU Justice and Home Affairs Law* (n 50) 224.

[94] ibid 308. See also V Chetail, 'The Common European Asylum System: *Bric-à-brac* or System?' in V Chetail, P de Bruycker and F Maiani, *Reforming the Common European Asylum System: The New European Refugee Law* (Leiden, Brill Nijhoff, 2016) 20.

however retain the right to adopt higher standards, but they can do so only if they are compatible with the relevant directives. This may explain the sensitivity of the reform of the Common European Asylum System and the lack of agreement among Member States and EU institutions, freezing the negotiations for an undefined period of time.

On the other hand, the competence of the Union is far more limited in other fields, such as for instance regarding the approximation of substantive and procedural criminal law. Approximation and the extent of the EU's competence is in this field counterbalanced with the principle of mutual recognition which plays an essential part. This principle is widely understood as being based 'on the thought that while another state may not deal with a certain matter in the same or even similar way as one's own state, the results will be such that they are accepted as equivalent to decisions by one's own state'.[95] Its implementation may diminish the need for the adoption of common rules, as it is reflected in the Treaty (Articles 82(2) and 83(1) TFEU). Minimum procedural rules shall only be adopted 'to the extent necessary to facilitate mutual recognition of judgments and judicial decisions, and police and judicial cooperation in criminal matters', and the EU institutions may only adopt minimum rules approximating national legislations. Although the two terms are often used as synonyms, the presence of the term 'approximation' rather than of the term 'harmonisation' can be seen as an indicator of a more restricted Union competence in these fields. Such an interpretation is supported by the reference to the establishment of 'minimum rules',[96] which rules out the full harmonisation of criminal law rules, and leaves Member States free to introduce or maintain higher standards.[97]

The competences of the Union to adopt and implement rules in the internal dimension of the AFSJ can thus be qualified as complex, depending on the degree of harmonisation foreseen in each instrument and the margin of appreciation left to Member States for the adoption of specific national legislation. Such variations in the Union's competences do not however impair the identification of the AFSJ acquis. Their impact is limited to the presence of common rules, whose binding force differs, but which nevertheless constitutes the core of the AFSJ acquis.

From an internal perspective, the AFSJ acquis is adopted and implemented in a complex legal framework, marked with differentiated integration among the Member States and with variations in the scope of the Union's competences. Yet this complexity does not impair the constitution of an internal AFSJ acquis, composed of a comprehensive ensemble of common and uniform rules, binding

---

[95] Commission, 'Communication on mutual recognition of final decisions in criminal matters', COM (2000) 495 final, quoted in A Weyembergh, I Armada and C Brière, 'Critical Assessment of the existing European Arrest Warrant Framework Decision', study realised for the LIBE Committee of the European Parliament (2014) 1.

[96] Art 82, para 2; and Art 83, para 1 TFEU.

[97] Peers, *EU Justice and Home Affairs Law* (n 50) 762 (substantive criminal law) and 669 (procedural criminal law). For more details, see also F Galli and A Weyembergh (eds), *Approximation of Substantive Criminal Law in the EU: The Way Forward* (Brussels, Editions de l'Université de Bruxelles, 2013).

upon Member States unless they obtained a specific derogation that is strictly organised. It is, however, questionable as to whether a similar finding will also be valid when considering the external dimension of the AFSJ acquis.

b. The External Dimension of the AFSJ Acquis

From a general perspective, the external dimension of the acquis can be differentiated from its internal dimension on the basis of the objective it pursues. The latter is indeed traditionally perceived as the objective to

> push candidate countries to the forefront of the acquired level of economic, political and legal cooperation within the EU. In other words, it is to export as much as possible of the acquis, which is sometimes not yet binding towards the EU Member States, with the aim of preparing candidate and potential candidate countries for democratic standards and competitive economy pressures within the EU.[98]

Whereas the notion is inextricably linked to the pre-accession policy, it shall hide the fact that the EU is also engaged in a broader exercise of rule transfer towards third countries, including in AFSJ matters, through which the EU engages in the external projection of EU rules, standards or policies.[99]

The development of the external dimension of the AFSJ has only taken place since the entry into force of the Treaty of Amsterdam as the logical consequence of the cross-border nature of the issues at stake. The process is inseparable from the perception that the migratory phenomena and the security threats tend to emanate from countries surrounding the Union, providing justification for addressing these issues, first via increased cooperation with these neighbouring countries, and later extended to more distant countries. The development of the external dimension of the AFSJ thus

> mainly aims at serving the internal policy by creating a secure external environment ... in order to combat illegal immigration, terrorism and organised crime (and, to that end) the European Union must foster cooperation with its neighbours and other partners throughout the world.[100]

This movement of inclusion of third countries in the pursuit of the EU's Internal Security Strategy has been addressed by numerous scholars, especially in political sciences or international relations, who have conceptualised this movement under various expressions, such as 'externalisation', defined as 'an extension of an internal policy through the projection of its rules and norms beyond the members

---

[98] Petrov, 'The Dynamic Nature of the acquis communautaire' (n 29) 747–48.

[99] E Fahey, *The Global Reach of EU Law* (Abingdon, Routledge, 2016) 9. See also B Ryan, 'The Migration Crisis and the European Union Border Regime' in M Cremona and J Scott (eds) *EU Law beyond EU Borders: The Extraterritorial Reach of EU Law* (Oxford, Oxford University Press, 2019).

[100] P de Bruycker and A Weyembergh, 'The external dimension of the European Area of Freedom, Security and Freedom' in M Telo, *The European Union and Global Governance* (Abingdon, Routledge, 2009) 210.

of the Union to third countries',[101] or 'rule-transfer' referring to the analysis of the conditions under which one single non-EU country selects, adopts and eventually implements part of the European legal system.[102]

EU's External Governance as the Vehicle for the Exportation of the Acquis

The concept of external governance encompasses the development of the external dimension of the AFSJ, which is inextricably linked to the definition of the external dimension of the AFSJ acquis. Preliminary remarks are thus necessary to present the ideas and arguments that have been invoked by the EU institutions to justify and legitimise the elaboration and implementation of an external policy designed to ensure the internal security of the Union.

In the early 1990s, while the EU was engaged in the development of the internal dimension of the AFSJ based on close cooperation and mutual trust between the EU Member States, policymakers became aware of the limits of such an approach. Practice indeed revealed that, for certain issues, such as police cooperation, the fight against international organised crime and asylum and immigration, 'the effectiveness of internal action often depends to a large extent also on parallel external action'.[103] While in the 1990s, EU external action remained limited to 'efforts by the Presidency to ensure a minimum of coordination between national positions on the international stage and a number of formally adopted common positions',[104] the European Council stressed for the first time the importance for the Union 'to develop a capacity to act and be regarded as a significant partner on the international scene' and set guidelines for reinforced external action at the special summit of the European Council at Tampere in October 1999.[105] The following European Council meeting in Feira was the occasion to approve the EU's external priorities in the field of Justice and Home Affairs.[106]

The European Security Strategy, referred to as the 'Solana Security Strategy', adopted in 2003, drew further attention to the global challenges faced by the EU as 'the post-Cold War environment is one of increasingly open borders in which the internal and external aspects of security are indissolubly linked'.[107] Even though the Strategy covered both Common Foreign and Security Policy (CFSP) and AFSJ

---

[101] Lavenex, 'Channels of Externalisation of EU Justice and Home Affairs' (n 7) 121, and see references quoted in fn 1. The expression of 'external governance' has also been used by this author.

[102] M Rousselin, 'The EU as a Multilateral Rule Exporter. The Global Transfer of European Rules via International Organizations', KFG Working Paper Series No 48 (2012) 5.

[103] J Monar, 'The EU as an International Actor in the Domain of Justice and Home Affairs' (2004) 4 *European Foreign Affairs Review* 395.

[104] ibid.

[105] Council, *Tampere Conclusions*, 15–16 October 1999, available at: www.europarl.europa.eu/summits/tam_en.htm#c.

[106] Council, *Feira Conclusions*, 19 and 20 June 2000, para 51, available at: www.europarl.europa.eu/summits/feil_en.htm. See H Labayle, 'L'espace pénal européen et le monde: instrument ou objectif ?' in G de Kerchove and A Weyembergh (eds), *Sécurité et justice: enjeu de la politique extérieure de l'Union européenne* (Brussels, Editions de l'Université de Bruxelles, 2003) 18.

[107] Council, 'A secure Europe in a better world, European Security Strategy', 12 December 2003, 2.

matters, it set the path for an integrated and coherent EU external security policy. The Hague Programme, adopted by the European Council in 2004, considered the development of a coherent external dimension of the AFSJ 'as a growing priority'.[108] As instructed, the Commission and the Council of the EU adopted, in 2005, two separate but complementary policy documents, both dealing with the external dimension of the AFSJ.[109] In its Strategy, the Commission emphasised how 'the external dimension of the AFSJ contributes to the establishment of the internal AFSJ and at the same time supports the political objectives of the EU's external relations'.[110] In the same text, the Commission highlighted the significant development of the acquis through the adoption of legislation in the different policy fields included in the AFSJ and stated that this internal acquis has to be considered as 'a broad basis for cooperating for third countries'.[111]

The EU's Internal Security Strategy, which was adopted by the European Council in March 2010,[112] later complemented by a Communication from the Commission,[113] also illustrates once more how the EU institutions continuously highlight the interdependence between the internal and external aspects of the Union's security. For the Commission, 'internal security-related priorities should feature in political dialogues with third countries and regional organisations where appropriate and relevant for combating multiple threats, such as trafficking in human beings'.[114] The importance of these elements was then repeatedly upheld in the following JHA five-year programmes[115] and in their implementing acts.[116] In its most recent programme for the period from 2015 to 2020,[117] the European Council insisted on 'the need for a fundamental link between the justice and home affairs and external policies ... as one of the most important priorities, (that) should elicit appropriate proposals, going further than a statement of intentions'.[118] In the same document, the European Council stressed that 'for geographical, economic and historical reasons, Europe is increasingly a zone of stability surrounded by a turbulent neighbourhood, (and as a consequence) the EU should play a stronger

---

[108] Council, 'The Hague Programme, strengthening freedom, security and justice', 5 November 2004, 33.
[109] Commission, Conclusions, 'A Strategy on the External Dimension of the Area of Freedom, Security and Justice' (n 9). Council, Conclusions, 'A Strategy for the External Dimension of JHA: Global Freedom, Security and Justice', Council Doc No 14366/3/05, rev 5.
[110] Commission, ibid 4.
[111] ibid 3.
[112] Council, 'Internal Security Strategy for the European Union', March 2010; and Council, Conclusions, 'Internal Security Strategy for the European Union: Towards a European Security Model', Council Doc No 5842/2/10.
[113] Commission, 'The EU Internal Security Strategy in Action: Five steps towards a more secure Europe' (Communication), COM (2010) 673 final.
[114] ibid 3.
[115] Council, 'The Stockholm Programme – An open and secure Europe serving and protecting citizens' [2010] OJ C115/1.
[116] Commission, 'Delivering an area of freedom, security and justice for Europe's citizens, Action Plan Implementing the Stockholm Programme' (Communication), COM (2010) 171 final, 8.
[117] Council, Conclusions of 26 and 27 June 2014, EUCO 79/14.
[118] ibid 5.

role in promoting its values and its interests towards its neighbours and partners'.[119] In 2015, on the occasion of the adoption of the European Agenda on Security, the Commission insisted again on the need to bring together all internal and external dimensions of security as 'EU internal security and global security are mutually dependent and interlinked'.[120] These elements are once more addressed in the 2020 EU Security Union Strategy, published in July 2020, in which the Commission highlighted how protecting the Union and its citizens is no longer about ensuring security within EU borders, but also about addressing the external dimension of security.[121] It further stressed how central is cooperation with third countries and at a global level to an effective and comprehensive response.[122] Further elements might be given in the future Agenda for tackling organised crime and the New Pact on Migration and Asylum, whose publication was announced for 2020,[123] but is potentially delayed due to the Covid-19 pandemic.[124]

The commitment of the Union's institutions and Member States in favour of the implementation of the external dimension of the AFSJ thus remains stable and firm, such as the perception of surrounding countries as a 'source or at least transit areas' for the criminal activities and migration issues addressed by JHA cooperation.[125] The cooperation with third countries appears thus necessary and unanimously supported as both EU institutions and Member States share the view that 'crime and terrorism challenges can only be effectively tackled if the countries from which they originate or through which they transit agree with the EU on the need to tackle them effectively on their own territories'.[126] Aware of the diversity of its relations with non-EU countries, the EU does not apply a single model for cooperation on AFSJ matters, but it adapts the content and the modalities of its cooperation according to the specific economic, political and social situation of each third country.

Complexity and Diversity in the Promotion of its Policy to Third Countries   In its relations with its external partners, the transposition of the Union's internal AFSJ acquis and its implementation constitutes the most advanced form of cooperation that the EU can obtain from a third country. In the field of AFSJ, the 'relevant acquis' covers some 1,500 to 1,600 measures, comprising the TREVI acquis, the Maastricht acquis, the Amsterdam acquis and the Lisbon acquis, except

[119] ibid 6.

[120] Commission, 'The European Agenda on Security' (Communication), COM (2015) 185 final, 4–5.

[121] Commission, 'The EU Security Union Strategy' (Communication), COM (2020) 605 final, 2.

[122] ibid.

[123] Commission, 'Work Programme 2020. A Union that strives for more' (Communication), COM (2020) 37 final, 7–8.

[124] Commission, 'Adjusted Commission Work Programme 2020' (Communication), COM (2020) 440 final.

[125] Lavenex, 'Channels of Externalisation of EU Justice and Home Affairs' (n 7) 120.

[126] J Monar, *The External Dimension of the EU's Area of Freedom, Security and Justice: Progress, Potential and Limitations after the Treaty of Lisbon* (Swedish Institute for European Policy Studies, 2012) 18.

where superseded.[127] Third countries concerned have to accept, transpose and implement the relevant acquis in full. However, the EU does not rely on a single framework to obtain such an extended form of cooperation, which can take place in complex and diverse forms. In these circumstances, an in-depth analysis of the external dimension of the AFSJ acquis reveals a differentiated 'transposition' of the acquis in third countries, a characteristic shared with other types of sectorial acquis exported to third countries.

The EU uses several means to promote the transposition of the acquis into third countries legal systems, and these means are closely interlinked with the objectives pursued in the cooperation with each third country.

Complexity Linked to the Content of the Acquis   First, the objectives pursued differ substantially from one external agreement to another and they influence the scope of the acquis exported to third countries. Whereas all external agreements concluded between the Union and third countries are designed to enhance cooperation between their parties, they constitute a vast array of instruments aimed at establishing different degrees of cooperation, ie, association in view of preparing accession, establishment of a customs union, sectorial cooperation or cooperation limited to maintaining a partnership relationship between the parties and creating a friendly environment for European investments and traders in third countries. Consequently, the scope of the acquis considered as 'relevant' and to be adopted by third countries is not uniform. 'Third countries are (thus) bound to adopt the "relevant" acquis in order to achieve specific objectives of agreement with the EU'.[128] In other words, it can be said that the closer the type of cooperation a country wishes to obtain from the EU, the more extended the scope of the acquis that it has to integrate within its national legal order will be.

Second, a distinction can be made within the content of the acquis exported. While stressing their dynamic nature, Petrov distinguishes two types of acquis most frequently applied within EU external agreements.[129] The first category of acquis 'encompasses vague legal categories, such as essential elements, common or shared values, principles of international public law and international trade law', or European standards, neither of them being precisely defined.[130] The second category of acquis comprises the 'relevant acquis', which usually means the EU sectorial legislation enshrined in the text of an EU external agreement and/or in its annexes.

Third, an additional source of complexity arises from the existence of various status and types of relationship between the EU and third countries, which influences the substance of the rules exported. By way of example, just for candidate

---

[127] Tony Bunyan, 'How the EU works and justice and home affairs decision-making' (*Statewatch Analysis* January 2013) 2, available at: www.statewatch.org/analyses/no-205a-cleu.pdf.
[128] Petrov, 'The Dynamic Nature of the acquis communautaire' (n 29) 749–50.
[129] ibid.
[130] ibid.

countries, several mechanisms coexist, potentially leading to the non-application of certain measures of the acquis to these countries. The bargaining power of each candidate country may influence the definition of the scope of the Union's acquis exported. In other words, whereas on paper every candidate country has to accept the whole acquis, the Union may in practice grant temporary and even permanent exemptions, subject to strict conditions, ie, they will not undermine the intrinsic foundations of the Union acquis.[131] In practice such exemptions have only been applied when they are 'justified by the need to protect a candidate country's essential characteristics or preferences, or to safeguard seminal national economic or social interests'.[132] Furthermore these exemptions are counterbalanced by another mechanism: the introduction of safeguard clauses. These clauses are considered as a mechanism of conditionality, applicable after the accession of the countries to the EU. Their application allows the suspension of the application of certain parts of Union law in case of potential violations by certain Member States. Such safeguard clauses have for instance been introduced in the accession treaties with Bulgaria and Romania, and they provide that, within three years following their accession in case of serious shortcomings or imminent risks relating to mutual recognition in criminal matters, the Commission would be able to adopt, after consulting the Member States, safeguard measures including the suspension of the application of provisions on judicial cooperation.[133] Finally, an additional post-accession conditionality mechanism exists: the requirement imposed on the Member States that joined the EU in 2007 and 2013 to reach a satisfactory level of 'Schengen readiness' prior to the full application of the Schengen acquis. Such mechanisms illustrate that, although the candidate countries are required to transpose and implement the AFSJ acquis in full, the EU reserves the right to suspend or postpone the application of the acquis in a specific field, when new Member States cease to satisfy the requirements imposed.

Finally, the content of the acquis to be transposed varies depending on the nature of the country's cooperation with the EU. For instance, countries taking part in the Agreement establishing the European Economic Area,[134] which receive access to the EU internal market and the right to exercise the fundamental freedoms it contains, are not only bound to adopt the 'relevant' acquis in force at the time of their signature of the Agreement. The Agreement organises, through the application of the principle of homogeneity, a specific procedure to ensure the 'actual adaptation of the dynamic post-signature acquis communautaire

---

[131] Petrov, 'The External Dimension of the Acquis Communautaire' (n 35) 16.

[132] For further discussions and examples of such exemptions, see Petrov, 'The External Dimension of the Acquis Communautaire' (n 35) 14–16. The possibility for a third country to negotiate exemptions mirrors somehow the possibility offered to the Member States to individualise the acquis through the argument of specific national circumstances (eg, Spain which refused to participate in the EU patent because of the language regime).

[133] Lavenex, 'Channels of Externalisation of EU Justice and Home Affairs' (n 7) 126.

[134] European Economic Agreement [1994] OJ L1/3.

into the legal orders of the EFTA Member States'.[135] This is all the more true for Schengen-associated countries, which are bound by revisions of the Schengen acquis,[136] and with which the EU has entered into agreements replicating to a certain extent EU internal cooperation mechanisms.[137] On the contrary, external agreements that target neither full EU membership nor common economic structures do not impose binding harmonisation commitments, and they only provide for cooperation between the parties on specific issues.[138] These considerations do not apply to the agreements signed with the countries participating in certain regional frameworks, especially for those participating in the Stabilisation and Association process in the Western Balkans. The EU promotes the complete transposition of its acquis in these third countries, in particular its acquis in JHA, as it wishes to strengthen their cooperation in this field.

Complexity Linked to the Different Leverages and Incentives at the Disposal of the EU   Considerable leverage is required to motivate third countries not only to cooperate on sensitive issues, such as keeping migration under control or tackling crime, but also to transpose and implement legislation drawn up without their participation or consent.

Accession conditionality has proven to be an efficient point of leverage for exporting norms when negotiating the accession to the Union of Central and East European countries, which joined the Union in 2004 and 2007.[139] Nowadays this accession conditionality leverage is more delicate to use as an incentive for candidate and potential candidate countries of the Western Balkans to transpose and implement the AFSJ acquis, especially given the ambiguity of the promise of membership. Whereas in 2014, the President of the Commission, Jean-Claude Juncker, clearly stated 'the next five years will be a period of consolidation, with no further enlargement taking place',[140] the Council adopted in March 2020 conclusions opening accession negotiations with the Republic of North Macedonia and the Republic of Albania,[141] a decision endorsed by the European Council a few days later. However, such a decision was initially barred by some Member States,

---

[135] Art 93, para 2 EEA Agreement. Detailed analysis in R Petrov, 'Exporting the Acquis Communautaire into the Legal Systems of Third Countries' (2008) 13 *European Foreign Affairs Review* 33, 37 f.

[136] See below the reference to 'guillotine clauses'.

[137] See, eg, Agreement between the European Union and the Republic of Iceland and the Kingdom of Norway on the application of certain provisions of the Convention on Mutual Assistance in Criminal Matters between the Member States of the European Union and the 2001 Protocol thereto [2004] OJ L26/3.

[138] Petrov, 'Exporting the Acquis Communautaire' (n 135) 41.

[139] For an analysis of the challenges faced, see J Monar 'EU Justice and Home Affairs in the Eastward Enlargement: The Challenge of Diversity and EU Instruments and Strategies', Zentrum für Europäische Integrationsforschung, Universität Bonn, Discussion Paper C 91 (2001).

[140] J-C Juncker, Mission Letter to Johannes Hahn, Commissioner for European Neighbourhood Policy and Enlargement Negotiations (2014) 4, available at: ec.europa.eu/commission/sites/cwt/files/commissioner_mission_letters/hahn_en.pdf.

[141] Council, 'Conclusions on Enlargement and Stabilisation and Association Process', 25 March 2020, Council Doc No 7002/20.

and it constitutes the first step in long negotiations.[142] Such leverage is even absent from its relations with countries concerned by the European Neighbourhood Policy (ENP).

The EU is thus increasingly relying on a new form of leverage based on policy conditionality: the prospect of visa-free travel,[143] which constitutes a very relevant issue for the daily life of the people and for the public authorities of both Western Balkans and ENP countries. As a mean of pushing for further reforms, the EU conditions the opening and the conduct of negotiations for visa facilitation agreements to the guarantee of smooth functioning visa facilitation and readmission practices, together with clearly demonstrable efforts to root out corruption and improve cross-border police cooperation.[144] Moreover, whereas the EU continues to apply the enlargement model characterised by strict conditionality and the obligation to adopt the EU acquis to the Western Balkans countries, it has set out a specific model for ENP countries. Although the ENP requires legislative adaptation by the neighbours to the EU AFSJ acquis, the different agreements and action plans implementing this policy tend to refer to approximation of laws.[145] The EU institutions have also adapted the leverage they offer to the needs of each country willing to obtain closer cooperation with the EU. For instance, the European Free Trade Association (EFTA) States willing to be associated with the Schengen area, such as Norway, Iceland, Liechtenstein and Switzerland, are also bound to transpose and implement the Schengen acquis before they can benefit from the abolition of border controls.[146] As candidate countries, or ENP countries, the Schengen associated countries have no say in the adoption of the Schengen acquis and in case of disagreement, they only have at their disposal the 'guillotine clauses'.[147]

Finally, the transposition of the AFSJ acquis on the basis of an external agreement may be enforced through various mechanisms. Depending once more on the degree of cooperation established, mechanisms to ensure the enforceability of the Agreement's provisions on approximation of legislation change. In agreements establishing advanced forms of cooperation, such as the European Economic Area (EEA) Agreement, specific institutions (for example, the EFTA Court)[148]

---

[142] N Fallon, 'New Moves: Opening up EU Prospects for North Macedonia and Albania' (April 2020) IIEA Briefing Paper, available at: www.iiea.com/eu-affairs/new-moves-opening-up-eu-prospects-for-north-macedonia-and-albania/.

[143] On this form of conditionality, see F Trauner, 'Deconstructing the EU's Routes of Influence in Justice and Home Affairs in the Western Balkans' (2009) 31 *Journal of European Integration* 65, 75–77.

[144] ibid 77.

[145] Lavenex, 'Channels of Externalisation of EU Justice and Home Affairs' (n 7) 130.

[146] Norway, Iceland and Liechtenstein have also signed agreements on the 'Dublin system' and on EURODAC (fingerprint database).

[147] This clause, present in each bilateral agreement between the EU and the country concerned, provides for the possibility to terminate the agreement in case an EEA EFTA country decided not to accept the content of an act or measure under the Schengen acquis.

[148] The EFTA Court fulfils the judicial function within the EFTA system, interpreting the Agreement on the EEA with regard to the EFTA States party to the Agreement. Like the Court of Justice, the EFTA

have been established and received the mandate to monitor the adoption and implementation of rules exported outside the EU legal framework closely. On the contrary, when the agreement establishes looser forms of cooperation, it may not include specific mechanisms of enforcement of the acquis. Under such agreements, only national constitutional courts, within their jurisdiction to ensure the respect of international agreements, are competent to monitor the adoption and implementation of the Union acquis within their national legal orders. They can thus exercise broad discretion in interpreting the relevant acquis[149] and the Union has no capacity to ensure an interpretation consistent with the one applicable within the EU legal order. Once more such factors of diversity and complexity are, however, not present in the framework of the policies foreseeing the export of the acquis under the regional frameworks with its neighbours (the Stabilisation and Association process in the Western Balkans and the ENP). The strict monitoring carried out by the Commission to review their correct adoption and implementation of the AFSJ acquis may be the occasion to pinpoint potential shortcomings in the judicial interpretation of the acquis. Recommendations may thus be addressed to the competent authorities to change national legislation in order to avoid problems.

iii. Conclusion

In conclusion, the identification of the acquis in the field of the AFSJ may appear prima facie as a complex and difficult exercise. However, the study of both the internal and external dimensions of this acquis proves the contrary. In terms of its internal dimension, the elaboration and identification of the AFSJ acquis is not affected by the differentiated integration among Member States and, thanks to the subsequent constitutional changes, it is now subject to a uniform legal regime. In its external dimension, diversity and complexity may arise because of the diverse types of cooperation and relationships that the EU has established with third countries. However, since the objective of exporting the AFSJ acquis is mainly pursued with the countries surrounding the EU, diversity and complexity are diminished thanks to the elaboration of regional frameworks, structuring the cooperation of these countries with the Union and the export of the AFSJ acquis along similar patterns. Even though a differentiated approach reflecting the situation of each country is designed on a case-by-case basis, the countries participating in the same regional framework are likely to be subjected to similar types of instruments and to similar demands from the EU. This search for a coherent approach is particularly noticeable in the external dimension of the EU's policy against trafficking in human beings, especially when analysing the acquis that is promoted outside the EU's borders.

Court is competent for dealing with infringement actions, for giving advisory opinions to courts in the EFTA States, and for appeals of decisions taken by the EFTA Surveillance Authority.
[149] Petrov, 'The Dynamic Nature of the acquis communautaire' (n 29) 748–49.

B. What is the Acquis in the Field of the Prevention and Fight against Trafficking in Human Beings?

Since the entry into force of the Maastricht Treaty and thanks to the subsequent constitutional amendments, the dynamism of the EU legislator in the field of the AFSJ has never weakened and has become even stronger in the last decade. Its dynamism leads to the existence of an ever-changing legal landscape, composed of instruments corresponding to different 'generations' of legislative instruments adopted in different institutional and decision-making frameworks, that have sometimes evolved under the influence of external norms. The legislative dynamism within the EU sometimes echoes the development of international standards that are provided for in international agreements binding upon the EU. It is accompanied by the adoption of a so-called 'soft acquis', composed of policy documents, such as strategies, action plans or conclusions, defining, among other things, general objectives or best practices.[150]

The promotion of the AFSJ acquis thus requires untangling the complex normative landscape and identifying the acquis in a specific policy area. In that regard, the identification of the acquis relating to the prevention of and the fight against trafficking in human beings is further complicated by the EU's approach. Despite the increasing importance of the protection of fundamental rights of victims and the introduction of a gender perspective, the Union's policy to counter trafficking in human beings remains somehow oriented by a perception of trafficking in human beings as organised crime and migration issues. Consequently, most of the relevant texts may be identified in the vast array of texts that are part of the establishment of a common migration policy and/or among the texts aimed at preventing and combating crime. However, no field shall be a priori excluded. Measures adopted in the field of social and labour law may be part of the EU's response to fight trafficking for labour exploitation. Those adopted in favour of the equality between men and women, or to fight against discrimination, may help to address the root causes of trafficking. Academic rigour and cautions are thus required to carry out this exercise of identification of the acquis. For the purposes of clarity, the different components of the acquis, ie, international standards, legislative and soft law instruments, will now be examined.

i. Importance and Import of International Standards

Trafficking in human beings is unfortunately a source of concern for all countries and all levels of governance. The approach pursued at EU level, which is characterised by equal attention being granted to the prevention of trafficking, the prosecution of the traffickers and the protection of its victims, is also the approach

---

[150] The expression has notably been employed by Petrov, 'Exporting the Acquis Communautaire' (n 135) 36.

that is followed by other international and regional actors. Whereas the first conventions dealing with trafficking in human beings focused on criminal justice measures, human rights considerations have gained in importance over the years, either by the renewed interpretation given to general human rights instruments or by the adoption of new instruments following a human rights-based approach. As a consequence, the list of instruments relevant for the prevention of and the fight against trafficking in human beings is a long list,[151] including in particular many instruments adopted in the framework of the United Nations[152] and UN-affiliated organisations.[153]

Whereas these international instruments are important to define the internationally agreed standards relevant for the prevention of and the fight against human trafficking, not all of them belong to the Union acquis in this field. Several alternative conditions may lead to the inclusion of an external agreement in the acquis.

The category that is the easiest to identify is composed of the agreements duly concluded by the EU, in accordance with current Article 216, paragraph 2 TFEU, which became an integral part of the acquis from the date of their entry into force. Mixed agreements concluded jointly by the Union and its Member States, or more precisely the parts falling within the Union's competences, are also part of the category of acquis, and as a consequence promotion of the EU's approach resides in persuading third countries to accede in due course to these agreements.[154]

The UN Protocol to Prevent, Suppress and Punish Trafficking in Persons, Especially Women and Children[155] falls within that category, qualifying both as a mixed agreement concluded by the Community[156] and as an agreement relevant for the prevention of and the fight against trafficking in human beings. This Protocol is attached to the UN Convention on Transnational Organized Crime, which aims at denying safe havens to persons engaged in transnational organised criminal activities. Both the Convention and the Protocol are open for signature

---

[151] For a detailed, yet not exhaustive list, see V Roth, *Defining Human Trafficking and Identifying its Victims: A Study on the Impact and Future Challenges of International, European and Finnish Legal Responses to Prostitution-related Trafficking in Human Beings* (Leiden, Martinus Nijhoff Publishers, 2011) 132–50.

[152] Relevant agreements are for instance the Convention on the Elimination of all forms of discrimination against women (1979), or the Supplementary Convention on the abolition of slavery, the slave trade and institutions and practices similar to slavery (1956).

[153] Relevant agreements are for instance those adopted under the auspices of the International Labour Organization, such as the Forced Labour Convention (1930) and the Abolition of Forced Labour Convention (1957).

[154] Petrov, 'The External Dimension of the Acquis Communautaire' (n 35) 12.

[155] UN General Assembly, Protocol to Prevent, Suppress and Punish Trafficking in Persons, Especially Women and Children, Supplementing the United Nations Convention against Transnational Organized Crime, 15 November 2000, 2237 UNTS 319, Doc A/55/383.

[156] The Protocol is attached to the UN Convention against Transnational Organised Crime, in which the Community participates alongside the Member States (Council Decision 2004/579/EC, 29 April 2004 [2004] OJ L261/69).

by regional economic integration organisations,[157] a possibility used at the time of their adoption by the European Economic Community. The Commission had been particularly active, first to obtain the right to negotiate the Protocol,[158] and then to be authorised to ratify the Protocol's provisions falling under Community competence, such as the provisions envisaging measures to be taken at borders or concerning travel documents.[159] Two Council Decisions authorised the conclusion of the Protocol on behalf of the Community[160] and they both recalled in their Annex II the extent of the Community's competence, which corresponded to the crossing of external borders, development cooperation and to measures on immigration policy.[161] The Protocol is thus a mixed agreement, signed by both the Community and the Member States, forming an integral part of the acquis. The EU, together with international actors, thus invite third countries to join the Protocol, as well as the Convention it is attached to, and follows its implementation, for instance as part of the monitoring of the States participating in the Stablisation and Association Process.

By contrast, the vast majority of the relevant international agreements do not foresee the participation of regional organisations, preventing the Union from joining. Under certain conditions, these agreements may become part of the Union acquis despite the fact that they have been concluded by the Member States. Agreements concluded by the Member States may indeed have binding force[162] if the Union has assumed under the Treaties the powers previously exercised by the Member States in the field to which the agreement applies[163] or if the Treaties provide that the Union must exercise its powers in accordance therewith.[164] As a consequence, when an international agreement becomes part of the acquis, the EU attaches particular importance to the ratification of the agreement by third

---

[157] Convention, Art 36, para 2; and Protocol, Art 16, para 2.

[158] Council Decision of 14 February 2000 not published.

[159] Commission, 'Proposal for a Council Decision on the conclusion on behalf of the European Community of the Protocol to Prevent, Suppress and Punish Trafficking in Persons, Especially Women and Children, supplementing the United Nations Convention Against Transnational Organised Crime', COM (2003) 512 final.

[160] Council Decision 2006/618/EC of 24 July 2006 [2006] OJ L262/44; and Council Decision 2006/619/EC of 24 July 2006 [2006] OJ L262/51.

[161] The Annex refers to measures on immigration policy regarding conditions of entry and residence and measures to counter illegal immigration and illegal residence, including repatriation of illegal residents, notably on the basis of Art 62, para 2 and Art 63, para 3 TEC. The text stresses that 'in these fields the Community has adopted rules and regulations and, and, where it has done so, it is hence solely for the Community to enter into external undertakings with third States or competent international organisations', meaning that the Community competence in these fields is exclusive.

[162] For more details on this delicate issue, see F Casolari, 'EU Member States' international engagements in AFSJ domain: Between subordination, complementarity and incorporation' in C Flaesch-Mougin and L Rossi (eds), *La dimension extérieure de l'Espace de Liberté, Sécurité et Justice de l'Union Européenne après le Traité de Lisbonne* (Brussels, Bruylant, 2013).

[163] See the famous precedent of the GATT Agreement, Case 21–24/72, *International Fruit Company* [1972] EU:C:1972:115.

[164] See the example of the Geneva Convention and the Protocol relating to the status of refugees binding on the Union in the matters of asylum policy by virtue of Art 78, para 1 TFEU.

countries. This is particularly true for international and regional conventions which explicitly refer to the functioning of the Union and/or aim at the establishment of uniform rules throughout the EU and/or fall to a certain extent within the Union's objectives.[165]

In that regard, the EU places particular emphasis on the ratification and implementation of international standards in criminal matters and especially on the regional instruments drawn up by the Council of Europe. These conventions have a particular status since they have often been used as models for the EU's internal instruments in the past.[166] The EU has been granted competences in fields covered by these Council of Europe conventions and it has exercised them to develop its internal acquis in these fields further.[167] In practice, the EU negotiates disconnection clauses from certain aspects of these Conventions in order to avoid conflicting obligations for its Member States. The latter are furthermore sometimes deemed to comply with the Council of Europe conventions as long as they comply with EU law. By contrast, third countries, and especially candidate and neighbouring countries, are strongly encouraged to ratify and adopt these conventions, which are viewed as a laboratory of EU membership and as a first step towards taking on EU obligations in full.[168]

In addition to the instruments designed to foster cooperation in the fight against crime,[169] and the instruments protecting human rights,[170] the Convention on Action against Trafficking in Human Beings[171] is particularly important for guaranteeing a common basis for cooperation to prevent and combat human trafficking. Although the text contains a disconnection clause excluding its application in the mutual relations between EU Member States,[172] it can be considered that

---

[165] Petrov, 'The External Dimension of the Acquis Communautaire' (n 35) 13.

[166] S Miettinen, *Criminal Law and Policy in the European Union* (Abingdon, Routledge, 2011) 80.

[167] V Mitsilegas, 'The European Union and the Implementation of International Norms in Criminal Matters' in M Cremona, J Monar and S Poli (eds), *The External Dimension of the European Union's Area of Freedom, Security and Justice* (Brussels, Peter Lang, 2011) 268.

[168] ibid.

[169] Such as the European Convention on Extradition, CETS No 24, 13 December 1957; the European Convention on Mutual Assistance in Criminal Matters, CETS No 30, 20 April 1959; the Convention on the Transfer of Sentenced Persons, CETS No 112, 21 March 1983 and the Convention on Laundering, Search, Seizure and Confiscation of Seizure of Proceeds from Crime, CETS No 141, 8 November 1990.

[170] The European Convention on Human rights is also relevant for the prevention of and the fight against trafficking in human beings, the latter being prohibited by its Article 4 as interpreted by the Court. See ch 3, III.A.iii 'Organisations Active in the Protection of Human Rights'.

[171] Convention signed in Warsaw, 16 May 2005, CETS No 197.

[172] Art 40, para 3 of the Convention provides that EU Member States 'shall, *in their mutual relations*, apply Community and European Union rules in so far as there are Community or European Union rules governing the particular subject concerned and applicable to the specific case' (emphasis added). Furthermore, a Declaration made upon the adoption of the Convention specifies that 'the disconnection clause is necessary for those parts of the Convention which fall within the competence of the Community/Union, in order to indicate that European Union Member States cannot invoke and apply the rights and obligations deriving from the Convention directly *among themselves (or between themselves and the European Community/Union)*' (emphasis added) (source: Note of the Secretariat, Convention on Action against THB).

most of the provisions contained in the Convention have been integrated within the EU's legal order, as the Directive adopted in 2011 'imports' them. A second instrument has recently been adopted in the framework of the Council of Europe: the Convention against Trafficking in Human Organs, adopted in 2015.[173] Although trafficking in human organs must be distinguished from trafficking for the purposes of organ removal, this Convention seeks to supplement the existing international legal instruments in the field of trafficking in human beings.[174] It identifies distinct activities that constitute 'trafficking in human organs' and obliges ratifying States to criminalise them. This new instrument will also be integrated into the Union's acquis, and several provisions organise the possibility for any State of the EU to reserve the right not to apply them or to apply them only in certain cases.[175]

International standards thus form a very specific category of acquis. The acquis in the field of the prevention of and the fight against trafficking in human beings includes the instruments relating directly to this issue, namely the UN Protocol and the Council of Europe Convention. These specialised instruments are complemented by other more general international and regional standards relating not only to cooperation in the fight against crime but also to the protection of human rights and dignity.[176]

ii. Legislative Instruments

Trafficking in human beings constitutes one of the criminal activities whose transnational character spurred on the development at European level of cross-border police and judicial cooperation in criminal matters. The instruments adopted by the European legislator reflect not only the evolution of the competences conferred on the EU but also the evolution of the Union's policy to prevent and combat human trafficking.

Whereas the first instruments were aimed at strengthening and fostering cross-border cooperation in criminal matters, the development of a multidisciplinary, integrated and holistic approach led to the adoption of legislative instruments in other spheres of Union competences. The legislative dynamism of the EU obtained throughout the years an additional raison d'être. Criminal justice measures remain justified by the need to fight crime but the constitutional evolutions of the Union, in particular with regard to the protection of fundamental rights, gave a new impetus to the development of a human rights-based approach to trafficking in human beings. The EU is indeed founded on the values of respect for human

---

[173] Council of Europe, Convention against Trafficking in Human Organs, CETS No 216, 25 March 2015.

[174] Preamble, para 7.

[175] Art 4, para 2 (illicit removal of illegal organs); Art 9, para 3 (aiding, abetting or attempting); Art 10, para 3 (jurisdiction); Art 29 (territorial application); and Art 30 (reservations).

[176] For more details, see ch 3, III.A.iii 'Organisations Active in the Protection of Human Rights'.

dignity and other fundamental rights which are violated in trafficking situations. Trafficking in human beings is, moreover, prohibited under Article 5, paragraph 3 of the Charter of Fundamental Rights of the European Union, which was binding on EU institutions even before its incorporation into primary Union law by the Treaty of Lisbon.

The European legislator has had several reasons to propose, negotiate and adopt instruments designed to prevent and fight trafficking in human beings. Its dynamism results in the existence of an important corpus of legislative instruments, directly pursuing the objective of eradicating trafficking in human beings, or relevant to a lesser extent for the elaboration of the most efficient framework for its detection and sanction.

Actions at European level had been conducted even before the entry into force of the Maastricht Treaty.[177] They were, however, limited to soft law instruments, such as European Parliament resolutions[178] or recommendations adopted, under the Belgian presidency of the EU, by the Justice and Home Affairs Council of 29 and 30 November 1993 concerning the trafficking of human beings for the purposes of prostitution.[179]

The adoption of the Treaty of Maastricht did not expressly confer competences on the Union with regard to trafficking in human beings, as its Article K.1 only provided that Member States shall regard 'as matters of common interest' areas that are potentially connected with trafficking in human beings, such as rules governing the crossing by persons of external borders of the Member States, immigration policy, judicial cooperation or police cooperation for the purposes of preventing and combating serious forms of international crime. The context was nevertheless marked by a growing awareness regarding trafficking in human beings, especially with the holding of two major international conferences, respectively in Vienna[180] and in Stockholm,[181] during which the need for concerted action at national, regional and international levels was highlighted. Awareness also existed concerning the importance to improve the effectiveness and cooperation of the competent national authorities, and under the Europol Convention adopted in 1995, Europol was invited to 'initially act to prevent and combat ... trade in human beings'.[182]

---

[177] A Weyembergh and C Brière, 'L'Union européenne et la traite des êtres humains' in D Bernard, Y Cartuyvels, C Guillain, D Scalia and M van de Kerchove (eds), *Fondements et objectifs des incriminations et des peines en droit européen et international* (Limal, Anthémis, 2013) 67.

[178] European Parliament, Resolution on the exploitation of prostitution and the traffic in human beings [1989] OJ C120/352; and Resolution on trade in women [1993] OJ C268/141.

[179] See Press release of the Council 10550/93; the text of the five recommendations can be found in the Annex to the Commission's 'Communication on trafficking in women for the purpose of sexual exploitation, COM (1996) 567 final, 35.

[180] European Conference on Trafficking in Women, which was held in Vienna on 10 and 11 June 1996 on the initiative of the European Commission.

[181] World Congress against the Sexual Exploitation of Children, which took place in Stockholm from 27 to 31 August 1996.

[182] Art 2, para 2 of the Europol Convention [1995] OJ C316/1.

The first legislative instrument was adopted in 1997: Joint Action 97/154/JHA of 24 February 1997 concerning action to combat trafficking in human beings and sexual exploitation of children.[183] Its provisions were mainly aimed at bringing national criminal legislation closer into line with each other. The text defined the offence of trafficking in human beings, but the offence referred indistinctly to criminal behaviours that now correspond to the two different offences of smuggling and trafficking. The content of its provisions was rather modest, as Member States were only required to review their existing national law and practice with a view to providing that trafficking and sexual exploitation (of a person and of children) were classified as criminal offences, punishable by effective, proportionate and dissuasive criminal penalties. The text aimed as well at boosting cooperation between Member States, through exchange and communication of information, or a better coordination for the execution of rogatory letters.[184] The text also invited Member States to ensure appropriate protection for witnesses and assistance for victims.[185]

The Treaty of Amsterdam changed the setting, as the treaty reform not only conferred more competences on the EU, but it also separated the competences linked to immigration policy from those relating to police and judicial cooperation in criminal matters. As a consequence, actions to prevent and fight trafficking in human beings could be taken on the basis of two different legal bases: Article 63, paragraph 3(b) of the Treaty Establishing the European Community (TEC) providing for the adoption of measures on illegal immigration and illegal residence,[186] and Article 29 TEU providing for the development of common action among Member States by 'preventing and combating crime, organised or otherwise, in particular ... trafficking in persons and offences against children'. On the basis of these two legal bases, the legislator adopted legislative instruments belonging to two categories of sectorial acquis: the acquis related to the EC's migration policy and the acquis related to the EU's measures in the fields of police and judicial cooperation in criminal matters.

The acquis adopted on the basis of the migration policy's provisions is rather modest, but the instruments it contains are all still in force. Directive 2004/81/EC on residence permits issued to third-country nationals who are victims of trafficking in human beings and who cooperate with the competent authorities[187] is the

---

[183] [1997] OJ L63/2.

[184] Council Joint Action 97/154/JHA of 24 February 1997 adopted by the Council on the basis of Article K.3 of the TEU concerning action to combat trafficking in human beings and sexual exploitation of children [1997] OJ L63/2, Title III, D, E, F, G and H.

[185] ibid Title II, F.

[186] Another legal basis for EU instruments with a more tenuous link can be found in Art 62 TEC, and in particular its para 2, which provides for the adoption of measures on the crossing of external borders. Such measures can include for instance the competence granted to border guards to detect potential victims of human trafficking.

[187] Council Directive 2004/81/EC of 29 April 2004 on the residence permit issued to third-country nationals who are victims of trafficking in human beings or who have been the subject of an action to facilitate illegal immigration, who cooperate with the competent authorities [2004] OJ L261/19.

only text exclusively dealing with trafficking in human beings. Even though the text is adopted on the basis of Article 63, paragraph 3 TEC, and its prima facie objective is to regulate the situation of migrants, its underlying objective is to ensure the presence of crucial witnesses, ie, the victims themselves, for the duration of the criminal proceedings by offering them an incentive to cooperate with the competent authorities.[188] Its rationale can be summarised as follows: it is assumed that victims who are also third-country nationals fear being swiftly deported and they do not share the details of their experience with national law enforcement authorities. Their silence prevents them from raising awareness among other potential victims and it prevents national authorities from collecting first-hand testimonies and evidence against traffickers. It is thus necessary to persuade them to cooperate with the authorities and to that end victims are offered incentives to cooperate, supposedly tailored to their concerns. It nevertheless grants access to victims of trafficking to a particular protection regime, which goes beyond the 'standard protection' regime defined in instruments forming part of the Common European Asylum System. The latter include references to trafficking in human beings, especially with regard to the vulnerability of its victims.[189] By way of example, and as the most comprehensive rule in this regard, the Reception Conditions Directive[190] refers to the necessity to take into account the situation of vulnerable persons, among whom are included victims of human trafficking,[191] and to assess the best interests of a child on the basis of safety considerations where there is a risk of the minor being a victim of human trafficking.[192] These elements are not subject to substantial amendments in the context of the attempted reform of the Common European Asylum System.[193]

Very few other legislative instruments belong to this category of the acquis, but even though they may seem to have a very tenuous link with the prevention of and the fight against human trafficking, their relevance to pursue these objectives is highlighted by the legislator. In the Council Directive defining the facilitation of unauthorised entry, transit and residence,[194] the legislator indicates without doubt

---

[188] For a more detailed analysis of the text, see for instance, T Obokata, 'EU action against Trafficking in Human Beings: Past, Present and Future' in E Guild and E Minderhoud, *Immigration and Criminal Law in the European Union: The Legal Measures and Social Consequences of Criminal Law in Member States on Human Trafficking and Smuggling in Human Beings* (Leiden, Martinus Nijhoff Publishers, 2006) 403.

[189] See, eg, Directive 2011/95/EU of the European Parliament and of the Council of 13 December 2011 on standards for the qualification of third-country nationals or stateless persons as beneficiaries of international protection, for a uniform status for refugees or for persons eligible for subsidiary protection, and for the content of the protection granted [2011] OJ L337/9, Art 20 (3).

[190] Directive 2013/33/EU of the European Parliament and of the Council of 26 June 2013 laying down standards for the reception of applicants for international protection [2013] OJ L180/96.

[191] ibid Art 21.

[192] ibid Art 23, para 2(c).

[193] See, eg, 'Proposal for a Regulation of the European Parliament and of the Council on standards for the qualification of third-country nationals or stateless persons as beneficiaries of international protection', COM (2016) 466 final, Art 22.

[194] Council Directive 2002/90/EC of 28 November 2002 defining the facilitation of unauthorised entry, transit and residence [2002] OJ L328/17.

its intention to 'combat the aiding of illegal immigration ... for the purpose of sustaining networks which exploit human beings', and to supplement with this text the other instruments adopted in order to combat trafficking in human beings.[195] Moreover, considering the evolution of trafficking, and notably the increasing number of irregular migrants who become victims of trafficking for the purpose of labour exploitation, the EU legislator made use of its powers to adopt, on the basis of Article 63, paragraph 3(b), the Employers' Sanctions Directive.[196] The text provides that Member States shall incriminate the behaviour of an employer who, although not being charged with trafficking in human beings, uses work or services exacted from an illegally staying third-country national with the knowledge that he or she is a victim of trafficking in human beings.[197] It constitutes an alternative way to fight trafficking in human beings, focusing on the demand of certain employers for a cheap labour force, favouring exploitative working situations. In that regard, other instruments adopted in the field of social and labour law are potentially relevant, such as the instruments dealing with working time[198] or working conditions.[199] Considering that most low-skilled workers or illegally staying migrants are pushed into low-end jobs or into the (quasi) illegal markets, they are more vulnerable to exploitation by traffickers.[200] Therefore, the correct implementation of rules protecting workers constitutes a way to prevent the existence of exploitative working situations, which may amount to trafficking in human beings for the purpose of labour exploitation.

By contrast, the acquis adopted on the basis of provisions on police and judicial cooperation in criminal matters is much more important. The legislative instruments relating to this sectoral acquis are traditionally divided into three categories: the instruments setting up mechanisms covering police and judicial cooperation in criminal matters, for example, those implementing the mutual recognition principle; the instruments pursuing the approximation of substantive and procedural criminal law; and finally the instruments establishing specialised actors at European level, such as Europol and Eurojust.[201] Most of these instruments are relevant for preventing and combating trafficking in human beings.

---

[195] Preamble, points (2) and (5), Directive 2002/90/EC.

[196] Directive 2009/52/EC of the European Parliament and of the Council of 18 June 2009 providing for minimum standards on sanctions and measures against employers of illegally staying third-country nationals [2009] OJ L168/24.

[197] ibid Art 9, para 1(d).

[198] Directive 2003/88/EC of the European Parliament and of the Council of 4 November 2003 concerning certain aspects of the organisation of working time [2003] OJ L299/9.

[199] Directive 96/71/EC of the European Parliament and of the Council of 16 December 1996 concerning the posting of workers in the framework of the provision of services [1997] OJ L18/1.

[200] A Middelburg and C Rijken, 'The EU legal framework on combating THB for labour exploitation' in C Rijken (ed), *Combating Trafficking in Human Beings for Labour Exploitation* (Nijmegen, Wolf Legal Publishers, 2011) 377.

[201] Although the number and content of instruments has considerably evolved since its publication, a more detailed presentation of the Police and Judicial Cooperation in Criminal Matters (PJCCM) acquis according to these distinctions can be found in S de Biolley, 'Panorama du droit pénal de l'Union' in G de Kerchove and A Weyembergh, *Sécurité et justice: enjeu de la politique extérieure de l'Union* (Brussels, Editions de l'Université de Bruxelles, 2003).

They provide the competent national authorities with the tools to enable them to investigate and prosecute trafficking cases outside the limits of their national territory. The frequently multilateral dimension of trafficking cases means that law enforcement bodies need to go beyond the national dimension of these cases in order to disrupt criminal networks that are active in trafficking. In that regard, the approximation of substantive criminal legislation plays an important role, not only in waiving the requirement of double criminality in cross-border cooperation between Member States,[202] but also in avoiding the transformation of certain Member States into safe havens for criminals.[203] Establishing a common definition of the offence of trafficking in human beings is thus essential and constituted the main objective of Council Framework Decision 2002/629/JHA on combating trafficking in human beings, which is no longer in force.[204] The EU recognised that seeking functional cooperation between the Member States was not sufficient and pursued more ambitious objectives: addressing the continuing inconsistencies in legal approaches in the Member States and promoting a common EU approach to trafficking in human beings. The instrument provides for the transposition of several key elements by the Member States: a common definition of trafficking in human beings; a uniform threshold for minimum penalties to be imposed; and protection and assistance to the victims. The text was, however, criticised for the limited ambition of the provisions dealing with the protection and assistance of victims of trafficking in human beings.[205] Other critics are concerned about its focus on the criminal justice measures (definition of the offence, jurisdiction etc), which only aim at improving the prosecution of traffickers. Under the Amsterdam Treaty, the counter-trafficking acquis was also completed through the adoption of instruments aimed at fighting migrant smuggling, referred to as the facilitation of unauthorised entry, transit and residence by the EU. Due to the subject, and its relevance both for the First and Third Pillars, the EU legislator decided to adopt two instruments on 28 November 2002: a Directive defining the offences covered by the facilitation of unauthorised entry, transit and residence; and a Framework Decision providing for punishment by effective, proportionate and dissuasive criminal penalties of the infringements.[206]

---

[202] In that regard, trafficking in human beings is listed among the 32 offences for which such requirement is waived, see, eg, Art 2, para 2 of Council Framework Decision 2002/584/JHA of 13 June 2002 on the European arrest warrant and the surrender procedures between Member States [2002] OJ L190/1.

[203] ibid 108. See also Commission, 'Towards an EU Criminal Policy: Ensuring the effective implementation of EU policies through criminal law' (Communication), COM (2011) 573 final, 5.

[204] Council Framework Decision 2002/629/JHA of 19 July 2002 on combating trafficking in human beings [2002] OJ L203/1.

[205] See for instance, A Gallagher, 'Recent Legal Developments in the Field of Human Trafficking: A Critical Review of the 2005 European Convention and Related Instruments' (2006) 8 *European Journal of Migration and Law* 163, 167; or Obokata (n 188) 401.

[206] Council Directive 2002/90/EC of 28 November 2002 defining the facilitation of unauthorised entry, transit and residence [2002] OJ L 328/17 and Council Framework Decision 2002/946/JHA of 28 November 2002 on the strengthening of the penal framework to prevent the facilitation of unauthorised entry, transit and residence [2002] OJ L328/1.

The entry into force of the Treaty of Lisbon fundamentally changed the legal bases for the Union's action against trafficking in human beings as it communitised all the legal bases remaining in the Third Pillar. The instruments available, ie, directives and regulations, as well as the legislative procedure applicable for their adoption, ie, the ordinary procedure, with the European Parliament and the Council of the EU acting as co-legislators, are now aligned to those of the previous First Pillar. The constitutional reform also introduced direct references to the phenomenon in the Treaties. The first legal basis can be found in Article 79, paragraph 1 TFEU relating to the development of a common immigration policy aimed at ensuring enhanced measures to combat illegal immigration and trafficking in human beings. The same provision, ie, Article 79, paragraph 2(d) TFEU, gives a mandate to the Parliament and the Council for the adoption of measures in the area of combating trafficking in human beings, in particular women and children. The second legal basis can be found in Article 83, paragraph 1 TFEU dealing with the approximation of substantive criminal law. The European Parliament and the Council can establish minimum rules concerning the definition of criminal offences and sanctions in areas of particularly serious crime with a cross-border dimension, such as trafficking in human beings.

The Union's counter-trafficking acquis in the field of migration policy continues to be made up mainly of instruments adopted prior to the entry into force of the Lisbon Treaty, as only one relevant new instrument has been adopted: the Directive on the conditions of entry and stay of third-country nationals for the purpose of employment as seasonal workers.[207] This text aims indirectly at reducing the risks of trafficking for labour exploitation by ensuring 'decent working and living conditions for seasonal workers, ... setting out fair and transparent rules for admission and stay and ... defining the rights of seasonal workers'. In addition, whereas the opportunity to revise the two instruments relating to the facilitation of unauthorised entry, transit and residence, had been raised by the European Commission,[208] the idea never materialised.[209]

However, the Union's counter-trafficking in the former Third Pillar has been subject to more evolution as important instruments developing new tools have been adopted and contribute further to the effective investigation and prosecution of the multilateral dimension of trafficking cases.[210] Furthermore, following a

---

[207] Directive 2014/36/EU of the European Parliament and the Council of 26 February 2014 on the conditions of entry and stay of third-country nationals for the purpose of employment as seasonal workers [2014] OJ L94/375.

[208] Commission, 'EU Action Plan against migrant smuggling (2015–2020)' (Communication), COM (2015) 285 final, 4.

[209] Commission, REFIT 'Evaluation of the EU legal framework against facilitation of unauthorised entry, transit and residence: The Facilitators Package (Directive 2002/90/EC and Framework Decision 2002/946/JHA)', SWD (2017) 117 final, 37.

[210] Instruments such as Directive 2014/41/EU of the European Parliament and of the Council of 3 April 2014 regarding the European Investigation Order in criminal matters [2014] OJ L130/1; or Directive 2014/42/EU of the European Parliament and of the Council of 3 April 2014 on the freezing and confiscation of instrumentalities and proceeds. of crime in the European Union [2014] OJ L127/39.

reflection launched in 2008 on the weaknesses of Framework Decision 2002/629/ JHA, the EU legislator negotiated and adopted a major new instrument: Directive 2011/36/EU on preventing and combating trafficking in human beings and protecting its victims.[211] This instrument is the first adopted on the basis of Article 83, paragraph 1 TFEU, with the European Parliament and the Council as co-legislators. Furthermore, it is subject to the new legal framework introduced by the Lisbon Treaty, especially regarding the powers of the Commission to conduct infringement proceedings.[212] The text is worth analysing for two reasons.

On the one hand, Directive 2011/36/EU reflects the new competences conferred on the EU in the approximation of criminal legislation. The obligation to criminalise the offence of trafficking in human beings is not a novelty. It is nevertheless important as it extends the definition to new forms of exploitation and Member States are for the first time required to adopt penalties of a maximum of at least five years, in line with the system of 'the minimum level of the maximum penalty'.[213] Provisions dealing with the liability of legal persons, jurisdiction or investigation and prosecution are also present, as well as a very innovative provision dealing with the non-prosecution or non-application of penalties to the victims.[214]

On the other hand, Directive 2011/36/EU also reflects the evolution of the EU approach towards trafficking in human beings as it contains detailed provisions on the protection of victims and the prevention of trafficking. Concerning the protection of victims, even though the text only makes reference to Directive 2004/81/EC for adult victims, provisions are much more detailed for minor victims, who benefit from a more favourable regime. Concerning the prevention of trafficking,

---

[211] Directive 2011/36/EU of the European Parliament and of the Council of 5 April 2011 on preventing and combating trafficking in human beings and protecting its victims and replacing Council Framework Decision 2002/629/JHA [2011] OJ L101/1.

[212] The Commission indeed launched severe infringements proceedings against Member States that failed to transpose the Directive after the expiration of the transposition period. Commission, 'Mid-Term implementation report of the EU strategy towards the Eradication of Trafficking in Human Beings', SWD (2014) 318 final, 4.

[213] From the entry into force of the Treaty of Amsterdam, on the basis of Art 31(e) TEU, the European legislator started to become more ambitious. The approach taken consists of setting sentences that deprive someone of their freedom whose minimum level of the maximum sentence cannot be lower than the number of years of fixed imprisonment. This approach, which is somewhat complex, can be partly explained by declaration No 8 in the Treaty of Amsterdam (Declaration No 8 on Article K.3, point (e), of the Treaty on European Union), by virtue of which the treaties in force do not need to oblige a Member State whose legal system does not foresee minimum penalties to adopt them. The possibility for the European legislator to set minimum penalties is de facto ruled out.

[214] This provision draws inspiration from a similar formulation in Art 26 of the Council of Europe Convention. For more details on this issue, see OSCE, Office of the Special Representative and Coordinator for Combating Trafficking in Human Beings, *Policy and legislative recommendations towards the effective implementation of the non-punishment provision with regard to victims of trafficking* (2013).

Member States are required to take measures such as education or training to discourage and reduce demand. Less stringent provisions encourage States to conduct awareness raising campaigns, to promote regular training for officials, or to envisage the criminalisation of the use of services that are the object of exploitation (for example, criminalising the clients of prostitutes).[215]

Directive 2011/36/EU is further complemented by other instruments reinforcing the rights of victims of crime, and especially Directive 2012/29/EU, known as the Victims' Rights Directive.[216] This text establishes minimum standards enabling victims of crime to receive appropriate information, support and protection and to be able participate in criminal proceedings, and it does 'not affect more far reaching provisions contained in other Union acts which address the specific needs of particular categories of victims', such as victims of trafficking in human beings.[217] It nevertheless stresses the due consideration authorities ought to pay to victims of human trafficking in the course of individual assessments aimed at determining whether a victim presents specific protection needs, and may benefit from special protection measures, such as measures to avoid visual contact between victims and offenders, or measures allowing a hearing to take place without the presence of the public.[218]

In conclusion, the implementation of the EU's multidisciplinary, integrated and holistic approach is particularly apparent when considering the legislative instruments that form part of the Union's acquis in the field of prevention of and the fight against trafficking in human beings. Although very few texts deal directly and exclusively with trafficking in human beings, the acquis in the field is diverse and covers a heterogeneous ensemble of legal texts, which have been adopted in the framework of various policy fields, such as migration, fighting crime or social and labour law.

iii. Soft Law Instruments

Last but not least, the Union's acquis in the field of the prevention of and tackling trafficking in human beings includes a large dimension of 'soft acquis', ie, soft law instruments that are not legally binding. This category also covers a heterogeneous ensemble of documents, referred to under different nominations, such as strategies, communications, declarations, manuals etc. These instruments

---

[215] For a critical analysis of the text, see E Symeonidou-Kastanidou, 'Directive 2011/36/EU on Combating Trafficking in Human Beings: Fundamental Choices and Problems of Implementation' (2016) 7 *New Journal of European Criminal Law* 465.

[216] Directive 2012/29/EU of the European Parliament and of the Council of 25 October 2012 establishing minimum standards on the rights, support and protection of victims of crime, and replacing Council Framework Decision 2001/220/JHA [2012] OJ L315/57.

[217] ibid Preamble, para 69.

[218] ibid Art 22(3).

'have not been attributed legally binding force as such, but nevertheless may have certain (indirect) legal effects and that are aimed at and may produce practical effects'.[219] These documents are essential to stress the political objectives pursued, to promote best practices and to participate in the development of a common approach towards the prevention of and fight against trafficking in human beings, which are shared not only among the EU Member States, but also with third countries. As for legislative instruments, soft law instruments can be found in diverse policy fields. Here, we will look at a selection of them, focusing on those dealing exclusively with trafficking in human beings, as this is necessary for the purpose of clarity.

However, despite a careful selection, the corpus of relevant texts remains too broad for an exhaustive discussion of them all and it is necessary to categorise them in three different groups:

- The first category includes all the soft law instruments accompanying the development of the EU's 'counter-trafficking' legislative framework, either announcing or reacting to the proposals for new instruments,[220] or monitoring the implementation of the existing legislative instruments.[221]

- The second category is composed of the instruments creating new bodies that will support the institutions in the elaboration of the EU 'counter-trafficking policy'[222] or establishing networks to facilitate the exchange of information.[223] The opinions formulated by these specialised bodies also form part of the EU counter-trafficking acquis.[224]

---

[219] Definition by L Senden, *Soft Law in European Community Law* (Oxford, Hart Publishing, 2004) 112, quoted in J Larik and RA Wessel, 'Instruments of EU External Action' in RA Wessel and J Larik (eds), *EU External Relations Law: Text, Cases and Materials*, 2nd edn (Oxford, Hart Publishing, 2020) 104.

[220] See for instance, Commission, 'Combating trafficking in human beings and combating the sexual exploitation of children and child pornography' (Communication), COM (2000) 854 final, 2. See also European Parliament, Resolution on strategies to prevent the trafficking of women and children who are vulnerable to sexual exploitation, [2006] OJ C287/75. See also Council Resolution of 20 October 2003 on initiatives to combat trafficking in human beings, in particular women [2003] OJ C260/4.

[221] See for instance, Commission, 'Report based on Article 10 of the Council Framework Decision of 19 July 2002 on combating trafficking in human beings', COM (2006) 187 final.

[222] Commission, Decision 2003/209/EC of 25 March 2003 setting up a consultative group, to be known as the 'Experts Group on Trafficking in Human Beings' [2003] OJ L79/25; Commission Decision 2007/675/EC of 17 October 2007 setting up the Group of Experts on Trafficking in Human Beings [2007] OJ L277/29.

[223] Council, 'Conclusions on establishing an informal EU network of National Rapporteurs or Equivalent Mechanisms on THB', available at: www.consilium.europa.eu/uedocs/cms_data/docs/pressdata/en/jha/108312.pdf.

[224] Commission, 'Report of the Experts Group on Trafficking in Human Beings', 22 December 2004; Experts Group on Human Trafficking, 'Opinion No 1/2008 on the revision of the Council Framework Decision of 19 July 2002 on combating Trafficking in human beings', 17 October 2008; Experts Group on Human Trafficking, 'Opinion No 4/2009 on a possible revision of Council Directive 2004/81/EC on the residence permit issued to third-country nationals who are victims of trafficking in human beings or who have been the subject of an action to facilitate illegal immigration, who cooperate with the competent authorities', 16 June 2009.

- The third category brings together instruments with a strategic dimension,[225] aimed at providing guidelines to the EU policymakers and legislator, also accompanied by reports evaluating their implementation.[226]

Within this last category, several strategic instruments deserve further attention, because they concern more particularly the external dimension of the EU policy against trafficking in human beings.

The first document worth mentioning is the Brussels Declaration[227] adopted in 2002 after a European Conference, initiated by the Commission, which brought together the EU Member States, candidates, neighbouring and other third countries, international organisations, intergovernmental organisations, NGOs and the EU institutions. These participants called upon themselves to take concrete measures and to intensify cooperation in the fields of prevention, protection of victims and police and judicial cooperation. The Declaration was later endorsed by the Council,[228] which addressed specific recommendations to the Member States and can be seen as one of the first mentions of the importance of closer cooperation between EU Member States and non-Member States in the prevention of and fight against trafficking in human beings.

A few years later, in 2009, the Council adopted another crucial document: the Action-Oriented Paper on strengthening the EU external dimension on action against trafficking in human beings.[229] The Action-Oriented Paper aimed at strengthening the commitment and coordinated action of the EU and the Member States, in partnership with third countries, regions and organisations at international level.[230] The Action-Oriented Paper remains particularly important, as its implementation has been carefully monitored[231] and was notably the occasion

---

[225] Commission, 'Fighting trafficking in human beings: an integrated approach and proposals for an action plan' (Communication), COM (2005) 514 final; Council, 'EU Plan on best practices, standards and procedures for combating and preventing trafficking in human beings' [2005] OJ C311/1; and European Parliament, 'Recommendation to the Council on fighting trafficking in human beings – an integrated approach and proposals for an action plan' [2006] OJ C314/355.

[226] Commission, 'Evaluation and monitoring of the implementation of the EU Plan on best practices, standards and procedures for combating and preventing trafficking in human beings' (Communication), COM (2008) 657 final.

[227] Brussels Declaration on Preventing and Combating Trafficking in Human Beings, 29 November 2002, Council Doc No 14981/02.

[228] Council, Conclusions of 8 May 2003 on trafficking in persons [2003] OJ C137/1.

[229] Council, 'Implementing the Strategy for the External Dimension of Justice and Home Affairs: Global Freedom, Security and Justice – Action-Oriented Paper on Strengthening the EU External Dimension on Action against Trafficking in Human Beings: Towards Global EU Action against Trafficking in Human Beings', Council Doc No 6865/10.

[230] ibid 10.

[231] Council, 'Action-Oriented Paper on strengthening the EU external dimension on action against trafficking in human beings – First implementation report/update of information on Member States' external action', 31 May 2011, Council Doc No 9501/3/11. Council, 'Action-Oriented Paper on strengthening the EU external dimension on action against trafficking in human beings – Second implementation report/update of information on Member States' external action', 3 December 2012, Council Doc No 13661/3/12. And see more recently, Commission, 'Mid-Term implementation report' (n 212) 14.

to identify priority countries and regions for the external dimension of the EU's external counter-trafficking policy.[232]

The Global Approach to Migration and Mobility further implements the objectives of developing a more coherent external policy.[233] The document focuses on the external migration policy of the EU and includes as one of its four equally important pillars, preventing and reducing irregular migration and trafficking in human beings. The Commission insists on the importance of making counter-trafficking measures a visible dimension of the pillar on irregular migration,[234] and on the need to consider irregular migration in connection with organised crime and lack of rule of law and justice, feeding on corruption and inadequate regulation.[235] The first implementation report, published in February 2014, reveals that the Global Approach to Migration and Mobility became the framework for dialogue and cooperation with third countries within bilateral and regional programmes.[236] Mutual cooperation in fighting against trafficking in human beings has been discussed, and even led to mutual commitments with some countries.[237] These objectives are further evidenced in a later policy document. The European Agenda on Migration,[238] published in 2015, considers cooperation with third countries in the fight against smugglers and traffickers of critical importance,[239] and connects it with the necessity to develop safe and legal pathways to reach Europe for vulnerable persons who are otherwise left to resort to the criminal networks of smugglers and traffickers.[240]

Finally, the EU Strategy towards the Eradication of Trafficking in Human Beings 2012–2016 built an interesting impetus, and remains an important instrument.[241] It was published by the Commission in 2012 and welcomed by both the Council[242] and the Parliament.[243] Considering the wide range of legislative and policy measures relating to trafficking in human beings, the risk of overlapping and duplication of initiatives exists. Consequently, the objective of this Strategy is 'to provide a coherent framework for existing and planned initiatives, to set

---

[232] ibid 'Second implementation report', 6.

[233] Commission, 'The Global Approach to Migration and Mobility' (n 4).

[234] ibid 6.

[235] ibid 15.

[236] Commission, 'Report on the implementation of the Global Approach to Migration and Mobility 2012–2013', COM (2014) 96 final, 2.

[237] The Commission's 'Report on the implementation of the Global Approach to Migration and Mobility (2010–2012)' mentions discussions with Tunisia (6) Nigeria (7), with countries in South East Asia (8) and mutual commitments with Morocco (6).

[238] Commission, 'A European Agenda on Migration' (Communication), COM (2015) 240 final.

[239] ibid 8.

[240] ibid 4.

[241] Commission, 'The EU Strategy towards the Eradication of Trafficking in Human Beings 2012–2016' (Communication), COM (2012) 286 final.

[242] Council, Conclusions on the new EU strategy towards the eradication of trafficking in human beings 2012–2016, 25 October 2012.

[243] European Parliament, Resolution of 13 December 2012 on the annual report on Human Rights and Democracy in the World 2011 and the European Union's policy on the matter, 2012/2145 (INI), para 137.

priorities (and) to fill gaps'. The Strategy is particularly interesting as it highlights some key features of the EU's counter-trafficking policy, which are also exported towards third countries. Such key features are, for instance, the establishment of national and transferral mechanism; the setting up of procedures to better identify, refer, protect and assist victims; and the establishment of national multidisciplinary law enforcement units. The Strategy also envisages actions belonging to the external dimension of the EU's counter-trafficking policy, such as increasing cooperation beyond borders (Priority C, Action 4) or coordinating EU external policy activities (Priority D, Action 2). The EU Anti-Trafficking Coordinator, appointed in 2011 by the Commission,[244] has a mission to oversee the implementation of this Strategy.[245] The first implementation report of the Strategy, published in October 2014, highlighted in particular the efforts made to strengthen the external dimension of EU counter-trafficking, in line with the Action-Oriented Paper and the Global Approach to Migration and Mobility.[246] The Strategy is furthermore complemented by other documents published by the Commission and also forming an integral part of the soft acquis, such as the *Guidelines for the identification of victims of trafficking in human beings*,[247] or the *EU rights of victims of trafficking in human beings*.[248] The Commission has announced its intention to complete the initiatives foreseen in the current Strategy,[249] and to develop a new strategy that builds on the existing framework.[250] Yet in 2017, the Commission, reporting on the follow-up of the Strategy, stressed the evolution of the socio-political context, and proposed a set of targeted priorities rather than a new Strategy.[251] Of particular interest, is the objective to intensify a coordinated and consolidated response, both within and outside the EU. The text notably highlights the systematic inclusion of an anti-trafficking angle in all aspects of the EU's relations with non-EU countries and in all relevant policy areas, supporting not only building strong law enforcement and prosecution capacity, but also protecting victims and reintegrating them into society.[252] Further reports have stressed the steps taken for the implementation of that objective, including in its external dimension, without identifying new priorities.[253] These limits shall be addressed in the course of 2020,

---

[244] Council, 'First implementation report' (n 231) 2.

[245] This position has moreover been formalised by Art 20 of Directive 2011/36/EU, which provides that 'in order to contribute to a coordinated and consolidated Union Strategy against THB, Member States shall facilitate the tasks of an anti-trafficking coordinator'.

[246] Commission, 'Mid-Term implementation report' (n 212) 14–17.

[247] Commission, *Guidelines for the identification of victims of trafficking in human beings, especially for consular services and border guards* (2013).

[248] Commission, *The EU rights of victims of trafficking in human beings* (2013).

[249] Commission, 'The Global Approach to Migration and Mobility' (n 4) 9.

[250] Commission, 'The European Agenda on Security' (n 120) 18.

[251] Commission, 'Reporting on the follow-up to the EU Strategy towards the Eradication of trafficking in human beings and identifying further concrete actions' (Communication), COM (2017) 728 final, 2.

[252] ibid 6–7.

[253] Commission, 'Staff Working Document accompanying the Second report on the progress made in the fight against trafficking in human beings (2018) as required under Article 20 of

as the Commission announced its intention to publish a new Strategy towards the eradication of trafficking in human beings.[254]

The identification of the policy documents relating to the prevention of and the fight against trafficking in human beings suffers from an inevitable bias. As a result of the increasing trend of addressing smuggling and trafficking together, the issue is frequently addressed from a security issue. In addition to the examples mentioned above, the European Agenda on Security, adopted in 2015, constitutes another illustration of the phenomenon. Trafficking is addressed as part of the second core priority of the Agenda, the disruption of organised crime,[255] and the EU's dedicated legal and policy framework is only referred to once.[256] Such assessment shall nevertheless be nuanced in light of other initiatives, addressing trafficking in human beings through other lenses, including as a form of violence against women,[257] and a human rights issue.[258] This results from the EU's approach, under which many policy instruments partially and/or indirectly address trafficking in human beings. The previous section only contains those expressly referring to trafficking in human beings and forming the core of the 'soft acquis' of the EU's policy against trafficking in human beings. Cooperation with third countries is repeatedly mentioned, as well as the insertion of counter-trafficking objectives and measures throughout the EU's external activities.

C. Conclusions

The identification of the core components of the EU's policy against trafficking in human beings raises several legal issues. Whereas the differentiated levels of integration among the Member States does not prevent the elaboration of the acquis within the AFSJ, the promotion of these norms outside the EU legal order comes against the backdrop of a complex political landscape. The image of concentric circles illustrates that the more a third country wishes to cooperate with the EU, the more the scope of the acquis it would have to transpose will broaden. However, this image does not correspond exactly to the reality, as the content of the relevant acquis to be transposed varies from one external agreement to another and from one third country to another. Regional frameworks appear as

---

Directive 2011/36/EU on preventing and combating trafficking in human beings and protecting its victims', SWD (2018) 473 final, 74–76.

[254] Commission, 'Work Programme 2020' (n 123) Annex I, 4.

[255] The agenda also contains several references to the importance of developing the external dimension of the Union's policies and of cooperation with third countries (see for instance ibid 4 and 5).

[256] ibid 18.

[257] Commission and High Representative for Foreign Affairs and Security Policy, 'Gender Equality and Women's Empowerment: Transforming the Lives of Girls and Women through EU External Relations 2016–2020' (Joint Staff Working Document), SWD (2015) 182 final, 6.

[258] Council, 'EU Priorities in UN Human Rights Fora in 2019 (Conclusions)', Council Doc No 6339/19, 9, para 17.

an exception since, in a quest for coherence and rationalisation, the EU tends to impose the transposition of similar acquis to the groups of countries participating in each framework.

When focusing on the review of the different sources and the core components of the EU's policy for the prevention of and the fight against trafficking in human beings, the following intermediary conclusions can be reached. First, the texts adopted reflect the commitment of the EU to prevent and fight trafficking in human beings in accordance with the multidisciplinary, holistic and integrated approach it adopted. Whereas the majority of the counter-trafficking measures have been developed within the EU's migration and criminal policies, counter-trafficking measures can also be identified outside these policy areas, such as in the EU's social and labour policy, or in the EU's activities addressing violence against women. This diversity is important to keep in mind when analysing in detail the external competences at the disposal of the Union as different types of external competences, whose scope is more or less extensive, may be used to develop and implement the external dimension of the EU's counter-trafficking policy.

Second, the texts adopted contain elements that can be qualified as the key features of the EU's counter-trafficking policy and which can be summarised as follows: whereas measures of criminal justice remain predominant and constantly developed and improved, increasing attention is now being granted to the protection of victims and the prevention of trafficking. Legislative instruments contain legally binding provisions imposing the adoption of various measures, going beyond the pursuit of the objective of prosecuting traffickers more effectively, and the special needs of victims of trafficking are at least acknowledged.

Finally, on the basis of soft law instruments, the EU also develops what could be qualified as a model policy to prevent and fight trafficking in human beings, including, for instance, the promotion of specific institutions, such as multidisciplinary law enforcement teams or national and transnational referral mechanisms. The promotion of this model policy is supported through funding programmes, which play an essential role in the transformation of national counter-trafficking responses both within the EU Member States and within third countries.

III. External Competences at the Disposal of the EU

Whereas the EU's intention is well established concerning its desire to develop the external dimension of its policy against trafficking in human beings,[259] the realisation of such a desire depends to a large extent on the existence and the scope of its external competences. As in internal matters, the external action of the Union is strictly framed by the principle of conferral of competences enshrined in Article 4 TEU, obliging the Union to continuously give precedence to considerations of

---

[259] See Introduction, II.C 'The External Dimension of the EU's Policy Against Trafficking'.

competence over considerations of effectiveness.[260] In this regard, the successive treaty reforms modified the framework in which the external dimension of the EU's policy against trafficking in human beings is developed.

The concretisation of a single legal personality for the EU brought under the same framework the different external policies carried out previously under different regimes. The Treaty of Lisbon clarified in its Article 21 TEU the values that the Union will promote in its external relations, such as the rule of law and respect for human dignity. The Treaty also imposes on EU institutions a duty to ensure consistency between the different areas of its external action and between these and its other policies, which may have a favourable impact on the coherent development and implementation of the external dimension of the EU's counter-trafficking policy. The latter does not constitute an independent external policy, such as development cooperation or the common defence and security policy, and the multidisciplinary, holistic and integrated approach of the EU requires the development of external actions in a variety of policy fields, leading to a risk of fragmentation and inconsistencies.

The evolution of the constitutional treaties allowed the EU to obtain new express external competences, in particular in the field of the AFSJ. Yet the majority of the Union's external competences remain based on the theory of implied powers, initially developed by the Court of Justice and now codified in Article 216, paragraph 1 TFEU. In that regard, the identification of the Union's counter-trafficking acquis plays an essential role in determining the scope and nature of the Union's external competences in the fields relevant for the prevention of and the fight against trafficking in human beings.

The following section will thus be devoted to the discussion of the competences the Union can rely on to promote its policy against trafficking in human beings outside its legal order. The challenges potentially arising because of the multi-disciplinary character of this policy will also be addressed. First, the specificities and scope of the Union's external competences in the AFSJ will be addressed in general terms (A). Second the Union's express external competences in migration and security issues will then be examined (B), as these two fields are most relevant for the export of the EU's counter-trafficking acquis. The theory of implied powers as well as its application in the fields of migration and police and judicial cooperation in criminal matters will be discussed (C). This analysis will be the opportunity to define the scope of the EU's external competences in these fields and to assess whether autonomous external actions are undertaken on their basis. Finally, the way in which the inherent risks of fragmentation of the EU's external action in the field of the prevention of and fight against human trafficking may be mitigated by the duty of consistency enshrined in Article 21, paragraph 3 TEU will be analysed (D).

---

[260] G De Baere, *Constitutional Principles of EU External Relations* (Oxford, Oxford University Press, 2008) 10 and the literature cited therein.

A. Specificities of the Union's External Competences Linked to the Area of Freedom, Security and Justice

The external actions of the EU are developed in very diverse policy fields, ranging from the common commercial policy to development cooperation. Complexity arises because of the interdependence between these different fields of actions, illustrated for instance by the presence of human rights clauses in trade agreements.[261] It is not surprising to refer to the EU external policies as an ensemble of intertangled objectives and actions. Although integrated among the Union's external actions, the external dimension of the AFSJ possesses certain specificities.

First, unlike certain policies defined since the beginning as external ones, like the common commercial policy or development cooperation, the AFSJ was initially envisaged as an internal policy. Before the entry into force of the Treaty of Lisbon, even its internal dimension did not possess overall objectives. Scholars have pointed out that, unlike the Internal Market or the European Monetary Union, 'there is no clearly defined overall project implicit in the very idea of Area of Freedom, Security and Justice'.[262] When the Treaty of Amsterdam introduced the notion of an AFSJ, it brought together a number of disparate objectives and fields of actions, ranging from asylum and international protection to judicial cooperation in civil matters. The impetus for their development came from internally defined goals, such as the establishment of the internal freedom of movement for persons or the abolition of internal border controls, and from perceived external challenges, such as transnational organised crime or terrorism. The latter led to the development of the external dimension of this area,[263] but without creating an external policy in its own right with its own distinctive objectives. Moreover, even though the Treaty of Lisbon provided for overall internal objectives, ie, in Article 3, paragraph 2 TEU, its entry into force did not alter the fact that the external dimension of the AFSJ does not constitute an external policy on its own and still possesses a two-fold purpose.[264]

The AFSJ's external dimension remains developed to help fulfil internal objectives, and in particular ultimately the protection of EU citizens and their rights and freedoms.[265] External actions aimed at dismantling transnational criminal networks are, for instance, developed in so far as they are necessary in order to combat organised crime and to achieve the internal objective of ensuring a high

---

[261] See, eg, L Bartels, *Human Rights Conditionality in the EU's International Agreements* (Oxford, Oxford University Press, 2005).

[262] N Walker, 'In Search of the Area of Freedom, Security and Justice: A Constitutional Odyssey' in N Walker (ed), *Europe's Area of Freedom, Security and Justice* (Oxford, Oxford University Press, 2004) 4, quoted in M Cremona, 'EU External Action in the JHA Domain: A Legal Perspective' in M Cremona, J Monar and S Poli (eds), *The External Dimension of the European Union's Area of Freedom, Security and Justice* (Brussels, Peter Lang, 2011) 81.

[263] See above II.A.iii.b 'The External Dimension of the AFSJ Acquis'.

[264] Cremona, 'EU External Action in the JHA Domain' (n 262) 79. See also Labayle (n 106) 18.

[265] Matera, 'The External Dimension of the Area of Freedom, Security and Justice' (n 90) 406.

level of security within the AFSJ. Such a characteristic is not contradictory to the overall external objectives of EU external relations listed in Article 21 TEU, and the AFSJ's external dimension is also developed to help fulfil the objectives of other external policies. Most, if not all, EU external policies need to include measures relating to AFSJ policy fields in order to attain their own objectives. In other words, as pointed out by Marise Cremona,

> insofar as the external AFSJ has as its objective the furtherance of other EU external policy objectives, existing policy legal bases and instruments from both EU treaties (such as legal bases in CFSP, development cooperation or trade policy) could be used.[266]

This insertion of AFSJ measures in broader external policies has been recognised by the Court.[267] Called to pronounce itself on the appropriate legal bases for the conclusion of the Framework Agreement on Partnership and Cooperation with the Philippines, the Court stressed that the EU policy in the field of development cooperation is not limited to measures directly aimed at the eradication of poverty, but also pursues the objectives referred to in Article 21(2) TEU.[268] The Court further highlighted that the measures relating to cooperation on migration and readmission of nationals contribute to the pursuit of objectives of development cooperation,[269] and do not contain obligations so extensive that they may constitute objectives distinct from those of development cooperation.[270] As a consequence, the Court considered that the Council wrongly selected additional legal bases, including Article 79(3) TFEU on readmission agreements, to complement Articles 207 and 209 TFEU. Even though subsequent institutional practice revealed the political sensitivity of the question,[271] this judgment gives us valuable indications about how the need for additional separate legal bases can be appraised in the multifaceted cooperation with third countries.

Second, before the entry into force of the Lisbon Treaty, the development of the external dimension of the AFSJ would have implied the use of legal bases and competences to be found in the different pillars. In other words, external actions in the field of the AFSJ could be conducted on the basis of provisions found either in the Community pillar or in the Third Pillar (police and judicial cooperation in criminal matters) and even perhaps under the CFSP (Second Pillar). This situation meant that different policymaking rules were applicable for the implementation of external actions, such as the conclusion of international agreements, and that the source and the scope of the EU's external competences would vary from one pillar to another. Measures adopted in the framework of the external competence provided for in the Third Pillar were, for instance, negotiated and

---

[266] Cremona, 'EU External Action in the JHA Domain' (n 262) 84.
[267] Case C-377/12, *European Commission v Council (PCA with the Philippines)* [2014] EU:C:2014:1903.
[268] ibid para 37.
[269] ibid para 55.
[270] ibid para 59.
[271] A Ott, 'The Legal Bases for International Agreements Post-Lisbon: Of Pirates and the Philippines' (2014) 21 *Maastricht Journal of European and Comparative Law* 739, 744–48.

adopted without any involvement of the European Parliament, which did not even need to be consulted.[272] For the external actions relating to the policy fields transferred to the Community pillar (migration, asylum, visas etc), no provision granted external competence to the Community. External actions would thus have to be conducted on the basis of the doctrine of implied powers, as developed in the case law of the Court of Justice.[273] In practice, the external actions conducted on the basis of these implied external competences have mainly appeared in the conclusion of readmission agreements. A few international agreements have also been signed and ratified on behalf of the Community, such as the UN Convention against Transnational Organised Crime, and the Protocols attached to it, notably against Smuggling of Migrants and against Trafficking in Persons.[274] Under the Third Pillar, ie, the former Title VI TEU, an express external competence was foreseen. Article 38 TEU provided that agreements referred to in Article 24 TEU, ie, agreements in the field of the CFSP, may cover matters falling under Title VI. In other words, in the context of the Third Pillar, the Council could make use of the CFSP provision, enabling it to negotiate and conclude agreements with third countries or international organisations.[275] In practice, this external competence has been used for the conclusion of agreements on extradition or mutual legal assistance.[276] Finally, external action conducted under the CFSP included, for instance, dialogue, declarations and cooperation with third countries aimed at preventing and combating terrorism,[277] or trafficking in human beings.[278]

The Treaty of Lisbon profoundly modified the legal framework in which the external dimension of the AFSJ is developed and implemented. The Treaty introduced institutional changes, such as the 'constitutionalisation' of the role of the High Representative for Foreign Affairs and Security Policy or the extension of the role of the European Parliament. Furthermore, in addition to the introduction of

---

[272] Monar, 'The EU as an International Actor' (n 103) 405.

[273] ibid 397–99.

[274] ibid 407.

[275] ibid 400. See also Peers, *EU Justice and Home Affairs Law* (n 50) 132–33.

[276] Such as the EU–US Agreement on extradition [2003] OJ L181/181, or the EU–US Agreement on mutual legal assistance [2003] OJ L181/134. For a detailed analysis of these agreements, see V Mitsilegas, 'The New EU–USA Cooperation on Extradition, Mutual Legal Assistance and the Exchange of Police Data' (2003) 8 *European Foreign Affairs Review* 515.

[277] Monar, 'The EU as an International Actor' (n 103) 412–13. Examples of CFSP-actions with a counter-terrorism dimension can be found in Council Joint Action 2008/124/CFSP of 4 February 2008 on the European Union Rule of Law Mission in Kosovo, EULEX KOSOVO [2008] OJ L42/92; or Council Joint Action 2007/150/CFSP in cooperation with the African Centre for Study and Research on Terrorism [2007] OJ L185/31. For a more detailed analysis see C Matera, 'The External Dimension of EU Counter-Terrorism Policy: An Overview of Existing Agreements and Initiatives' in E Herlin-Karnell and C Matera (eds), 'External dimension of the EU counter-terrorism policy', CLEER Working Paper 2014/2, 18–21.

[278] Provisions in CFSP Instruments sometimes refer to the fight against organised crime, including implicitly the fight against trafficking in human beings. See for instance, Art 3 of Council Joint Action 2008/124/CFSP establishing EULEX Kosovo, which provides that the EULEX Kosovo shall ensure that cases of organised crime are properly investigated, prosecuted, adjudicated and enforced.

a single legal personality for the Union, the Treaty also suppressed the pillar structure, thus unifying the legal framework applicable to the Union's external actions. However, the impact of the latter change is still being debated. Some scholars consider that the new regime has a negative impact as it causes a fuzzier demarcation between the external aspects of the AFSJ and other external competences. As pointed out by Lucia Serena Rossi,

> the external dimension (of the AFSJ) might in some cases overlap not only with CFSP action, such as the fight against international terrorism, but also with the external dimension of other non-CFSP policies, like development cooperation, emergency aids … In this context, problems may raise with regard to the competences, the legal bases and the coherence of the external actions in the field of Freedom, Security and Justice.[279]

On the contrary, other scholars, like Marise Cremona, consider that the removal of the pillar, together with the introduction of a single structure, a single legal order and a single personality, 'will simplify policy-making internally, … and improve policy coherence'.[280] 'Although the provisions relating to AFSJ external action are still to be found in several different places, we no longer have special decision-making rules for the third pillar as it is integrated into the TFEU'.[281] A common concern resides in the difficulties arising because of the remaining dichotomy between the CFSP and non-CFSP external actions. Whereas Article 40 TEU provides for the equal protection of the various types of EU external actions,[282] CFSP external actions are still subject to a different legal framework. Such a difference might lead to 'new challenges of delimitation in the field of EU external action', as the application of a centre of gravity test is not an easy and straightforward exercise in this field,[283] in particular for measures falling within the scope of both the CFSP and AFSJ, such as restrictive measures (smart sanctions) against individuals and non-State entities.[284] Until recently, the CFSP integrated considerations relating to trafficking in human beings in a very marginal way, and that question of potential overlap was unlikely to be problematic when analysing the external dimension of the EU's counter-trafficking policy. However, over the last years several developments may

---

[279] LS Rossi, 'From EU Pillar to Area: The Impact of the Lisbon Treaty' in C Flaesch-Mougin and LS Rossi, *La dimension extérieure de l'Espace de Liberté, Sécurité et Justice de l'Union Européenne après le Traité de Lisbonne* (Brussels, Bruylant, 2013) 8.

[280] Cremona, 'EU External Action in the JHA Domain' (n 262) 97 and 98.

[281] ibid 98.

[282] Equal protection differs from the previous legal regime, under which the former Art 47 TEU, as interpreted by the Court of Justice, 'reduced the CFSP to a narrowly defined, residual category of external relations activities'. P Van Elsuwege, 'EU External Action after the Collapse of the Pillar Structure: in search of a new balance between delimitation and consistency' (2010) 47 *Common Market Law Review* 987, 1002.

[283] ibid 1003.

[284] However, the sensitivity of the delimitation in the case of smart sanctions is unlikely to be present in other aspects of the AFSJ, since the existence of two legal bases for smart sanctions, ie, Art 75 TFEU (AFSJ) and Art 215 TFEU (CFSP), is a unique situation. For more details, see Van Elsuwege (n 282) 1009–12.

attenuate this argument. By way of example, the CFSP mission, EUNAVFOR MED, also known as Operation Sophia,[285] aims at contributing to the disruption of the business model of human smuggling and trafficking networks in the southern central Mediterranean. Its operations, based on enhanced cooperation between a wide range of organisations, have notably helped to apprehend suspected traffickers and smugglers, who were handed over to Italian criminal justice authorities.[286] It thus participates in strengthening the nexus between internal and external security and between the Common Security and Defence Policy (CSDP) and Justice and Home Affairs actors, a trend requiring a critical analysis of its own.[287]

The external dimension of the AFSJ thus presents certain specificities, which are particularly important when discussing the scope of the competences at the disposal of the Union for the external promotion of its policy against trafficking in human beings. The first specificity, especially the insertion of AFSJ considerations into the Union's external policies, is particularly relevant, as it may lead to the insertion of counter-trafficking measures in the Union's external policies whenever it is relevant. Second, the complexity of the legal regime applicable, with the possibility to identify AFSJ-related measures in various external policy areas, impacts the identification and definition of the external competences at the disposal of the EU. The scope of EU powers varies from one sector to another,[288] and thus requires a thorough analysis.

B. The Union's Relevant Express Competences

Addressing trafficking in human beings effectively calls 'for a policy response going beyond the external dimension of Justice and Home Affairs (and) including external relations, development cooperation, social affairs and employment, migration policy, gender equality, capacity building and non-discrimination'.[289] Express competences, potentially relevant to promote the Union's counter-trafficking policy externally, can thus be found throughout the TFEU.

Express external competences have been conferred on the Union to conduct its development cooperation policy under Article 208 TFEU. The Community has always been pursuing its own development policy, autonomously from the Member States,[290] which retain their capacity to act on their own.[291] Development

---

[285] Council Decision (CFSP) 2015/778 of 18 May 2015 on a European Union military operation in the Southern Central Mediterranean (EUNAVFOR MED) [2015] OJ L122/31.

[286] Commission, 'Staff Working Document accompanying the Second report on the progress made in the fight against trafficking in human beings (2018)' (n 253) 75.

[287] See ch 4, II 'Militarisation of the Response to Trafficking in Human Beings'.

[288] Matera, 'The External Dimension of the Area of Freedom, Security and Justice' (n 90) 405.

[289] Council, 'Action-Oriented Paper on strengthening the EU external dimension on action against trafficking in human beings' (n 229) 10.

[290] Lenaerts and Van Nuffel (n 36) 990, para 25-032.

[291] Art 4, para 4 TFEU. Art 210, para 1 TFEU nevertheless foresees an obligation for the Union and the Member States to coordinate their policies and to consult each other on their aid programme.

policy aims notably at eradicating poverty, institution and capacity building and conflict prevention, elements that directly address the root causes of trafficking in human beings.[292] The conclusion of the UN Protocol on Trafficking in Persons contained provisions relating to development cooperation, prompting the adoption of a specific Council Decision, building upon the competence of the Community in development cooperation to justify its participation in the Agreement.[293] In addition, the Union makes use of this legal basis to develop dialogues and strategies relating to human trafficking, including measures dealing with freedom, security and justice matters. For instance, in the framework of its relations with African countries, the EU notably endorsed the EU–Africa Plan of Action on Trafficking in Human Beings.[294] This Action Plan not only integrated measures belonging to diverse policy fields, from peace and security, to trade and regional integration, but it also included measures reflecting the key features of the Union's counter-trafficking policy, ie, prevention and awareness raising, victims' protection and assistance, and law enforcement capacity building. Whereas the Action Plan failed to indicate in detail how the Union's development policy must be shaped or how the EU can help address the root causes of trafficking in human beings,[295] the EU also endorsed the Joint Africa–EU Declaration on Migration and Development,[296] in which the EU extended its support for building capacity and developing projects in countries of origin and transit, for boosting efforts to criminalise trafficking,[297] and for protecting the human rights of all migrants.[298] The integration of human trafficking issues in the framework of the Union's development policy was further evidenced in the Africa–European Union Strategic Partnership,[299] signed in 2007. Together with the participating African States, the EU made a commitment to deepen

---

[292] Development cooperation with third countries indeed addresses issues such as poverty, social exclusion of certain social groups, or inequality between men and women, which are all circumstances in which persons are vulnerable to trafficking. C Rijken, 'The External Dimension of EU Policy on Trafficking in Human Beings' in M Cremona, J Monar and S Poli (eds), *The external dimension of the European Union's Area of Freedom, Security and Justice* (Brussels, Peter Lang, 2011) 233–34.

[293] Council Decision 2006/618/EC of 24 July 2006 on the conclusion, on behalf of the European Community, of the Protocol to Prevent, Suppress and Punish Trafficking in Persons … in so far as the provisions of this Protocol fall within the scope of Articles 179 and 181a of the EC Treaty [2006] OJ L262/44.

[294] 'Ouagadougou Action Plan to combat Trafficking in Human Beings, Especially Women and Children', as adopted by the Ministerial Conference on Migration and Development, Tripoli, 22–23 November 2006.

[295] C Rijken and C de Volder, 'The EU's Struggle to Realize a Human Rights-Based Approach to Trafficking in Human Beings. A Call on the EU to take THB-Sensitive Action in the Relevant Areas of Law' (2009) 45 *Connecticut Journal of International Law* 49, 77.

[296] Joint Africa–EU Declaration on Migration and Development, Tripoli, 22–23 November 2006, available at: www.africa-eu-partnership.org/sites/default/files/AU-UE-22.11.06.pdf.

[297] ibid 10, 8. Illegal or irregular migration.

[298] ibid 8, 5. Concern for human rights and the well-being of the individual.

[299] The Africa–EU Strategic Partnership, A Joint Africa EU Strategy, available at: www.africa-eu-partnership.org/sites/default/files/eas2007_joint_strategy_en.pdf.

the frank and constructive dialogue by taking forward the implementation of the Ouagadougou Action Plan and to indicate its intention to foster the linkages between migration and development.[300] In 2015, during the Valetta Summit on Migration, European and African heads of state and government adopted a common Action Plan.[301] As in previous declarations, the prevention of and fight against trafficking in human beings is mentioned, alongside the fight against irregular migration and migrant smuggling,[302] and other fields of cooperation, such as development cooperation.[303] The Rabat and the Khartoum Processes[304] further participate in the implementation of those declarations and objectives. Whereas their geographical scopes differ, both processes aim at stimulating cooperation between regional groups of countries, not only in the field of police and judicial cooperation in criminal matters, but also in the protection and promotion of rights of vulnerable persons and victims of trafficking.[305] These political declarations are important as they serve as a basis for the introduction of measures relating to the prevention of and the fight against human trafficking in subsequent agreements and funding schemes. Furthermore, similar texts and cooperation may also be developed with other regions and countries of origin, such as South America. However, the insertion of counter-trafficking measures in development cooperation with third countries may cause certain problems of coherence and consistency, as this external policy is developed and implemented on its own, and coordination with the actors in charge of the development of the external dimension of the AFSJ may not always be present.

Express competences in the field of the AFSJ might have the advantage of enabling the adoption of external measures addressing human trafficking directly and exclusively. However, a close reading of the current Title V of the TFEU reveals that the only two provisions constituting express legal bases for EU external action in Freedom, Security and Justice matters may not be particularly relevant to do so. These two provisions constitute the only two explicit legal bases for external action in the AFSJ, but they do not create new competences. They 'are in fact only

---

[300] ibid para 69: 'maximise the development impact of remittances, facilitate the involvement of diasporas/migrant communities in development processes, promote the protection of the human rights of migrants, assist and protect asylum seekers and refugees and help countries of origin, transit and destination in Africa build capacity to better manage migration'.

[301] Joint Valetta Action Plan on Migration, 11–12 November 2015, available at: www.consilium. europa.eu/en/press/press-releases/2015/11/12-valletta-final-docs/.

[302] ibid 11–15.

[303] ibid 2–7.

[304] These two processes are the two regional dialogues that form the Valletta Framework and have as their mandate the monitoring of the implementation of the Joint Valletta Action Plan.

[305] States participating in the Rabat Process, Marrakesh Political Declaration and Action Plan, 2 May 2018, available at: www.rabat-process.org/images/documents/EN_MarrakeshDeclarationand ActionPlanRabatProcess.pdf. 6–7, and Ministerial Conference of the Khartoum Process, Rome Declaration, available at: www.khartoumprocess.net/about/tackling-human-trafficking-and-people-smuggling, 3–4.

a codification of existing practices as the European Union – acting as the European Community as these were former "first pillar" matters – had already been active on both accounts'.[306]

Article 79, paragraph 3 TFEU provides for the conclusion of agreements 'for the readmission to their countries of origin or provenance of third-country nationals who do not or who do no longer fulfil the conditions for entry, presence or residence in the territory of one of the Member States'. This express competence codifies the practice under which the EU institutions had received the mandate to negotiate such agreements and concluded readmission agreements with third countries on the basis of the doctrine of implied powers.[307] However, the link of readmission agreements with counter-trafficking considerations is tenuous. It is true that these agreements can provide a framework under which identified victims of trafficking benefit from the possibility of returning voluntarily to their countries of origin, but they do not foresee measures relating to victims' assistance, or to their safe return and their reintegration. Moreover, they could even be considered as favouring the eventuality of trafficking situations, when they are, for instance, concluded with third countries that do not respect migrants' rights, placing the persons in situations in which they are more vulnerable and thus more likely to be recruited by traffickers.

The other provision, Article 78, paragraph 2(g) TFEU, foresees the possibility of partnership and cooperation with third countries for the purpose of managing inflows of people applying for asylum, subsidiary or temporary protection. However, it does not qualify as an explicit external competence to conclude international agreements in the field of asylum and constitutes rather an objective formulated as an internal competence. This is further reinforced by the limited conventional character of the external dimension of asylum,[308] the latter consisting mostly in the EU encouraging third countries to ratify and implement the Refugee Convention as well as to establish effective asylum procedures.[309] This provision has once more a tenuous link with the external promotion of the EU's policy against trafficking, even though international standards pay attention to the specific needs and protection of trafficking victims.[310]

Therefore, two specific legal bases for external actions in the field of the AFSJ offer limited ground for the EU to externally promote some of the key features of its policy to prevent and fight against human trafficking. The express external

---

[306] Monar, *The External Dimension of the EU's Area of Freedom, Security and Justice* (n 126) 26.

[307] For readmission agreements, see Peers, *EU Justice and Home Affairs Law* (n 50) 586–89.

[308] P Garcia Andrade, 'EU External Competences in the Field of Migration: How to Act Externally When Thinking Internally' (2018) 55 *Common Market Law Review* 157, 160.

[309] M Maes, D Vanheule, J Wouters and M-C Foblets, 'The International Dimension of EU Asylum and Migration Policy: Framing The Issues' in P de Bruycker, M-C Foblets and M Maes (eds), *External Dimensions of European Migration and Asylum Law and Policy* (Brussels, Larcier, 2011) 30.

[310] F Novak-Irons, 'Unable to return? The protection of victims of trafficking in need of international protection' in R Piotrowicz, C Rijken C and B Heide Uhl (eds), *Routledge Handbook of Human Trafficking* (New York, Routledge, 2018) 200.

competences at its disposal, notably in the field of development cooperation, may allow for the insertion of some counter-trafficking-related measures, but they are far from sufficient to promote key elements of the EU's approach in the matter. In the current state of EU primary law, it is thus necessary to examine the implied external competences at the disposal of the EU.

C. The Union's Relevant Implied Competences

The theory of implied powers was created by the Court of Justice of the EU back at the time when the treaties did not contain many provisions on the external dimension of the European integration process. The Court 'exploited the embryonic legal framework to read external competences into the Treaties'.[311] In addition to an extensive interpretation of the few provisions dealing with Common Commercial Policy, the Luxembourg judges introduced with the ERTA case[312] the doctrine of implied powers, 'a solid basis for an ever-expanding competence ... in external relations'.[313] Since the early 1970s, this doctrine has not been challenged, and has been constantly developed by the Court.[314] The Treaty of Lisbon even constitutionalised the doctrine in its Article 216 TFEU, which may, read together with Article 3, paragraph 2 TEU, confer on the Union implied external competences for the realisation of the external dimension of the AFSJ. In order to determine whether the doctrine of implied powers may give rise to the possibility to enter into international agreements in the fields of migration and prevention of and combating of crime, general considerations are necessary to recall the different situations in which the doctrine applies, especially in light of the case law developed by the Court of Justice after the entry into force of the Lisbon Treaty (i). Its application in the two fields, in which the EU has developed most of its counter-trafficking measures, will then be examined in detail (ii and iii).

i. The Doctrine of Implied Powers and its Codification

Before examining the case law of the Court of Justice and its constitutionalisation in the Lisbon Treaty, a few preliminary remarks have to be made. It is first important to stress the two-step approach applicable when determining the existence of an implied external competence: the first step consists of establishing the existence of an external competence (substance); the second determining the nature

---

[311] I Govaere, 'External Competence: What's in a Name? The Difficult Conciliation between Dynamism of the ECJ and Dynamics of European Integration' in P Demaret, I Govaere and D Hanf (eds), *European Legal Dynamics/Dynamiques juridiques européennes* (Brussels, Peter Lang, 2007) 461.

[312] Case 22/70, *Commission v Council* [1971] EU:C:1971:32.

[313] Govaere, 'External Competence: What's in a Name?' (n 311) 461.

[314] For an extensive study, see P Eeckhout, *EU External Relations Law*, 2nd edn (Oxford, Oxford University Press, 2012) 70–119.

of this competence (ie, exclusive or shared competence). In the following developments we will distinguish between these two steps, attempting to characterise each policy field within the AFSJ according to this approach. Second, it is important to highlight that the identification of a Union's external competence on the basis of implied powers does not necessarily imply that the Union will exercise this competence extensively or that the Member States would be prevented from acting externally, especially in the field of the AFSJ.[315]

The description of the abundant case law of the Court on the issue of implied external competences would be irrelevant in the framework of this research,[316] and the choice has been made to focus on the most important judgments/opinions of the Court of Justice, recalling briefly their detailed factual background, and explaining their contribution to the doctrine of implied powers. Summarising the Court's case law, it can be said that three situations may lead to the recognition of an external implied competence.

The first situation in which implied competences are recognised is the one highlighted in the *AETR/ERTA* case,[317] in which the doctrine of implied powers was invoked and applied for the first time. The case concerned the negotiation and conclusion of the revised Agreement concerning the work of crews of vehicles engaged in international road transport. Considering that work on similar issues had been undertaken at Community level,[318] the Commission proposed that the Community, and not the Member States, should negotiate the revised Agreement. After the Council's refusal, the Commission brought an action before the Court of Justice for the annulment of the Council's decision. The arguments brought before the Court focused on the scope to be given to the current Article 91 TFEU on transport policy, and on the possibility to extend its scope to the external dimension of this policy field. Whereas the Council claimed that only an explicit provision could give the Community the power to enter into international agreements, the Commission claimed that the provision applied to external relations as well. In its answer, the Court started to refer to (then) Article 210 EEC, providing for the legal personality of the Community. The place of this provision at the head of the Treaty's General and Final Provisions 'means that in its external relations, the Community enjoyed the capacity to establish contractual links with third countries over the whole field of objectives defined in Part One of the Treaty'.[319] The authority of the Community to enter into international agreements

---

[315] See in this regard, Declaration No 36 on Article 218 TFEU concerning the negotiation and conclusion of international agreements by Member States relating to the area of freedom, security and justice.

[316] For an analysis see, inter alia, M Dony, 'Retour sur les compétences externes implicites de l'Union' (2018) 1 *Cahiers de droit européen* 109; or M Chamon, 'Implied Exclusive Powers in the ECJ's Post-Lisbon Jurisprudence: The Continued Development of the ERTA Doctrine' (2018) 55 *Common Market Law Review* 1101.

[317] Case 22/70, *Commission v Council* (n 312).

[318] This work led to the adoption of Regulation (EEC) No 543/69 on the harmonisation of certain social legislation relating to road transport [1969] OJ 170/49.

[319] Case 22/70, *Commission v Council* (n 312) para 14.

thus arose not only from an explicit reference in the Treaty, but could equally flow from other provisions of the Treaty and from measures adopted within the framework of those provisions by the Community institutions.[320] The Court thus established that the existence of the Community's external competence does not exclusively depend on an explicit provision in the Treaty and the Community may obtain the right to act externally if it possesses the right to do so internally. In this first situation, the recognition of an implied external competence thus relies on the existence of internal rules. The Court subsequently went into further details concerning the nature of the Community's competence. According to the Court, each time the Community adopted provisions laying down common rules in order to implement a common policy, 'the Member States no longer have the right, acting individually or even collectively, to undertake obligations with third countries which affected those rules'.[321] As a consequence, when such common rules come into being, the Community alone is in a position to assume and carry out contractual obligations towards third countries.[322] The implied external competence of the Community is thus of an exclusive nature.

The *AETR* judgment was considered both pragmatic and innovative, as it recognised an external Community competence to conclude an international agreement, despite the absence of an explicit provision in the Treaty. It remains until today one of the cases in which the Court of Justice made an extensive interpretation of the Treaties, and the parallelism made by the Court between internal and external competences has been referred to as 'a bold act of judicial engineering'.[323] Such interpretation proved particularly useful to enable the European Community, and then the EU, to develop the external dimension of some of its internal policies.

In its Opinion 1/76,[324] the Court of Justice further extended the doctrine of implied powers, as it identified a second situation in which an implied power to conclude an external agreement may be recognised despite the absence of internal Community legislation. The Opinion examined a draft Agreement concerning the establishment of a fund compensating the temporary laying-up of naval transport capacity on the Rhine and the Moselle. The Commission negotiated the Agreement on behalf of the Community and, exercising the possibility foreseen in (current) Article 218, paragraph 11 TFEU, the Commission requested the Opinion of the Court on the compatibility of the draft Agreement with the Treaty and on the competence to conclude the Agreement. The Court started to stress that the objective of the Agreement, ie, the rationalisation of the economic situation of the inland waterway transport industry and the system it set up were important factors in the common transport policy, which was included in the activities of the

---

[320] P Eeckhout, *EU External Relations Law*, 2nd edn (Oxford, Oxford University Press, 2012) 72–73.

[321] Case 22/70, *Commission v Council* (n 312) para 17.

[322] ibid para 18.

[323] A Ott, 'EU External Competence' in RA Wessel and J Larik (eds), *EU External Relations Law: Text, Cases and Materials*, 2nd edn (Oxford, Hart Publishing, 2020) 67.

[324] Opinion 1/76, Opinion of the Court on the Draft agreement establishing a European laying-up fund for inland waterway vessels [1977] EU:C:1977:63.

Community. The (current) Article 91 TFEU instructed the Council to lay down common rules applicable to international transport to or from the territory of one or more Member State. On the basis of this Article, the Community has the legal basis to establish the system foreseen in the draft Agreement.[325] However, the presence of Switzerland in the system was necessary and should be secured by means of an international agreement.[326] The Court conceded the absence of an explicit provision conferring competence on the Community for the conclusion of such an agreement but recalled that the authority to enter into international commitments could 'flow implicitly from the (Treaty) provisions'.[327] The judges recalled the *AETR* reasoning, stating that

> whenever Community law has created for the institutions of the Community powers within its internal system for the purpose of attaining a specific objective, the Community has authority to enter into the international commitments necessary for the attainment of that objective even in the absence of an express provision in that connection.[328]

More importantly, the Court added that whereas 'this is particularly so in all cases in which internal powers have already been used in order to adopt measures', it is 'not limited to that eventuality'. The power to bind the Community vis-a-vis third countries may indeed flow 'by implication from the provisions of the Treaty creating the internal power and in so far as the participation of the Community in the international agreement is … necessary for the attainment of one of the objectives of the Community'.[329]

The Court departed from the *AETR* reasoning, which required the existence of prior internal legislation. In Opinion 1/76, the Court confirmed that there is no requirement of prior internal Community legislation for the recognition of an external implied competence, and this recognition is possible on the sole condition that the conclusion of an agreement is necessary for the attainment of one objective of the Community. Concerning the nature of the external competence, the Court did not give a precise answer. The judges focused their attention on a 'special problem', ie, the participation of six Member States in the draft Agreement, explained by the fact that they were parties to two older international conventions, and had to undertake to amend them for the implementation of the future Agreement. For the Court, under these specific circumstances, their participation 'is not such as to encroach on the external power of the Community'.[330]

Opinion 1/76 is generally regarded as establishing a parallelism between the Community's internal and external powers.[331] Even though the Court did not

---

[325] ibid para 1.
[326] ibid para 2.
[327] ibid para 3.
[328] ibid para 4.
[329] ibid.
[330] ibid para 7.
[331] Eeckhout (n 320) 81 and the references quoted in fn 37.

extend the Community's powers in matters of transport, the judges recognised the possibility to exercise these powers through an international agreement rather than through the adoption of internal legislation.[332]

Finally the third situation in which the Community could rely on implied powers to act externally appeared in Opinion 1/94 concerning the conclusion of the Agreements annexed to the Agreement establishing the World Trade Organization, especially those on trade in services and trade-related aspects of intellectual property rights.[333] The importance of the Opinion concerning the scope of the Community's external competence in the framework of the Common Commercial Policy is well known. However, we will restrict our analysis to the elements within the Opinion dealing with the implied powers of the Community. These powers are to be found in the discussion about the General Agreement on Trade in Services, where the Court examines the arguments put forward by the Commission to support the existence of an external Community competence. The Commission relies on the use made by the Community institutions of the powers conferred on them in the chapters on the right of establishment and on freedom to provide services 'in order to specify the treatment which is to be accorded to nationals of non-member countries'.[334] The Court accepts that practice and concludes that

> whenever the Community has included in its internal legislative acts provisions relating to the treatment of nationals of non-member countries or expressly conferred on its institutions powers to negotiate with non-member countries, it acquires exclusive external competence in the spheres covered by those acts.[335]

With such a statement, the Court thus identified the third source of implied powers, ie, the existence of provisions in internal legislative acts providing for the conclusion of external agreements, and also defined at the same time the exclusive nature of this external competence.[336] The recognition of an exclusive external competence in such circumstances was however referring to a situation of 'complete harmonisation' of the internal rules,[337] and restricted to such fully harmonised areas. This constituted a somewhat more restrictive application of the *AETR* principle, which was later confirmed in the *Open Skies* judgments of 2002.[338] These concerned the conformity with EU law of bilateral air transport

---

[332] ibid 82.

[333] Opinion 1/94 on the competence of the Community to conclude international agreements concerning services and the protection of intellectual property [1994] EU:C:1994:384.

[334] ibid para 90.

[335] ibid para 94.

[336] ibid para 95.

[337] A Rosas, 'EU External Relations: Exclusive Competence Revisited' (2015) 38 *Fordham International Law Journal* 1073, 1084–85.

[338] Case C-466/98, *Commission v United Kingdom* [2002] EU:C:2002:624; Case C-467/98, *Commission v Denmark* [2002] EU:C:2002:625; Case C-468/98, *Commission v Sweden* [2002] EU:C:2002:626; Case C-469/98, *Commission v Finland* [2002] EU:C:2002:627; Case C-471/98, *Commission v Belgium* [2002] EU:C:2002:628; Case C-472/98, *Commission v Luxembourg* [2002] EU:C:2002:629; Case C-475/98,

agreements concluded by some Member States. Whereas the Court recognised an exclusive competence for the Community, this competence only covered certain concrete issues.[339]

When considering those three situations in which the Court recognised implied external Community competences, it is important to remember that the Court follows a step-by-step approach, meaning that great attention is given to the specific circumstances in which the recognition of an implied external competence is envisaged. The Court's judgments, including those building upon those landmark cases, were often submerged with case-specific technicalities, leaving the general conditions of treaty-making power and exclusive competences rather obscure.[340]

Such elements of complexity were also present in cases concerning the development of the external dimension of the AFSJ. Before the entry into force of the Lisbon Treaty, AETR-type and Opinion 1/76-type competences had been invoked for the conclusion of agreements: AETR-type competences for the conclusion of visa facilitation agreements for instance, and Opinion 1/76-type competences for the conclusion of readmission agreements.[341] The existence of AETR-type competences was, for instance, confirmed by the Court in Opinion 1/03,[342] in which the Court for the first time applied the doctrine of implied powers and more precisely the *AETR* reasoning in the AFSJ's field of judicial cooperation in civil matters. The case concerned the conclusion of the Lugano Convention on jurisdiction and recognition and enforcement of judgments in civil and commercial matters. The question before the Court was to determine whether the conclusion of the Convention came within the Community's exclusive AETR-type implied competence by virtue of its proximity with internal legislation, ie, Regulation 44/2001.[343] In its general analysis, after recalling its previous case law, notably the *AETR* case and Opinion 1/76, as well as the importance of the principle of conferral of competences, the Court further explored the test of 'an area which is already covered to a large extent by Community rules' (AETR-like situation).[344] The Court concluded that a

> comprehensive and detailed analysis had to be carried out, ... and in doing so account had to be taken not only of the area covered by the Community rules and by the provisions of the agreement envisaged, but also of the nature and content of those rules and those provisions, to ensure that the agreement is not capable of undermining the

---

Commission v Austria [2002] EU:C:2002:630; and Case C-476/98, *Commission v Germany* [2002] EU:C:2002:631.

[339] Rosas (n 337) 1085.

[340] Ott, 'EU External Competence' (n 323) 63.

[341] Cremona, 'EU External Action in the JHA Domain' (n 262) 83–84.

[342] Opinion 1/03 on the Competence of the Community to conclude the new Lugano Convention on jurisdiction and the recognition and enforcement of judgments in civil and commercial matters [2006] EU:C:2006:81.

[343] Council Regulation (EC) No 44/2001 of 22 December 2000 on jurisdiction and the recognition and enforcement of judgments in civil and commercial matters [2001] OJ L12/1.

[344] Eeckhout (n 320) 109. Opinion 1/03 (n 342) paras 126–28.

uniform and consistent application of the Community rules and the proper functioning of the system they established.[345]

The emphasis of the Court was thus on safeguarding the uniformity and effectiveness of Community law and, for that reason, the Court concluded that the Lugano Convention came within the Community's exclusive competence. The second step of the Court's reasoning, ie, the definition of the nature of the external competence, is particularly important as the recognition of an exclusive external agreement leads to the application of the principle of pre-emption, which prevents Member States from undertaking international obligations that would affect the common rules adopted by the Union. In that regard, Opinion 1/03 provided a welcomed clarification on the Court's case law and the sequence to be followed when applying the *AETR* pre-emption[346] and the formalistic approach of the Court may positively contribute to the coherence of EU external relations.[347]

The entry into force of the Treaty of Lisbon intervened in a complex landscape. The Treaty codified the case law in which the Court recognised the existence of implied external competences through two provisions. Article 216, paragraph 1 TFEU codifies a first dimension, namely the existence of an external competence. It distinguishes the existence of an express competence ('where the Treaty so provides') from three situations where such external competence is implicit, which may intervene

> where the conclusion of the agreement is necessary in order to achieve, within the framework of the Union's policies, one of the objectives referred to in the Treaties, or is provided for in a legally binding act or is likely to affect common rules or alter their scope.

This provision is complemented by Article 3, paragraph 2 TFEU, which provides further details regarding the nature and scope of the EU's external competences, listing situations in which the Union possesses an exclusive external competence for the conclusion of an international agreement, namely 'when its conclusion is provided for in a legislative act of the Union, or is necessary to enable the Union to exercise its internal competence, or in so far as its conclusion may affect common rules or alter their scope'. As pinpointed by several authors, and as illustrated by the abundant case law of the Court on implied external competences,[348] these two provisions fail to achieve the objective of clarification. The differences of wording between the two provisions have led to numerous discussions and critics,[349]

---

[345] Eeckhout (n 320) 110. Opinion 1/03 (n 342) para 133.

[346] Opinion 1/03 (n 342) para 133. See also Dony (n 316) 131.

[347] B Van Vooren, 'The Principle of Pre-emption after Opinion 1/03 and coherence in EU readmission policy' in M Cremona, J Monar and S Poli (eds), *The External Dimension of the European Union's Area of Freedom, Security and Justice* (Brussels, Peter Lang, 2011) 176.

[348] S Adam et al, 'Chronique de la jurisprudence de l'Union, Les relations extérieures (1er Janvier 2013–31 décembre 2016)' (2017) 3 *Cahiers de droit européen* 737, 756–63.

[349] See the references and discussions in Dony (n 316) 144; Ott, 'EU External Competence' (n 323) 64; or Chamon (n 316) 1121–22.

even though their relationship has been partially clarified by the Court, which considered that the last scenarios in both Articles are one and the same.[350]

From a more general perspective, the constitutionalisation of the doctrine of implied powers did not resolve the lack of clarity regarding the existence of EU external competences. If in the past Member States could have preferred implied powers over express powers since 'the transfer of competences is less intrusive ... and goes hand in hand with the adoption of internal measures',[351] their attempt in codifying them restrictively in the Lisbon Treaty failed.[352] The formulation of the current provisions fails to provide a definitive clarification of questions relating to Union competences and the division of competences between the Union and its Member States. Moreover, the Treaty does not touch upon the issue of application of the principle of pre-emption of a given field, once the Union's implied external competence is recognised. As a consequence, the Court maintains a large room of manoeuvre, as it was for instance evidenced in Opinion 1/13 on the extent of the respective powers of the EU and its Member States to declare the acceptance of the accession of third States to the 1980 Hague Convention on the civil aspects of international child abduction. In its Opinion, the Court had a broad interpretation of the criteria for the recognition of an implicit exclusive external competence.[353] The Court clearly indicated that it refused to detract from its prior case law and would continue to subject treaty provisions to its specific purposive method of interpretation.[354]

These general considerations are crucial not only for determining the existence of the Union's implied external competence in relation to its policy against human trafficking, but also for reflecting on the nature of the Union's competence, which may influence its capacity to develop the external dimension of its counter-trafficking policy coherently. The internal instruments that are part of the Union's counter-trafficking acquis are also particularly relevant and identifying them can prove to be useful. Their adoption may indeed trigger the recognition of implied external competences to the benefit of the EU, in application of the Court's jurisprudence.

ii. *The Union's Implied Competences in the Field of Migration*

Before entering into considerations relating to the scope and nature of the EU's implied competence in the field of migration, it is important to stress that most of the legislative instruments belonging to the 'internal' counter-trafficking acquis

---

[350] Opinion 2/15, Free Trade Agreement *Singapore* [2017] EU:C:2017:376, paras 171–72, quoted in Chamon (n 316) 1123.

[351] Govaere, 'External Competence: What's in a Name?' (n 311) 462.

[352] I Govaere, '"Setting the International Scene": EU External Competence and Procedures Post-Lisbon Revisited in the Light of ECJ Opinion 1/13' (2015) 52 *Common Market Law Review* 1036.

[353] Rosas (n 337) 1091.

[354] Govaere, '"Setting the International Scene"' (n 352).

concern non-EU citizens, ie, third-country nationals already present in the Union's territory or willing to join this territory. As Eeckhout stressed, 'one can say that they form an externally-oriented policy of the European Union, even if it mostly consists of the adoption of internal legislation'.[355] Measures such as the Directive on residence permits for victims of trafficking,[356] the Employers' Sanctions Directive[357] and the Seasonal Workers Directive[358] are relevant examples of that trend, as they directly target third-country nationals, and are de facto inapplicable to Union citizens.

That being said, the existence of these internal rules is inextricably linked to the development of agreements and cooperation with third countries. Due to the limits of the EU's express external competences in this field addressed above, the identification of the EU's external implicit competences in the field of migration is a necessary exercise. Among the different possibilities for the recognition of implied competences, it seems clear that the EU's competence to conclude international agreements with third countries would facilitate the achievement of the internal objectives assigned to the common immigration policy, including the prevention of, and enhanced measures to combat illegal immigration and trafficking in human beings.[359] However, the difficulty arises when determining the nature of such implicit competences in the field of migration, in which coexist exclusive and concurrent external competences, making it often necessary to resort to the conclusion of agreements as mixed agreements/mixity.

The ratification of the UN Protocol against Trafficking in Persons, especially Women and Children reflect such tension, and the need to resort to mixity for the conclusion of agreements including measures addressing trafficking from a migration perspective. The Commission identified a certain number of provisions and developed a lengthy argument,[360] justifying Community participation in the Protocol with regard to its competence in immigration and borders laws.[361] The adoption of the Council Decision approving the ratification of the Trafficking Protocol was delayed because of discussion between the Council and the Commission on the extent of Community competence with regard to

---

[355] Eeckhout (n 320) 157–58.

[356] Directive 2004/81/EC (n 187) intends to 'define the conditions for granting residence permits of limited duration, linked to the length of the relevant national proceedings, to third-country nationals who cooperate in the fight against trafficking in human beings'.

[357] Directive 2009/52/EC (n 196) prohibits the employment of illegally staying third-country nationals, and to this end lays down minimum common standards on sanctions and measures to be applied on the Member States against employers who infringe that prohibition.

[358] Directive 2014/36/EU (n 207) defines the conditions of entry and stay of third-country nationals for the purpose of employment as seasonal workers.

[359] Art 79 (1) TFEU. Garcia Andrade, 'EU External Competences in the Field of Migration' (n 308) 163.

[360] Monar, 'The EU as an International Actor' (n 103) 407–08.

[361] Commission, 'Proposal for a Council Decision on the conclusion, on behalf of the European Community, of the Protocol to Prevent, Suppress and Punish Trafficking in Persons, Especially Women and Children, supplementing the United Nations Convention Against Transnational Organised Crime', COM (2003) 512 final.

this Protocol.[362] Interestingly, the legal bases evolved from those included in the initial proposal for a decision authorising the ratification of the Trafficking Protocol, and those included in the Council Decision authorising it.[363] As it is common practice in other mixed agreements, the ratification instrument set down by the Community was accompanied by declarations of competence, delimiting the scope of its competence.[364] The latter included crossing of external borders of the Member States (border checks, rules on visas for intended stays of no more than three months); measures on immigration policy regarding conditions of entry and residence; measures to counter illegal immigration; as well as measures to ensure cooperation between relevant national and EU administrations.[365]

iii. *The Union's Implied Competences in the Field of Police and Judicial Cooperation in Criminal Matters*

The competence of the EU to enter agreements with third countries in criminal matters evolved with revisions of EU treaties. The Treaty of Amsterdam introduced an explicit external competence allowing the EU to conclude international agreements covering matters falling within the scope of the Third Pillar, including police and judicial cooperation in criminal matters.[366] The Treaty of Lisbon deleted this provision and thus unified the regime applicable to international agreements covering matters falling under the former First and Third Pillars. This means that under the current state of EU law, the EU's external competence in the field of police and judicial cooperation can be identified in application of the doctrine of implied powers, as codified by the Lisbon Treaty and interpreted by the Court of Justice. The delimitation of the EU's external competences requires a careful examination, distinguishing judicial cooperation in criminal matters from police cooperation.

In the field of judicial cooperation in criminal matters, the EU has been conferred two types of internal competences: Article 83, paragraph 1 provides for the adoption of rules approximating substantive criminal law, whereas Article 82,

---

[362] Commission, 'Amended proposal for a Council Decision on the conclusion, on behalf of the European Community, of the Protocol to Prevent, Suppress and Punish Trafficking in Persons', COM (2005) 503 final.

[363] Legal bases were initially Art. 62 point 2, 63 point 3, and Art 300 TEC, and the amended proposal added Art. 66, 179 and 181a C.

[364] P Garcia Andrade, 'EU external competences on migration: which role for mixed agreements?' in S Carrera, J Santos Vara, M Strik and A Hermina (eds), *Constitutionalising the External Dimensions of EU Migration Policies in Times of Crisis* (Cheltenham, Edward Elgar Publishing, 2019) 50–51.

[365] Council, Decision 2006/618/EC of 24 July 2006 on the conclusion, on behalf of the European Community, of the Protocol to Prevent, Suppress and Punish Trafficking in Persons, especially Women and Children ... in so far as the provisions of this Protocol fall within the scope of Part III, Title IV of the EC Treaty [2006] OJ L262/51, Annex II. The Annex also includes a reference to the competence of the Community in development cooperation.

[366] Former Art 38 TEU – see above III.A 'Specificities of the Union's External Competences Linked to the Area of Freedom, Security and Justice'.

paragraph 2 TFEU foresees the adoption of measures approximating procedural criminal law, each of them pursuing different objectives. Although these two provisions possess a clear internal dimension, and are linked to the principle of mutual recognition, which applies only between EU Member States, they have not prevented the EU from developing an external dimension of this policy field. These treaty provisions could be invoked for the recognition of implied external competences in the situation in which the agreement is necessary in order to achieve one of the objectives referred to in the Treaties. Even though the agreements on mutual legal assistance had been signed under the previous legal framework, ie, on the basis of former Articles 24 and 38 TEU,[367] the agreements concluded after the entry into force of the Lisbon Treaty can confirm the recognition of an implied competence. By way of example, the Council Decision authorising the conclusion of the Agreement on the surrender procedure between EU Member States, Iceland and Norway, which deals with the facilitation of cooperation between judicial or equivalent authorities in relation to proceedings in criminal matters and the enforcement of decisions, is based on Article 82, paragraph 1(d) TFEU.[368] In addition, the instruments adopted on the basis of Articles 82 and 83 could also be considered as potential bases for the recognition of AETR-type implied powers to conclude international agreements, in so far as the provisions of such agreements come within the EU's substantive powers.[369] According to Monar,

> the enhanced action potential on common rules regarding criminal procedure and seven 'new' fields of approximation of substantive criminal law … could, via the strengthening of the internal EU acquis, provide a stronger common platform for mutual legal assistance agreements with third-countries and the defence of common positions in the criminal justice domain in the relevant international organisations.[370]

This argument is supported by the practice of the EU institutions, notably when the Council adopted its Decision on the signing on behalf of the EU of the Istanbul Convention[371] with matters relating to judicial cooperation in criminal matters.[372] The Council Decision stressed that the Convention was signed on behalf of the Union as regards matters falling within its competence in so far as

---

[367] See, eg, Council Decision 2010/88/CFSP/JHA of 30 November 2009 on the signing, on behalf of the European Union, of the Agreement between the European Union and Japan on mutual legal assistance in criminal matters [2010] OJ L39/19.

[368] Council Decision 2014/835/EU of 27 November 2014 on the conclusion of the Agreement between the European Union and the Republic of Iceland and the Kingdom of Norway on the surrender procedure between the Member States of the European Union and Iceland and Norway [2014] OJ L343/1.

[369] Eeckhout (n 320) 163.

[370] Monar, *The External Dimension of the EU's Area of Freedom, Security and Justice* (n 126) 26.

[371] Council of Europe Convention on preventing and combating violence against women and domestic violence, CETS No 210, signed in Istanbul on 11 May 2011.

[372] Council Decision (EU) 2017/865 of 11 May 2017 on the signing, on behalf of the European Union, of the Council of Europe Convention on preventing and combating violence against women and domestic violence with regard to matters related to judicial cooperation in criminal matters [2017] OJ L131/11.

the Convention may affect common rules or alter their scope.[373] The legal bases of the text, Articles 82(2) and 84 TFEU, remained unchanged since the publication of the Commission's Proposal, both institutions agreeing on the fact that the predominant purpose of the Convention lies in the prevention of violent crimes against women.[374] Although some argued in favour of considering adding other legal bases, the choice of these legal bases and the existence of an EU's implied competence is currently reviewed by the Court of Justice.[375]

In the field of police cooperation, a similar reasoning applies, and Opinion 1/76-type of implied competences, ie, when the agreement is necessary in order to achieve one of the objectives referred to in the Treaties, could be recognised on the basis of Article 87 TFEU. After the entry into force of the Treaty of Lisbon, the Commission for instance proposed the conclusion of several external agreements dealing with policing and criminal law issues, such as for instance the Agreement with Iceland and Norway on the application of certain provisions relating to the fight against terrorism and organised crime.[376] Its conclusion was authorised by the Council in its Decision of 26 July 2010, an instrument based on both Article 82, paragraph 1(d) and Article 87, paragraph 2(a) TFEU, the latter referring to the adoption of measures concerning the collection, storage, processing, analysis and exchange of relevant information. The same legal bases were used, together with Article 16 TFEU on data protection, for the conclusion of the agreements between third countries and the EU on the use and transfer of Passenger Name Record,[377] until the Court of Justice clarified in its Opinion 1/15 on the PNR Agreement with Canada that such agreements could not be based on Article 82 TFEU, as none of the provisions of the envisaged agreement refer to facilitating such judicial cooperation.[378] As a consequence a subsequent Council Decision relating to PNR agreements, such as the Decision authorising

---

[373] ibid Preamble, para 6.

[374] Commission, 'Proposal for a Council Decision on the signing, on behalf of the European Union, of the Council of Europe Convention on preventing and combating violence against women and domestic violence', COM (2016) 111 final, 9.

[375] See European Parliament Resolution of 12 September 2017 on the proposal for a Council decision on the conclusion, by the European Union, of the Council of Europe Convention on preventing and combating violence against women and domestic violence, P8_TA(2017)0329, para 2; and S De Vido, 'The ratification of the Council of Europe Istanbul Convention by the EU: a step forward in the protection of women from violence in the European legal system' (2017) 9(2) *European Journal of Legal Studies* 69, 84–85. Opinion 1/19 (pending) [2019] OJ C413/19.

[376] Commission, 'Proposal for a Council Decision on the conclusion of the Agreement between the European Union and Iceland and Norway on the application of certain provisions of Council Decision 2008/615/JHA on the stepping up of cross-border cooperation, particularly in combatting terrorism and cross-border crime and Council Decision 2008/616/JHA on the implementation of Decision 2008/615/JHA on the stepping up of cross-border cooperation, particularly in combatting terrorism and cross-border crime, and the Annex thereto', COM (2009) 707. Council Decision of 26 July 2010 [2010] OJ L238/1.

[377] Council Decision 2012/472/EU of 26 April 2012 on the conclusion of the agreement between the between the USA and the EU on the use and transfer of Passenger Name Record to the US Department of Homeland Security, [2012] OJ L215/4.

[378] Opinion 1/15 of 26 July 2017 [2017] EU:C:2017:592, paras 102–03.

the opening of negotiations with Japan, was based on the dual legal bases of Articles 16 and 87 TFEU.[379]

However, whereas the existence of a Union implied external competence in the fields of police and judicial cooperation in criminal matters has been established, defining its nature is more complex. According to Article 4, paragraph 2(j) TFEU, the AFSJ is a domain of shared competence between the Union and the Member States. Such a situation implies that only in areas where the EU has exercised its competences to the extent of full harmonisation, will the EU enjoy exclusive powers on related external action. In practice, in areas where the EU has not achieved full harmonisation, such as police and judicial cooperation in criminal matters, the Member States can continue to exercise their competence, meaning that they can not only participate in any international agreement together with the EU, but also conclude international agreements on their own. The nature of the EU's internal competence in criminal matters counts among the elements militating against the emergence of an exclusive EU external competence. This is further reinforced by Declaration 36 annexed to the Treaty of Lisbon, which expressly provides that

> the Conference confirms that Member States may negotiate and conclude agreements with third countries or international organisations in the areas (of judicial cooperation in civil and criminal matters, and of police cooperation) in so far as such agreements comply with Union law.[380]

With this declaration, Member States seem to have sought to ensure that the competence to conclude international agreements remains shared between them and the EU. This may imply first that international agreements in this field might often be concluded as mixed agreements, potentially causing delays in their entry into force, or variable geometry in the application of certain provisions due to national reservations.[381] A second potential consequence is the capacity of Member States to remain free to conclude bilateral agreements with third countries,[382] inside or outside a framework defined by the EU.[383] By way of example, the Agreement on mutual legal assistance concluded with Japan was concluded by the EU alone, as a self-standing agreement without any provision on bilateral agreements with EU Member States.[384] Nevertheless, it allows Japan and

---

[379] Council Decision authorising the opening of negotiations with Japan for an agreement between the European Union and Japan on the transfer and use of Passenger Name Record (PNR) data to prevent and combat terrorism and serious transnational crime, Council Doc No 5378/20.

[380] Declaration No 36, Declaration on Article 218 TFEU concerning the negotiation and conclusion of international agreements by Member States relating to the AFSJ [2008] OJ C115/349.

[381] See, eg, D Brodowski, 'Judicial Cooperation between the EU and Non-Member States' (2011) 2 *New Journal of European Criminal Law* 21, 33–34.

[382] Monar, *The External Dimension of the EU's Area of Freedom, Security and Justice* (n 126) 61.

[383] The validity of these agreements shall nevertheless be dependent on their full compliance with EU law and the Court of Justice can declare them, or certain of their provisions, contrary to Union rules (see for instance, the famous *Open Skies* judgments, Cases C-466/98, C-467/98, C-468/98, C-469/98, C-471/98, C-472/98, C-475/98 and C-476/98 [2002] Rec 2002 I-09427 and f.

[384] Matera, 'The External Dimension of the Area of Freedom, Security and Justice' (n 90) 431

the Member States to cooperate on the basis of other international conventions, and conclude agreements confirming, supplementing, extending or amplifying the provisions of the EU–Japan Agreement.[385]

Finally, to close our examination of the external competences at the disposal of the EU, it is also necessary to review its competences to externally promote standards belonging to the field of social policy, which is relevant to address trafficking in human beings for the purpose of labour exploitation. In Opinion 2/91,[386] the Court of Justice confirmed that the definition of the Community's internal legislative competence in the field of health and safety of workers in rather subsidiary terms did not prevent the recognition of a Community external competence in that field.[387] However, the Court carefully examined the scope of the envisaged convention and the texts already adopted by the Community, and concluded that the competence to conclude the envisaged international convention was shared between the Community and the Member States.[388] This absence of exclusivity was further reinforced by the treaty provision allowing Member States from maintaining or introducing more stringent protective social measures, as long as they are compatible with the Treaties (Article 153(4) TFEU). The conclusion and ratification by the EU of international agreements in this field may nevertheless be restrained by external factors. For instance, the Union cannot become a member of the International Labour Organization (ILO), or participate in the conclusion of ILO Conventions. It can only exercise its competence through the medium of the Member States acting jointly in the Community interest,[389] which requires cooperation with the Member States in the procedure of ratification of the international agreements and in their implementation. Measures in favour of the respect of international social standards can also be found in trade agreements adopted in the framework of the Common Commercial Policy.[390]

iv. Conclusion on the EU's Implied Competences

Our examination of potential implied external competences demonstrates that the EU possesses the capacity to act externally in migration matters and/or in police and judicial cooperation in criminal matters. The existence of these implied external competences is particularly important for the development and implementation of the external dimension of the Union's policy against trafficking in human beings. They allow the EU to participate, where possible, in the relevant

---

[385] ibid.
[386] Opinion 2/91, Convention No 170 of the International Labour Organisation concerning safety in the use of chemicals at work [1993] EU:C:1993:106.
[387] ibid paras 16–17.
[388] ibid paras 26 and 32.
[389] ibid para 5.
[390] As an example, and for an analysis of such measures, see A Navasartian, 'EU–Vietnam Free Trade Agreement: Insights on the Substantial and Procedural Guarantees for Labour Protection in Vietnam' (2020) 5 *European Papers* 561.

international agreements setting important standards and to conclude agreements with third countries containing provisions relating to justice, freedom and security matters. However, they present several challenges. First, the complexity inherent to the AFSJ is reflected in the external competences at the disposal of the EU. The recognition of an exclusive external competence is much more difficult than in other policy fields of external relations, especially in light of the wording of relevant treaty provisions and the specific steps taken by the Member States to retain their competence to act externally. The Member States often maintain their capacity to conclude their agreements with third countries, for instance in border management, or on judicial cooperation in criminal matters.[391] They also remain in full possession of their enforcement and operational prerogatives, and the EU's competences appear to be put to use rather to define a common reference framework.[392] Second, their nature as implied competences leaves a certain lack of predictability in the identification and definition of the Union's competence. In its case law following the entry into force of the Lisbon Treaty, the Court of Justice reaffirms itself in its decisive role as the final arbiter on competences,[393] and disputes still arise concerning the existence, nature and scope of the Union's competence. This leads at best to variations in the competences at the disposal of the EU to develop the external dimension of its policy against trafficking in human beings. Such diversity is further reinforced by the fact that relevant counter-trafficking measures may be relevant and adequately integrated into many of its external policies, including those for which the EU possesses an express external competence.

D. Constitutional Principles Guiding the EU's External Counter-Trafficking Activities

The capacity of the EU to act externally on the basis of express and implied competences is particularly important for the development and implementation of the external dimension of its policy against trafficking in human beings. The latter does not constitute an external policy of its own and is implemented through the insertion of counter-trafficking considerations and measures in various external policies. In line with the approach defined at EU level, built on a multidisciplinary and comprehensive answer to trafficking, and as provided for in strategic documents, external actions will be conducted in all relevant areas. The overall picture of these actions is not only broad in its outlook but is also quite complex to manage as it will include actions pursuing different objectives and/or developed in different policies, including in areas in which the EU shares its competence to act externally with the Member States. Addressing all aspects

---

[391] Matera, 'The External Dimension of the Area of Freedom, Security and Justice' (n 90) 414, 431.
[392] ibid 431.
[393] Ott, 'EU External Competence' (n 323) 68.

of counter-trafficking policy thus implies the involvement of and the reliance on various EU and national actors, each of them willing to enact and implement counter-trafficking measures within its respective competences, which may vary depending on the policy field concerned. How can it be ensured that their actions do not contradict each other or that they at least participate together in the pursuit of the external objectives assigned to the EU? Constitutional principles of EU law are essential in this regard, as they are to understand the internal activities of the EU. The principle of conferral of competences, mentioned above, is crucial to understand and identify the scope and nature of the EU's external competences relevant to counter trafficking in human beings. Other constitutional principles are relevant in guiding how the EU can develop the external dimension of its counter-trafficking policy, and their examination is thus required (i). They are furthermore to be considered in relation to the institutional dimension of the EU's external activities. While the topic is rich, and has been the object of many discussions,[394] we will focus here on one specificity of the EU's counter-trafficking policy: the nomination of an EU Anti-Trafficking Coordinator whose role and mandate will also be analysed (ii).

i. Guiding Constitutional Principles and Duties

In the field of external relations, the Treaty of Lisbon sought to correct several faults identified in the previous legal framework. In terms of substance, the introduction of a single legal personality for the Union is equally important as it establishes the unitary conception of the EU legal order, and it is accompanied by the introduction of general provisions concerning the Union's external action as a whole. Article 21, paragraph 1 TEU sets out the principles that shall guide the EU's action on the international scene, which include in particular the rule of law, the universality and indivisibility of human rights and fundamental freedoms and respect for human dignity. The same Article states in its paragraph 2(a) that the Union shall define and pursue common policies and actions in order to safeguard its values, fundamental interests, security, independence and integrity. Finally, in Article 21, paragraph 3 TEU, the treaty makers provide that such objectives shall be pursued 'in the development and implementation of the different areas of the Union's external action ... and of the external aspects of its other policies'. The impact of these novelties for the external dimension of the AFSJ and, in particular, of the EU's counter-trafficking policy, deserves further analysis.

A first advantage lies in the recognition of the rule of law and respect for human dignity as principles that shall guide the Union's external action. Trafficking in human beings being a clear violation of victims' human rights and in particular of their dignity, this recognition provides an additional argument

---

[394] In the field of AFSJ see, eg, Matera, 'The External Dimension of the Area of Freedom, Security and Justice' (n 90) 415–21.

in support of the implementation of the EU's multidisciplinary, holistic and integrated approach towards trafficking in human beings in all external policies of the Union. Second with Article 21 paragraph 2(a) TEU, the Union receives a clear mandate to define and pursue common external policies and actions in particular to safeguard its security. The reference to the Union's security and not to security in general might indicate that the security dimension of the Union's external policy can address external challenges that may affect its (internal) security. The considerable extent to which the external dimension of the AFSJ instrumentalises other EU external policies[395] is acknowledged and somehow legitimised. Finally, the Treaty of Lisbon introduces the requirement that the development and implementation of external aspects of the Union's other policies will respect the principles and pursue the objectives previously mentioned. This requirement is particularly important for the external dimension of the EU's policy against trafficking in human beings, as it leads to its integration in the common legal framework. It is also important in so far as it means that, whenever the EU uses external competences based on other policy fields to develop and implement the external dimension of its counter-trafficking policy, it would be bound by these overall principles and objectives, which may potentially reduce the risk of fragmentation and disparities.

However, two elements may undermine the positive impact of the proclamation of common principles and objectives for the coherence of the Union's external policy. First, these common principles and objectives shall not hide the remaining dichotomy between CFSP and non-CFSP external actions, which are still subject to different legal frameworks. Under the pre-Lisbon legal framework, Article 47 TEU granted to the Court of Justice the competence to decide when measures adopted under the Second and Third Pillars 'affected' the Treaty on the European Community. This provision underlined the primacy of Community competences and it indicated a hierarchical relationship between the pillars, reducing the CFSP to a narrowly defined, residual category of external relations activities.[396] By contrast Article 40 TEU, which was introduced by the Treaty of Lisbon, provides for equal protection in the various types of EU external action.[397] This might lead to 'new challenges of delimitation in the field of EU external action', as the application of a centre of gravity test is not an easy and straightforward exercise in this field.[398] The difficulty of the exercise is particularly apparent for measures falling within the scope of both the CFSP

---

[395] For further details, see P Koutrakos, 'The External Dimension of the AFSJ and Other EU External Policies' in M Cremona, J Monar and S Poli (eds), *The External Dimension of the European Union's Area of Freedom, Security and Justice* (Brussels, Peter Lang, 2011) 160.

[396] Van Elsuwege (n 282) 1002.

[397] Equal protection differs from the previous legal regime, under which the former Art 47 TEU, as interpreted by the Court of Justice, 'reduced the CFSP to a narrowly defined, residual category of external relations activities'. Van Elsuwege (n 282) 1002.

[398] ibid 1003.

and AFSJ, in particular for restrictive measures against individuals and non-State entities (smart sanctions),[399] or when AFSJ measures are included in CFSP activities.[400] The case law of the Court of Justice is here of relevance, notably in order to test and identify the centre of gravity of the instrument adopted,[401] and will prove essential to address the insertion of counter-trafficking measures in CFSP instruments.[402] Second, the risk of fragmentation may remain, especially considering the simultaneous insertion of counter-trafficking considerations and measures in policies designed as purely external, such as trade, development cooperation and CFSP, as well as in policies developing the external dimension of an internal policy, such as the AFSJ. The principle of coherence in EU external relations is in this regard essential. While the issue of coherence in EU external relations has been the subject of numerous discussions, our analysis would here be limited to its source, definition and role in framing the external dimension of the EU's policy against human trafficking.

Prior to the entry into force of the Lisbon Treaty, coherence was already present in EU primary law, with Article 1 TEU stating that the task of the Union shall be to organise the relations between the Member States and their people in a manner demonstrating consistency. The importance of horizontal and vertical coherence within the EU legal order had been highlighted and it is of no surprise that the principle has found 'its way into EU external relations when legal conflicts, interpretational problems, delineation issues and so arise'.[403] The Treaty of Lisbon strengthened the constitutionality of this principle. It enounced in a provision having general application, Article 7 TFEU, that the Union shall have consistency between its policies and activities taking all its objectives into account. It further included an additional provision, Article 21, paragraph 3, subparagraph 2 TEU, specific to the EU's external relations, which provides that 'the Union shall ensure consistency between the different areas of its external action and between these and its other policies'.

Before discussing the interpretation to be given to this provision, the linguistic difficulty that arises because of the discrepancy between the English language version of the Treaty and others must be addressed, the English language version

---

[399] For more details, see ibid 1009–12. The sensitivity of the delimitation in the case of smart sanctions is unlikely to be present in other aspects of the AFSJ, since the existence of two legal bases for smart sanctions, ie, Art 75 TFEU (AFSJ) and Art 215 TFEU (CFSP), is a unique situation.

[400] See for instance, Council Decision 2012/392/CFSP of 16 July 2012 on the European Union CSDP mission in Niger (EUCAP Sahel Niger) [2012] OJ L187/48. The tasks of the mission defined in Art 3 provide for the support of the development of comprehensive regional and international coordination in the fight against terrorism and organised crime, and for the strengthening of the rule of law through the development of the criminal investigations' capacities.

[401] Case C-658/11, *Parliament v Council (Mauritius Agreement)* [2014] EU:C:2014:2025; and Case C-263/14, *Parliament v Council (Tanzania Agreement)* [2016] EU:C:2016:435.

[402] See, eg, the EUNAVFOR MED mission (n 285).

[403] B Van Vooren, *EU External Relations Law and the European Neighbourhood Policy: A Paradigm for Coherence* (Abingdon, Routledge, 2012) 67.

referring to consistency when the other language versions refer to the notion of coherence.[404] This discrepancy led to different interpretations. Some authors, such as Peter Van Elsuwege, considered that it has important implications from a legal point of view. According to him, 'whereas the term "consistency" points to the absence of contradictions between the various external policies, "coherence" refers to the positive obligation to ensure synergy between the different elements of the EU's external action'.[405] The two terms cannot be used interchangeably as consistency can be understood to mean forming a first degree of coherence. However, a consensus seems to emerge in the literature that the references to consistency ought to be interpreted broadly. Consequently, 'it has been argued that the requirement of "consistency" foreseen in the English language version entails more than avoiding legal contradictions and presupposes a quest for synergy and added value between the different actions of the Union'.[406]

Further complexities arise when a more substantial definition of the notion is sought, given the multilayered nature of the concept,[407] which has been the subject of political and academic debates throughout the years, stressing its connection with other EU constitutional principles. Those governing relations between Member States and the EU institutions, and between the EU institutions themselves, also apply in the field of EU external relations. In an attempt to give it shape, Marise Cremona proposes an analysis of the concept as encompassing three levels of rule, each supported by its own legal rules and principles. The first level includes rules pertaining to conflict avoidance between potentially conflicting norms and to conflict resolution, supported by the primacy of EU law and the hierarchy of norms in EU law.[408] The second level gathers rules pertaining to ensuring the effective allocation of tasks between actors and instruments, avoiding both duplication and gaps. Principles of conferral and institutional balance, as well as the doctrine of pre-emption, are important to address the EU's competences and the role of each institution and State.[409] Finally, the third level is composed of rules aimed at synergy between norms, actors and instruments, requiring cooperation and complementarity, supported by the principle of sincere cooperation.[410] The latter enshrined in Article 4, paragraph 3 TEU, is essential as it imposes an obligation to cooperate not only for the Member States, required to cooperate

---

[404] As an example, the French language version of the provision reads as follows: 'L'Union veille à la cohérence entre les différents domaines de son action extérieure et entre ceux-ci et ses autres politiques'.
[405] Van Elsuwege (n 282) 1013 and the references quoted therein.
[406] C Hillion, 'Tous pour un, un pour tous! Coherence in the External Relations of the European Union' in M Cremona (ed), *Developments in EU External Relations Law* (Oxford, Oxford University Press, 2008) 12–16, quoted in Van Elsuwege (n 282) 1013, fn 124.
[407] For a description of the different analytical prisms, see Van Vooren, *EU External Relations Law and the European Neighbourhood Policy* (n 403) 68.
[408] M Cremona, 'Coherence through law: what difference will the Treaty of Lisbon make?' (2008) 3 *Hamburg Review of Social Sciences* 11, 14.
[409] ibid 15.
[410] For more details on the duty of cooperation, see Eeckhout (n 320) 241–55.

with the EU institutions, but also on the EU institutions themselves.[411] Cremona further adds another dimension: the vertical and horizontal coherence, the former referring to the coherence between Member State and Union action, the latter referring to inter-policy (and inter-pillar) coherence.[412] All these principles help to define the legal structure in which the EU can operate as an international actor, and whereas they may be held in tension with one another and pull in different directions, they are not contradictory or conflicting.[413] Bart Van Vooren connects them with the legal obligation of coherence in EU external relations entrenched in Article 21, paragraph 3 TEU and summarises Cremona's proposal as follows: 'To attain coherence between norms, actors and instruments towards a common objective, between them conflicts should be avoided and resolved (first level), tasks should be allocated effectively (second level) and positive synergy should be achieved (third level).[414] Other scholars, such as Mireia Estrada Coñamares, further identify new dimensions to the notion of coherence in EU external relations law, namely the negative and positive dimensions. Whereas the latter refers to the complementarity between the different policies and activities of the EU without pointing at a specific outcome, the former aims at avoiding contradiction and overlaps, requiring the EU actors to justify why they act externally and what they will do.[415] These theoretical discussions may appear abstract and complex, but they are grounded on the case law of the Court of Justice which had multiple occasions to clarify in the context of EU external relations the substance and articulation of these principles. This abundance of judgments even prompted some authors to pinpoint the complexity of its case law, qualified as impenetrable for anyone but specialists of external relations law.[416] Nevertheless, they provided the Court, in particular in its cases regarding the choice of the appropriate legal basis, the opportunity to stress the requirements of clarity, consistency and rationalisation under the Lisbon Treaty and how the EU must ensure, in accordance with Article 21(3) TEU, consistency between the different areas of its external actions.[417]

The principle of coherence thus appears rather as a systemic principle, which serves to guide and shape the interpretation of the other principles and their implementation;[418] it participates, together with the other key EU constitutional

---

[411] Cremona, 'Coherence through law' (n 408) 16. See in this regard, Case C-204/86, *Greece v. Council* [1988] EU:C:1988:450, para 16.

[412] Cremona, 'Coherence through law' (n 408) 16 and 19.

[413] M Cremona, 'Structural Principles and their Role in EU External Relations Law' in M Cremona (ed), *Structural Principles in EU External Relations Law* (Oxford, Hart Publishing, 2018) 14.

[414] Van Vooren, *EU External Relations Law and the European Neighbourhood Policy* (n 403) 68–69.

[415] M Estrada Coñamares, '"Building Coherent EU Responses": Coherence as a Structural Principle' in M Cremona (ed), *Structural Principles in EU External Relations Law* (Oxford, Hart Publishing, 2018).

[416] B de Witte, 'Too Much Constitutional Law in the European Union's Foreign Relations?' in M Cremona and B de Witte, *EU Foreign Relations Law: Constitutional Fundamentals* (Oxford, Hart Publishing, 2008) 11.

[417] Case C-263/144, *European Parliament v Council* [2016] EU:C:2016:435, paras 68 and 72.

[418] Cremona, 'Structural Principles and their Role in EU External Relations Law' (n 413) 28.

principles, in building a set of norms of a procedural and substantive nature in order to ensure a coherent EU response to complex issues. Relying on such principles, and in particular on the principle of coherence, is important for our analysis of the external dimension of the EU's policy against trafficking in human beings. The different dimensions of the principle, which are encompassed by this broad definition, somehow resonate with the soft law requirements included in the multidisciplinary, holistic and integrated approach defined in the Union counter-trafficking policy. Implementing the external dimension of this policy in a coherent way thus becomes an obligation that flows from EU primary law. Although the sole existence of the principle of coherence does not suffice to solve the risks of fragmentation and inconsistencies arising in the implementation of the external dimension of the Union's counter-trafficking policy, it nevertheless provides essential guidance for the EU's and Member States' external actions, which could be subject of judicial review before the Court of Justice.

ii. Institutional Dimension of the Quest for Coherence

In addition to the concretisation of new constitutional principles, the Treaty of Lisbon provided an opportunity to reinforce the institutional dimension of the quest for coherence in the EU's external relations. Diverse institutions and actors are indeed involved in the external dimension of the EU's policy against trafficking in human beings. The main EU institutions, the Commission, the Council and the European Parliament, play an important role in the negotiation and conclusions of external agreements, and they also face internally a fragmentation of actors, as relevant counter-trafficking measures may be dealt with in different directorates or committees. Other EU actors, such as the EU agencies competent in the field of migration and criminal justice, also participate in such external activities.

In recent years, new positions have been created in order to coordinate as much as possible the diverse external activities that may be developed to address human trafficking. In EU primary law, the main innovation consists of the constitutionalisation of the role of the High Representative for Foreign Affairs and Security Policy, belonging to both the Commission and the Council and assisted by the European External Action Service (Articles 18 and 27 TEU). The creation of this new actor aims in particular at addressing the 'dualist nature of EU external relations' as well as the fragmentation of responsibility for the conduct of EU external actions, which was shared between the Commission on the one hand, and the Council on the other. The High Representative has a clear and strong mandate to ensure the consistency of the Union's external action. First, under Article 21, paragraph 3 TEU he or she assists the Council and the Commission in ensuring consistency between the different areas of the EU's external action and between these and its other policies. Second, in connection with his or her double hat, he or she is entrusted under Article 18, paragraph 4 TEU with the task of ensuring the consistency of the Union's external actions. These two provisions read together clearly make he or she 'the first watchdog over the consistency principle'.[419]

Moreover, the High Representative receives the assistance of ad hoc actors, designated as coordinators, whose missions especially concern the coherent development and implementation of the external dimension of certain aspects of the AFSJ, namely the fight against terrorism and the fight against trafficking in human beings. A short comparison of the missions and mandates of both coordinators is relevant, especially to stress the somewhat reduced function of the EU Anti-Trafficking Coordinator.

The position of EU Counter-Terrorism Coordinator was created by the European Council in 2004 and assigned it the tasks of coordinating the work of the Council and maintaining an overview of all the instruments at the Union's disposal.[420] In 2007, the appointment of Gilles de Kerchove by Javier Solana, EU Representative for the CFSP, became the moment to extend its mandate. In addition to previous tasks, the EU Counter-Terrorism Coordinator is also in charge of closely monitoring the implementation of the EU's Counter-Terrorism Strategy,[421] but also of coordinating with the relevant preparatory bodies of the Council, the Commission and the European External Action Service (EEAS), and sharing information with them on his activities.[422] The role of the EU Counter-Terrorism Coordinator was reaffirmed by the European Council in its multi-annual strategic guidelines for 2014–19, in particular as an effective EU counter-terrorism policy is needed whereby all relevant actors work closely together, integrating the internal and external aspects of the fight against terrorism.[423] Even though the Strategic Agenda for 2019–2024 does not mention its role,[424] the terrorist attacks on European soil have reinforced the commitment of the EU institutions and Member States towards a coordinated counter-terrorism policy, especially with regard to its external dimension.[425] This was, for instance, reaffirmed in June 2020 in the Council's conclusions, calling upon the relevant EU bodies to continue strengthening the synergy and improving coordination between the internal and external dimensions of counter-terrorism.[426] The EU Counter-Terrorism Coordinator thus remains a key actor in EU counter-terrorism policy, its distinctive characteristic probably being its extensive

---

[419] Van Elsuwege (n 282) 1013.

[420] Council, Declaration on combating Terrorism, Brussels 25 March 2004, 13, available at: www.consilium.europa.eu/uedocs/cmsUpload/DECL-25.3.pdf.

[421] Council, 'The European Union Counter-Terrorism Strategy', 30 November 2005, Council Doc No 14469/4/05.

[422] Council, 'Policies, Fight against terrorism', available at: www.consilium.europa.eu/en/policies/fight-against-terrorism/counter-terrorism-coordinator/.

[423] Council, Conclusions of 26 and 27 June 2014 (n 117) 5, para 10.

[424] Council, Conclusions, 20 June 2019, EUCO 9/19.

[425] Commission, 'Delivering on the European Agenda on Security to fight against terrorism and pace the way towards an effective and genuine Security Union' (Communication), COM (2016) 230 final, 16.

[426] Council, 'Council's Conclusions on EU External Action on Preventing and Countering Terrorism and Violent Extremism, 15 June 2020', Council Doc No 8868/20, 16, para 35.

mandate to coordinate the work of the relevant services within the Commission, the Council and the EEAS.

In contrast, the role and mandate of the EU Anti-Trafficking Coordinator appears less ambitious. The establishment of the position was initiated by the European Council, in order to also ensure better coherence.[427] The first EU Anti-Trafficking Coordinator, Dr Myria Vassiliadou, was appointed by the European Commission in 2010,[428] and her mandate came to an end in February 2020, without (as of May 2020) a new coordinator being appointed.[429] In the course of her mandate, she carried out her mission of ensuring consistent and coordinated strategic planning at EU level and with international organisations and third countries. The adoption of the EU Strategy in 2012 was a first step in the implementation of such a mandate, as evidenced by the implementation reports which offer several examples of the way in which the EU Anti-trafficking Coordinator 'provides strategic policy guidance to ensure consistent and coordinated planning to address trafficking in human beings'.[430] Furthermore, the EU legislator decided, thanks notably to the efforts of the European Parliament,[431] to insert in Directive 2011/36/EU several references to the EU Anti-Trafficking Coordinator. The main reference can be found in Article 20 on the coordination of the EU's Strategy, which provides that on the basis of information communicated by Member States, the EU Anti-Trafficking Coordinator contributes to the Commission's biennial report on its counter-trafficking policy.[432] In practice, the EU Anti-Trafficking Coordinator assumed its internal coordination role through the establishment of the Inter-Service Group on Trafficking in Human Beings, bringing together representatives of the 16 European Commission services, the EEAS and the European Statistical Office.[433] Her office also collaborated with EU agencies, notably to support the signature of Joint Statements in 2011 and 2018.[434] However, the role and powers of the EU Anti-Trafficking Coordinator are not identical to those of the EU Counter-Terrorism Coordinator and the two functions are not perceived as similar by Member States. The latter perceive the EU Anti-Trafficking Coordinator as being the coordinator for the Commission's activities.[435] Such a perception can

---

[427] Council, 'The Stockholm Programme' (n 115).

[428] Commission, 'The Commission appoints an EU Anti-Trafficking Coordinator', Press release IP/10/171 of 14 December 2010, available at: europa.eu/rapid/press-release_IP-10-1715_en.htm.

[429] Mr Olivier Onidi, Deputy Director-General of DG Migration and Home Affairs, will serve as acting coordinator, in charge notably of developing a new EU Strategy against trafficking. La Strada International, Newsletter Issue 56, 2020, 4, available at: lastradainternational.org/lsidocs/3352-LSI%20 Newsletter%2030%20March%202020%20-%20final.pdf.

[430] Commission, 'Mid-Term implementation report' (n 212) 14.

[431] Z Sakelliadou, 'EU Anti-trafficking Coordinator: Trajectory of a Unique Mandate' in J Winterdyk and J Jones (eds), *The Palgrave International Handbook of Human Trafficking* (Basingstoke, Palgrave Macmillan, 2020) 1310–11.

[432] Art 20 of Directive 2011/36/EU, Coordination of the Union Strategy against trafficking in human beings.

[433] Sakelliadou (n 431) 1315.

[434] ibid.

[435] Commission, Press release IP/10/171 (n 428).

somehow be reinforced by the fact that the EU Anti-Trafficking Coordinator reports directly to the Director-General of DG Home Affairs, not to the Council or the European Council, like the EU Counter-Terrorism Coordinator.

These institutional innovations, formalised since the entry into force of the Lisbon Treaty, are to be considered together with the constitutionalisation of the principle of coherence. Their impact on the risk of fragmentation of the external dimension of the AFSJ may yet be difficult to grasp, as 'coherence is and remains essentially a policy imperative which largely depends on the political will of the Member States and the EU institutions'.[436] Yet the creation of the position of EU Anti-Trafficking Coordinator, together with the budget and staff associated with the position, contributes in ensuring, at the very least, a certain coordination within the Commission, and with the EEAS.

E. Conclusions

The analysis of the external competences at the disposal of the EU to externally promote its policy against trafficking in human beings has allowed us to identify several issues.

The first issue relates to the abundance of external competences on which the EU can rely. Its competences are not limited to the competences expressly foreseen in the Treaties and several implied external competences have been identified. This abundance of competences serves the implementation of the approach advocated by the EU but it also encompasses certain disadvantages and challenges. A first challenge resides in identifying the appropriate instrument and legal basis to promote a specific counter-trafficking measure and ensure that the external action undertaken complies with EU constitutional principles. A second challenge arises from the specificities of AFSJ and the special status of certain Member States, currently only Ireland and Denmark. These Member States may indeed retain their capacity to act externally, even in areas in which the EU has decided to exercise its external competences. The protocols regulating their relations with the development of the AFSJ both provide that no provision of international agreements concluded by the EU in this field shall be applicable to them.[437] In practice, their participation in the EU's external activities in that field follow a piecemeal approach. Denmark is not bound by an international agreement concluded by the EU in AFSJ matters and it may be required in certain cases to conclude a separate agreement with third countries. For Ireland (and previously for the UK), participation in any proposed internal measure implies acceptance of the EU's external competence to conclude international agreements on the same

---

[436] Van Elsuwege (n 282) 1015.
[437] Protocol No 21, Arts 2, 3 and 4; Protocol No 22, Arts 1 and 2.

issue, and it is also possible to opt in to international agreements.[438] This results mostly in procedural hurdles,[439] as each Council Decision needs to be precise about which State is bound by the text. The Decision authorising the ratification of the Istanbul Convention by the EU is a good illustration: whereas Denmark is not taking part in this Decision, the UK and Ireland are, as a consequence of their participation in the relevant EU internal instruments (Directives 2011/36/EU and 2011/93/EU (child pornography)).[440] These specific regimes may nevertheless require additional efforts from the EU to ensure that its external actions are not undermined with those initiated by these Member States prior to entering into negotiations, notably to ensure sufficient coordination, relations and especially the external dimension of its policy against trafficking in human beings. This need for coordination is not limited to countries with a specific relationship with the development of the AFSJ, but it concerns all EU Member States. The third challenge can thus be identified: namely the fact that in those matters the Member States often retain a competence of their own to develop cooperation with third countries and external partners. The duty of loyal cooperation is here crucial, especially considering how it may, in the field of external relations, restrict the capacity of Member States to develop independent initiatives or conclude bilateral agreements, even in areas of shared competences.[441]

The second issue lies in the importance of ensuring a coherent external dimension of the EU's policy against trafficking in human beings. Not only is coherence a duty binding the EU institutions and the Member States by virtue of the TEU, but coherent external actions are also essential to ensure the effectiveness of the EU's external promotion of its policy. Without coherence, there is a risk that cooperation with third countries in that field will remain limited or, worse still, will be impaired by contradictory demands. The appointment of an Anti-Trafficking Coordinator is to be welcomed but its limited mandate reveals the wish of the Member States to keep its role limited to the coordination of the actions of the EU institutions. In this regard, the adoption of numerous soft law instruments, especially those relating to the combat against trafficking in human beings, such as the future second EU Strategy towards the eradication of trafficking, may be relevant in shaping the EU's response to the phenomenon. Such instruments are beneficial

---

[438] J Santos Vara and E Fahey, 'Transatlantic relations and the operation of AFSJ flexibility' in S Blockmans (ed), *Differentiated Integration in the EU: From the Inside Looking Out* (CEPS, 2014) 116.

[439] C Matera, 'Much ado about opt-outs? The impact of variable geometry in the AFSJ on the EU as a Global Security Actor' in S Blockmans (ed), *Differentiated Integration in the EU: From the Inside Looking Out* (CEPS, 2014) 82.

[440] Council Decision (EU) 2017/865 (n 372) Preamble, paras 10 and 11.

[441] On possible restrictions in AFSJ fields, see JHA Council, 'Conclusions on readmission agreements and the consequences of the entry into force of the Amsterdam Treaty', Council Doc No 8654/99, 27–28 May 1999; and on the obligations binding on Member States see, eg, Case 266/03 *Commission v Luxembourg* [2005] EU:C:2005:341, para 60, both discussed in M Cremona, 'Defending the Community Interest: the Duties of Cooperation and Compliance' in M Cremona and B de Witte (eds), *EU Foreign Relations Law: Constitutional Fundamentals* (Oxford, Hart Publishing 2008) 160–64.

for several reasons. They serve to ensure that external activities reflect and implement the objectives and the approach pursued internally, and they also participate in a certain allocation of tasks between various EU institutions and actors within their respective scope of competences, and may even participate in coordinating Member States' responses.[442]

IV. Conclusions on the EU's Policy against Trafficking in Human Beings and its External Competences

The EU has developed an ambitious approach to address trafficking in human beings, and it has in that respect mobilised various types and sources of competences to adopt counter-trafficking measures, enshrined in international agreements, EU legislative instruments or soft law documents. The principle of conferral of competences limits the actions it can undertake, and our analysis of the counter-trafficking acquis, developed within the competences the Treaties conferred on the EU, shows that the measures it adopted are clearly enshrined within the AFSJ. As within the TFEU, the only provisions referring explicitly to trafficking in human beings and enabling the adoption of measures are those granting competences to the EU in migration and criminal matters; the issue remains very much addressed from these two perspectives. This is especially true concerning the main EU legislative instrument, Directive 2011/36/EU. Even though the Directive includes a wide range of provisions on the rights of victims of trafficking, and complies in that regard with a series of positive human rights obligations identified by the European Court of Human Rights, the relevant provisions continue to be framed in whole or in part under a logic of prosecutorial efficiency.[443] Recent policy documents do not correct this assessment, even though they mark a step in the right direction. The EU Strategy on victims' rights for 2020–2025[444] refers to the difficulties for victims of crime to fully rely on their rights in the EU, and the particular challenges faced by the most vulnerable victims, including victims of trafficking, to go through criminal proceedings and to deal with the aftermath of crime.[445] Yet when addressing potential measures, it only announces that 'the Commission is working on a new strategic approach towards the eradication of trafficking in human beings *as part of the Security Union* (emphasis added)'.[446] Similarly, comparable language is used in the EU

---

[442] See in this regard, Council, 'Action-Oriented Paper on strengthening the EU external dimension on action against trafficking in human beings' (n 229).

[443] V Mitsilegas, *The Criminalisation of Migration in Europe, Challenges for Human Rights and the Rule of Law* (London, Springer, 2015) 51.

[444] Commission, 'EU Strategy on victims' rights (2020–2025)' (Communication), COM (2020) 258 final.

[445] ibid 2.

[446] ibid 13.

Gender Equality Strategy for 2020–2025.[447] If the text mentions that the concerns of women and girls affected by trafficking have to be at the centre of policy development, it also stresses that countering the impunity of users, exploiters and profit-makers is a priority.[448] This supports the idea that the EU is not yet ready to depart from the security-based approach under which trafficking in human beings remains addressed as a criminal threat and a form of serious and organised crime.[449] The question of victims' protection remains connected to security measures, something evidenced by the fact that victim protection continues to be disassociated from security of residence. The 2004 Directive on residence permits for victims of trafficking remains in force, and residence remains conditional on the victim's collaboration in the criminal proceedings.[450]

Such a security-based approach may as a consequence be reflected in the external dimension of the EU's policy against trafficking in human beings. Internally, the EU has limited competences in the field of the promotion of human rights, and even though trafficking in human beings is prohibited under Article 5 of the EU Charter of Fundamental Rights, the EU has mostly developed measures falling into migration and criminal matters. Externally, the EU's actions ought to be guided by the principles which have inspired its own creation, including the universality and indivisibility of human rights and fundamental freedoms and respect for human dignity (Article 21, paragraph 1 TEU); and that the EU shall contribute to the protection of human rights (Article, 3 paragraph 5 TEU). However, these general provisions do not create or automatically extend the competences of the EU, and any external action in the pursuit of these objectives must rely on other legal bases in the Treaties.[451] The recent EU Action Plan on Human Rights and Democracy 2020–2024 announces efforts to integrate the protection of human rights in all areas of external action, especially in the areas of migration and security.[452] However, once more the two dimensions of countering impunity and protecting victims are closely intertwined.[453]

The purpose of the next steps of our analysis will thus be twofold. We will explore the ways through which the EU can ensure that it complies with its own constitutional principles and objectives when developing the external dimension of its counter-trafficking policy. Our attention will be particularly focused on the

---

[447] Commission, 'A Union of Equality: Gender Equality Strategy 2020–2025' (Communication), COM (2020) 152 final, 5: '*As part of the Security Union*, the Commission will present a new EU strategy on the eradication of trafficking in human beings' (emphasis added).

[448] ibid 5.

[449] Mitsilegas, *The Criminalisation of Migration in Europe* (n 443) 48–49.

[450] ibid 51.

[451] L Pech and J Grogan, 'EU External Human Rights Policy' in RA Wessel and J Larik (eds), *EU External Relations Law: Text, Cases and Materials*, 2nd edn (Oxford, Hart Publishing, 2020) 333.

[452] Commission and High Representative for Foreign Affairs and Security Policy, 'EU Action Plan for Human Rights and Democracy 2020–2024' (Joint Communication), JOIN (2020) 5 final, 4.

[453] Commission and High Representative for Foreign Affairs and Security Policy, 'Annex to EU Action Plan for Human Rights and Democracy 2020–2024', (Joint Communication), JOIN (2020) 5 final, 5.

duty of coherence, whose respect may thus be sought in alternative ways, such as support for the promotion of the EU's policy in regional frameworks, in which the EU engages in dialogue and cooperation with third countries in a vast array of policy fields, or via its participation in multilateral initiatives. We will also examine whether, in its external activities, the EU upholds and promotes a human rights-based approach to trafficking in human beings, or whether its actions are marked by a security-based approach.

2

Unilateral Promotion of the
EU's Policy: Case Study
of the Western Balkans

In order to externally promote its policy against trafficking in human beings, the European Union (EU) can engage in various types of external activities. As indicated in the Introduction, two main ways to achieve that aim have been identified: on the one hand, the unilateral promotion, through which the EU addresses specific demands to certain third countries, and relies on specific EU-incentives to support cooperation; and on the other, the multilateral promotion through which the EU interacts and collaborates with other actors also engaged in counter-trafficking efforts in order to build synergies and avoid duplication of efforts. The two techniques are not exclusive of one another and they are often used together. Nevertheless, it is worth analysing them both in detail in order to analyse how the EU relies on its external competences to promote its own policy and whether it manages to do so in compliance with its constitutional principles.

In order to achieve its objective to promote its policy against trafficking in human beings externally, the EU must ensure that it addresses its cooperation with third countries in a coherent and comprehensive way. The fight against this crime cannot be a stand-alone area of cooperation and it must insert itself into a broader set of policy areas in which the EU cooperates with the third countries concerned. Such a requirement is further reinforced by the approach that the EU applies internally. This approach is reflected in the external dimension of the EU's policy against trafficking in human beings and implies the promotion of a scope of measures extending beyond those only addressing trafficking in human beings. These requirements can in principle be fulfilled in most of the relationships that the EU has developed with third countries as it is rare that cooperation with a third country does not encompass more than a policy area.

The EU has, since the early 1950s, developed its relationships with third countries, pursuing various objectives, such as the preparation of third countries prior to the accession to the European Community and later to the European Union, the establishment of customs unions or free trade areas and the creation of economic partnerships etc. The intensity and the content of the cooperation with the EU varies from one third country to another, depending for instance on its geographical position, its geostrategic importance and its economic power.

These relationships are cemented through association agreements with third countries, particularly in order to facilitate access to the Union's internal market for goods, and to commit the EU to cooperate with them economically and financially.[1] The Treaties leave a wide margin of discretion to the EU institutions and the Member States to define the scope of these agreements. Article 217 of the Treaty on the Functioning of the European Union (TFEU) only provides that these agreements involve 'reciprocal rights and obligations, common action and special procedure' and the Court of Justice has judged that the Union has the power to 'guarantee commitments in all fields covered by the Treaties'.[2] On the basis of this provision, association agreements constitute the main instruments used to develop cooperation between the EU and third countries. Because of their large scope, they are almost always mixed agreements, signed by both the EU and the Member States. The EU will rely on its external competences, such as those analysed in the previous chapter, to insert provisions relating to migration and security matters, and any other issue relevant to prevent and combat trafficking in human beings.

The provisions contained in association agreements, and the cooperation developed on their basis indeed cover a broad scope of policy areas and are not restricted to trade and commercial cooperation. Human rights considerations are always present,[3] as well as elements relating to the Area of Freedom, Security and Justice (AFSJ),[4] such as provisions on the movement of workers or the possibility to grant visa-free travel to the countries' businessmen. These agreements may also include general provisions aimed at developing and strengthening an institutional framework guaranteeing the rule of law and access to justice, elements which are also relevant to address trafficking in human beings and protect its victims.[5]

Political considerations have a major influence on the content of the agreements and in particular the ultimate objective of the countries' cooperation with the EU, ie, accession, access to the internal market or development of a special relationship (Article 8 of the Treaty on European Union (TEU)). The objectives of the Union's cooperation with third countries that are parties to these agreements exercise considerable influence, especially because the EU has developed regional frameworks of cooperation based on them. These regional frameworks are addressed

---

[1] K Lenaerts and P Van Nuffel, *European Union Law*, 3rd edn (London, Sweet & Maxwell, 2011) 980, para 25-021.

[2] Case 12/86, *Meryem Demirel* [1987] EU:C:1987:400, para 9.

[3] See for instance, the Cotonou Partnership Agreement [2000] OJ L317/3, which contains a human rights clause (Art 9) and a procedure to apply in case a party fails to fulfil an obligation stemming from respect for human rights, democratic principles or the rule of law (Art 96 – consultation procedure which may at the last resort result in the suspension of the Agreement). Lenaerts and Van Nuffel (n 1) 985, para 25-025.

[4] Cotonou Agreement, Art 11A on the fight against terrorism and Art 13 on Migration.

[5] ibid Art 33 on institutional development and capacity building.

to groups of third countries with which the EU intends to cooperate in a similar way. These frameworks, which are not foreseen in the Treaties, result from a political decision. The main ones are: the Stabilisation and Association Process (SAP) concerning the Western Balkans countries; the European Neighbourhood Policy (ENP) concerning countries in the 'neighbourhood' of the EU; and the African, Caribbean and Pacific Group of States. The association agreements concluded in these frameworks are often designated under a certain label, for example, Stabilisation and Association agreements or the Mediterranean agreements, and their content is very similar, if not identical. Yet, although these frameworks refer to groups of countries as regions, they do not presuppose homogeneity among the third countries they cover. A tailor-made approach is developed and reflects the political, economic and social situation of each country. The cooperation under these frameworks nevertheless pursues similar general objectives, ie, ensuring stable and consistent cooperation with third countries and aims at developing a common methodology and a set of tools to frame the arrangements for their cooperation with the EU in various policy fields, from economic cooperation to cooperation in security matters.

The exhaustive analysis of the EU's efforts to externally promote its policy against trafficking in human beings will include the analysis of all the agreements and cooperation initiatives launched with third countries. Yet the added value of such an exhaustive analysis is limited. The issue of trafficking in human beings, or more broadly of the fight against crime, is not addressed in detail in the EU's relations with every third country. Moreover, certain forms of cooperation are too sectoral to assess whether the EU manages to promote the multidisciplinary, holistic and integrated approach that it advocates externally. A selection is thus necessary, and the application of the criteria set out in section I, led to us choosing the Stabilisation and Association Process, which concerns the Western Balkans countries. The following sections will be devoted to the analysis of the promotion of the EU's policy against trafficking in human beings in the policy documents (II), and the agreements (III) concluded with these countries. The support for regional cooperation initiatives and especially those in the field of police and judicial cooperation in criminal matters will also be examined (IV).

I. Selection of the Case Study

In the following section, we will proceed to the delicate exercise of selecting the most relevant regional framework to analyse the efforts of the EU to externally promote the transposition and implementation of its policy against trafficking in human beings. This selection is based on an objective criterion, which limits the choice of the relevant frameworks between two options (A). A more detailed analysis leads to the selection of one specific framework, the Stabilisation and Association Process, which will be presented in detail (B).

A. The Desire of the EU to Establish Close Cooperation in the Fight against Crime

The EU institutions have been prolific in publishing a vast corpus of strategic and policy documents indicating the objectives to be pursued in the external dimension of the AFSJ and more particularly in the external dimension of its counter-trafficking policy and the regions on which the EU's efforts should focus. The Stockholm Programme provided that the development of a consolidated Union policy in this matter includes 'building up and strengthening partnerships with third countries, improving coordination and cooperation within the Union and with the mechanisms of the Union external dimension as an integral part of such a policy'.[6] The Commission even received the task of examining whether 'ad hoc cooperation agreements with specific third countries … could be a way to enhance the fight against trafficking'.[7] Trafficking in human beings was furthermore envisaged as one of the continued thematic priorities, for which the European Council repeated the invitation made to the Commission to examine the conclusion of ad hoc cooperation agreements.[8] The importance of developing cooperation with third countries was also mentioned in the strategic guidelines for the AFSJ, adopted by the European Council in June 2014, in which heads of state and governments insisted on the need to address smuggling and trafficking in human beings more forcefully, with a focus on priority countries and routes.[9] This priority has been repeated in the EU Strategic Agenda, in which the European Council stressed that the EU will continue and deepen its cooperation with countries of origin and transit to fight illegal migration and human trafficking.[10] New strategic guidelines for Justice and Home Affairs (JHA), currently under preparation within the Council aiming to integrate the priorities of the EU Strategic Agenda into its work, might further reflect this ambition and give it more substance. However, while the guidelines were supposed to be adopted within the JHA Council in March 2020, the absence of a full consensus postponed their adoption.[11]

This process of selecting priority countries was initiated long ago, and the list of countries concerned is regularly updated. Whereas, from the early 1990s onwards, priority was placed on the countries that joined the EU in 2004 and 2007, their accession pushed the geographical focus eastwards and southwards.[12]

---

[6] Council, 'The Stockholm Programme – An open and secure Europe serving and protecting citizens' [2010] OJ C115/1, 21.

[7] ibid 22. It is important to stress that for the European Council, 'such agreements could involve full use of all leverage available to the Union, including use of financing programmes, cooperation for the exchange of information, judicial cooperation and migration tools'.

[8] ibid 35.

[9] Council, Conclusions of 26 and 27 June 2014, EUCO 79/14, 3.

[10] Council, EU Strategic Agenda for 2019–2024, Conclusions of 20 June 2019, EUCO 9/19, 7.

[11] Council, 'Outcome of the Council meeting JHA on 13 March 2020', Council Doc No 6582/20, 3.

[12] S Lavenex, 'Channels of Externalisation of EU Justice and Home Affairs' in M Cremona, J Monar and S Poli (eds), *The External Dimension of the European Union's Area of Freedom, Security and Justice* (Brussels, Peter Lang, 2011) 119.

The accession of 10 new Member States and the displacement of the EU's external borders led to a certain instrumentalisation of cooperation in criminal matters. For the Member States, the emergency was to establish as soon as possible a safe zone around the EU's external borders and to find partners that would contribute to keeping criminals away from EU territory, even though these partners are not completely trustworthy.[13] In other words, neighbouring countries became, 'in a sense, the Union's external buffer zone ("*glacis sécuritaire*") when it comes to preventing crime and migration challenges from reaching and crossing the EU's external borders'.[14]

By 2005 the Council had put a special emphasis on the candidate countries and countries with EU membership prospects and European neighbouring countries.[15] Since then, diverse policy documents repeated this need to focus on these neighbouring countries, both for the external dimension of the AFSJ in general[16] and for the external dimension of the Union's counter-trafficking policy.[17] They have been included in the list of priority countries and regions drawn up by the Council.[18] The Global Approach on Migration and Mobility also stressed, 'the first priority should be the EU neighbourhood, ... where the migration and mobility dimensions are closely interwoven with the broader political, economic, social and security cooperation'.[19] The objectives of the EU nevertheless differ slightly, considering the different political leverages at its disposal. The main objective of the EU in its cooperation with candidate countries and countries with EU membership prospects is to assist them in transposing the acquis. By contrast in its relations with the ENP countries, the EU 'only' seeks to establish cooperation on some policy areas belonging to the AFSJ.

Despite these differences and the fact that the SAP and the ENP do not belong to the same areas of the Union's external policy,[20] several patterns are common to both frameworks and will now be analysed.

---

[13] H Labayle, 'L'espace pénal européen et le monde: instrument ou objectif?' in G de Kerchove and A Weyembergh (eds), *Sécurité et justice: enjeu de la politique extérieure de l'Union européenne* (Brussels, Editions de l'Université de Bruxelles, 2003) 22–23.

[14] J Monar, *The External Dimension of the EU's Area of Freedom, Security and Justice: Progress, Potential and Limitations after the Treaty of Lisbon* (Swedish Institute for European Policy Studies, 2012) 64.

[15] Council, Conclusions, 'A Strategy for the External Dimension of JHA: Global Freedom, Security and Justice', Council Doc No 14366/3/05 rev 5, 6.

[16] Council, 'The Stockholm Programme' (n 6) 35.

[17] Council, 'Action-Oriented Paper on strengthening the EU external dimension on action against trafficking in human beings – Second implementation report/update of information on Member States' external action', 3 December 2012, Council Doc No 13661/3/12, 6. See also Commission, 'The EU Strategy towards the Eradication of Trafficking in Human Beings 2012–2016' (Communication), COM (2012) 286 final, 13.

[18] ibid 'Second implementation report', 6.

[19] Commission, 'The Global Approach to Migration and Mobility' (Communication), COM (2011) 743 final, 8.

[20] The SAP belongs to the pre-accession policy, whereas the ENP belongs to the more general foreign policy aimed at fostering cooperation between the Union and third countries.

Before analysing their common patterns, it is important to highlight that we will not discuss the cooperation of the EU with Turkey, even though the country participates in the pre-accession policy, together with the Western Balkans countries. The exclusion of Turkey is justified by the fact that the country constitutes a partner with special treatment from an EU perspective, as is clear for a number of reasons:

- Although the process of pre-accession started much earlier, ie, in the 1960s, and the prospect of accession is constantly repeated,[21] the question is politically sensitive and a special provision has been introduced in national laws subjecting the accession to a referendum in certain EU Member States, for example, France and Austria.[22]

- The country has obtained the conclusion of specific provisions granting preferential treatment to its nationals, for instance with regard to the movement of workers.[23]

- Its relations and the intensity of its cooperation with the EU in security and migration issues have become particularly topical in the last few years, and they are subject to frequent changes, which complicates the analysis of the impact/influence of the EU's efforts to promote its counter-trafficking policy.

Now that we have explained this methodological point, we will briefly present the patterns common to the SAP and the ENP.

First, the two frameworks have been launched in the same context and pursue the same overall objectives. Concerning the former, both frameworks have been launched in the context of the upcoming enlargement of the EU towards the East (enlargements of 2004 and 2007). The policy documents steering the two processes stress how much the upcoming enlargement, prepared since the early 1990s, would move eastwards and southwards of the external borders of the Union and thus lead to closer geographical proximity with 'neighbouring countries'. The EU thus has an interest in strengthening its relations and cooperation with its new neighbours.[24] Furthermore, although the long-term perspectives of the countries participating in each framework differ, the EU and the countries concerned share the same interests in developing cooperation with the EU. The overall objectives are also similar as their cooperation aims not only at enjoying

---

[21] Council, 'Enlargement and Stabilisation and Association Process – Conclusions', 15 December 2015, Council Doc No 15356/15, 6.

[22] On this issue see Foreign Affairs Committee, *UK–Turkey relations and Turkey's regional role* (HC 2010–12, 1567) para 174.

[23] Additional Protocol (title II, chapter 1) signed on 23 November 1970, annexed to the Agreement establishing the Association between the European Economic Community and Turkey and on measures to be taken for their entry into force [1972] OJ L293/3.

[24] R Prodi, President of the European Commission at the time, referred to 'a ring of friends'. See for instance, Romano Prodi, Speech 'A Wider Europe – A Proximity Policy as the Key to Stability', Peace, Security and Stability International Dialogue and the Role of the EU, Sixth ECSA-World Conference, Jean Monnet Project, 5–6 December 2002, available at europa.eu/rapid/press-release_SPEECH-02-619_en.htm.

political stability and security, but also seeks prosperity and the development of their economies. In order to pursue these objectives, the fields of cooperation are broad in both frameworks, ranging from the approximation of legislation in order to benefit from access to the EU's Internal Market and fundamental freedoms, to cooperation in justice and home affairs and strengthening democracy, the rule of law and civil society. All these objectives are inextricably linked. For instance, the independence and impartiality of judges is a key element in the fight against organised crime and corruption, but it is also essential to reassure potential foreign investors.[25] Nevertheless, a difference arises concerning the requirements of the EU: whereas the SAP countries are required to adopt and implement the EU acquis, the ENP countries are more often encouraged to participate in relevant European and international instruments.

Second, the two frameworks are both characterised by the fact that they have been designed in order to offer coherent frameworks for the development of the Union's cooperation with groups of third countries while respecting the individual specificities of each third country. The rationale behind this design resides in the heterogeneity among the countries concerned by each framework and the EU's response to this lack of homogeneity. The EU institutions are very prompt to recognise 'the variety and intensity of the Union's existing relations with and among the countries of its new neighbourhood'.[26] Whereas some already benefit from certain contractual relationships, cemented through the conclusion and implementation of cooperation agreements, others do not yet have such a 'contractual relationship' with the EU and were only engaged in dialogue(s) with the EU and its Member States. Their heterogeneity is also present in the political will and desire to boost their cooperation with the EU. Such a desire may vary from one country to another, depending for instance on its proximity with other important strategic partners, such as Russia, or on the acceptance by national governments of the reforms required by the EU. In the SAP,[27] as in the ENP,[28] countries willing to obtain advantages from the EU, such as the conclusion of an association agreement, or the benefits of a visa-free regime, are obliged to demonstrate their willingness to carry out the actions required by the EU. This strong

---

[25] Along the same line of reasoning, the fight against organised crime and corruption is also an important element of ensuring optimal conditions for economic development, as it serves to ensure fair competition and to avoid money laundering in the legitimate economy, which may disrupt its sustainable development.

[26] Commission, 'Wider Europe – Neighbourhood: A new framework for relations with our Eastern and Southern Neighbours' (Communication), COM (2003) 104 final, 4.

[27] The SAP Communication provides that 'the perspective of contractual relations should be progressive in nature and should be seen as complementary to other stabilization efforts in the political, economic, diplomatic, humanitarian and even military fields' (Commission, 'Communication on the Stabilisation and Association Process for countries of South East Europe', COM (1999) 235 final, 3).

[28] The ENP Communication mentions that closer economic integration with the EU would come 'in return for concrete progress demonstrating shared values and effective implementation of political, economic and institutional reforms, including aligning legislation with the *acquis*' (Commission, 'Wider Europe – Neighbourhood' (n 26) 10).

conditionality leads to the Union having a close look at the internal affairs of its neighbours, which may explain why certain countries 'lose their faith' in cooperating with the Union, precisely because the demands made by the Union are considered to exceed what they would be ready to commit to.[29] As a reaction to such heterogeneity, the EU develops a tailor-made approach adapted to the situation of each country, conceptualised by the principle of differentiation. Such differentiation is given concrete form by drafting political instruments setting up objectives to be attained by each country, ie, the SAP's European partnerships and the ENP's actions plans, which are tailored to each country's political, economic and social situation and specific needs.[30] The importance of differentiation is particularly clear in the framework of the ENP, since the addition of new ENP beneficiaries and the development of an eastern and a southern partnership[31] may have eventually diluted the political value of the new Policy, and pushed certain neighbours such as Ukraine to require further differentiation.[32]

Third, the SAP and the ENP share the common characteristic of being 'cross-pillar policies'. The third countries concerned have not only to be ready to observe former Community rules, encompassing the Internal Market acquis and the acquis developed in sectoral policies, but they also have to accept measures dealing with common foreign and security policy, and with justice, freedom and security. Both frameworks are thus characterised as being comprehensive processes, establishing a system whereby the EU institutions follow and closely scrutinise the reforms carried out.[33] In that regard, attributing EU funding for capacity building is essential. Financial assistance to SAP and ENP countries started even before the two frameworks were set up, and specific instruments[34] aimed at streamlining and organising the funding directed to the EU's neighbours have been adopted. The funding instruments that have been adopted for the period from 2014 to 2020 are the Instrument for Pre-Accession Assistance (IPA) for Western Balkans

---

[29] Various elements may lead to the freezing of cooperation between the EU and a given country. It was for a certain period of time in the Western Balkans the unwillingness of certain countries to cooperate with the International Tribunal for the Former Yugoslavia and to extradite suspects to the Netherlands for their trial. It can also be the demands made to change the political regime of the country towards more democracy, which in certain countries such as Belarus, which has an authoritarian regime, may be considered impossible.

[30] Council, Conclusions and Annex, 'The Thessaloniki Agenda for the Western Balkans: moving towards European Integration', Council Doc No 10369/03, 14.

[31] Commission, 'Eastern Partnership' (Communication), COM (2008) 823 final, 15; and Commission and High Representative for Foreign Affairs and Security Policy, 'A Partnership for Democracy and Shared Prosperity with the Southern Mediterranean' (Communication), COM (2011) 200, 2.

[32] M Cremona and C Hillion, 'L'Union fait-elle la force? Potential and Limitations of the European Neighbourhood Policy as an Integrated EU Foreign and Security Policy' (2006) EUI Working Paper Law 2006/39, 16.

[33] For an extensive comparison of the two systems, stressing their similarities, see ibid 8–15.

[34] Council Regulation (EC) No 1085/2006 of 17 July 2006 establishing an Instrument for Pre-Accession Assistance (IPA) [2006] OJ L210/82. Regulation (EC) No 1638/2006 of the European Parliament and of the Council of 24 October 2006 laying down general provisions establishing a European Neighbourhood and Partnership Instrument [2006] OJ L310/1.

countries,[35] and the European Neighbourhood Instrument (ENI).[36] Under these funding instruments, programmes, named either Country Strategy Papers (IPA) or Bilateral Programmes for Neighbourhood Countries (ENI), fix more concrete and precise actions to be undertaken by the EU and the countries concerned for the period from 2014 to 2020.

Last but not least, both frameworks are characterised by their comprehensive approach of cooperation, as they both include a multilateral dimension, which favours regional integration/regional cooperation among the groups of States they bring together, ie, a multilateral track.[37] In the Western Balkans, the past atrocities explain the objectives to stabilise and transform the region, encompassing the objective of 'further reconciliation and the development of peaceful and good neighbourly relations among the countries concerned, and thus laying the ground for south-eastern Europe's political, economic and security integration in Europe'.[38] The intensified cross-border cooperation at the intra-Balkan level was destined to serve as a catalyst to the aspirations of the countries in the region to integrate themselves into broader structures.[39] For the ENP countries, the importance granted to regional cooperation increased over time. Whereas at the initial phase of the policy, regional cooperation was addressed in rather general and vague terms,[40] the 2011 Joint Communication of the Commission and the High Representative for Foreign Affairs and Security Policy adopt more ambitious language and objectives. It is clearly stated that 'the eastern and southern dimension of the ENP seek to complement that single policy by fostering regional cooperation and developing regional synergies and responses to the specific geographic, economic and social challenges of each region'.[41] Consequently, specific regional actions are supported by the EU, ranging from the establishment of a free trade area among the countries of one region to the promotion of cross-border cooperation in security issues. The development of such regional cooperation initiatives also involves current EU Member States, especially those sharing borders with those neighbouring countries.

The two frameworks demonstrate the clear intention of the EU institutions and the Member States to cooperate in a comprehensive and coherent way with

---

[35] Regulation (EU) No 231/2014 of the European Parliament and of the Council of 11 March 2014 establishing an instrument for Pre-Accession Assistance [2014] OJ L77/11.

[36] Regulation (EU) No 232/2014 of the European Parliament and of the Council of 11 March 2014 on Establishing a European Neighbourhood Instrument [2014] OJ L77/27.

[37] D Hanf and P Dengler, 'Accords d'association' (2004) College of Europe Research Papers in Law 1/2004, 14.

[38] ET Fakiolas and N Tzifakis, 'Transformation or Accession? Reflecting on the EU's Strategy Towards the Western Balkans' (2008) 13 *European Foreign Affairs Review* 377, 382.

[39] ibid.

[40] Cremona and Hillion (n 32) 24: 'the promotion of good neighbourly relations is one of the common values underpinning the proposed relationship and the peaceful settlement of disputes is said to be one of the "essential aspects of the EU's external action" on which commitments will be sought'. The authors regret that the ENP does not provide for any institutionalisation of the regional dimension.

[41] Commission and High Representative for Foreign Affairs and Security Policy, 'A new response to a changing Neighbourhood' (Communication), COM (2011) 303 final, 12.

neighbouring countries. Even though the concrete implementation of the two frameworks they designed can potentially lead to a patchwork, composed of different types of instruments and agreements pursuing general and/or specific objectives in a vast array of policy areas, clear objectives and uniform tools have been designed. Furthermore, the Commission received a clear mandate to monitor the efforts of the SAP and ENP countries, allowing the EU institutions and the Member States to have an overview of the actions undertaken in these regions.

On the basis of the criterion chosen, two regional frameworks may thus be considered as potentially relevant to analyse the modalities of the EU's efforts to externally promote its policy against trafficking in human beings. Nevertheless, a closer look might lead us to dismiss one of them.

B. The SAP with the Western Balkans as the Selected Case Study

The pursuit of our analysis of the EU's efforts to externally promote its counter-trafficking policy requires an additional element. Not only shall the EU seek to ensure the cooperation of the countries concerned in security and migration matters, but it shall also be able to do so in a coherent and comprehensive way. The latter requirement implies that there is a certain similarity in policy areas covered by the cooperation between the EU and the countries concerned and in the intensity of their relationship.

In this regard, whereas all the countries of the Western Balkans, with the exception of Kosovo, which is still subject to Common Foreign and Security Policy (CFSP) missions, have developed similar relations with the EU, the relations between the EU and the countries participating in the ENP are much more heterogeneous, which does not allow us to select this framework for two main reasons. First, the heterogeneity in their relations with the EU can be seen in the content of the association agreements that some ENP countries have signed with the EU. Some of these agreements were signed when the EU's actions and competences in JHA were limited and very few provisions deal with security issues.[42] Those signed in 2014 with Eastern partners, namely Georgia, Moldova and Ukraine, contain more detailed and precise provisions relating to justice and home affairs issues[43] and some even refer directly to trafficking in human beings.[44] These provisions

---

[42] See in this regard the so-called 'Euro–Mediterranean agreements' signed within the framework of the Barcelona process launched in 1995. Very few provisions deal with security issues, and this one concerns money laundering and drug trafficking (Arts 61 and 62, Association Agreements with Tunisia and with Morocco) and only provisions providing for dialogue on social matters may be relevant for the fight against labour exploitation (Art 69, Association Agreements with Tunisia and with Morocco).

[43] Provisions on the fight against organised crime and corruption, money laundering and terrorism financing and legal cooperation.

[44] Art 15, Association Agreement with Georgia; Art 14, Association Agreement with Moldova; and Art 16, Association Agreement with Ukraine.

reflect a clear evolution, such as the conclusion of Mobility Partnerships,[45] with ENP countries concerned by the management of migration flows towards the EU. Some countries, namely Georgia, Moldova, Ukraine,[46] Jordan, Morocco and Tunisia, have committed themselves to taking 'specific measures and initiatives seriously to combat migrant smuggling and human trafficking, in line with the Council of Europe Convention … and the relevant protocols of the United Nations' Convention on transnational organised crime'.[47] Second, the limited influence of the EU's efforts has been acknowledged. Whereas the offer of a closer relationship with the EU that is conditional upon reforms in terms of governance has encouraged change in some countries, current practice and policy has not proven to be a sufficiently strong incentive to create a commitment to reform where there is insufficient political will.[48]

As a consequence, the SAP appears to be the most appropriate regional framework for our analysis of the EU's efforts to externally promote its policy against trafficking in human beings.

The chronological development of this framework, which we will present in more detail below, allows for cooperation between the EU and the countries concerned in a big array of policy areas, allowing for the promotion of all aspects of the EU's multidisciplinary, integrated and holistic approach. Furthermore, the EU institutions have reiterated the EU's 'unequivocal commitment to the European perspective of the Western Balkans', and the prospect of accession to the EU thus constitutes an incentive for the countries concerned to transpose and implement the Union's acquis in the field of trafficking in human beings. It also offers the EU a tool with which to monitor their efforts.

Blighted by political and inter-ethnic conflicts resulting from the dissolution of Yugoslavia and the crisis in Kosovo in 1999, the region of the Western Balkans represented a challenge for the foreign policy of the EU and of its international partners. The characteristics of the Union's external actions were defined at that time. In the Stability Pact for South East Europe, which was proclaimed by the international community and whose aim was to promote stability and growth in the region, the Union was given a leading role in the attainment of these objectives.

---

[45] These partnerships are not however reserved to third countries participating in the European Neighbourhood Policy. Participating countries are selected according to strict criteria: 'The eligibility criteria applied were the geographical balance between Eastern Europe and Africa, the importance of migration flows from or through the country to the EU, the readiness to cooperate on readmission and fight against illegal migration, the interest of EU Member States to cooperate with the country in question and its interest to enter such a partnership' – Commission, 'Mobility partnership as a tool of the Global Approach to Migration', SEC (2009) 1240 final, 3.

[46] Ukraine is a particular case, not only because of its current political situation, but also because it refused to negotiate a mobility partnership with the EU. The country has however concluded a detailed Association Agreement with the EU.

[47] Commission, 'Communication on circular migration and mobility partnership between the European Union and third countries', COM (2007) 248 final, 4.

[48] Commission and HRFASP, 'Review of the European Neighbourhood Policy' (Joint Communication), JOIN (2015) 50 final, 2 and 5.

The EU institutions and Member States made a commitment to bring the region closer to the prospect of full integration, especially through 'a new kind of contractual relationship taking fully account of the individual situations of each country with the perspective of membership, once the Copenhagen criteria are met'.[49] In practice, the Union developed a comprehensive approach to invest in post-conflict stabilisation, peace and security:[50] on the one hand, Common Security and Defence Policy missions and operations were launched to ensure peace in the short term and to avoid the resurgence of conflicts. On the other hand, the EU institutions presented and adopted a new framework for cooperation with the countries of the region (the SAP) in order to promote stability and security in the long term.[51] The EU thus sees the SAP 'as its central policy framework for the Western Balkans countries, all the way to their eventual accession'[52] and as a complement to the Stability Pact.

The Thessaloniki Summit of 2003 represents a pivotal moment in the EU's approach towards the region as the latter 'shifted from post-conflict stabilisation and reconstruction (security) to democratic consolidation and European integration (enlargement)',[53] meaning that the EU policy in the region partially departed from the framework of the CFSP and joined the general framework of the pre-accession policy.[54] The tools at the disposal of the EU institutions changed, as they built upon the tools developed in the preparation of previous enlargements, such as parliamentary cooperation or institution-building mechanisms like TAIEX. Inspired by the Accession Partnerships adopted for Central and Eastern European candidate countries, the EU institutions adopted European Partnerships,[55] which identify short and medium-term priorities which the countries need to address,[56] and serve as a checklist against which the countries' progress is

---

[49] Stability Pact for South East Europe, Cologne, 10 June 1999, paras 18–20.

[50] E Prifti, 'Introduction: from stabilisation to integration' in E Prifti (ed), *The European future of the Western Balkans: Thessaloniki @ 10 (2003–2013)* (EU Institute for Security Studies, 2013) 14.

[51] Commission, 'Communication on the Stabilisation and Association Process for countries of South East Europe' (n 27). Process later endorsed by the European Council (Council, Cologne, 3 and 4 June 1999, Conclusions, paras 72–77) and the Council of the EU (Council of the EU, 21 and 22 June 1999, Conclusions on the development of a comprehensive policy based on the Commission's Communication on the 'SAP for countries of SEE').

[52] Fakiolas and Tzifakis (n 38) 384.

[53] Prifti (n 50) 15.

[54] This policy aims at preparing the accession of future EU Member States. Countries of the Western Balkans are the largest group. This policy is of a very particular nature, as the accession to the EU is first and foremost an area of competence of the Member States, the latter having agreed for the EU institutions to be more involved but keeping the final word. For more details on the renationalisation of the accession procedure, see C Hillion, 'EU Enlargement' in P Craig and G de Burca (eds), *The Evolution of EU Law* (Oxford, Oxford University Press, 2011).

[55] Council, 'The Thessaloniki Agenda' (n 30) 11–19.

[56] Legal basis: Council Regulation (EC) No 533/2004 of 22 March 2004 on the establishment of European partnerships in the framework of the stabilisation and association process [2004] OJ L86/1, later amended by Council Regulation (EC) No 269/2006 of 14 February 2006 amending Regulation (EC) No 533/2004 on the establishment of European partnerships in the framework of the stabilisation and association process [2006] OJ L47/7.

monitored and judged. The institutions also drew up a specific type of association agreement:[57] the Stabilisation and Association Agreements (SSAs), whose particularity lies in the emphasis placed on the countries' status as potential candidates for EU membership.[58] These agreements are accompanied by other means such as EU financial assistance provided through successive programmes,[59] trade concessions (Autonomous Trade Measures) and cooperation in JHA issues (visa liberalisation agreements).

A few years later, following the Union's expansion to the East and against the backdrop of the rejection of the Constitutional Treaty, the EU and its Member States adjusted their approach towards enlargement and thus towards the accession of the Western Balkans countries. In its Enlargement Strategy of 2006,[60] the Commission envisaged that 'rigorous but fair conditionality' is applied to all candidate and potential candidate countries.[61] The acquis to be transposed during the accession negotiations phase is divided into chapters, for which 'the Council defines benchmarks on the basis of a Commission recommendation, which the candidate country has to meet for the EU to open and/or close a particular negotiating chapter'.[62] The enhanced conditionality of the EU approach is particularly noticeable in the Chapters relating to security matters, ie, Chapter 23 on Judiciary and Fundamental Rights and Chapter 24 on Justice, Freedom and Security. Considered as belonging to the most difficult areas of reforms and to the toughest negotiation chapters, the EU favours opening them early on in the accession process and closing them at the end in order to give maximum time to the countries to establish the necessary legislation, institutions and solid track record of implementation.[63]

However, the adoption and implementation of a coherent framework, defining common patterns for cooperation with all the countries of the region, does not mean that the EU gives up judging each country according to the principle of

[57] The expression is in fact an umbrella expression encompassing a heterogeneous *ensemble* of external agreements concluded with third countries. Their legal basis can be found in the Treaties, at the current Art 217 TFEU (former Art 310 TEC), which does not define precisely the substance of the agreements. P Eeckhout, *EU External Relations Law*, 2nd edn (Oxford, Oxford University Press, 2012) 123.

[58] See for instance, SAA with Albania [2009] OJ L107/166/168; SAA with FYROM [2004] OJ L84/14.

[59] Since the mid-1990s, the Community provided its assistance through the OBNOVA (Council Regulation (EC) No 1628/96) and the Phare (Council Regulation (EEC) No 3906/89) programmes. The CARDS Regulation (Council Regulation (EC) No 2666/2000) was introduced in 2000 and established a single framework for assistance. The Instrument for Pre-Accession then replaced it in 2007 (Council Regulation (EC) No 1085/2006), now organised by Regulation (EU) No 231/2014 of the European Parliament and of the Council of 11 March 2014 establishing an instrument for Pre-Accession Assistance ([2014] OJ L77/11).

[60] Commission, 'Enlargement Strategy and Main Challenges 2006–2007' (Communication), COM (2006) 649. The Strategy was later endorsed by the European Council (Brussels, European Council of 14 and 15 December 2006, 'Presidency Conclusions' Council Doc No 16879/1/06, 12 February 2007).

[61] Commission, 'Enlargement Strategy and Main Challenges 2006–2007' (n 60) 6.

[62] Hillion, 'EU Enlargement' (n 54) 201.

[63] L Topic, 'Regional cooperation' in E Prifti (ed), *The European Future of the Western Balkans: Thessaloniki @ 10 (2003–2013)* (EU Institute for Security Studies, 2013) 70.

'own merits'. Nor does it mean that the EU gives up linking the pace of progress in the accession process with the political will and the performance of each country in meeting the EU's conditions for accession.[64] This is why the Western Balkans countries have reached different stages in the accession process: Croatia became the twenty-eighth Member State of the EU in July 2013,[65] four countries have obtained the status of candidate countries[66] and two countries remain potential candidate countries.[67] The negotiations for the accession of candidate and potential candidate countries are still ongoing, and yet have recently gained new impetus. In 2014, Jean-Claude Juncker, then President of the European Commission, stated in his Political Guidelines that 'the Western Balkans will need to keep a European perspective but no further enlargement will take place over the next five years'.[68] Yet, in 2018, the Commission announced its readiness to prepare recommendations to open negotiations with Albania and the Republic of North Macedonia, while stressing the possibility for Montenegro and Serbia to be ready for membership in a 2025 perspective with real and sustained efforts.[69] After a veto by some Member States at the October 2019 European Council,[70] and the publication of a Communication reforming the accession process,[71] the Council[72] and the European Council[73] in March 2020 approved the decision to open negotiations with Albania and the Republic of North Macedonia.

Although cooperation in security and migration issues had been initiated from the early stages of the SAP, recent events, and in particular the refugee crisis and the use of the Balkan route by large numbers of refugees, have demonstrated and underlined the importance of cooperation in these matters. As pointed out by the Commission in its 2018 Communication, organised crime's foothold on the Western Balkans remains strong, notably in terms of trafficking in

---

[64] Prifti (n 50) 15.

[65] On the accession of Croatia, all relevant documents are published in [2012] OJ L112/3. (Commission's Opinion, European Parliament's legislative resolution, and Decision of the Council of the EU.) The Treaty of Accession signed between the Member States and the Republic of Croatia was signed on 9 December 2011.

[66] FYROM (Council, Presidency Conclusions of 14–15 December 2006, Council Doc No 16879/1/06, 8); Montenegro (Council, Conclusions of 16–17 December 2010, EUCO 30/1/10, 4); Serbia (Council, Conclusions of 1–2 March 2012, EUCO 4/3/12, 15); and Albania (Council, Conclusions of 26–27 June 2014, EUCO 79/14, 13).

[67] Bosnia–Herzegovina and Kosovo.

[68] Jean-Claude Juncker, 'A New Start for Europe, Political Guidelines for the next European Commission', Opening statement in the European Parliament Plenary Session, 15 July 2014, 12.

[69] Commission, 'A credible enlargement perspective for and enhanced EU engagement with the Western Balkans' (Communication), COM (2018) 65 final, 2.

[70] N Fallon, 'New Moves: Opening up EU Prospects for North Macedonia and Albania' (April 2020) IIEA Briefing Paper, available at: www.iiea.com/eu-affairs/new-moves-opening-up-eu-prospects-for-north-macedonia-and-albania/.

[71] Commission, 'Enhancing the accession process – A credible EU perspective for the Western Balkans' (Communication), COM (2020) 57 final.

[72] Council, 'Conclusions on Enlargement and Stabilisation and Association Process', 25 March 2020, Council Doc No 7002/20.

[73] Council, 'Joint statement of the members of the European Council, 26 March 2020', available at: www.consilium.europa.eu/media/43076/26-vc-euco-statement-en.pdf.

human beings.[74] As an additional sign of the political attention given to these issues, the Western Balkans partners stressed in the Zagreb Declaration that in cooperation with the EU and with each other, they will continue to take resolute actions against human trafficking.[75]

While the political objectives and shared ambitions strongly support a close cooperation between the EU, its Member States and the Western Balkans countries in addressing trafficking in human beings, it is necessary to analyse how such cooperation is promoted, supported and strengthened. Our analysis will distinguish between the promotion of the EU's policy against trafficking in human beings through the adoption of soft law instruments (II), the conclusion of various types of agreement (III), and the support of regional cooperation (IV).

II. Promotion of the Fight against Trafficking Via Soft Law

Although the SAP was designed as a comprehensive framework for cooperation, a major feature of it continues to be its emphasis on security considerations. These considerations may concern, in some rare cases, security as envisaged in the framework of the CFSP, ie, the preservation of peace through peace-building military operations and missions, such as the CFSP EU-Lex mission in Kosovo.[76] However, more often they concern soft security threats, ie, criminal activities such as trafficking in drugs, weapons and human beings, or smuggling of migrants. Cooperation with these countries is perceived as essential in order 'to avoid that the existence of borders in relation to policing and judicial activities while border checks are being loosened may advantage criminal and terrorist organisations to flee justice'.[77]

Policy documents concerning countries participating in the SAP insist on the importance of AFSJ issues in their cooperation with the Union and in particular the importance of their cooperation in the fight against trafficking in human beings. Considering the large number of documents and their broad scope, our focus will be on the measures and discussions directly referring to trafficking in human beings. Other elements are also important and relevant, such as the adoption of adequate labour standards, the training of police officers, prosecutors and judges etc, but they will not be analysed here.

The emphasis on trafficking in human beings in the cooperation with Western Balkans countries is related to a specific context regarding the history of this

---

[74] Commission, 'A credible enlargement perspective' (n 69) 4.

[75] Zagreb Declaration, 6 May 2020, available at: www.consilium.europa.eu/media/43776/zagreb-declaration-en-06052020.pdf.

[76] See ch 4, II 'Militarisation of the Response to Trafficking in Human Beings'.

[77] C Matera, 'The External Dimension of EU Counter-Terrorism Policy: An Overview of Existing Agreements and Initiatives' in E Herlin-Karnell and C Matera (eds), 'External Dimension of the EU Counter-Terrorism Policy' (2014) CLEER Working Paper 2014/2, 22.

crime in the region. It functioned primarily as a transit zone for sexual trafficking flows in the early 1990s, but the Yugoslav wars brought them a source of domestic demand for sexual services – the international peacekeepers. The wars not only favoured the involvement of locals as perpetrators, but they also increased the vulnerability of local women, who often became victims of trafficking.[78] Despite the actions carried out since then, trafficking in human beings remains a problematic issue for the countries of the region.[79] Even though the number of victims detected has decreased since 2012, victims from south-eastern Europe have been recorded in large numbers in almost every Western European country.[80] Considering the importance of combating human trafficking in that region, the EU integrated it in its external policy in that region. As a consequence, references to human trafficking can be found in numerous policy documents, addressed to all the countries of the region or to a specific country.

Many policy documents have been adopted to discuss recommendations made to the region as a whole, but the initial documents did not refer directly to trafficking in human beings. Although the text is very much concerned with CFSP considerations in ensuring peace and stability within the region, the signatories of the Stability Pact for South East Europe[81] pledge themselves to 'cooperate towards … combating organised crime, corruption and terrorism and all criminal and illegal activities'.[82] Similarly, when initiating the SAP for countries of south-eastern Europe, the Commission proposed consideration of 'initiatives in the field of justice and home affairs, (including) assistance for capacity-building in increasing the efficiency of … the fight against organised crime'.[83]

In subsequent years, the development of a policy focusing only on trafficking in human beings became apparent. In September 2002, the Brussels Declaration on preventing and combating trafficking in human beings[84] identified the phenomenon 'as a criminal activity increasingly penetrated by trans-national organised crime that generates substantial illicit proceeds, often laundered and fed into licit markets, with too low a risk of prosecution and confiscation'.[85] The signatories, including EU institutions and Member States, as well as countries participating in the SAP, were called to work 'towards a comprehensive, multidisciplinary and effective coordinated policy that involves factors from all fields concerned'.[86] In its

---

[78] UNODC, *Crime and its Impact on the Balkans and affected countries* (2008) 74.

[79] UNODC, *Global report on Trafficking in Persons* (2018) 56–60.

[80] ibid 53. Caveat: the evaluation made in this report includes data from the region of Western Balkans broadly defined, as it includes not only the countries participating in the SAP but also Bulgaria, Romania, Poland and Latvia.

[81] Stability Pact for South East Europe (n 49) paras 18–20.

[82] ibid para 10.

[83] Commission, 'Communication on the Stabilisation and Association Process for countries of South East Europe' (n 27) 5.

[84] European Union, 'Brussels Declaration on Preventing and Combating Trafficking in Human Beings', 29 November 2002, Council Doc No 14981/02.

[85] ibid 3.

[86] ibid 4.

Annex, the Declaration further details the recommendations, standards and best practices, starting with mechanisms for cooperation and coordination, followed by the prevention of trafficking and victim protection and assistance and addressing police and judicial cooperation at the very end. The ratification and the implementation of the UN Convention against Transnational Organised Crime and its supplementing Protocol against Trafficking in Persons are considered as 'an immediate priority for the achievement of a converged legislative platform and a basis for intensified cooperation'.[87] The other actions envisaged are quite far-reaching considering the large number of countries participating in this declaration and include in particular the establishment of specialised joint investigative teams of investigators and prosecutors and the use of proactive and intelligence-led investigative techniques.

However, these counter-trafficking guidelines were increasingly developed in instruments addressing trafficking in human beings alongside other criminal activities, demonstrating the initial focus of the EU institutions in favour of a criminal justice approach to the issue. First, in 2003, the Thessaloniki Agenda[88] focused on cooperation in fighting organised crime as the latter 'must constitute a key priority (and) particular focus should be placed upon fighting all forms of trafficking, particularly of human beings, drugs and arms, as well as smuggling of goods'.[89] Nevertheless, a specific paragraph is devoted to trafficking in human beings, in which the EU 'urges the countries of the region to act both domestically and regionally in line with the principles of the EU and proposals contained in the Brussels Declaration of September 2002'. The text goes even further as it explicitly lists the areas considered of high priority by the EU, ie, the areas of victim assistance, training programmes of competent bodies, intelligence and exchange of information, public awareness and strategy development. The wording used is certainly strong ('urges') and it must be stressed that trafficking in human beings is the only serious and organised criminal activity subject to such detailed recommendations, which signals the importance that the EU gives to combating this particular phenomenon. Second, the Action-Oriented Paper on Improving Cooperation on Organised Crime, Corruption, Illegal Immigration and Counter-terrorism between the EU, Western Balkans and relevant ENP countries, adopted by the Council in 2006,[90] stressed once again the strategic importance of the fight against organised crime and other related phenomena in the region since developments in this area 'have an immediate and mutual impact on the security situation within the EU and vice versa'.[91] The Balkans were

---

[87] ibid 18, point 16.
[88] Council, 'The Thessaloniki Agenda' (n 30) 11–19, later endorsed by the European Council (Presidency Conclusions – Thessaloniki', 19 and 20 June 2003, Council Doc No 11638/03, 13).
[89] Council, 'The Thessaloniki Agenda' (n 30) 15.
[90] Council, 'Action-Oriented Paper on Improving Cooperation on Organised Crime, Corruption, Illegal Immigration and Counter-terrorism between the EU, Western Balkans and relevant ENP countries', 12 May 2006, Council Doc No 9272/06, 34 pages.
[91] ibid 2.

known to be a transit and source region for human trafficking into the EU and organised crime groups from the region are involved in trafficking in human beings in close cooperation with other international organised crime groups.[92] The Council addressed numerous recommendations to the Western Balkans countries, on general issues[93] as well as on actions directly targeting human trafficking.[94]

The trend of addressing trafficking in human beings from a security perspective is still noticeable, as it remains mentioned as one of the priorities for the cooperation with the Western Balkans. However, potentially as a consequence of the evolution of the migratory routes after 2015, and the importance taken by the Western Balkans route,[95] more recent policy documents refer more and more to smuggling of migrants alone, or together with trafficking in human beings, and to border management. As a first example, the 2018 Communication on a credible European perspective for the Western Balkans refers briefly to human trafficking to stress the strong foothold of organised crime in the region, but the text does not then include specific or tailored-made measures to prevent and combat human trafficking.[96] Similarly, the Sofia Declaration stresses the common security challenges shared by the EU and the Western Balkans, requiring individual and collective action,[97] and the EU welcomed their commitment to take resolute action, in cooperation with the EU and with each other against human trafficking and smuggling of migrants.[98] The Priority Agenda attached to this Declaration further supports the significant enhancement of operational cooperation in the fight against international organised crime in priority areas such as smuggling of migrants and trafficking in human beings.[99]

These general policy documents are somewhat frustrating as they seem to repeat the same messages without deviating much from the same general wording. By way of example, the 2019 Communication on EU Enlargement Policy stressed how the refugee crisis and irregular migration have been key challenges for the EU and the Western Balkans, and how smuggling and trafficking of persons

---

[92] ibid 5.

[93] ibid 6–7. Recommendations on improving regional cooperation, or the exchange and sharing of criminal information and intelligence.

[94] ibid 8. Recommendations on increasing cooperation at operational level notably in the area of the trafficking in human beings, including the elaboration of threat assessments documents, the cooperation with EU Member States in the format of joint teams or through the exchange of specialist, or the development and implementation of effective national and regional protection programmes for witnesses and victims of human trafficking.

[95] Commission, 'EU Enlargement Strategy', COM (2015) 611 final, 3.

[96] Commission, 'A credible enlargement perspective' (n 69) 5.

[97] Sofia Declaration, 17 May 2018, available at: www.consilium.europa.eu/media/34776/sofia-declaration_en.pdf.

[98] ibid para 12.

[99] Annex to the Declaration, Sofia Priority Agenda, Reinforcing engagement on security and migration, 4. The priority actions identified echo those defined in the Action Plan in Support of the Transformation of the Western Balkans (Commission, 'A credible enlargement perspective' (n 69), COM (2018) 65 Annex, 1– 2).

remain of concern,[100] but did not necessarily provide for more precise objectives or measures. Such elements can nevertheless be found in country-specific policy recommendations and documents.

Initially, country-specific guidelines were developed in the European Partnerships, identifying short and medium-term priorities that the countries needed to address.[101] Four European Partnerships have been concluded with North Macedonia,[102] Bosnia–Herzegovina,[103] Albania,[104] Montenegro and Serbia.[105] When comparing these European Partnerships, a clear differentiation appears between the priorities on which each country has to focus. Whereas for some countries, like Albania, trafficking in human beings receives less attention than drug trafficking,[106] other countries agree to much more detailed priorities, such as the ratification of the Council of Europe Convention,[107] the implementation of the National Strategy for the prevention of trafficking[108] or the adoption of measures to protect victims.[109] These differences can be easily explained through the differences in the development of the national counter-trafficking policy and legislation. Albania may, for instance, receive less precise demands (probably) because its

[100] Commission, '2019 Communication on EU Enlargement Policy', COM (2019) 260, 7.

[101] Legal basis: Council Regulation (EC) No 533/2004 of 22 March 2004 on the establishment of European partnerships in the framework of the stabilisation and association process [2004] OJ L86/1, later amended by Council Regulation (EC) No 269/2006 of 14 February 2006 amending Regulation (EC) No 533/2004 on the establishment of European partnerships in the framework of the stabilisation and association process [2006] OJ L47/7.

[102] The Council had concluded a European Partnership in 2004 (Council Decision 2004/518/EC of 14 June 2004 [2004] OJ L222/20), amended in 2006 (Council Decision 2006/57/EC of 30 January 2006 [2006] OJ L35/57), but the Council since then has adopted an Accession Partnership with North Macedonia (Council Decision 2008/212/EC of 18 February 2008 on the principles, priorities and conditions contained in the Accession Partnership with FYROM [2008] OJ L80/32).

[103] The Council concluded a first European Partnership in 2006 (Council Decision 2006/55/EC of 30 January 2006 [2006] OJ L35/19), now replaced by a new one concluded in 2008 (Council Decision 2008/211/EC of 18 February 2008 [2008] OJ L80/18).

[104] The Council concluded a first European Partnership in 2004 (Council Decision 2004/519 of 14 June 2004, [2004] OJ L 223/20), amended in 2006 (Council Decision 2006/54/EC of 30 January 2006 [2006] OJ L35/1), now replaced by a new one concluded in 2008 (Council Decision 2008/210/EC of 18 February 2008 [2008] OJ L80/1).

[105] The two countries, constituting together a State union, were initially subject to the same European Partnership (Council Decision 2004/520/EC of 14 June 2004 [2004] OJ L227/21), amended in 2006 (Council Decision 2006/56/EC of 30 January 2006 [2006] OJ L35/32). With their transition into two independent nations in 2006, 'individual partnerships' have thus been concluded for Serbia on the one hand (Council Decision 2008/213/EC of 17 February 2008 [2008] OJ L80/46) and for Montenegro on the other (Council Decision 2007/49/EC of 22 January 2007 with Montenegro [2007] OJ L20/16).

[106] In the European Partnerships, there is always a specific section relating to drug trafficking, and trafficking in human beings is rarely mentioned (once with regard to migration in Albania's European Partnerships of 2006, 10). The medium priorities set in the most recent European Partnerships must however be noted: to strengthen domestic and international cooperation on preventing THB and the staffing of the police anti-trafficking unit (11).

[107] European Partnership with Bosnia–Herzegovina (2008) 27.

[108] European Partnership with Bosnia–Herzegovina (2006) 26; European Partnership with Serbia (2008) 56.

[109] European Partnership with Montenegro (2007) 10.

policy to prevent and fight trafficking in human beings was launched earlier than in other countries.

Country-specific recommendations and objectives are also formulated in the framework of the pre-accession policy and in the documents defining and monitoring the EU Enlargement Strategy, in which the Commission regularly addresses trafficking in human beings, notably to point out the progress made by the Western Balkans countries in meeting the defined priorities and to monitor the correct implementation of national laws and action plans. As a consequence, the recommendations formulated by the Commission are tailored-made to the policy and legal framework of each country, and the development of its counter-trafficking efforts. By way of example, in 2019, whereas Albania was invited to make determined efforts in the fight against drug trafficking and cultivation,[110] Serbia was yet to establish a convincing track-record of effective final convictions in organised crime cases, as the number of convictions, notably in the fight against trafficking in human beings remains low,[111] and Montenegro was called upon to address the shortcomings in the critical area of trafficking in human beings, one of the more complex types of organised crimes where local interests are at stake.[112] The progress realised by North Macedonia was stressed in meeting previous recommendations on improving the track record, stepping up law enforcement cooperation and substantially improving the operational capacity to fight trafficking in human beings.[113]

Further detailed recommendations are then made in yearly country reports, and they illustrate how closely the Commission monitors the efforts made by its partners in preventing and combating trafficking in human beings. Various elements of the national counter-trafficking response are analysed: the criminal law provisions; the number and severity of final convictions; the institutional framework with the existence of specialised law enforcement units and prosecutors; or the establishment of multidisciplinary task force etc.[114] Attention is also paid to victims of trafficking, and the Commission monitors for instance whether the non-prosecution clause benefits victims who committed offences in the course of or as a consequence of being trafficked,[115] or whether they receive adequate protection and assistance.[116] Interestingly, in these reports, trafficking in human beings is also addressed in connection with violence against women,[117] including when relevant, from a crime prevention perspective.[118]

---

[110] Commission, '2019 Communication on EU Enlargement Policy' (n 100) 15.
[111] ibid 32.
[112] ibid 13 and 29.
[113] ibid 34.
[114] See, eg, Commission, 'Montenegro 2019 Report', SWD (2019) 217 final, 36.
[115] Commission, 'North Macedonia 2019 Report', SWD (2019) 218 final, 34.
[116] Commission, 'Serbia 2019 Report', SWD (2019) 219 final, 35.
[117] ibid 30.
[118] Commission, 'Montenegro 2019 Report' (n 114) 29: 'Montenegro did not adopt measures to counter stereotypes and discriminatory practices, or the trafficking and exploitation of prostitution'.

The analysis of these policy documents reveals first that trafficking in human beings has been initially addressed as a criminal justice issue relating to the fight against organised crime. This focus remains present until today, as trafficking in human beings is mostly addressed under the section on the fight against organised crime. Yet in recent years, smuggling of migrants has being receiving increased attention, in connection with the evolution of migratory routes to Europe, and smuggling is now often addressed alongside trafficking in human beings. A second characteristic of these documents is the differentiation in the priorities identified. While since the early 2000s, trafficking in human beings is consistently addressed in both general and country-specific documents, the latter include variations in the degree of detail, the precision and the intensity of the measures recommended. Differentiation is particularly noticeable in country-specific documents, in which tailored-made recommendations are made to national governments and authorities. Interestingly, it is mostly in these documents that the measures recommended reflect to a certain extent the broader approach developed within the EU. Measures relating to the protection, assistance and support of victims are indeed encouraged and monitored, even though a strong emphasis remains on criminal justice objectives, such as the need to secure a convincing track-record of final convictions in trafficking cases. A third and final characteristic resides in the nature of these policy documents, which may suffer from an identical flaw: they are soft law instruments, not directly binding for the third countries they concern, and the existence of monitoring mechanisms may be a limited incentive for their effective implementation. They are nevertheless important for two reasons. They introduce a conditionality relating to the prevention and combat of trafficking in human beings in the discussions between the EU and the Western Balkans countries. They indeed form the basis for the Council's decisions, for instance on the opening of accession negotiations, or new negotiation chapters, deepening the relationship between the EU and these countries. They furthermore include a steering function, indicating the direction of future policy and the principles on which it is based,[119] and the objectives they define are often translated into practice through the conclusion of specific agreements.

III. Promotion of the Fight against Trafficking Via the Conclusion of Agreements

In addition to soft law guidelines developed and monitored by the EU institutions, the EU has at its disposal a range of instruments with a certain binding legal force. The external competences it has obtained, either through express treaty provisions or through implied powers, are in this regard crucial as they will enable

---

[119] J Larik and RA Wessel, 'Instruments of EU External Action' in RA Wessel and J Larik (eds), *EU External Relations Law: Text, Cases and Materials*, 2nd edn (Oxford, Hart Publishing, 2020) 107.

the Union, alone or together with the Member States, to conclude agreements containing measures relevant for the prevention and fight against trafficking in human beings. Furthermore, as a consequence of the nature and scope of the EU's external competences, the Member States still possess a capacity to act on their own externally. The following section will be devoted to the analysis of the provisions of legally binding instruments and agreements in order to analyse the elements of the counter-trafficking policy that the EU promotes externally. After analysing the association agreements establishing cooperation between the EU and each third country in a variety of fields (A), the agreements concluded by the EU agencies, which form an integral part of the EU's external policy, will be analysed (B). Finally, the external actions carried out by the Member States will be examined (C).

A. Association Agreements

The classical and traditional means through which the Union establishes cooperation mechanisms with third countries consists of the conclusion of association agreements, based on the current Article 217 TFEU. These agreements are defined in very broad terms and they thus refer virtually to any international agreement concluded by the Union.[120] These agreements also have the specificity of being concluded as mixed agreements. Although association agreements have continued to be a preferred instrument for preparing non-Member countries for accession, they are also used for privileged links with third countries across a broad spectrum of EU policies. It is no surprise therefore that the EU and the Member States concluded association agreements with the countries taking part in the SAP. The presence of counter-trafficking measures, as well as their content, will now be analysed.

Within the framework of the SAP, the EU decided in favour of reaching SAAs, which constitute a sui generis category of external agreements especially envisaged for cooperation between the EU and the Western Balkans countries. They are based on the general treaty provision on Association Agreements and possess most of the common characteristics of these agreements.[121] Almost all the countries of the Western Balkans have concluded SAAs with the EU and its Member States, albeit with different timelines. The entry into force of the first concluded agreements took place in 2004 for North Macedonia,[122] in 2009 for Albania,[123]

---

[120] Eeckhout (n 57) 123.

[121] Such as the creation of a Stabilisation and Association Council able to take binding decisions within the scope of the Agreement and to be used in disputes between parties, and of a Stabilisation and Association Committee and a Stabilisation and Association Parliamentary Committee, both providing a forum for discussions.

[122] [2004] OJ L84/3.

[123] [2009] OJ L107/166.

in 2010 for Montenegro[124] and in 2013 for Serbia.[125] The Agreement with Bosnia–Herzegovina was signed in 2008 and ratified by all EU Member States but its entry into force was postponed until June 2015, notably because Bosnia–Herzegovina failed to address the European Court of Human Rights ruling in the so-called *Sejdic-Finci* case.[126] Kosovo is subjected to a specific regime as the EU has established under the CFSP a mission for the rule of law in Kosovo (EULEX). The Stabilisation and Association Agreement with Kosovo, which entered into force in 2016,[127] stands out as it was concluded as an EU-only agreement to avoid problems during the ratification process, and with the explicit provision that it does not constitute recognition of Kosovo as an independent State.[128]

These SAAs contain very similar, if not identical, provisions relating to justice and home affairs, and approximation of laws shall focus at an early stage on the acquis in this field.[129] Specific measures referring to trafficking in human beings can be found in the Titles on Justice and Home Affairs. In addition to a general provision on reinforcement of institutions, in particular for law enforcement and the judiciary,[130] references to trafficking in human beings are present in two provisions. The first provision concerned dealing with the prevention and control of illegal immigration and readmission, which provide that the Stabilisation and Association Council (of each agreement) 'shall establish joint efforts that can be made to prevent and control illegal immigration, including trafficking and illegal migration'.[131] This provision reflects the reference made in the Lisbon Treaty to the prevention and fight against trafficking in human beings as one of the components of the EU's migration policy. It furthermore acknowledges the interdependence between the smuggling of human beings, which is an aspect of illegal immigration, and trafficking in human beings, as the two offences are often part of a larger set of criminal activities carried out by organised criminal networks. The latest SAA concluded with Kosovo includes a slightly different wording as it refers to joint efforts to prevent and control illegal immigration, including trafficking

---

[124] [2010] OJ L108/3.

[125] [2013] OJ L278/16.

[126] *Sejdic and Finci v Bosnia and Herzegovina*, App Nos 27996/06 and 34836/06 (ECtHR, 22 December 2009). The case concerns the right for national minorities to stand for election to the House of Peoples or for the presidency. Two citizens complained of their ineligibility on the grounds of their Roma and Jewish origin. The Court considered that their ineligibility lacked objective and reasonable justification and was therefore discriminatory, in breach of Art 14. The Council in its Conclusions of 21 March 2011 stresses that 'as a matter of priority the country needs. to bring the Constitution in compliance with the ECHR. A credible effort in this regard is key to fulfilling the country's obligations under the Interim/Stabilisation and Association Agreement'.

[127] [2016] OJ L71/3.

[128] For an analysis of the agreement, see P Van Elsuwege, 'Legal Creativity in EU External Relations: The Stabilisation and Association Agreement between the EU and Kosovo' (2017) 22 *European Foreign Affairs Review* 393.

[129] See, eg, Art 72(3) SAA Serbia.

[130] Art 74 SAA North Macedonia; Art 78 SAA Albania; Art 80 SAA Montenegro; Art 80 SAA Serbia; and Art 83 SAA Kosovo.

[131] Art 76, para 4 SAA North Macedonia; Art 81, para 5 SAA Albania; Art 83, para 4 SAA Montenegro; and Art 83, para 3 SAA Serbia. Although the numbering varies, the text of the provision is identical.

and smuggling in human beings, while ensuring respect for and protection of the fundamental rights of migrants.[132] This additional reference to fundamental rights is to be welcomed, even though its practical consequences may be limited. The second reference to trafficking in human beings can be found in the provisions relating to preventing and combating crime and other illegal activities. In this provision, the parties 'agree to cooperate on fighting and preventing criminal and illegal activities, organised or otherwise, such as trafficking in human beings or ... smuggling'.[133] The list of criminal activities includes other forms of serious crimes, such as drug trafficking, terrorism or illicit arms trafficking. In that regard, some differences can be identified among the SAAs in force. The list of criminal activities concerned by such cooperation is more developed for the most recent agreements as it includes corruption, identity theft, forging documents and cyber-crime. This can easily be explained because new criminal activities have emerged in the EU, in its Member States as well as in the Western Balkans countries and these justify an extension of the scope of the cooperation. Furthermore, it must be stressed that certain forms of crime are subject to specific provisions, reflecting the evolution of criminal threats,[134] but that none of these provisions relate to trafficking in human beings. The Agreement concluded with Kosovo stands out once more as the provision organising cooperation in combating organised crime does not refer to trafficking in human beings but only to forms of serious crime with a cross-border dimension.[135]

The content of the provisions relating to trafficking in human beings may at first glance appear limited and not very ambitious. With the exception of the general reference to respect for democratic principles and human rights as essential elements of these agreements,[136] and the provision on the rule of law,[137] human rights considerations are very much absent from the provisions framing the cooperation in criminal matters between the EU, its Member States and the Western Balkans countries. The rights of victims of crime and/or vulnerable persons are scarcely addressed, via references to access to justice,[138] social cooperation for the protection of minorities and vulnerable persons,[139] and the protection

---

[132] Art 87 SAA Kosovo.

[133] Art 78, para 1 SAA North Macedonia; Art 85 SAA Albania; Art 86 SAA Montenegro; Art 86 SAA Serbia; and Art 84 SAA BiH.

[134] Whereas the Agreement with North Macedonia signed in 2001 only contains one provision dealing exclusively with drug trafficking, the agreements concluded with Albania, Montenegro, Serbia and BiH contain additional provisions on counter-terrorism, and money laundering and terrorism financing.

[135] Art 91 SAA Kosovo.

[136] Art 2 SAA North Macedonia; Arts 2 and 5 SAA Serbia; Arts 2 and 5 SAA BiH; Art 2 SAA Albania; Arts 2 and 5 SAA Montenegro; and Arts 3 and 4 SAA Kosovo.

[137] Art 74 SAA North Macedonia; Art 80 SAA Serbia; Art 78 SAA Albania; Art 80 SAA Montenegro; Art 78 SAA BiH; and Art 83 SAA Kosovo.

[138] Art 78 SAA BiH.

[139] Art 46 SAA North Macedonia; Art 101 SAA Serbia; Art 99 SAA BiH; Art 99 SAA Albania (which does not refer to minorities or vulnerable persons); Art 101 SAA Montenegro; and Art 106 SAA Kosovo.

of workers.[140] Trafficking in human beings remains perceived and addressed from a criminal justice perspective. Yet the clauses on combating organised crime appear 'as programmatic and habilitating clauses, ie clauses that mark the first step towards the establishment of future means of cooperation,'[141] as they only create an obligation to establish cooperation without envisaging more concrete instruments and mechanisms.[142] Their vagueness can be compensated by different means, including but not limited to, the ratification of international conventions, adopted within the United Nations or the Council of Europe, and the adoption of the international standards contained therein.[143] These international conventions offer an additional basis for the EU's cooperation with the Western Balkans countries, and they are complemented by the cooperation developed by the EU agencies.

B. Agreements with EU JHA Agencies

The EU created a number of specialised agencies in order to support and enhance the development of the AFSJ, among which three that can play a crucial role in preventing and combating trafficking in human beings, namely those supporting police cooperation (Europol), judicial cooperation in criminal matters (Eurojust) and border management (Frontex). These specialised agencies have developed, within their respective mandates, key competences not only to support cross-border cooperation between EU Member States, but also to support cooperation between the EU and third countries in the fight against trafficking in human beings. While each agency has been developed in its own rhythm and is subject to reforms in its structure and competences on the basis of various factors, the entry into force of the Lisbon Treaty, as well as reflections among EU institutions, have pushed for a certain rationalisation of their activities, and in particular of their external activities. The 2012 Common Approach on decentralised agencies insists on the importance of streamlining their international relations, notably to ensure that the agencies operate within their mandate and the existing institutional framework,[144] and in the last five years the three agencies concerned have been the

---

[140] Treatment free of any discrimination as regards working conditions: Art 49(1)(a) SAA Montenegro; Art 46(1) SAA Albania; Art 49(1)(a) SAA Serbia; Art 44(1) SAA North Macedonia; and Art 47(1) SAA BiH.

[141] Matera, 'The External Dimension of EU Counter-Terrorism Policy' (n 77) 23.

[142] ibid. The author analyses clauses relating to the fight against terrorism, but his analysis can be extended to the provisions on police and judicial cooperation in criminal matters. His analysis goes further: 'the clauses are not executive and enforceable since these do not envisage concrete activities but only express the intention to cooperate in relation to specific dossiers'.

[143] V Mitsilegas, 'The European Union and the Implementation of International Norms in Criminal Matters' in M Cremona, J Monar and S Poli (eds), *The External Dimension of the European Union's Area of Freedom, Security and Justice* (Brussels, Peter Lang, 2011) 267. See ch 1, II.B.i 'Importance and Import of International Standards'.

[144] Commission, Council of the EU and European Parliament, 'Joint Statement and Common Approach on decentralised agencies', 19 July 2012, 8, para 25.

object of ambitious reforms, which have substantially modified their competences, including to develop their cooperation with international organisations and third countries.[145]

The latter takes notably the form of agreements concluded with the relevant EU agencies, by virtue of secondary legislation, under which these agencies can 'establish and maintain cooperative relations with third countries in so far as it is necessary for the performance of their tasks'.[146] The possibility for EU agencies to possess a treaty-making capacity was not provided for in the Treaties, and it remains so, even for those subject to explicit treaty provisions like Eurojust and Europol. The capacity to enter agreements is thus based on the Union's secondary law, which raised doubts and debates regarding the constitutionality of these agreements.[147] These agreements may concern any relevant third country considered as a strategic partner for the EU. Whereas the US or Canada are often preferred as parties, the EU agencies also negotiate and conclude cooperation agreements with countries participating in the SAP. These agreements are complemented by other techniques to foster cooperation, such as the appointment of liaison officers or liaison magistrates, as well as specific arrangements.

The next sections will be devoted to analysing the means at the disposal of the EU agencies, which are particularly relevant for the promotion of EU standards in fields related to the fight against organised crime and trafficking in human beings. Compliance with standards in data protection and/or independence of law enforcement and judicial authorities count among the elements relevant for the EU's agencies' decision to conclude cooperation agreements with third countries. Part of our analysis will include the importance of ensuring the protection of fundamental rights.

i. Cooperation with Europol

Europol is the agency in charge of supporting cross-border police cooperation. Its competences and tasks are defined in a recently adopted instrument, Regulation of 11 May 2016 on the European Union Agency for Law Enforcement Cooperation,[148]

---

[145] At the time of writing the relevant instruments are: Regulation (EU) No 2016/794 of the European Parliament and of the Council of 11 May 2016 on the European Union Agency for Law Enforcement Cooperation (Europol) and replacing and repealing Council Decisions 2009/371/JHA, 2009/934/JHA, 2009/935/JHA, 2009/936/JHA and 2009/968/JHA [2016] OJ L135/53; Regulation (EU) 2018/1727 of the European Parliament and of the Council of 14 November 2018 on the European Union Agency for Criminal Justice Cooperation (Eurojust) and replacing and repealing Council Decision 2002/187/JHA [2018] OJ L295/138; and Regulation (EU) 2019/1896 of the European Parliament and of the Council of 13 November 2019 on the European Border and Coast Guard and repealing Regulations (EU) No 1052/2013 and (EU) 2016/1624 [2019] OJ L295/1.

[146] Legal bases for such agreements can be found, for instance, in Art 23 Europol Regulation; in Art 47 Eurojust Regulation; and in Art 68 Frontex Regulation.

[147] Eeckhout (n 57) 163. See also M Chamon and V Demedts, 'Constitutional limits to the EU agencies' external relations' in M Chamon, HCH Hofmann and E Vos (eds), *The External Dimension of EU Agencies and Bodies: Law and Policy* (Cheltenham, Edward Elgar Publishing, 2019) 29.

[148] Regulation (EU) No 2016/794 (n 145) 53.

which repealed the previous instruments. Despite the recent reform of its legal framework, the European Commission has announced in its Work Programme for 2020 a legislative proposal to 'strengthen the Europol mandate in order to reinforce operational police cooperation'.[149]

Europol's external relations are politically very sensitive. The data stored in Europol's databases is itself very sensitive because of its subject matter, ie, information on presumed criminals that could lead to someone's criminal conviction and/or because of the way it has been obtained, ie, information obtained via phonetapping or supplied by informants. The rules on data protection applicable within the Union ensure that the exchange of information between Member States takes place in a secure environment. Similar guarantees have to be present to allow the transfer of data to third countries and international organisations. Furthermore, cooperation with third countries includes the receipt of data by Europol which has been obtained by competent national authorities and in this regard particular attention must be paid to the way information has been obtained as it may in certain countries have been obtained in violation of human rights. As a consequence, compliance with standards in data protection and/or relating to the independence of law enforcement and judicial authorities has always been high up the agenda in terms of the elements relevant for a decision to conclude cooperation agreements with third countries and organisations. Such requirements are the legal framework and the types of agreement.

a. Legal Framework

The possibility of Europol cooperating with third countries is foreseen in secondary legislation, which provides that Europol can establish and maintain cooperative relations with third countries in so far as it is necessary for the performance of its tasks.[150] These cooperative relations are formalised through the conclusion of cooperation agreements, whose legal framework has evolved significantly over time.

Initially Europol was set up on the basis of a convention, which had the form of a traditional international public law treaty, making it a fully-fledged international organisation with full legal personality.[151] Europol's capacity to enter into binding agreements was established in Article 42 of the Convention, which explicitly provided for Europol's right to 'establish and maintain relations with third States and third bodies'. Reference to rules dealing with the receipt of data[152] and

---

[149] Commission, 'Adjusted Commission Work Programme 2020' (Communication), COM (2020) 440 final, Annex 1, 4.

[150] Art 23 Europol Council Decision, now Art 23 Europol Regulation.

[151] D Heimans, 'The external relations of Europol – Political, Legal and Operational Considerations' in B Martenczuck and S van Thiel (eds), *Justice, Liberty and Security: New Challenges for EU External Relations* (Brussels, VUB Press, 2008) 369.

[152] Art 10, para 4 Europol Convention: 'Europol may request that third states, international organisations, and their subordinate bodies, or Interpol forward the relevant information to it by whatever

the transmission of data[153] were also present, illustrating the careful approach adopted by the Member States and the importance granted to compliance with data protection standards. The Council of the EU played a major role in defining the procedure and standards applicable in Europol's external relations since the institution was in charge of drawing up more detailed rules governing Europol's external relations. Three Acts have been adopted in this regard, establishing the procedure to be followed[154] and detailing the rules applicable for the receipt[155] and transmission of data.[156] Cooperation between Europol and third States and bodies was based on the conclusion of formal agreements, which were necessary not only for the secondment of liaison officers[157] but also for the receipt and the transmission of information. The procedure to be followed for the conclusion of such agreements was characterised by the predominant role granted to the Council of the EU, which was responsible for all major steps of the process: it determined the third States/bodies with which agreements are to be negotiated; it authorised the Director of Europol to enter into negotiations; and it had to unanimously approve the conclusion of the Agreement.[158]

In 2000, the Council adopted a Decision authorising the Director of Europol to enter into negotiations on agreements with third States and non-EU related bodies.[159] The Decision provided for provisions to be contained in the agreements to be negotiated. For the agreements containing provisions on the transmission of personal data, the Council needed to be satisfied with the absence of obstacles to such a transmission, ie, a satisfactory level of compliance with data protection rules, taking into account the law and administrative practice of relevant third States/bodies in the field of data protection.[160] More importantly, the Council established the first list of third States and bodies with which negotiations should start. The list contained no less than 23 States and

means may be appropriate. It may also under the same conditions and by the same means accept information provided by those various bodies on their own initiative'.

[153] Art 18 Europol Convention: 'Communication of data to third states and bodies is authorised if three conditions are met: where this is necessary in individual cases for the purposes of preventing or combating criminal offences, an adequate level of data protection is ensured in that State or that body, and this is permissible under the general rules contained in the implementing decisions'.

[154] Council Act of 3 November 1998 laying down rules governing Europol's external relations with third States and non-European-related bodies [1999] OJ C26/4.

[155] Council Act of 3 November 1998 laying down rules concerning the receipt of information by Europol from third countries, adopted on 3 November 1998 [1999] OJ C26/3.

[156] Council Act of 12 March 1999 laying down rules governing the transmission of personal data by Europol to third States and third bodies [1999] OJ C88/1.

[157] Art 3, Rules governing Europol's external relations.

[158] Art 2, Rules governing Europol's external relations; Art, 2 paras 2 and 4, Rules concerning the receipt of information; and Art 2 paras 2 and 4, Rules governing the transmission of personal data. The Council must also give its agreement for any exchange of classified information – Art 8, Rules governing Europol's external relations.

[159] Council Decision of 27 March 2000 authorising the Director of Europol to enter into negotiations on agreements with third States and non-EU related bodies [2000] OJ C106/1.

[160] ibid, Preamble, Recital 5, and Art 1, para 5. See also Council Declaration concerning the relations between Europol and third States and non-European-Union-related bodies [2000] OJ C106/3.

three organisations[161] but, in a declaration, the Council provides that priority shall be given to the accession candidates, the Schengen cooperation partners, Switzerland and Interpol.[162]

The adoption of the Europol Council Decision in 2009 slightly changed the legal framework of Europol's external relations.[163] Its Article 23 reiterated the capacity of Europol to establish and maintain cooperative relations with third countries and international organisations. In addition, Article 26, which dealt exclusively with the implementing rules governing Europol's relations, again foresaw a predominant role for the Council. The latter remained competent for adopting, after consulting the European Parliament, not only the list of third countries and organisations with which Europol concludes agreements,[164] but also for implementing rules governing Europol's relations with third parties.[165] Furthermore, the approval of the Council was necessary for the conclusion of the agreement.[166] The rules concerning the procedure for the conclusion of a cooperation agreement provided for new responsibilities for Europol's organs: the Management Board[167] becomes the body responsible for the decision to enter into negotiations with third parties and the opinion of the Joint Supervisory Body[168] has been required at each step of the procedure. Yet the mechanism lacked flexibility and the procedure to conclude an agreement was time consuming and thus not particularly suited to operational activities.[169] This mechanism has nevertheless been considered as a 'valid tool to control and programme the activities of the Agency in advance with external partners under the scrutiny of institutions and bodies that are politically accountable for their action'.[170]

---

[161] Art 2, Council Decision of 27 March 2000. The list has been subsequently amended to add new third States and bodies in 2001 ([2001] OJ C358/1); in 2002 ([2002] OJ C150/1); in 2004 ([2004] OJ L342/27); in 2005 ([2005] OJ L56/14); in 2006 ([2006] OJ C311/10); and in 2007 ([2007] OJ L51/18).

[162] Council Declaration concerning the priority to be given to third states and non-European-Union-related bodies [2000] OJ C106/4.

[163] Council Decision 2009/371/JHA of 6 April 2009 establishing the European Police Office (Europol) [2009] OJ L121/37.

[164] The list was first established by Council Decision 2009/935/JHA of 30 November 2009 [2009] OJ L325/12, amended, inter alia, by Council Implementing Decision 2014/269/EU of 6 May 2014 [2014] OJ L138/104.

[165] Council Decision 2009/934/JHA of 30 November 2009 adopting the implementing rules governing Europol's relations with partners, including the exchange of personal data and classified information [2009] OJ L325/6.

[166] Art 6, Rules governing Europol's relations with partners.

[167] Composed of representatives of the Member States and a representative from the Commission, the Management Board was given the task to adopt a strategy for Europol and to oversee the Director's performance (Art 37 Europol's Council Decision).

[168] The Joint Supervisory Body, an independent body, has been set up to review the activities of Europol, in order to ensure that the rights of the individual are not violated by the storage, processing and use of data held by Europol (Art 34 Europol's Council Decision).

[169] Intervention of B de Buck, during the ECLAN 10th Anniversary Conference, Brussels, 25–26 April 2016.

[170] C Matera, 'The Influence of International Organisations on the EU's Area of Freedom, Security and Justice: A First Inquiry' in RA Wessel and S Blockmans (eds), *Between Autonomy and Dependence: The EU Legal Order Under the Influence of International Organisations* (The Hague, TMC Asser Press, 2013) 289.

The newly adopted Regulation, based on Article 88 TFEU, introduces several changes in the approach towards Europol's external relations. First, its Article 23 still foresees that Europol may establish and maintain cooperative relations, ie, exchange information with the law enforcement authorities of third countries and international organisations, but such relations can also include private parties, which cannot however transfer personal data to Europol. Second, Article 25 of the Regulation foresees three situations in which Europol may transfer personal data to third countries and international organisations. Whereas two were already foreseen in the Council Decision, the Regulation now provides for the possibility to transfer personal data to third countries on the basis of Article 25 of Directive 85/36/EC,[171] on the basis of a decision of the Commission, ensuring that the third country or an international organisation ensures an adequate level of protection.[172] This possibility is particularly welcomed by practitioners as it allows for the exchange of data with a third country in the absence of an agreement and on a more flexible basis. The adequacy decision can indeed be adapted to the content, the nature or the purpose of the exchange of information. For instance, an adequacy decision could be obtained for an exchange of information in which the data is not stored afterwards in Europol's databases. A concern could be the variable application of the standards on data protection, but since the text will be aligned with the data protection package, minimum guarantees shall apply.[173] The Regulation also foresees the transfer of personal data in a fourth hypothesis: such transfer may intervene on a case-by-case basis in exceptional circumstances, such as the prevention of an immediate and serious threat to public security.[174] Third, the Regulation modifies the procedure for the conclusion of an agreement with a third country or an international organisation. The procedure is no longer to be defined in a separate Council Decision. On the contrary, the procedure set up in Article 218 TFEU will apply, which means that Europol's external agreements would fall within the general legal framework applicable to the conclusion of all the EU's international agreements.[175] For the Commission, 'the Lisbon Treaty has changed the way in which the European Union conducts its external relations and these changes also affect the agencies, (which) shall no longer be able to negotiate international agreements themselves'.[176] The Council retains an important role,

---

[171] Directive 94/46/EC of 24 October 1995 on the protection of individuals with regard to the processing of personal data and on the free movement of such data [1995] OJ L281/31. Text now replaced by Regulation (EU) 2016/679 of 27 April 2016 on the protection of natural persons with regard to the processing of personal data and on the free movement of such data, and repealing Directive 95/46/EC (General Data Protection Regulation) [2016] OJ L119/1. The possibility offered by this text has only been applied three times; intervention of B de Buck (n 169).

[172] Art 25, para 1(a) Europol Regulation.

[173] Intervention of B de Buck (n 169).

[174] Art 25, para 5 Europol Regulation.

[175] This abolition of *sui generis* procedures for the conclusion of external agreements also concerns Eurojust, as the proposal for a regulation on Eurojust, currently negotiated, also foresees that the conclusion of future agreements will be carried out pursuant Art 218 TFEU (see below).

[176] Commission, 'Proposal for a Regulation of the European Parliament and of the Council on the European Union Agency for Criminal Justice Cooperation (Eurojust)', COM (2013) 535 final, 6.

as the institution authorises the opening of negotiations, addresses directives to the negotiators and authorises the conclusion of the agreement. Similarly, in line with the intention of EU institutions to streamline the structure and the international relations of EU agencies, the Management Board retains a significant role.[177] It is competent to decide on the conclusion of working and administrative arrangements,[178] and it can also suggest to the Council that it draws the attention of the Commission to the need for an adequacy decision or for a recommendation for a decision authorising the opening of negotiations.[179] Nevertheless, the procedure of Article 218 brought an important change as it grants new powers to the European Parliament, which has to give its consent to the conclusion of Europol's agreements.[180] The attention granted to compliance with data protection standards, already enshrined in Europol's Regulation,[181] will be reinforced by the scrutiny of the European Parliament on the negotiation process, and its power to block the conclusion of the Agreement whenever it considers that the third question concerned does not respect data protection rules and/or human rights enough.[182] The agency remains competent to conclude working arrangements, but these instruments shall not form the basis for allowing the exchange of personal data and shall not bind the EU or its Member States.

After a few years of implementation, the current legal framework has been portrayed by the Commission as a potential problem, since 'the long and complex negotiations to reaching an international agreement have prevented Europol from engaging in operational cooperation with third countries in the last two years and half'.[183] This is reflected in the recent practice of the agency. Its latest cooperation agreements with Georgia and Brazil were concluded in April 2017, a few weeks before the entry into force of the Regulation and the switch in the regime applicable to its external relations. Since then, the Commission recommended to the Council the opening of negotiations with eight countries (Algeria, Egypt, Israel, Jordan, Lebanon, Morocco, Tunisia and Turkey), and while the Council authorised the negotiation mandates in June 2018, no agreement has been yet finalised.

---

[177] Common Approach on decentralised agencies, para 25.

[178] Art 11(1)(f) Europol Regulation.

[179] Art 11(2) Europol Regulation.

[180] Art 218, para 6(a)(v) TFEU. The consent of the European Parliament is required for agreements covering fields to which the ordinary legislative procedure applies, which is the case in the field of police cooperation. It can thus be deduced that the European Parliament's consent will be required for the conclusion of Europol's agreements.

[181] The Proposal states that transfer of personal data may be done 'adducing adequate safeguards with respect to the protection of privacy and fundamental rights and freedoms of individuals' (Art 31, para 1(b) Proposal for Europol's regulation).

[182] As an example of the European Parliament's new negotiating powers, see the example of the Passenger Name Record Agreement with the US, described in C Eckes, 'How the EP's Participation in International Relations Affects the Deep Tissue of the EU's Power Structures' (2014) Jean Monnet Working Paper 12/2014, 12–18.

[183] Commission, Inception Impact Assessment Europol Regulation, 14 May 2019, ref Ares(2020) 2555219, 2.

The European Parliament that gave its consent to the opening of the negotiations, made very clear that its consent to the conclusion of the agreement would be conditional, especially on a level of protection of individuals' rights essentially equivalent to the level of protection in EU law.[184] As a result, the agency instead established working arrangements with new partners,[185] including those with whom negotiations are ongoing. The policy options envisaged by the Commission to 'correct' this limit consist of adding the possibility in the absence of a cooperation agreement to transfer personal data in cases where the existence of appropriate safeguards is provided in the third country concerned, and in cases where the existence of such safeguards is assessed by Europol after having ascertained the specific circumstances that apply to the specific transfer.[186] However, these new possibilities raise concerns, especially in light of the fundamental rights violations in some of the countries concerned, and the lack of adequate data protection laws.[187]

The evolution of the legal framework of Europol's external relations can be summarised as a movement from a sui generis regime to its integration into the EU's general external relations regime. Such movement reinforces the scrutiny of EU institutions and provides additional guarantees concerning respect for data protection rules, although the applicable regime seems to be portrayed as an obstacle to operational cooperation, and it could be further improved. The importance of compliance with data protection rules is reflected by the elaboration by Europol of two types of agreement, allowing for a differentiated approach.

b. Types of Agreement

In practice, the agency has concluded two types of agreement: Strategic Cooperation Agreements on the one hand and Agreements on Strategic and Operational Cooperation on the other.[188]

The agency has concluded Strategic Cooperation Agreements with Bosnia–Herzegovina and Montenegro. These Strategic Cooperation Agreements contain very similar, if not identical, provisions. Their purpose is to enhance the cooperation of the parties in preventing, detecting, suppressing and investigating serious forms of international crime, notably in the area of trafficking in human beings.[189] In addition to the designation of a national contact point

---

[184] eg, European Parliament, Resolution of 4 July 2018, Opening of negotiations for an EU-Algeria Agreement on the exchange of personal data for fighting serious crime and terrorism, P8-TA(2018)0302 [2018] OJ C118/104, paras 3 and 4.

[185] See the working arrangements concluded with Israel on 17 July 2018, Japan on 3 December 2018 and New Zealand on 17 April 2019.

[186] Commission, Inception Impact Assessment Europol Regulation (n 183) 4.

[187] See 'Submission to the European Commission's consultation on revising Europol's mandate' (*Statewatch*, 8 July 2020) F53679, available at: ec.europa.eu/info/law/better-regulation/have-your-say/initiatives/12387-Police-cooperation-stronger-mandate-for-Europol/F536792, 5.

[188] The list and the texts of the different agreements are available on the Europol website: www.europol.europa.eu/content/page/external-cooperation-31.

[189] Arts 1 and 3 (read together) of both agreements.

in the country, the agreement covers different forms of cooperation. First, the exchange of strategic and technical information is regulated, ie, its use is limited for the investigation, prosecution and prevention of criminal offences and in proceedings relating to criminal matters.[190] However, the agreement does only authorise the exchange of information of a general nature (modus operandi, threat assessments etc), and does not authorise the transmission of data relating to an identified individual or identifiable individuals. Second, the agreements provide that cooperation shall take the form of written requests for assistance, for which the requested Party must ensure prompt and complete execution.[191] Finally, the agreements foresee an exchange of expertise as well as the possibility to appoint liaison officers.[192]

Europol has also concluded Agreements on Operational and Strategic Cooperation, signed with Albania, the Former Yugoslav Republic of Macedonia (FYROM) and Serbia. They represent a more advanced form of cooperation for several reasons. Whereas they pursue similar objectives and foresee methods of cooperation existing in less ambitious agreements, such as the appointment of national contact points, the deployment of liaison officers and the exchange of information, these agreements go further. They allow the transmission of personal data and classified information[193] and thus include much more detailed measures on data protection.[194] The agreements with Albania and Serbia, more recent than the Agreement with FYROM, even provide for the association of national experts to Analysis Groups, granting them the possibility to attend analysis group meetings, to be informed of the development of the Analysis Working Files concerned,[195] and to receive analysis results concerning them.[196] These two agreements also foresee mutual support between their national authorities and Europol in the facilitation of the establishment and operation of Joint Investigation Teams (JITs).[197] These more advanced agreements have the preference of third countries as they provide for a more extensive cooperation, ie, the exchange of personal data. Nevertheless, the authorisation for their conclusion depends on respect for the EU's standards in the field of data protection, which are higher than those developed within the Council of Europe. Consequently, it is not surprising that the signatories of these agreements are all countries participating in the SAP which, in

---

[190] Art 6, Agreement with Serbia; Art 6, para 3, Agreement with Montenegro.
[191] Arts 7 and 8 of both agreements.
[192] Arts 9 and 12, Agreement with Serbia; Arts 10 and 11, Agreement with Montenegro.
[193] Art 10, Agreements with Serbia and with Albania; and Art 7, Agreement with FYROM.
[194] Arts 11–16, Agreements with Serbia and with Albania; and Arts 8 and 9, Agreement with FYROM.
[195] AWFs are information-processing systems that simultaneously store, process and analyse factual information (hard data) and intelligence (soft data) on specific crime areas. For more details, see D Drewer and J Ellerman, 'Europol's data protection framework as an asset in the fight against cybercrime' (2012) 13 *ERA Forum* 381, 387–89, available at: link.springer.com/article/10.1007/s12027-012-0268-6.
[196] Art 17, Agreements with Serbia and with Albania.
[197] Art 18, Agreements with Serbia and with Albania.

the process of approximating their national legislations with the EU acquis, have already adopted and implemented to a certain extent the EU standards on data protection.[198]

In practice, cooperation with the Western Balkans countries is well developed. Mobile offices with Europol officials' support were deployed in most of the countries of the region,[199] and they are also involved in large operations, such as the Joint Action Day Western Balkans 2018, during which they collaborated with EU Member States and agencies to address a certain number of priorities, such as illegal immigration.[200] These third countries are also already integrated in some of the EU's initiatives to combat serious and organised crime, such as the EU policy cycle which aims at facilitating cooperation in operational activities on the ground.[201] Finally, Europol opened liaison bureaux in the Western Balkans, the first one being opened in Tirana, Albania in July 2019, and the two others in Bosnia–Herzegovina and Serbia. The ambition pursued by such initiative is to further enhance the exchange of information between Europol and competent national authorities, which are increasingly involved in operational cooperation in combating serious organised crime including trafficking in human beings.[202]

ii. Cooperation with Eurojust

Eurojust is the agency in charge of supporting judicial cooperation in criminal matters between two or more Member States. Its history is slightly different from the history of Europol, as it has been established later,[203] but it also aims at supporting the cooperation and coordination between national authorities. Its legal framework has been subject to a recent reform, which was motivated not only by the entry into force of the Lisbon Treaty, but also by the establishment of the European Public Prosecutor's Office, which partially explained the delay taken in the negotiations of its Regulation.[204] Its competences are today defined

---

[198] Interview No 1.

[199] Europol, *Europol in brief* (2018) 5.

[200] Europol, 'Operational centre at Europol: 30 countries team up to combat crime in the Western Balkans', Press release of 9 September 2019, available at: www.europol.europa.eu/newsroom/news/operational-centre-europol-30-countries-team-to-combat-crime-in-western-balkans.

[201] Council, 'Presidency Discussion Paper on Enhancing Cooperation with the Western Balkan Countries: Combating Migrants Smuggling' (Brussels, January 2020) (not publicly available).

[202] Europol, 'Tirana hosts Europol's first liaison office in the Western Balkans', Press release of 11 July 2019, available at: www.europol.europa.eu/newsroom/news/tirana-hosts-europol%E2%80%99s-first-liaison-office-in-western-balkans.

[203] Council Decision 2002/187/JHA of 28 February 2002 setting up Eurojust with a view of reinforcing the fight against serious crime [2002] OJ L63/1. Council Decision 2009/426/JHA of 16 December 2008 on the strengthening of Eurojust (and amending Decision 2002/187/JHA [2009] OJ L138/14.

[204] C Brière, 'Protecting the EU's financial interests together: cooperation between EU actors' in I Sammut and J Agranovska, *Implementing and Enforcing EU Criminal Law: Theory and Practice* (The Hague, Eleven International Publishing 2019).

in a Regulation, adopted in 2018,[205] which also provide for the possibility for the agency to establish and maintain cooperation with authorities of third countries and international organisations.[206]

Under the previous legal regime, Eurojust could conclude agreements with third countries, on the basis of Union's secondary law, concerning the exchange of information, including personal data, and the secondment of liaison officers or liaison magistrates to Eurojust.[207] The conclusion of these agreements was a requirement to allow the exchange of personal data, which could in their absence only take place between competent national authorities.[208] The third countries with which such an agreement may be concluded were identified by the College of Eurojust, in consultation with the European Commission. The Council of the EU was kept informed every six months about ongoing negotiations and any plans to enter into negotiations and it was able to draw any conclusions it deemed appropriate.[209]

The procedure for the conclusion of a cooperation agreement was divided into several steps.[210] The College of Eurojust discussed and approved a list of priorities for its external relations every year. On the basis of this list, the decision to open negotiations with a third country was approved by the College without a prior approval by the Council of the EU. In practice the agency informed the Presidency of the Council about its decision by letter, specifying its reasons for engaging such negotiations and the planned date of their initiation. A reasonable period of approximately two months was applied in order to allow the Council to communicate its conclusions. The negotiations officially opened the day that Eurojust formally sent the third country concerned its Model Agreement. An agreement containing provisions on the exchange of personal data could be concluded only once two conditions are satisfied. The first condition related to an adequate level of data protection. Eurojust's Joint Supervisory Body must had concluded favourably on the existence of an adequate level of data protection in the country concerned. Pursuant to Article 26a para 3 of the Eurojust Council Decision, this first condition was deemed to be respected after an assessment carried out by Eurojust confirmed the existence of an adequate level of data protection. No assessment took place if

---

[205] Regulation (EU) 2018/1727 of the European Parliament and of the Council of 14 November 2018 on the European Union Agency for Criminal Justice Cooperation (Eurojust) and replacing and repealing Council Decision 2002/187/JHA [2018] OJ L295/138.

[206] Art 52 Eurojust Regulation.

[207] Art 26(a), para 2 Eurojust Council Decision.

[208] L Surano, 'L'action extérieure d'Eurojust' in M Dony (ed), *La dimension externe de l'espace de liberté, de sécurité et de justice au lendemain de Lisbonne et de Stockholm: un bilan à mi-parcours* (Brussels, Editions de l'Université de Bruxelles, 2012) 213. See also M Coninsx, 'The fight against terrorism and the role of Eurojust: cooperation with third countries' in E Herlin-Karnell and C Matera (eds), 'External Dimension of the EU Counter-Terrorism Policy' (2014) CLEER Working Paper 2014/2, 61.

[209] Art 26(a), para 2 of the Eurojust Council Decision. Eurojust has also issued an opinion on the practical implementation of the provision (published as Council Doc No 12479/10).

[210] Surano (n 209) 214.

the third country concerned was subject to the Council of Europe Convention on Data Protection.[211] The second condition depended on the Council of the EU, which had, in a vote by qualified majority, to give its approval.

The regime and the procedure applicable changed with the entry into force of the Regulation in December 2019, and a clear will to standardise the procedure through EU agency to conclude cooperation agreements can be seen. The relevant provisions build upon the previous legal framework, as it is still possible for Eurojust to post liaison magistrates to third countries, whose tasks shall include

> any activity designed to encourage and accelerate all forms of judicial cooperation in criminal matters, in particular by establishing direct links with the competent authorities of the host State, and the exchange of operational personal data with the competent authorities of the State concerned.[212]

It is also still possible for the agency to coordinate, with the agreement of the Member States concerned, the execution of requests for judicial cooperation issued by a third country where these requests require execution in at least two Member States as part of the same investigation.[213] Regarding the transfer of operational personal data to third countries, it may take place in different situations, which are identical to those foreseen in the Europol Regulation.[214] Such transfer would take place on the basis of a decision of the Commission adopted in accordance with the Data Protection Police Directive,[215] on the basis of an international agreement concluded between the EU and that third country pursuant to Article 218 TFEU or on the basis of a cooperation agreement signed under the previous regime. As with Europol, the transfer of operational personal data can also occur on a case-by-case basis, notably when it is 'absolutely necessary to safeguard the essential interest of one or more Member States'.[216] The agency remains competent to conclude working arrangements, but like those concluded by Europol, these instruments shall not form the basis for allowing the exchange of personal data and shall not bind the EU or its Member States.[217]

As with Europol, the procedure under which Eurojust may conclude cooperation agreements changed in favour of the procedure applicable for the conclusion of agreements under Article 218 TFEU, ie, negotiations by the European Commission

---

[211] Convention for the Protection of Individuals with regard to Automatic Processing of Personal Data, 28 January 1982, CETS No 108.

[212] Art 53 Eurojust Regulation.

[213] Art 55 Eurojust Regulation.

[214] Art 56(2) Eurojust Regulation.

[215] Directive (EU) 2016/680 of the European Parliament and of the Council of 27 April 2016 on the protection of natural persons with regard to the processing of personal data by competent authorities for the purposes of the prevention, investigation, detection or prosecution of criminal offences or the execution of criminal penalties, and on the free movement of such data, and repealing Council Framework Decision 2008/977/JHA [2016] OJ L119/89.

[216] Art 59 Eurojust Regulation. See also Preamble, para 52: 'Those derogations should be interpreted restrictively and should not allow frequent, massive and structural transfers of personal data, or large-scale transfers of data, but should be limited to data strictly necessary'.

[217] Art 47(3) Eurojust Regulation.

and subsequent approval by the Council after consulting the European Parliament. This change must be welcomed. It will not only grant a stronger role to the Commission and the European Parliament,[218] but it will also facilitate negotiations with third countries. Taking an outsider's perspective, they will only deal with one negotiator, ie, the Commission, and at the same time may discuss the conclusion of cooperation agreements with both Europol and Eurojust.[219] Finally, the possibility of exchanging data on the basis of an adequacy decision will help the agency to respond to operational needs in a better way. Yet the agency's structure calls for certain specificities. The College of Eurojust retains a leading role in defining the posting of liaison magistrates who report to it,[220] and in defining the Strategy for cooperation with the authorities of third countries and international organisations.[221] The College, like the Management Board of Europol, is also competent to suggest that the Council draw the attention of the Commission to the need for an adequacy decision or for a recommendation for the opening of negotiations on an international agreement.[222]

In practice, Eurojust has concluded a number of cooperation agreements, in particular with Western Balkans countries. The first ones concluded were an Agreement on Cooperation with FYROM, signed in 2008 and which entered into force in 2010,[223] and with Montenegro signing in 2016.[224] These agreements pursue the objectives of developing close and dynamic cooperation to meet the present and future challenges posed by serious transnational crime. Their cooperation can take place in the fields of Eurojust's competence, including trafficking in human beings. The agreements foresee several forms of cooperation: first, the possibility to second a liaison prosecutor to Eurojust[225] and the appointment of at least one contact point,[226] who may attend operational and strategic meetings. Second, cooperation takes the form of the exchange of information through the liaison prosecutor/contact point or directly with the judicial authority in charge of the case. This exchange of information can concern personal data, justifying the insertion of strict data protection rules in the agreement.[227] Contacts designed to start negotiations for the conclusion of similar agreements have been made since 2010 with Serbia, Bosnia–Herzegovina and Albania.[228] The negotiations have resulted

---

[218] According to Art 218, para 6(a)(v) TFEU, the consent of the European Parliament will be necessary.
[219] Intervention of de Buck (n 169).
[220] Art 53(5) and (6) Eurojust Regulation.
[221] Art 15(4) Eurojust Regulation.
[222] Preamble, para 50 Eurojust Regulation.
[223] The list and the texts of the different agreements are available on the Eurojust website: www.eurojust.europa.eu/about/legal-framework/Pages/eurojust-legal-framework.aspx#partners.
[224] Eurojust, 'Eurojust and Montenegro sign cooperation agreement', Press release, 4 May 2016, www.eurojust.europa.eu/press/PressReleases/Pages/2016/2016-05-04.aspx.
[225] Art 5 Eurojust–FYROM Cooperation Agreement.
[226] Art 6 Eurojust–FYROM Cooperation Agreement.
[227] Arts 9–16 Eurojust–FYROM Cooperation Agreement.
[228] Council, 'Action-Oriented Paper on strengthening the EU external dimension on action against trafficking in human beings – First implementation report/update of information on Member States' external action', 31 May 2011, Council Doc No 9501/3/11, 119–20.

in the conclusion of cooperation agreements with Albania in 2018[229] and Serbia in 2019.[230] These two agreements were submitted for consultation to the European Parliament,[231] and they entered into force before 12 December 2019, date of the entry into force of the new Eurojust Regulation.[232] By virtue of these agreements, three out of the seven liaison prosecutors appointed to Eurojust represent Western Balkans countries, namely North Macedonia, Montenegro and Serbia.[233] However, even though reinforcing operational cooperation is announced among the multi-annual strategic objectives of the agency,[234] neither the College, nor the European Commission have initiated steps for the identification of new potential partners.

In the absence of a cooperation agreement, the agency can still cooperate with third countries and assist investigations and prosecutions. In this regard the appointment of Eurojust's contact points in third countries has proven to be very useful to identify the competent authority. In 2018, Eurojust was able to rely on a network of 47 contact points, among neighbouring but also more distant third countries, including for instance Nigeria or Mauritius.[235]

In practice, Eurojust's operational activities frequently involve third countries, especially neighbouring countries. Bosnia–Herzegovina and Serbia are among the countries most requested to take part in operational activities.[236] Since January 2015, 330 cases have been registered at Eurojust involving Albania, Bosnia–Herzegovina, North Macedonia, Montenegro and Serbia, including the participation in 14 JITs. Serbia, Montenegro and Bosnia–Herzegovina rank among the top 10 third States that actively cooperate with Eurojust on criminal cases, in the role of a requesting or requested State.[237] Regarding more precisely their cooperation in the investigation and prosecution of cases of human trafficking,

---

[229] Eurojust, 'Eurojust and Albania take major step to strengthen the fight against cross-border organised crime', Joint press release of 5 October 2018, available at: www.eurojust.europa.eu/press/PressReleases/Pages/2018/2018-10-05.aspx.

[230] Eurojust, 'Cooperation agreement signed to strengthen the fight against cross-border organised crime in the Western Balkans', Joint press release of 12 November 2019, available at: www.eurojust.europa.eu/press/PressReleases/Pages/2019/2019-11-12.aspx.

[231] European Parliament legislative resolution of 13 September 2018 on the draft Council implementing decision approving the conclusion by Eurojust of the Agreement on Cooperation between Eurojust and Albania [2019] OJ C433/306. European Parliament legislative resolution of 10 October 2019 on the draft Council implementing decision approving the conclusion by Eurojust of the Agreement on Cooperation between Eurojust and Serbia, P9_TA(2019)0023.

[232] Agreement with Serbia entered into force on 11 December 2019, and Agreement with Albania entered into force on 1 November 2019.

[233] Eurojust, 'Questions and Answers, Eurojust's cooperation with Serbia and the Western Balkans', 10 March 2020, available at: www.eurojust.europa.eu/press/Documents/QnA_cooperation-Western-Balkans_2020-03.pdf. The other Liaison Prosecutors are from the USA, Norway, Switzerland and Ukraine.

[234] Eurojust, 'Eurojust Multi Annual Strategy 2019–2021', 3, available at: www.eurojust.europa.eu/doclibrary/programming-and-reporting/mas/Multi-Annual%20Strategy%202019-2021/MAS_2019-2021_EN.pdf.

[235] Eurojust, *Annual Report 2018*, 4 and 30.

[236] Surano (n 209) 217.

[237] Eurojust, 'Questions and Answers' (n 234).

Eurojust conducted for several years a project designed, inter alia, to increase the involvement of third States in trafficking cases, and its final report pinpoints the limits and difficulties encountered in pursuing that target.[238] It nevertheless mentioned an important milestone: the setting up in 2015 of the first JIT with a third State, Bosnia–Herzegovina, in a trafficking case.[239] The case, known as the *Hamidovic* case, concerned a Bosnian criminal network whose members were trafficking underage Bosnian girls, who committed theft, mainly on the Parisian public transport system. The network made profits of more €2 million, and the proceeds were used to buy luxury vehicles and property in Bosnia–Herzegovina.[240] The JIT was created on the basis of Article 20 of the Second Additional Protocol of the European Convention on Mutual Assistance in Criminal Matters, ratified by both Bosnia–Herzegovina and France. The case has been presented as a success story, not only because it demonstrates the preparation and the capacity of the Bosnian authorities to cooperate efficiently with their counterparts,[241] but also because it addressed complex legal issues.[242] The conduct of a JIT in this particular case is part of a larger context under which the EU promotes, through projects, the development of JITs to fight trafficking in human beings in southeastern Europe.[243]

iii. Cooperation with Frontex

Frontex, the agency in charge of supporting border management, has received important media coverage and public attention for its external activities, in particular at sea, and it has also experienced in the last few years important reforms of its legal framework. The latest revision led to the adoption of Regulation 2019/1896,[244] just a few years after a first important reform of its legal framework which granted to a certain extent operational powers to the agency. Although the main mission of the agency lies in supporting the management of

---

[238] Eurojust, *Implementation of the Eurojust Action Plan against THB 2012–2016*, Final evaluation report, January 2017, 31–33.

[239] Eurojust, 'French Bosnian human traffickers arrested', Press release of 10 July 2015, available at: www.eurojust.europa.eu/press/PressReleases/Pages/2015/2015-07-10.aspx.

[240] ibid.

[241] ibid, quotation of Mr Cyril Lacombe, assistant to the National member for France.

[242] One of the suspects was an employee of the Bosnian embassy in Paris, and the investigation required the search of his office at the embassy. By virtue of rules of diplomatic immunity, French police forces were unable to enter the premises, and Bosnian police forces had to travel to Paris to perform this investigative act. Source: www.sipa.gov.ba/en/news/sipa-searching-premises-of-bamph-embassy-in-paris/13180.

[243] A first project was conducted from 2011–13 and aimed at the introduction of the requirements for establishing JIT (HOME/2010/ISEC/FP/C1/4000001423). A second project was then launched in 2013, entitled 'Use of Joint Investigation Teams (JIT) to fight Trafficking in Human Beings in the Western Balkans at the local level' (HOME/2012/ISEC/FP/C2/4000003974). Europol and Eurojust, together with the UNODC, are partners to these projects. For more details see: jit-thb.pccseesecretariat.si/.

[244] Regulation (EU) 2019/1896 of the European Parliament and of the Council of 13 November 2019 on the European Border and Coast Guard and repealing Regulations (EU) No 1052/2013 and (EU) 2016/1624 [2019] OJ L295/1.

the EU's external borders, it has several responsibilities with regard to the fight against trafficking in human beings. Under the previously applicable instrument, Regulation 2016/1624,[245] in force until 1 January 2021, the agency had already received, as part of European integrated border management including measures to prevent and detect serious cross-border crime, the following missions: (1) the preparation of risk analysis[246] and the provision of adequate information and intelligence on the issue, so as to allow for appropriate measures to be taken and to tackle identified threats and risks; and (2) the initiation of joint operations and rapid border interventions as part of a multipurpose operation which may involve the fight against trafficking in human beings.[247] The latter constitutes a first form of external activities, as it may coordinate activities for one or more Member State and third countries at the external border, including joint operations with neighbouring third countries, and the deployment of teams to third countries.[248] To that regard the Commission drew up a draft Model Agreement in November 2016,[249] which serves as a basis for the conclusion of status agreements with Western Balkans countries. As of July 2020, such agreements have been concluded with Albania, Serbia and Montenegro, while agreements with Bosnia–Herzegovina and North Macedonia still need to be ratified by national governments and receive the assent by the European Parliament.[250] Frontex has already launched two missions outside the EU in Albania in 2019, and in Montenegro in 2020, one of the main aims of the second operation being to tackle cross-border crime including migrant smuggling and trafficking in human beings.[251]

In addition to this advanced form of operational cooperation, the agency can develop more 'traditional' forms of cooperation with third countries, within the framework of the external relations policy of the Union, including with regard to the protection of fundamental rights.[252] Its cooperation with third countries can for instance consist of the deployment of liaison officers[253] and the invitation of

---

[245] Regulation (EU) 2016/1624 of the European Parliament and of the Council of 14 September 2016 on the European Border and Coast Guard and amending Regulation (EU) 2016/399 of the European Parliament and of the Council and repealing Regulation (EC) No 863/2007 of the European Parliament and of the Council, Council Regulation (EC) No 2007/2004 and Council Decision 2005/267/EC [2016] OJ L251/1.

[246] Art 11 Regulation (EU) 2016/1624 and Preamble, para 18.

[247] Art 15 Regulation (EU) 2016/1624.

[248] Art 14 (1)(c) Regulation (EU) 2016/1624; and Art 54(4) and (5) Regulation (EU) 2016/1624.

[249] Commission, 'Model Status Agreement as referred to in Article 54(4) of Regulation (EU) 2016/1624' (Communication), COM(2016) 747 final.

[250] 'EU: Border externalisation: Agreements on Frontex operations in Serbia and Montenegro heading for parliamentary approval' (*Statewatch*, 11 March 2020), available at: www.statewatch.org/news/2020/march/eu-border-externalisation-agreements-on-frontex-operations-in-serbia-and-montenegro-heading-for-parliamentary-approval/.

[251] Frontex, 'Frontex launches second operation outside EU', Press release of 15 July 2020, available at: frontex.europa.eu/media-centre/news-release/frontex-launches-second-operation-outside-eu-1UZt3Q.

[252] Art 54 (3) Regulation (EU) 2016/1624.

[253] Art 55 Regulation (EU) 2016/1624.

observers from third countries,[254] but the main formal instrument is the conclusion of working arrangements.[255] These arrangements do not constitute international agreements and their content is very general. Operational cooperation between Frontex and each third country may only be further structured so that both sides commit resources to specific planned activities over a given time frame.[256] Nevertheless, they set the objectives pursued by the cooperation between both parties, including in particular the objective 'to counter illegal/irregular migration and related cross-border crime by means of border control, as well as to strengthen security at the borders' between the EU and each third country participating in such arrangements. From a procedural point of view, the 2016 Regulation introduced several important changes bringing Frontex's external activities in line with the procedures applicable to other agencies: the necessary approval of working arrangements by the Commission and the Frontex Management Board, and the duty to inform the European Parliament about the conclusion of such arrangements (and of all aspects of its international cooperation with third countries).[257] The fact that Frontex possesses operational capacities, even though limited, is a big difference, and significantly increases the attractiveness of concluding working arrangements for third countries. This is clear from the fact that working arrangements have been concluded with all the third countries concerned in the SAP.[258]

The new Regulation adopted in 2019 does not fundamentally change the form through which the agency will cooperate with third countries, even though it clarifies and details further the modalities of such cooperation. The Regulation now provides for a clearer articulation between Member States' cooperation with third countries and the external activities of the agency.[259] On the latter, working arrangements remain the main instrument of formal cooperation, which can be combined with status agreements organising the deployment of border management teams.[260] The novelty resides in the possibility for the exchange of information with third countries in the framework of EUROSUR, the integrated framework for the exchange of information.[261]

From a practical perspective, the external cooperation of Frontex remains subject to close attention, as evidenced for instance by a visit of a mission from

---

[254] Art 54 (7) Regulation (EU) 2016/1624.
[255] F Coman-Kund, 'The cooperation between the European Border and Coast Guard Agency and third countries according to the new Frontex Regulation: legal and practical implications' in M Chamon, HCH Hofmann and E Vos (eds), *The External Dimension of EU Agencies and Bodies: Law and Policy* (Cheltenham, Edward Elgar Publishing, 2019) 43.
[256] For more details see the Frontex website: frontex.europa.eu/partners/third-countries.
[257] Coman-Kund (n 256) 43–44.
[258] Working arrangements have been concluded with Albania, Bosnia–Herzegovina, Kosovo, Montenegro, North Macedonia and Serbia. Frontex, Working arrangements with non-EU countries, available at: frontex.europa.eu/about-frontex/key-documents/?category=working-arrangements-with-non-eu-countries.
[259] Art 72 Regulation (EU) 2019/1896.
[260] Art 73(3) and (4) Regulation (EU) 2019/1896.
[261] Art 75 Regulation (EU) 2019/1896.

the Committee on Civil Liberties, Justice and Home Affairs in February 2020, on the occasion of which its international cooperation was addressed.[262] Of particular interest were the details concerning the role of Frontex Liaison Officers in third countries, in particular in the Western Balkans countries in which the liaison officer supports, in particular, the implementation of the status agreements and prepares the ground for operations. These missions differ from those exercised by liaison officers in more distant countries, such as Niger, where the tasks focus more on information exchange and situational awareness.[263] Their mission is further reinforced by the adoption of a new Regulation establishing a network of European immigration liaison officers deployed in third countries by Member States, EU institutions and agencies.[264] These liaison officers are entrusted with a number of tasks relating to trafficking in human beings, such as the collection of information on the existence, activities and modi operandi of criminal organisations involved in this activity (Article 3 (4)(d)), sharing it with competent national authorities, including law enforcement authorities (Article 3(6)(d)) and the constitution of local and regional cooperation networks (Article 5).

The EU agencies, and in particular those competent for supporting the national authorities in charge of preventing and combating crime and irregular migration, have exercised the option to develop an external policy of their own. The legal basis for their own external activities found in EU secondary law instruments are relied upon to develop their cooperation with third countries and in particular with those participating in the SAP. Two elements deserve to be further emphasised. First, from an operational perspective, the EU institutions and Member States are particularly aware of the role these EU agencies can play in the external dimension of the EU's policy against trafficking in human beings. In the last few years, events, such as the extraordinary migratory pressure on the EU's external borders in the summer of 2015 or the terrorist attacks, have shown the transnational nature of security and migratory challenges. The frequent and successive reforms of their founding instruments, sometimes in a very short time line, reflect the importance granted to the necessity to equip them with the necessary tools to foster external cooperation with key partners. Not only do the EU agencies receive more competences, especially from an operational perspective, but they are also encouraged to develop their cooperation with neighbouring countries, and especially with Western Balkans countries which clearly emerge as priority third countries in relation to trafficking in human beings. As a side and more nuanced note, respect for fundamental rights remains a weak point. Even though their importance is highlighted, at the very least from a data protection

---

[262] European Parliament, 'Final Mission Report following the LIBE Mission to the European Border and Coast Guard Agency (Frontex) in Warsaw, Poland (24–25 February 2020)', 5 June 2020, www.statewatch.org/media/1231/final_mission_report_frontex_en.pdf, 14.

[263] ibid.

[264] Regulation (EU) No 2019/1240 of the European Parliament and of the Council of 20 June 2019 on the creation of a European network of immigration liaison officers [2019] OJ L198/88.

perspective, and more generally for Frontex the agency with the most advanced operational powers, the mandate and tasks attributed to the agencies reflect a clear security approach to trafficking in human beings. This reflects the internal imbalance within the EU area of criminal justice, in which the EU established agencies supporting cooperation between national authorities, and not yet between agencies supporting cross-border cooperation for defence lawyers or those representing victims.

Second, from an EU external relations law perspective, the evolution of the legal frameworks governing the external activities of the EU agencies is particularly interesting. The procedure for concluding the agencies' cooperation agreements is progressively being aligned with the ordinary procedure defined in Article 218 TFEU. This not only diminishes the risk of their incompatibility with the Treaties, but it is also an element in favour of more coherence and coordination in the EU's external activities. The role of the Commission in identifying potential partners supports the conclusion of cooperation agreements with specific countries, in line with broader cooperation frameworks. The limited role of the Commission regarding Frontex's arrangements is somehow compensated by the multiple references to the EU's external policy in its Regulations, and the role the Commission plays within the Management Board of the agency, notably responsible for approving the working arrangements it concludes.[265] Further coherence is reinforced by the obligation on EU agencies to adopt strategic programming documents, including priorities for their international cooperation, and the role of oversight given to EU institutions, in particular the European Parliament. Nevertheless, despite these elements, the complex nature of the EU's external competences in preventing and combating trafficking in human beings is reflected by the possibility for Member States to continue to develop their own external activities and their own cooperation initiatives with Western Balkans countries.

C. Agreements Concluded by the EU Member States

Whereas the EU may possess an exclusive external competence in certain aspects of its migration policy, such as for the conclusion of visa facilitation agreements, its external competence is shared with the Member States in the fields of police and judicial cooperation in criminal matters, fields particularly relevant for preventing and combating trafficking in human beings. The conclusion of mixed association agreements as well as the conclusion of cooperation agreements by the EU agencies do not prejudice the capacity of the Member States to conclude bilateral agreements with third countries in these fields. Indeed, in most of the fields relevant for the external dimension of its counter-trafficking policy, the EU Member States remain free to conclude bilateral agreements with third countries

---

[265] Art 62(2)(z) Regulation (EU) 2016/1624; and Art 100 (2)(a)–(b) Regulation (EU) 2019/1896.

on an individual basis,[266] and in particular with those participating in the SAP. Moreover, the Union does not yet possess 'operational capabilities' in the sense of deployable personnel (police, judicial or other) and technical means of its own to participate in joint operations (law enforcement, intelligence sharing, border protection, migration management, etc), as all these capabilities remain at the level of the Member States'.[267] As a consequence, the potential scope of the Union's agreements is reduced and third countries may find it more attractive to conclude bilateral agreements with Member States, through which they can achieve more effective operational cooperation arrangements.[268]

The following paragraphs will be devoted to the bilateral cooperation initiatives and agreements concluded between EU Member States and third countries, excluding the multilateral instruments through which they may also cooperate, as these will be analysed later. The bilateral agreements concluded by the EU Member States are worth analysing since they complement the cooperation developed by the EU institutions and agencies, in particular in operational matters. They can for instance be used to obtain personal data from and/or transfer it to a third country, when this data is required for the investigation and prosecution of trafficking cases, even in the absence of cooperation agreements between that third country and the EU agencies.

Although no exhaustive and up-to-date account of the bilateral agreements concluded by the Member States is available, the EU institutions have occasionally compiled information on their bilateral external actions so as to enable us to make some comments.

A first account of the initiatives conducted by the Member States can be found in the first implementation report of the Action-Oriented Paper on Improving Cooperation on Organised Crime between the EU, Western Balkans and relevant ENP countries. This report details, for instance, how police and judicial cooperation is mainly done through the exchange of information and identifies three methods of cooperation. First, bilateral or multilateral agreements can be concluded, which has been the choice made by several Member States,[269] or other means such as rogatory letters, the reciprocity rule and direct police contacts can be used. Second, Member States may station liaison officers in the Western Balkans region. Finally, Member States may also participate in the police missions in the region.[270]

---

[266] Monar, *The External Dimension of the EU's Area of Freedom, Security and Justice* (n 14) 59.

[267] ibid 60. This finding may not be valid once the Proposal for a Regulation on a European Border and Coast Guard Agency is adopted; as the text foresees the employment of 1,000 permanent staff, including field operatives (source: europa.eu/rapid/press-release_IP-15-6327_en.htm).

[268] ibid.

[269] Agreements have been concluded by Finland, Cyprus, Slovakia, Poland, Hungary, Germany, Austria and Sweden.

[270] Council, 'Report on the state of implementation by Member States and EU bodies of Action-Oriented Paper on Improving Cooperation on Organised Crime, Corruption, Illegal Immigration and Counter-terrorism, between the EU, Western Balkans and relevant ENP countries',

A second account of the agreements concluded by the EU Member States can be found in the Annex to the Action-Oriented Paper on Strengthening the EU External Dimension on Action against Trafficking in Human Beings,[271] which constitutes a summary of current action by the Member States and the Commission. Even though the document lists all actions carried out by Member States, including those carried out at internal level, numerous examples of cooperation between EU Member States and SAP and ENP countries can be found.

In relation to the SAP countries, several examples of bilateral cooperation are provided, such as the deployment of liaison officers by Austria in Bosnia–Herzegovina, FYROM, Kosovo and Serbia; the conclusion of an agreement for the protection and support of trafficking victims between Greece and Albania; and the strengthening of cooperation between Romania and neighbouring States.[272] Examples of the intensification of bilateral cooperation through the funding of specific projects or through the conclusion of new bilateral agreements are also mentioned.[273]

Despite the fragmentary information available, especially with regard to the content of these bilateral agreements and their potential relevance for the external promotion of the Union's counter-trafficking acquis, two remarks can be made concerning the rationale of Member States in deciding with which third country they will conclude an agreement. On the one hand, the desire of a Member State to conclude bilateral agreements seems to depend largely on specific operational needs. It is likely that such a desire arises only when and only if a Member State becomes the privileged destination country of a specific trafficking route, coming from or transiting though one of the Western Balkans countries. Cross-border cooperation may be initiated for the purpose of dismantling this route and, after informal exchanges, such cooperation may be formalised through the conclusion of a bilateral cooperation agreement at a later stage. On the other hand, the geographical proximity between one Member State and a third country seems to play an equally important role. In that regard Bulgaria, Romania and Slovenia seem very keen to conclude agreements with their south-eastern neighbours.[274] Such activism may be explained by operational needs, but it may also be explained by their participation in regional cooperation initiatives, in the framework of which the conclusion of bilateral cooperation agreements is foreseen and encouraged.

Council Doc No 15013/1/06, 21 November 2006, 4. The second implementation report does not note differences as regards the patterns of cooperation already observed, and no new agreement is listed.

[271] Council, 'Implementing the Strategy for the External Dimension of Justice and Home Affairs: Global Freedom, Security and Justice – Action-Oriented Paper on Strengthening the EU External Dimension on Action against Trafficking in Human Beings; Towards Global EU Action against Trafficking in Human Beings', Council Doc 6865/10, 24–90.

[272] ibid, 25, 50 and 78.

[273] Council, 'First implementation report' (n 229) 16 – Belgium discussed and signed police cooperation agreements with Serbia, Albania, FYROM, including a focus on human trafficking: 22–23; Bilateral agreements concluded by Bulgaria with FYROM, Serbia, Montenegro, Bosnia–Herzegovina and Albania; or at 82, Bilateral agreements concluded by Poland with Serbia.

[274] See below IV 'The Support of Regional Cooperation'.

However, these findings are based on documents predating the evolution of the migratory routes to the EU since 2015. Two main migratory corridors of irregular migration to the EU are located within the Western Balkans, namely the Greek–Albanian corridor and the Serbian centred corridor. In 2019 detections of irregular crossing grew up by 158 per cent compared with 2018, and most clandestine entry attempts the same year were again in this region.[275] As a consequence, the Western Balkan region turned into a region of great strategic importance for the EU as a whole, and a mapping exercise of Member States' non-EU funded cooperation, conducted in early 2020, reveals that Member States continue to have significant interest and engagement in the region.[276] This is further acknowledged in Council conclusions, which stressed the importance for Member States to keep supporting the Western Balkans on migration and security issues in order to reinforce their partners' ability to dismantle smuggling and trafficking networks, and to further improve their operational output by sharing information on major cases of cross-border criminal activities.[277]

The conduct by the Member States of their own external policies may however potentially endanger the coherence of their actions with the EU's external policies. In this regard, the principle of sincere cooperation may prevent external actions conducted by the Member States from running counter to the Union's own external policy, and it may also favour positive synergies among the activities carried out within national and European external policies. In practice, Member States respect the general guidelines decided at EU level and they exchange information on their bilateral initiatives, for instance in the framework of the Council's working groups, in particular in order to avoid any contradiction.[278] However, there seems to be room for improvement as 'the activities of Member States and EU agencies in their respective fields of competence tend to be directed at specific fields of interest, and are thus most likely to overlap'.[279]

D. Conclusion

Ensuring coherence in the external dimension of the EU's policy against trafficking in human beings may be a difficult task, particularly when considering the abundance of actors with which the Western Balkans countries can conclude agreements in this field, ie, the EU itself, the EU agencies and/or the EU Member States. Additional complexity indeed arises because of the development of

---

[275] Frontex, *Risk Analysis for 2020* (2020) 8 and 20.

[276] Council, 'Strengthening migration management capacities in the Western Balkan region' (Presidency discussion paper), 12 May 2010, Council Doc No 7896/20, 10.

[277] Council, 'Council conclusions on enhancing cooperation with Western Balkans partners in the field of migration and security', 5 June 2020, Council Doc No 8622/20, paras 27 and 31.

[278] Interview No 1.

[279] Council, 'Strengthening migration management capacities in the Western Balkan region' (n 277) 5.

external policies conducted by the EU agencies and bodies, such as Europol, Eurojust and Frontex. Even though these agencies act under the scrutiny of the EU institutions, they participate in the multiplication of competent actors and in the related risks of fragmentation and inconsistencies in the Union's external actions. Yet the strict respect of key constitutional principles, accompanied by the clear political will of both the EU institutions and Member States, leads to efforts to conduct coherent and coordinated external actions.

In this regard two further remarks must be made. First, full use will be made of the internal coordination mechanisms that exist within the EU to coordinate and ensure the coherence of the Member States' operational activities, such as the EU policy cycle against serious and organised crime[280] or the role of the Standing Committee on Internal Security (COSI).[281] Although their original objective is to foster synergies among the actions of Member States' national authorities, they may play a crucial role in ensuring the coherence, or at least the coordination, of the external actions conducted to fight against trafficking in human beings. Numerous reporting exercises, including joint reporting, and/or policy documents have revealed frequent exchanges of information about the external actions conducted by each competent actor, making it possible to reach a certain level of coordination.

A second remark more specifically concerns the coordination of the agencies' activities and the importance of inter-agency cooperation and coordination in external matters. Duplication of efforts had been, for instance, identified with regard to the assessment of the compliance of third countries with data protection standards, with Europol and Eurojust performing similar analyses. It must be welcomed that, under the new regulations governing the conclusion of cooperation agreements by both agencies, this duplication will no longer be present.

The EU agencies also cooperate on a regular basis in the field of the fight against trafficking human beings: a network of contact points on trafficking was created in 2011,[282] with one contact point appointed in each JHA agency (CEPOL, EASO, EIGE, Eurojust, Europol, FRA and Frontex).[283] These agencies regularly attend coordination meetings and exchange with the Anti-Trafficking Coordinator,[284]

---

[280] This policy cycle aims at tackling the most important criminal threats in a coherent and methodological manner through optimum cooperation between the relevant services of the MSs, EU institutions and EU agencies, as well as relevant third countries.

[281] Foreseen in Art 71 TFEU, the COSI's objective is to facilitate, promote and strengthen the coordination of operational cooperation of EU countries in the field of internal security. It was established by Council Decision 2010/131/EU of 25 February 2010 on setting up the COSI [2010] OJ L52/50.

[282] Joint Statement of the Heads of the EU Justice and Home Affairs Agencies, 18 October 2011, available at: ec.europa.eu/anti-trafficking/sites/antitrafficking/files/joint_statement_final_18_oct_2011_1.pdf.

[283] CEPOL – European Police College; EASO – European Asylum Support Office; EIGE – European Institute for Gender Equality; FRA – EU Agency for Fundamental Rights.

[284] Commission, 'Second activity report following the joint statement of the Heads of the EU JHA agencies, Annex to the Mid-term report on the implementation of the EU strategy towards the eradication of trafficking in human beings', SWD (2014) 318 final, 22.

who has for instance consulted them for the elaboration of the next EU's Strategy. These agencies also conduct joint activities, including in the external dimension of their activities.[285] Yet their cooperation is limited by the necessity to find in their different mandates areas where their respective competences are complementary. This limit is not specific to their cooperation in the fight against trafficking in human beings, and it can be witnessed in other policy areas. It is for instance the case in the field of migration. Joint initiatives involving more than one EU agency, and third countries, such as the Joint Operational Team (JOT) MARE,[286] or the European Migrant Smuggling Centre,[287] have been developed and they illustrate the desire of the agencies to improve their cooperation. Yet their cooperation depends on the emergence of specific operational needs, and do not automatically involve all EU JHA agencies.

IV. The Support of Regional Cooperation

Considering the frequent cross-border dimension of trafficking in human beings, especially between neighbouring countries, cross-border cooperation between them is essential. The EU has developed numerous instruments and agencies to support and strengthen police and judicial cooperation within its territory and between EU Member States. A part of the external dimension of its policy against trafficking in human beings, the EU also seeks to associate third countries, especially neighbouring countries, with such efforts. Furthermore, the 'cooperative reflex' is at the heart of the EU's approach against trafficking in human beings and it includes cooperation between national authorities in charge of fighting crime. Their cooperation across national borders is essential in ensuring that the whole 'trafficking chain' is disrupted in cases involving more than one country. Yet the investigation and prosecution of these cases is extremely time-consuming and complex, in particular because evidence must be obtained from several jurisdictions, requiring the application of mutual legal assistance instruments.[288] Within the EU, several initiatives have been launched to encourage not only cross-border

---

[285] ibid 26. 'Inter-agency coordination also concerns the external dimension, judicial cooperation with non-EU countries and facilitating investigations beyond the EU's borders. Training for those working in the field plays a very important role'.

[286] The JOT was created in March 2015 and focuses on organised crime groups involved in migrant smuggling by boat across the Mediterranean Sea towards Europe and the subsequent secondary movements. It involves Europol, key arrival, transit and destination countries in the EU, plus the US, Frontex and Interpol. Source: www.europol.europa.eu/content/jot-mare.

[287] The EMSC, located at Europol, was launched in February 2016: 'Working closely with relevant EU partners, INTERPOL and third countries, the EMSC aims to strengthen Europol's capacity to assist European Union Member States through enhanced information exchange, operational and strategic support' (source: www.europol.europa.eu/content/europol-and-interpol-take-steps-against-organised-crime-behind-migrant-smuggling).

[288] Eurojust, *Strategic Project on Eurojust's Action against Trafficking in Human Beings – Final Report and Action Plan* (2012) 21.

cooperation among EU Member States, but also with third countries.[289] By way of example, and of relevance for our analysis, the EU promotes regional cooperation among the Western Balkans countries, a form of cooperation which also involves the EU Member States geographically close to that region, such as Croatia, Slovenia, Bulgaria and Romania.

The importance of regional cooperation has been emphasised since the adoption of the Stability Pact for South East Europe,[290] in which its authors stressed their 'interest in viable regional initiatives and organisations which foster friendly cooperation between neighbouring states'.[291] Similarly, when launching the Stabilisation and Association Process, the EU institutions highlighted that most of the countries in the region face many of the same problems, which cannot be solved on a purely national basis. These countries and the EU must thus 'put more emphasis on cooperation, both bilateral, multilateral and regional'.[292] Summits gathering the EU and the Western Balkans countries continued to stress such elements, insisting on the fact that 'rapprochement with the EU will go hand in hand with the development of regional cooperation'.[293] Regional cooperation is regarded as a qualifying indicator of the countries' readiness to integrate into the EU,[294] and its importance was recalled at the occasion of the EU–Western Balkans Zagreb summit of 6 May 2020. The EU indicated its full support for the Western Balkans countries' pledge to inclusive cooperation and strengthening good neighbourly relations.[295] Regional cooperation also counts among the elements for which Western Balkans leaders must show further efforts and deliver more credibly on their commitment in order to progress towards accession.[296]

Numerous initiatives have been launched to strengthen regional cooperation, ranging from those dealing with a large range of issues, such as the Regional Cooperation Council,[297] to those relating to specific fields, for example, security

---

[289] ibid or the actions planned under the EMPACT priority 'THB' of the EU policy cycle against trafficking in human beings.

[290] Stability Pact for South East Europe (n 49) paras 33–40, Regional initiatives and organisations.

[291] ibid.

[292] Commission, 'Communication on the Stabilisation and Association Process for countries of South East Europe' (n 27) 3.

[293] See for instance, the Thessaloniki Declaration, made during the EU – Western Balkans Summit on 21 June 2003, text available at: europa.eu/rapid/press-release_PRES-03-163_en.htm.

[294] Commission, 'Regional cooperation in the Western Balkans: A policy priority for the European Union' (leaflet) 2005, 4.

[295] Zagreb Declaration, 6 May 2020, para 9.

[296] Commission, 'Enhancing the accession process – A credible EU perspective for the Western Balkans' (n 71) 2.

[297] The Regional Cooperation Council (RCC) was officially launched at the meeting of the Ministers of Foreign Affairs of the South-East European Cooperation Process in Sofia, on 27 February 2008, as the successor of the Stability Pact for South Eastern Europe. The RCC focuses on promotion and enhancement of regional cooperation in South East Europe (SEE), and in a large variety of fields, from economic and social development, energy and infrastructure, to media development and communication. Justice and Home Affairs issues are also addressed and the RCC provides a certain global overview of the different initiatives and of their successes and/or weaknesses (see for instance *Annual Report 2013–2014* of the Secretary General of the RCC on Regional

matters and police and/or judicial cooperation in criminal matters. These initiatives also take various forms: whereas some merely consist of informal discussions between high-ranking authorities, such as the Brdo Process,[298] others lead to the creation of autonomous institutions with decision-making powers. Finally, some initiatives concern cooperation within the macro-region, extending beyond the Western Balkans, such as the Central European Initiative,[299] which mostly concerns the region and neighbouring countries.

The following paragraphs will focus on the initiatives relevant for the fight against trafficking in human beings, which share a common pattern: their resemblance to the instruments and initiatives existing in the EU, whose aim is to support and strengthen police and judicial cooperation between the EU Member States. They are designed to prepare for the moment when potential/future candidate countries will join the EU and participate in the instruments of cooperation between law enforcement and judicial authorities.

A. Regional Initiatives Promoting Police Cooperation

Regional police cooperation initiatives are probably the most developed and the ones that function best. The Southeast Europe Police Chiefs Association (SEPCA) is to be disbanded as the Association, which was created in 2002,[300] in particular for the promotion and facilitation of 'measures to prevent and combat cross-border organized crime and to develop regional partnerships between police and the communities',[301] suffers from insufficient personnel resources and lack

Cooperation in South East Europe, Sarajevo, 24 April 2014, 31–36, available at: www.rcc.int/pubs/22/annual-report-of-the-secretary-general-of-the-regional-cooperation-council-on-regional-cooperation-in-south-east-europe-in-2013-2014.

[298] The Brdo Process is a counter-terrorism and organised-crime cooperation forum initiated in 2001 at Brdo pri Kranju, Slovenia, by a number of countries from Central and Eastern Europe (Austria, Albania, Bosnia–Herzegovina, Bulgaria, Croatia, FYROM, Greece, Hungary, Romania, Serbia and Montenegro, Slovenia, and Turkey). Representatives of interior and justice ministers, from EU Member States and Western Balkans countries, meet informally yearly to address current security challenges to the region and find common ways to tackle them. In 2012, the decision was taken to continue the process, although in a restructured framework. The Brdo process is important for the prevention and the fight against trafficking in human beings. It is for instance in this framework that it was decided in 2010 that National Anti-Trafficking Coordinators from South-East Europe will meet on a regular basis. ICMPD, 'News –The National Anti-Trafficking Coordinators of the South-East European Countries Issue Joint Declaration', available at: www.icmpd.org/News-results.1610.0.html?&cHash=77b0f31fbf08 3597e1f6268583cb955d&tx_ttnews%5Btt_news%5D=243.

[299] Founded in 1989, the CEI is a regional intergovernmental forum committed to supporting European integration through cooperation among its Member States, ie, Albania, Austria, Belarus, Bosnia–Herzegovina, Bulgaria, Croatia, the Czech Republic, Hungary, Italy, Macedonia, Moldova, Montenegro, Poland, Romania, Serbia, Slovakia, Slovenia and Ukraine. The CEI focuses on economic and political issues and not especially on the prevention and fight against crime.

[300] Its member countries are Albania, Bosnia–Herzegovina, Bulgaria, Croatia, North Macedonia, Moldova, Montenegro, Romania and Serbia.

[301] SEPCA, 'Articles of Association', Art III, para 1 (d), available at: www.sepcasee.eu/images/stories/files/sepca_legal_document.pdf.

of budget.[302] The two other initiatives are, on the contrary, examples of successful cooperation.

First, the Police Cooperation Convention for South East Europe (PCC SEE) establishes a very advanced form of regional police cooperation. Signed in May 2006, the Convention, which entered into force in 2007, envisages modern forms of cooperation such as joint threat analysis, hot pursuit, JITs etc. The parties to the Convention, including several EU Member States,[303] pursue the main objectives to cooperate in order to pursue common security interests and to effectively combat cross-border threats to public order and security and international crime.

The Convention was primarily designed to enable the approximation of the national legislation of aspiring candidates to the Union's acquis, which explains why certain provisions 'follow very much the language from police cooperation provisions contained in the EU acquis in the area of Justice and Home Affairs',[304] and also provide essential tools for cross-border investigations and prosecutions. This is, for instance, the case of the provision on JITs, which almost matches exactly Article 1 of the EU Framework Decision on JITs.[305]

In practice, the impact of the Convention is noticeable as the text offers modern tools for the fight against cross-border crime as well as an efficient legal basis for coordinated activities between its parties. Although trafficking in human beings is not expressly mentioned in the Convention, the cooperation it foresees, such as in terms of witness protection or regular exchange of information on illegal border crossing, is essential for the effective investigation and prosecution of cross-border cases of trafficking. Moreover, the Convention is complemented by bilateral agreements, signed between neighbouring countries that may or may not be EU Member States. Finally, the parties to the Convention also work closely with the EU institutions when specific operational needs arise. This was, for instance, the case prior to and in the immediate aftermath of the visa liberalisation process for the Western Balkans, when several Member States notably reported an increase in crimes associated with prostitution and trafficking in human beings, committed by suspects and criminal networks operating in the countries. The PCC SEE Secretariat received a specific mission in the framework of the EU Post-Visa Liberalisation Mechanism, working alongside Europol and Frontex.[306]

---

[302] SEPCA, 'Strategy and Action Plan (2011–2013)' 15 April 2011, 4, available at: www.sepca-see.eu/images/stories/SEPCA_Strategy_2011-2013.pdf.

[303] The following Member States are parties to the Convention: Romania, Bulgaria, Austria, Hungary and Slovenia. The other parties are Albania, Bosnia–Herzegovina, FYROM, Moldova, Montenegro and Serbia.

[304] PCC SEE Secretariat, 'Police Cooperation Convention for South East Europe 2006–2011', 2011, 2, available at: www.pccseesecretariat.si/index.php?item=9&page=static.

[305] Council Framework Decision 2002/465/JHA of 13 June 2002 on Joint Investigation Teams [2002] OJ L162/1.

[306] PCC SEE Secretariat, 'Police Cooperation Convention for South East Europe 2006–2011', 2011, 42, available at: www.pccseesecretariat.si/index.php?item=9&page=static.

Furthermore, the parties to the PCC concluded in 2018 an Agreement on the automated exchange of DNA data, dactyloscopic data and vehicle registration data, accompanied by a memorandum of understanding.[307] This text has been explicitly labelled as an EU–Prüm inspired framework for automated exchange of data, and it aims at extending to third countries the possibility to automatically compare data stored in national databases in order to strengthen cross-border police cooperation. Even though the full implementation of this text is a long-term objective, almost representing an 'aspirational regime',[308] it is an additional illustration of the trend of replicating EU-cooperation instruments to south-east Europe, especially considering that full EU–Prüm readiness is one of the preconditions for closing negotiations on Chapter 24 on Justice and Home Affairs.

From a more operational perspective, regional police cooperation is also supported through the Southeast European Law Enforcement Centre (the SELEC),[309] which replaced the SECI (South East Cooperation Initiative) Regional Centre for Combating Organised Crime in 2011.[310] The Convention creating the SELEC was concluded between 13 Member States,[311] working in close cooperation with 21 observers, countries and organisations.[312] The new Convention stresses the importance of cross-border cooperation given that 'criminals have no respect for borders and are disposed to exploit the same to the detriment of equity and justice'.[313]

Its objective is to boost coordination to prevent and combat crime, including serious and organised crime, where such crime involves or appears to involve an element of cross-border activity.[314] Since 2001, a specialised Task Force on the Trafficking of Human Beings and Migrant Smuggling, called Mirage, has been active and achieves good results, notably in the dismantling of illegal immigration

---

[307] PCC SEE, 'Agreement between the Parties to the Police Cooperation Convention for Southeast Europe on the Automated Exchange of DNA Data, Dactyloscopic Data and Vehicle Registration Data', 13 September 2018, available at: www.eu2018.at/latest-news/news/09-13-Westbalkan-Konferenz--Prm-Abkommen-f-r-S-dosteuropa-unterzeichnet-.html.

[308] V Toom, R Granja and A Ludwig, 'The Prüm Decisions as an Aspirational regime: Reviewing a Decade of Cross-Border Exchange and Comparison of Forensic DNA Data' (2019) 41 *Forensic Science International Genetics* 50.

[309] The Centre is established by a Convention of the same name. The text of the Convention is available at: www.selec.org/p521/Convention+of+the+Southeast+European+Law+Enforcement+Center+(SELEC).

[310] The Centre was established as the result of the Agreement of Cooperation to Prevent and Combat Trans-Border Crime, an agreement on cooperation between the law enforcement agencies and signed by the SEE countries The SECI Centre became operational in November 2000.

[311] Albania, Bosnia–Herzegovina, Bulgaria, Croatia, Greece, Hungary, FYROM, Moldova, Romania, Serbia, Slovenia, Montenegro and Turkey.

[312] Austria, Azerbaijan, Belgium, Canada, EUBAM, France, Georgia, Germany, Israel, Italy, Japan, the Netherlands, Poland, Portugal, Spain, Slovakia, Ukraine, UNDP Romania, the United Kingdom, UNMIK and the United States of America.

[313] Preamble SELEC Convention.

[314] Art 2 SELEC Convention.

networks.[315] It also plays an important role in the fight against human trafficking as it in particular supports the identification and protection of victims as well as their contribution to criminal proceedings in safety.[316]

B. Regional Initiatives Promoting Judicial Cooperation

Other initiatives have been developed. These are designed to support and strengthen judicial cooperation in criminal matters.

The Southeast European Prosecutors Advisory Group (SEEPAG) was established in 2005 and constitutes a mechanism for judicial cooperation.[317] SEEPAG is considered as a close partner to SELEC since, in order to dismantle organised criminal groups, proper and timely production of evidence, followed by successful court convictions, are required.[318]

SEEPAG pursues two functions: it first functions as 'a network of experienced prosecutors who assist the SELEC in operational matters and facilitate the rapid exchange of information and evidence in trans-border investigations ... through the proper execution of mutual legal assistance requests or through more informal channels'.[319] In respect of this first mission, SEEPAG can be compared to the European Judicial Network,[320] existing and operating within the EU and which also aims at facilitating judicial cooperation through the establishment of direct contacts between judicial authorities.[321]

SEEPAG's second function is to 'provide guidance, assistance and feedback to lawmakers in the region on justice and law enforcement issues'.[322] Such a function is unique and no equivalent can be found in the EU's judicial

---

[315] 1,301 victims identified, 191 victims assisted and 509 traffickers charged as a result of the information exchanged and tactical measures taken by the police forces during the Mirage operations in 2002, 2003 and 2004. Source: www.selec.org/p280/Task_Force_on_Human_Trafficking_and_Migrant_Smuggling.

[316] Victims may indeed benefit from enhanced protection regimes, and several initiatives enable them to strengthen the possibility of giving their testimonies (assisted travels to testify in another State (eg, from Romania to FYROM), anonymous testimony, use of video conference system, etc).

[317] The initiative was launched in 2003 by the Declaration of the prosecutor representatives of the first meeting of the Southeast European Prosecutors Advisory Group, Belgrade, 11–12 December 2003: www.seepag.info/download/Declaration%20of%20the%20prosecutors.pdf. However, the basic documents institutionalising the SEEPAG were only adopted in 2005. Most of the SELEC members are also members of the SEEPAG, which include Albania, Bosnia–Herzegovina, Bulgaria, Croatia, Greece, Hungary, the FYROM, the Republic of Moldova, Romania, the Republic of Serbia, the Republic of Montenegro, Slovenia and Turkey.

[318] Declaration of the prosecutor representatives of the first meeting of the Southeast European Prosecutors Advisory Group, Belgrade, 11–12 December 2003, Preamble, available at: www.seepag.info/download/Declaration%20of%20the%20prosecutors.pdf.

[319] SEEPAG website: www.seepag.info/index.php?section=about&id=1.

[320] Initially set up by Joint Action 98/428/JHA [1998] OJ L191/4, the EJN is now organised by Council Decision 2008/976/JHA of 16 December 2008 on the European Judicial Network [2008] OJ L348/130.

[321] Art 4, para 1 EJN Council Decision.

[322] SEEPAG website: www.seepag.info/index.php?section=about&id=1.

cooperation instruments.[323] It can be explained by the specific situation of the countries participating in SEEPAG, who are mostly candidate or potential candidate countries amending their national legislation and reforming their internal criminal justice systems in order to meet requirements set by the EU. Finally, SEEPAG receives the support of all judicial cooperation institutions/tools developed within the EU, such as Eurojust, the European Judicial Training Network and the European Judicial Network.[324] It illustrates once more the desire to prepare the countries of the region for the moment when they will be able to join the EU and more precisely the Union's specialised agencies and tools for judicial cooperation.

SEEPAG's work is complemented by another initiative: the Western Balkans Prosecutors' Network. Established in March 2005,[325] and supported by several EU-funded projects, this network aims to foster cooperation in repressing, investigating and prosecuting perpetrators of organised crime, criminal groups and criminal associations. In addition, its mandate also includes fostering cooperation in the fight against corruption. The functions of the Prosecutors' Network are twofold.

The network aims to foster cooperation in concrete cases through exchange of information, documents and evidence, swift and efficient work in cases of extradition and requests for mutual assistance and the development of mechanisms to help coordination in the investigation of cases. Additionally, the network can take general measures to ensure better cooperation, ie, training for public prosecutors, the organisation of regular professional contacts or the evaluation of national provisions and practices.[326] Areas of overlap in the missions/functions of SEEPAG and the Western Balkans Prosecutors' Network can be identified and should be addressed.[327]

C. Regional Cooperation Among National Anti-Trafficking Coordinators

Another initiative, which does not concern police or judicial cooperation, deserves our attention. It focuses exclusively on regional cooperation for the fight against

---

[323] The only approaching mechanism is the one by which Eurojust acting as a College can deliver a written opinion on recurrent refusals and difficulties concerning the execution of requests for and decisions on judicial cooperation (Art 7, para 4 Council Decision 2008; Art 4, para 5 Proposal for a Regulation).

[324] For instance, SEEPAG is invited to EJN annual meetings, or through the EJTN, prosecutors from EU Member States are invited to visit the SEEPAG's premises.

[325] Albania, Bosnia–Herzegovina, Croatia, FYROM, the Republic of Serbia and the Republic of Montenegro.

[326] Council of Europe, Support to the Prosecutors' Network in South Eastern Europe Regional PROSECO Project, Assessment of existing cooperation networks, contact points and legal frameworks for their operating, 28 May 2009, PC-TC (2009) 30, 8.

[327] ibid 14–15.

trafficking in human beings and consists of the organisation of regular meetings of National Anti-Trafficking Coordinators of south-east European countries.

Decided during the Ministerial Conference held in Brdo-Kanj on 20 October 2010, the national coordinators have been meeting regularly since 2011. Their meetings 'have served as forums for sharing good practices, discussing the needs of these countries and identifying areas for potential cooperation in the future'.[328] It is important to stress that national rapporteurs from neighbouring EU Member States, ie, Romania, Bulgaria and Croatia, participate in these meetings, leading to the development of synergies between the work carried out within the EU.[329]

As an illustration of such synergy, in 2012, the national coordinators adopted a Joint Declaration in which they recognised that the priorities set out in the EU Strategy reflect their own policy priorities in the last decade.[330] Similarly, the national rapporteurs from south-east European countries joined the annual meeting of the EU National Rapporteurs or Equivalent Mechanisms, held in October 2014, for the first time.[331] These elements need to be highlighted as these meetings serve as a forum for exchanges of best practices and constitute another way to prepare the integration of the Western Balkans countries into the EU policy for the prevention and the fight against trafficking in human beings. They can also be the framework of discussions on technical points such as data collection, referral mechanisms, training etc. They not only constitute a 'soft way' to export certain practices developed within the EU to candidate countries, but they also serve to establish a strong background in cooperation, which would allow that future EU Member States can effectively contribute to the EU's counter-trafficking efforts from the day of their accession.

Their contribution to the Union's counter-trafficking policy is furthermore reflected by the integration of the data collected by some south-east European countries in the reports prepared by Eurostat on Trafficking in Human Beings.[332] Such integration makes it possible to have a broader regional picture of trafficking, ie, information on the trends of human trafficking, thus enabling the identification of common patterns and potential synergies to be developed.

---

[328] ICMPD, an intergovernmental organisation based in Vienna, provides its services as the Secretariat of this platform. Information available at: www.icmpd.org/Meetings-of-the-National-Anti-trafficking-Coordinators.2669.0.html.

[329] Similarly, regular meetings of the informal EU Network of National Rapporteurs or Equivalent Mechanisms on Trafficking in Human Beings are organised since 2009 and give opportunities to exchange good practices to be implemented at national level, and to discuss with the Commission the EU policy against THB.

[330] Joint Declaration of National Anti-Trafficking Coordinators of South-East European countries on 'Enhancing Transnational Referral Mechanisms (TRM) and Strengthening Cooperation in cases of Human Trafficking', 4 October 2012, 2 pages.

[331] ICMPD, Meeting Report, 1, available at: www.icmpd.org/fileadmin/ICMPD-Website/ICMPD Website_2011/Capacity_building/THB/NATC_Platform/Past_Meetings/Istanbul__June_2014/ Meeting_report_NATC_SEE_Istanbul_2014.pdf.

[332] The reports include data from Montenegro and FYROM (2013) and Serbia (2014).

D. Regional Cooperation as a Preparation for Accession

One can welcome the abundance of initiatives designed to promote regional coop-eration in the fight against crime. Yet the same abundance can be problematic. As pointed out by the Regional Cooperation Council in 2014,

> the number of organisations, initiatives and other players is continually growing. Those regional cooperation structures are well known to the central authorities, but a very limited number of practitioners actually knows how to get the maximum from the tools that are available. On the other hand, we have a growing number of regional players in the region, which often duplicate and overlap the work. This is overburdening for the experts in the region.[333]

Further synergies are necessary, as well as more connection and coordination between the different initiatives.

Although regional cooperation initiatives seem to be more or less success-ful, they all share the same characteristic of preparing the national authorities of third countries to cooperate in criminal matters. This element is of crucial importance, especially when considering the difficulties faced, including within the EU, to convince national authorities of the well-founded necessity to coop-erate in the investigation and prosecution of cross-border criminal activities. These regional cooperation initiatives constitute not only an additional way for the EU to externally promote its acquis, for instance with regard to JIT teams, but they also allow for the export of a more diffuse 'acquis': the practice of cooperating with counterparts located in another country. When coupled with regular training for all relevant authorities, regional cooperation initiatives offer opportunities for practitioners to socialise and develop personal contacts with each other, which constitutes a successful example of cross-border cooperation. One could consider that protection of victims is somehow absent from these cross-border cooperation initiatives, but such an assumption must be dismissed, first, because some of the regional cooperation initiatives include provisions on the protection of victims and witnesses, such as the Police Cooperation Convention for South East Europe. Moreover, projects are conducted especially with the aim of developing mechanisms, ie, institutionalised cooperative frame-works, necessary for comprehensive transnational victim support, including the entire sequence of case measures from identification, assistance and protection, participation and support during legal proceedings and legal redress to return/resettlement and/or social inclusion of the victims in their destination, origin or third country.[334]

---

[333] 'Annual Report 2013–2014 of the Secretary General of the RCC on Regional Cooperation in South East Europe', Sarajevo, 24 April 2014, 32, available at: www.rcc.int/pubs/22/annual-report-of-the-secretary-general-of-the-regional-cooperation-council-on-regional-cooperation-in-south-east-europe-in-2013-2014.

[334] The project conducted between 2006 and 2009 by the ICMPD, with the financial support of USAID, focusing on the development of a Transnational Referral Mechanism for Trafficked Persons

V. Conclusions

The analysis of the different instruments used by the EU to develop its cooperation with the Western Balkans countries participating in the SAP confirms that this regional framework is a relevant case study to examine the way in which the EU externally promotes its policy against trafficking in human beings.

The policy documents we analysed show that the region has ranked among the priority regions with which the EU intensified its cooperation in this field, and it continues to be. Furthermore, the SAP countries are already closely associated with certain counter-trafficking activities implemented within the EU, such as the collection of data on trafficking (Eurostat annual reports), the EU policy cycle on serious and organised crime, or the annual meetings of the national anti-trafficking rapporteurs.

When focusing on the provisions contained in binding agreements, it cannot be concluded that the countries participating in the SAP enjoy special treatment compared with other neighbouring countries. Association agreements concluded, for instance, with third countries participating in the ENP also contain provisions relating to the fight against crime and trafficking in human beings. The agreements concluded with Georgia, Moldova and Ukraine in 2014 contain detailed and precise references to justice and home affairs issues,[335] and some even refer directly to trafficking in human beings.[336] A similar comment can be made with regard to the cooperation agreements and working arrangements concluded with the EU JHA agencies. All neighbouring countries have engaged in the conclusion, or at least the negotiations, of these forms of cooperation with the EU. The procedures and the content of the agreements signed with the SAP countries do not differ from the 'standard model' cooperation of these agencies with third countries. Countries not located at the EU external borders, such as the US or Canada, also enjoy a close relationship with the EU, as is witnessed by the negotiations of agreements on mutual legal assistance and on the exchange of passenger name record, a tool that is crucial for the prevention of crime. Along the same line of thinking, countries participating in the ENP, such as Mediterranean countries, also count among the key partners of the EU in preventing and combating trafficking in human beings.

---

in South East Europe. For more details, see ICMPD, *Guidelines for the development of a Transnational Referral Mechanism for Trafficked Persons* (2009) 10.

[335] Articles on the fight against organised crime and corruption (Art 17 AA with Georgia, Art 16 AA with Moldova and Art 22 AA with Ukraine); money laundering and terrorism financing (Art 19 AA with Georgia, Art 18 AA with Moldova and Art 20 AA with Ukraine); and on legal cooperation (Art 21, para 2 Association Agreement with Georgia, Art 20, para 2 Association Agreement with Moldova and Art 24, para 3 Association Agreement with Ukraine).

[336] Art 15, Association Agreement with Georgia; Art 14, Association Agreement with Moldova; and Art 16, Association Agreement with Ukraine: Art on cooperation on migration, asylum and border management, providing for the establishment/enhancement of 'an effective and preventive policy against illegal migration, smuggling of migrants and trafficking in human beings, including the issue of how to combat networks of smugglers and traffickers and how to protect the victims of such trafficking'.

Nevertheless, the countries participating in the SAP are still to be singled out as key partners for the EU. They constitute the countries benefiting from the most intensive relations with the EU and the degree of their cooperation with the EU exceeds the level of cooperation with any other of the EU's partners. Their close relationship with the EU is illustrated through the fact that the SAP countries cumulate all the instruments for cooperation available within the EU's toolbox, including the most advanced, such as the deployment of Frontex staff on the ground for assistance in border management. The promotion of regional cooperation initiatives with the participation of certain EU Member States demonstrates the willingness of the EU to make cooperation with them an everyday reality on the ground. The abundance of instruments and initiatives targeting these countries may be a source of confusion and overlap, yet the characteristic that unites them lies in the will of the EU to externally promote the rules, mechanisms and best practices it has developed internally. The rationale behind such promotion lies in the belief that cooperation with certain third countries, such as the SAP countries, is of strategic importance to ensure internal security within the territory of the Union. Furthermore, the Western Balkans countries are the only ones for which the EU implements the process of the transmission of the EU acquis and especially in the field of the AFSJ. This is inextricably linked with their prospects for accession to the EU in the future and the EU benefits from the large scope of policy fields covered to address important complementary measures, such as respect for the rule of law, the promotion of the independence of the judiciary or the integration of the Roma minority.[337] The perspective of accession is also particularly important to assess whether the EU manages to externally promote the transposition and the implementation of its policy against trafficking in human beings. Indeed, a challenge lies in the need to persuade the third countries targeted to engage in long and burdensome reforms in order to meet the requirements set by the Union. Once more, the EU institutions have proved their pragmatism and flexibility as they have adapted their approach to conditionality. Accession-based conditionality has proved to be less effective for the SAP countries, partially because enlargement fatigue within the EU and the renationalisation of the accession process render the prospects for accession more distant, if not unreachable. However, pre-accession conditionality has not been abandoned and continues to play an important role. This is especially true with the recent adoption of decisions opening up the accession negotiations for North Macedonia and Albania which might mark a new impetus in the reforms to be undertaken in these two countries. Furthermore, the EU institutions have developed new policy-based conditionality mechanisms that are proving satisfactory complements. They focus on granting advantages, such as free-visa travel regime, that can immediately be perceived by nationals of the countries concerned, thus improving the public's support for

---

[337] Intervention of Wouter van de Rijt, during the ECLAN 10th Anniversary Conference, Brussels, 25–26 April 2016.

cooperation between their country and the EU. The EU institutions have used them to develop new incentives for the transposition and implementation of the Union's counter-trafficking acquis. They have designed ambitious programmes to fund projects in the targeted regions, which participate in the development of a context that is favourable for the emergence of committed and trained national counter-trafficking actors, able to influence and implement national policies in line with the EU's approach.

This chapter illustrates well how the external activities carried out by the EU institutions, agencies and Member States participate in the unilateral external promotion of the EU's policy against trafficking in human beings. The case study of the Western Balkans shows how the EU relies on diverse policy and legal frameworks to identify strategic priorities and identify tools and instruments to put them into practice, while constantly adapting them to reflect among others the evolution in the modi operandi of traffickers. These mechanisms can be qualified as a unilateral form of promotion for two main reasons. First, the EU makes the development of cooperation conditional upon the transposition and implementation of EU standards, for instance in the field of data protection. Second, the standards promoted externally reflect to a large extent the policy and legal choices made internally by the EU when developing its own acquis and policy against trafficking in human beings. As a consequence, such unilateral promotion also reflects some of the limits identified in the components of the EU's internal policy against trafficking in human beings. The protection of fundamental rights, albeit present, remains far less addressed than crime prevention and the prosecution of traffickers. This can, in particular, be due to the fact that such protection is linked to more structural reforms far more difficult to promote and monitor than the transposition and/or conclusion of agreements and arrangements organising cooperation between criminal justice authorities.

In addition, and last but not least, the unilateral promotion of the EU's policy against trafficking in human beings does not intervene in an isolated context. If risks of inconsistency already arise because of the multiplicity of EU-related actors, ie, its institutions, its agencies and its Member States, such a risk is further reinforced by the intervention of other actors, being either non-EU Member States, or other international and regional organisations, that also have an interest and mandates to participate in the prevention and combating of trafficking in human beings. In a multilevel framework of governance, the EU must thus engage in other types of external activities, relying this time on more multilateral settings to promote its own counter-trafficking policy.

3

Multilateral Promotion of the EU's Policy

I. Introduction

The development by the European Union (EU) of an external policy of its own, independent from and yet complementary to the external policies of its Member States, is one example of the transformations of the legal architecture. Traditional legal concepts, such as the concept of the hierarchy of norms outlined by Hans Kelsen,[1] are no longer capable of explaining and encapsulating the new mechanisms through which legal norms are developed and implemented.

States still possess certain prerogatives which are inextricably linked to their sovereignty. However, different movements have pushed and are still pushing them to relinquish parts of their sovereignty to international and regional organisations and to include new actors in law-making processes. The EU possesses extended competences and EU Member States have relinquished substantive parts of their sovereignty to this sui generis regional organisation. Its history, its institutional framework and its subsequent reforms single it out from other international and regional intergovernmental organisations.

The EU makes use of its competences not only to develop and implement norms applicable internally to its Member States, but also to promote certain norms externally. With regard to the latter, and as we saw in the previous chapter, the unilateral promotion of the EU's acquis, in particular the acquis in the field of the fight against trafficking in human beings, towards third countries is one of the dimensions of the EU's external policy. Its participation in other intergovernmental organisations is an equally important dimension of the EU's external policy, notably to promote the adoption of international standards reflecting its own acquis.

The EU interacts with these organisations in many policy fields, such as combating trafficking in human beings, in which they are competent and have developed their own instruments and actions. These organisations play an important role in the definition of shared legal standards and carefully monitor their implementation by States parties. Private actors, considered as newcomers on the international scene, such as businesses and civil society organisations, also interact

---

[1] H Kelsen, *Théorie pure du droit*, 1934 puis 1960 (traduction française, Paris, LGDJ, 1999).

with the EU, States and other intergovernmental organisations. These private actors are active both in the adoption of new standards and the follow-up in terms of their implementation.

These evolutions on the international scene and, more particularly, the recognition of the EU as a key partner, illustrate the recent transformation of the legal architecture. They illustrate more precisely the fact that law is developed more and more outside national legal frameworks through a law-making process that involves a wide range of actors. This type of transformation is present, to different degrees, in almost all policy fields. International trade has been the subject of numerous academic analyses, in particular because of the specific role played by the European Community. The drafters of the Treaty on the European Economic Community had indeed conferred explicit external competences to the Community in order to develop a Common Commercial Policy. And in *International Fruit Company*, the Court of Justice considered that the Community had become a member of the General Agreement on Trade and Tariffs (GATT), succeeding to its Member States.[2] Over the years, the extension of the competences conferred on the European Community, and later the European Union, has led to the extension of its participation in instruments, policies and actions developed at international level in other policy fields. The frequent transnational character and global dimension of trafficking in human beings have made it one of the most dynamic fields, and the EU fully participates in the answers developed by the international community.

When developing the external dimension of its policy to combat trafficking in human beings, the EU interacts with the other actors active in this field and participates in the initiatives that they launch. For instance, the Community ratified the United Nations Protocol against Trafficking in Persons, a mixed agreement also ratified by its Member States.[3] The European Commission participated in the negotiations on the Council of Europe Convention on Action against Trafficking in Human Beings alongside the Member States (Council of Europe Convention).[4] These examples demonstrate that the EU does not develop its counter-trafficking policy in isolation from the actions and policies developed by other international and regional intergovernmental organisations.

---

[2] Case 21–24/72, *International Fruit Company* [1972] EU:C:1972:115; and P Eeckhout, *EU External Relations Law*, 2nd edn (Oxford, University Press, 2012) 226.

[3] Council Decision 2006/618/EC of 24 July 2006 on the conclusion, on behalf of the European Community, of the Protocol to Prevent, Suppress and Punish Trafficking in Persons, Especially Women and Children, supplementing the United Nations Convention Against Transnational Organised Crime concerning the provisions of the Protocol, in so far as the provisions of this Protocol fall within the scope of Articles 179 and 181a of the Treaty establishing the European Community [2006] OJ L262/44.

[4] Expert Group on Trafficking in Human Beings of the European Commission, Opinion on measures in the Council of Europe Convention on Action Against Trafficking in Human Beings to establish a Monitoring Mechanism, 2004, 1: 'considering the negotiations at the Council of Europe ... and the participation of the Commission in the negotiations'.

The EU interacts with them in the same way in which it interacts with third countries and for a number of reasons.

- First, EU Member States are active on the international scene and wish to participate in initiatives and actions set out in other legal frameworks. Given the competences that they have conferred on the EU, the latter must sometimes intervene alongside them, for instance in the negotiations and drafting of new agreements, in order to prevent conflicts of norms and objectives.

- Second, the third countries towards which the EU is promoting its own acquis, such as the countries of the Western Balkans, are also part of the international scene, and participate in initiatives and actions set out in other legal frameworks. The EU has thus also an interest in interacting with other intergovernmental actors, who are active at international or regional levels, in order to prevent the adoption of conflicting norms and objectives. Otherwise, these third countries would be placed in a delicate situation in which they may be forced to violate international standards in order to satisfy the EU's requirements. Ultimately, through its interactions with other intergovernmental organisations and other relevant actors, the EU inserts itself into the modern multilateral scene and participates in the development of new forms of elaboration and implementation of norms.

Legal scholars have developed new concepts to analyse these new mechanisms and to understand how they function. All share the view that words in ordinary legal language, such as order or system, hierarchy or autonomy, have difficulty expressing the phenomena of imprecision, inconsistencies and instability that accompany the transformations of the legal architecture.[5] This shift from one legal paradigm to another means that it is necessary to develop new theories of law that are capable of explaining and encapsulating this new reality, such as the concept of global law or legal pluralism.[6] Focusing on interactions, movements and ongoing processes, rather than on the models that result from them, the concept of legal pluralism seems to be the most suited to analyse the interactions between the diverse actors active in the field of the prevention and fight against trafficking in human beings. This chapter will thus be the opportunity to analyse the interactions between the EU, other intergovernmental organisations and all other relevant actors active in this field. These interactions constitute another aspect of the EU's efforts at the externalisation of its policy against trafficking in human beings and they form an

---

[5] 'C'est ainsi que les pauvres mots du langage juridique ordinaire – des mots pourtant si commodes comme 'ordre' ou 'système', 'hiérarchie' ou 'autonomie'- peinent à traduire les phénomènes d'indétermination, d'incohérence et d'instabilité qui accompagnent l'internationalisation du droit'. M Delmas-Marty, *Le pluralisme ordonné, Les forces imaginantes du droit (2)* (Paris, Editions du Seuil, 2006) 27–28 (author's translation).

[6] For a description of the concepts linked to legal pluralism, see N Levrat, 'Legal Studies and Global Governance' in M Telo, *Globalisation, Multilateralism, Europe: Towards a Better Global Governance?* (Farnham, Ashgate Publishing, 2013).

integral part of its external policy, developed on the basis of the external competences previously identified.

Our analysis will start with a short description of a necessary prerequisite,
the commitment of the EU to effective multilateralism, ie, the conceptualisation of its desire to engage and interact with the other actors on the international
scene (II). A presentation of these other actors, which together form a complex
and multilevel tapestry of actors, will follow. The actions that they take to counter
trafficking in human beings will also be briefly described (III). Our analysis will
then focus on the interactions between these actors with and without the EU.
Our objective will be twofold: determining how their interactions contribute to
legal pluralism, and assessing whether the risk of conflicts of norms has been
addressed (IV). Finally, we will focus on the coordination mechanisms set up to
address the risk of duplication of effort and to foster cooperation in the implementation of a counter-trafficking approach that is as comprehensive as possible (V).

II. The EU's Commitment to Multilateralism

From the very beginning of the European integration process, the Treaty drafters
envisaged that the European Community should have the competences to be active
on the international scene. The Treaty of Rome expressly foresaw the recognition
of the Community's legal personality[7] and its capacity to sign and ratify international agreements[8] in the fields in which it had received external competences,
such as the Common Commercial Policy. The Treaty even contained provisions
providing for the establishment of cooperation and collaboration with the Council
of Europe and the Organisation for Economic Cooperation and Development
(OECD).[9] On the basis of these provisions, the Community had become a member
of certain international organisations, established cooperative relationships with
others and became party to international conventions.[10] Moreover, the case law
of the Court of Justice, and especially the famous *ERTA* case establishing the
doctrine of implied powers,[11] contributed to the extension of the Community's
external competences. Numerous scholars have analysed the complex legal questions arising from such developments, such as the capacity of the Community to
become a member of international organisations alongside its Member States.[12]

---

[7] Art 210 Treaty establishing the European Community (TEC) (1957).

[8] Art 238 TEC (1957) 'La Communauté peut conclure avec un Etat tiers, une union d'Etats ou une organisation internationale, des accords créant une association caractérisée par des droits et des obliga-tions réciproques, des actions en commun et des procédures particulières'.

[9] Arts 230 and 231 TEC (1957).

[10] For more details, see S Adam et al, *L'Union européenne comme acteur international: Commentaire Mégret*, 3rd edn (Brussels, Editions de l'Université de Bruxelles, 2015) 133.

[11] Case 22/70, *Commission v Council* [1971] EU:C:1971:32.

[12] See for instance, A Orsini (ed), *The European Union with(in) International Organisations* (Farnham, Ashgate Publishing, 2014); or C Kaddous (ed), *The European Union in International Organisations and Global Governance* (Oxford, Hart Publishing, 2015).

Equal attention has been devoted to the changes brought about by the creation of the EU and its subsequent treaty reforms.[13]

The entry into force of the Treaty of Lisbon clarified several aspects of the EU's external competences and the framework in which it can act on the international scene. The EU obtained a single legal personality, which put an end to the complex situation where its external action was weakened by the ambiguity surrounding its legal personality, together with the complication of retaining a separate legal personality for the European Economic Community.[14] The conferral of legal personality on the EU clarifies that it has the ability to conclude and negotiate international agreements, become a member of international organisations and join international conventions.[15] Furthermore, in addition to the constitutionalisation of the doctrine of implied powers,[16] the Treaties also now provide for constitutionalised objectives to be pursued in the framework of the Union's external policy. In this framework, the EU, that is itself a product of integration that derives its existence from the transfer of powers to it by its Member States, can pursue the objective of integration and other forms of cooperation itself.[17] The latter reflects interestingly. According to Article 3, paragraph 5 of the Treaty on the Functioning of the European Union (TFEU), in its relations with the wider world the Union shall uphold and promote its values and interests and contribute to peace, security, eradication of poverty and the protection of human rights, as well as to the strict observance and the development of international law. These objectives are very ambitious since they refer to challenges that are typically beyond the powers of any single state or regional bloc, such as the EU.[18] Since these problems can be solved only by concerted actions that are undertaken on a global scale and that involve a plurality of actors, it is of crucial significance that the Treaties stress in Article 21, paragraph 1 of the Treaty on European Union (TEU) the importance of 'multilateral solutions to common problems'. The Union is called upon to 'develop relations and build partnerships with third countries, and international, regional or global organisations'. The Union shall, moreover, work for a high degree of cooperation in all fields of international relations in order to promote 'an international system based on stronger multilateral cooperation and good global governance'.[19] These provisions recognise constitutional tools at the disposal of the Union to act in pursuit of its global mission[20] and they set down a commitment

---

[13] See for instance, A Dashwood and M Maresceau (eds), *Law and Practice of EU External Relations: Salient Features of a Changing Landscape* (Cambridge, Cambridge University Press, 2011).

[14] J Brsakoska, 'The legal personality of the European Union' (2011) 2 *Iustianius Primus Law Review* 1, 2.

[15] Source: eur-lex.europa.eu/summary/glossary/union_legal_personality.html.

[16] See ch 1, III.C.i 'The Doctrine of Implied Powers and its Codification'.

[17] J Larik, 'The Substance of Constitutional Foreign Policy Objectives' in J Larik, *Foreign Policy Objectives in European Constitutional Law* (Oxford, Oxford University Press, 2016) 115.

[18] J Larik, 'Entrenching Global Governance: The EU's Constitutional Objectives Caught Between a Sanguine World View and a Daunting Reality' in B Van Vooren, S Blockmans and J Wouters, *The EU's Role in Global Governance: The Legal Dimension* (Oxford, Oxford University Press, 2013) 18.

[19] Art 21, para 2(h) TEU.

[20] Larik, 'Entrenching Global Governance' (n 18) 7.

to multilateral solutions in EU primary law. They are reinforced by provisions detailing the modalities of such cooperation, such as Article 217 TFEU foreseeing the possibility for the EU to conclude association agreements with international organisations, or Article 220 TFEU, calling upon the EU to establish cooperative relations with international organisations, among which are specifically named the UN System, the Council of Europe, the Organisation for Security and Cooperation in Europe (OSCE) and the OECD.[21]

These constitutional objectives formalise the support already given by the EU to multilateral solutions to global challenges, especially in the fields belonging to the Area of Freedom, Security and Justice (AFSJ).[22] In 2005, when defining the Strategy for the external dimension of Justice and Home Affairs (JHA), the Council stressed the importance of engaging with international organisations and of contributing to effective multilateralism and the promotion of international standards.[23] The Commission's Strategy, which was adopted the same year, also stressed the readiness of the EU 'to support multilateral approaches to strengthen policies in these areas, in order both to enhance its role in international bodies and to encourage the development of further international instruments',[24] as well as the encouragement addressed to third countries 'to ratify and implement international conventions, which become a cornerstone for developing international cooperation'. The Stockholm Programme adopted by the European Council in 2009 was an opportunity to 'reiterate its commitment to effective multilateralism that supplements the bilateral and regional partnership with third countries and regions'.[25] The United Nations and the Council of Europe are singled out as respectively 'the most important international organisation for the Union' (United Nations) and an organisation whose work is 'of particular importance' (Council of Europe). The EU is invited to 'continue to promote European and international standards and the ratification of international conventions, in particular those developed under the auspices of the UN and the Council of Europe'.[26] The importance of collaborating

---

[21] Larik, 'The Substance of Constitutional Foreign Policy Objectives' (n 17).

[22] The European integration among the EU Member States is based on the idea that a common policy may be preferable to address common problems, and the actions undertaken to address them are developed through a dialogue between several actors, representing different views and systems (national for the Member States and the Council; supranational for the European Commission and the European Parliament). Although such a mechanism does not correspond to the definition of multilateralism *stricto sensu* (the practice or principle of nations or parties trading or forming agreements on a multilateral basis), the EU follows its internal decision-making processes multilateral mechanisms.

[23] Council, Conclusions, 'A Strategy for the External Dimension of JHA: Global Freedom, Security and Justice', Council Doc No 14366/3/05, rev 5. The Strategy goes further and provides examples, 'as for example in developing an EC input into endeavours in the UN system on global governance of migration issues, in current work on refugee protection with UNHCR, or on counter-terrorism with UN CTED'.

[24] Commission, 'A Strategy on the External Dimension of the Area of Freedom, Security and Justice' (Communication), COM (2005) 491, 5.

[25] Council, 'The Stockholm Programme – An open and secure Europe serving and protecting citizens' [2010] OJ C115/1, 37.

[26] ibid.

with international partners remains frequently emphasised and acknowledged. The 2015 EU Internal Security Strategy stressed the ambition for the Union to further develop its relations with international organisations, such as the United Nations (UN), the Council of Europe and Interpol, and use multilateral forums more actively to promote best practices and meet common objectives.[27] The latest 2020 EU Security Union Strategy also highlights the importance of cooperating with international organisations, and in particular with Interpol.[28]

The approach defined in these policy documents lies in the unconditional support for multilateral solutions, perceived as opportunities for the promotion of European norms and values.[29] It illustrates not only the Union's commitment to multilateral solutions, but also its position in favour of the development of international and regional legal standards. These standards will not only complement the instruments developed for cooperation between EU Member States, but they may also serve as a basis for cooperation with third countries. They are thus integrated among the tools of the EU's external activity as a way to foster cooperation between the EU, its Member States and third countries.

The importance of supporting the development of multilateral solutions and of working together with other international and regional organisations to that end has also been expressed in policy documents directly concerning the EU's policy against trafficking in human beings. In the 2005 EU Plan on best practices, standards and procedures for combatting trafficking in human beings,[30] the importance of cooperation between the relevant international organisations (for example, the UN, OSCE and the Council of Europe) is highlighted. Furthermore, the EU is encouraged to put emphasis on multilateral counter-trafficking activities.[31] This support in favour of the EU's involvement in multilateral cooperation is crucial, as the EU's support may improve the chances of success for multilateral counter-trafficking activities. The EU remains an able and willing regional partner, which can alleviate financial and logistical burdens and/or provide political support for the implementation of the agendas, actions plans and/or instruments developed by its partners.[32] In its 2012 Strategy, the Commission stressed its intention to 'work towards strengthening and formalising partnerships with international organisations active in the field of trafficking in human beings to improve the exchange

---

[27] Commission, 'The European Agenda on Security' (Communication), COM (2015) 185 final, 5.

[28] Commission, 'The EU Security Union Strategy' (Communication), COM (2020) 605 final, 23.

[29] Political scientists have developed the concept of Europe as a 'normative power' and focus on the ability of the EU of shaping conception of 'normal' in international relations. See for instance, I Manners, 'Normative Power Europe: A Contradiction in Terms?' (2002) 40 *Journal of Common Market Studies* 235.

[30] Council, 'EU Plan on best practices, standards and procedures for combating and preventing trafficking in human beings' [2005] OJ C311/3.

[31] ibid. Annex, Point 8, External relations, (1)c).

[32] J Wouters, 'The United Nations and the European Union: Partners in Multilateralism' (2007) Working Paper No 1, Leuven Centre for Global Governance Studies, 2.

of information and ensure cooperation'[33] and reported on its efforts in pursuing this objective.[34]

Therefore, the EU also expresses its commitment to multilateral solutions in relation to trafficking in human beings, as in other fields of its external actions. It is of crucial importance in order to ensure that the Union does not implement the external dimension of its counter-trafficking policy in isolation. Instead of isolation, the EU's commitment to multilateral solutions supports the idea that the EU institutions and Member States will take into account initiatives and activities launched by the other relevant actors and thus offers fertile ground for interaction.

This perspective is further reinforced by the fact that there is also support for multilateral solutions to transnational challenges, like trafficking in human beings, and support for the idea of developing partnerships from other international organisations, States and actors.

Their shared commitment is, for instance, clear from the Brussels Declaration, which was adopted in 2002.[35] The actors combating trafficking in human beings were called on 'to provide an unambiguous and comprehensive response, at national, European and international levels, working towards a comprehensive, multidisciplinary and effectively co-ordinated policy that involves actors from all fields concerned'.[36] To that end, they were all invited 'to intensify their co-operation and exchange of information with a view to achieving a better co-ordinated response, to avoid overlaps and duplications of work and to maximise the impact of actions taken at international level'.[37]

Policy documents adopted by other organisations proclaim similar cooperation and coordination objectives. The OSCE Action Plan provides that the OSCE is uniquely placed to cooperate and coordinate effectively with relevant international actors.[38] Similarly the Global Plan of Action to combat trafficking in human beings, which was adopted by the UN General Assembly in 2010, reiterates the importance of promoting 'comprehensive, coordinated and consistent responses,

---

[33] Commission, 'The EU Strategy towards the Eradication of Trafficking in Human Beings, 2012–2016' (Communication), COM (2012) 286 final, 12. Cooperation should be particularly enhanced in the areas of policy planning, prioritisation, data collection, research and monitoring and evaluation.

[34] Commission, 'Mid-Term Implementation report of the EU Strategy towards the Eradication of Trafficking in Human Beings', SWD (2014) 318 final, 15.

[35] The Declaration has been adopted by the following actors: institutions at local, regional and governmental level; NGOs; international organisations; international governmental organisations; and the EU institutions.

[36] Brussels Declaration on Preventing and Combating Trafficking in Human Beings, Council Doc No 14981/02, 29 November 2002, 3–4.

[37] ibid. Annex – 1, International co-ordination and exchange of information, 5.

[38] Preamble, OSCE Permanent Council, OSCE 'Action Plan to Combat Trafficking in Human Beings', Decision No 557/Rev. 1, 7 July 2005. The list of relevant actors is almost exhaustive: the United Nations Office on Drugs and Crime; the United Nations High Commissioner for Refugees; the United Nations High Commissioner for Human Rights; the United Nations Children's Fund; the International Labour Organization; as well as the International Organization for Migration; the International Centre for Migration Policy Development; the EU; the Council of Europe; the Council of Baltic Sea States; the Southeast European Co-operative Initiative; Interpol; and Europol.

at the national, regional and international levels, to counter trafficking in persons' and to 'foster cooperation and coordination among all relevant stakeholders'.[39] Cooperation is envisaged in diverse contexts. On the one hand the UN will intensify its work with States and relevant organisations.[40] On the other hand, effective cooperation and coordination of efforts are encouraged at the national, bilateral, sub-regional, regional and international levels.[41] More recently, in the Political Declaration on the implementation of the Global Plan of Action, the UN General Assembly reiterated 'in the strongest terms possible' the importance of strengthening collective action, including through partnerships with the United Nations system and other regional and international organisations.[42]

This brief analysis of relevant provisions of the Treaties and policy documents reveals that the EU and its Member States are aware of the crucial importance of cooperation with third countries to address trafficking in human beings, and with other actors active in this field, especially with other international and regional organisations. The desire to engage in multilateral solutions to common challenges is not reserved to the EU alone and other intergovernmental organisations also wish to cooperate with other relevant actors. This shared commitment in favour of multilateralism constitutes a fertile ground for interaction and thus for the development of an ordered kind of pluralism in the fight against trafficking in human beings. Before analysing the interactions developed and implemented in practice, we will attempt to briefly describe who are the actors that are active in combating trafficking in human beings.

III. Institutional Multilateralism: Identification of Relevant Actors

Preventing and combating trafficking in human beings is a subject of concern for, and requiring action from, a wide range of actors, be they States, international and regional organisations, NGOs etc. In this multilayered system, each actor possesses its own area of competences and acts in accordance with them.

In a theoretical setting, they would carry out their own activities within a coherent multilateral framework. States would be the main actors and a hierarchy

---

[39] UN General Assembly, 'Global Action Plan to Combat Trafficking in Persons', Resolution 64/293 adopted on 12 August 2010, A/RES/64/293. The list of relevant actors includes Member States, international organisations, civil society organisations and the private sector, and within various entities of the United Nations system, taking into account existing best practices and lessons learned.

[40] ibid Point 24. The text reads as follows: 'Encourage the United Nations to intensify its work with Member States and relevant international, regional and sub-regional organizations to identify and share best practices to prevent trafficking in persons'.

[41] ibid Point 54.

[42] UN General Assembly, 'Political Declaration on the Implementation of the UN Global Plan of Action to Combat Trafficking in Persons', 27 September 2017, A/RES/72/1, para 24.

of norms and actors would be regulating their responses to trafficking in human beings.[43] The competences necessary to develop and implement a comprehensive international counter-trafficking policy would be clearly separated and attributed to different actors and an organisation/body, which is granted a leadership role, would ensure that they stick to their respective areas of competence. Elements of such a theoretical system are present in many policy fields involving transboundary movements across borders, such as climate change, international trade, finance and communicable diseases. To tackle these issues, States have developed institutionalised cooperation primarily through the UN. Their cooperation is often accompanied by international agreements, whose implementation is supervised by a specific organisation with monitoring powers. The EU, as a regional organisation, can claim a place in such a cooperation system and possibly become a full member of this international arrangement.[44]

However, despite its transnational nature and its global dimension, the field of international migration is one of the fields for which there was a glaring gap in terms of a multilateral framework. There was for a long time 'no UN Migration Organisation and no international migration regime, and sovereign states retain a significant degree of autonomy in determining their migration policies'.[45] Additional complexity stems from the division of the field of international migration into different policy categories, such as low-skilled labour migration, high-skilled labour migration, irregular migration, asylum and refugee protection. Each category is regulated differently at the global level and they vary along a spectrum in terms of the degree of formal institutional cooperation that exists – from asylum and refugee protection (which has a formal regime based on the Geneva Conventions and a UN organisation, the United Nations High Commissioner for Refugees (UNHCR)) to labour migration, which is largely unregulated at the global level. The incorporation of the International Organization for Migration (IOM) into the UN, as well as the adoption of Global Compacts for Safe, Orderly and Regular Migration and for Refugees, demonstrate the willingness of States to discuss international migration within a multilateral UN framework.[46]

---

[43] A Betts, 'Introduction: Global Migration Governance' in A Betts (ed), *Global Migration Governance* (Oxford, Oxford University Press, 2011) 1.
[44] This is particularly true in the field of international trade. On the basis of the exclusive competence, granted by the Treaties, in the field of the Common Commercial Policy, the Community and then the EU has not only obtained the right to substitute itself for the Member States in the GATT, but has also obtained full membership of the WTO. Although complex arrangements govern its actions within the WTO, allowing in certain cases Member States to step back in, the EU is now fully integrated into the comprehensive, coherent multilateral institutional framework governing trade relations between States. Many scholars have studied EU membership of the WTO and other international organisations (see for instance, J Wouters and B de Meester, *The World Trade Organisation: A Legal and Institutional Analysis* (Antwerp, Intersentia, 2010)).
[45] Betts (n 43) 1.
[46] A Betts and L Kainz, 'The history of global migration governance' (2017) Refugee Studies Centre Working Paper Series No 122, 11.

The field of the fight against trafficking in human beings is worth analysing because of its complexity and its hybrid nature. Human trafficking can be considered to be subject to an emerging multilateral framework based on an increasingly complex array of bilateral, regional and interregional institutions and instruments. The UN Protocol against Trafficking in Persons, attached to the Convention against Transnational Organised Crime,[47] could be considered as the basis for a formal regime as it is often referred to as the instrument establishing the first internationally agreed definition of trafficking. However, such a claim must be dismissed since the Protocol does not address the full range of issues affecting individuals who are at risk of being (or who have been) trafficked.[48]

As a consequence, the multilateral framework developed to tackle trafficking in human beings corresponds neither to a hierarchical framework, like that applicable for asylum, nor to a loose framework, like labour migration. Half way between these two extremes, the counter-trafficking framework is composed of a wide range of actors interacting without a hierarchical structure. These actors, that are international and regional intergovernmental organisations, States, NGOs and private companies, have developed policies and programmes designed to tackle trafficking in human beings.

The framework in which they interact is particularly complex. A first level of complexity emerges from the abundance of traditional international public law actors, such as UN-affiliated organisations (the United Nations Office on Drugs and Crime (UNODC), UNHCR, etc); international organisations (IOM, International Labour Organisation (ILO)); regional organisations (OSCE, Council of Europe) and States. Many of these intergovernmental organisations possess, in their mandate, competences that enable them to address, directly or indirectly, comprehensively or partially, trafficking in human beings. Furthermore, the support for a comprehensive approach to tackle human trafficking effectively leads to the involvement of actors that are not traditionally involved in security and migration matters. Actions in these fields have traditionally been considered as the exclusive prerogatives of public national authorities, but nowadays a larger range of actors is called upon to participate in counter-trafficking efforts, and more generally in the fight against crime. National public authorities, such as law enforcement services or borders guards, remain in a central position to combat trafficking in human beings. However, they must cooperate more and more with private actors. Banks are, for instance, called on to assist in tracing criminal assets and detecting money laundering. Transport companies, and in particular air transport companies, are invited to pay attention to false documents that smugglers and traffickers give to their clients/victims. The shift of trafficking to the virtual realm requires

---

[47] UN General Assembly, Protocol to Prevent, Suppress and Punish Trafficking in Persons, Especially Women and Children, Supplementing the United Nations Convention against Transnational Organized Crime, 15 November 2000, 2237 UNTS 319, Doc A/55/383.

[48] S Martin and A Callaway, 'Human Trafficking and Smuggling' in A Betts (ed), *Global Migration Governance* (Oxford, Oxford University Press, 2011) 233.

communication service providers and social media companies to cooperate with law enforcement and judicial authorities. Similarly, NGOs, which are active at a local level or at a transnational level, are also involved, in particular for identifying and helping victims of trafficking. The involvement of these diverse actors is necessary in order to respond to the evolution of the criminals' modus operandi and to tackle trafficking in human beings effectively, but it also introduces an additional layer of complexity.

In order to present the variety of actors active in the fight against trafficking in human beings in a dynamic way, they will be divided into different categories: first, international and regional intergovernmental organisations (A); second, private actors, ie, businesses and civil society organisations (B); and finally attention will be devoted to the actions taken by States (C). It is important to note that our analysis will be geographically limited and focuses on actors relevant for the actions conducted in Europe. Global actors are included as far as they conduct activities in Europe as in other regions of the world, but only European regional actors will be presented. The presentation of these actors will include a summary of their main characteristics and competences relating to the fight against trafficking in human beings.

A. Traditional Multilateral Actors: International and Regional Intergovernmental Organisations

The complex and multifaceted nature of trafficking in human beings obviously has an impact on the number of international and regional intergovernmental organisations active in preventing and combating the phenomenon. Global initiatives exist and are, for instance, led by UN-affiliated organisations. Similarly, many regional organisations have developed their own anti-trafficking programmes and instruments.[49] All these initiatives participate in the development of a multilateral regime whose aim is to prevent and combat trafficking in human beings at a global level. Our analysis will focus on the organisations active in Europe and more particularly those active in south-eastern Europe.

In this region, the EU is not the only intergovernmental organisation doing work to combat trafficking in human beings. Numerous intergovernmental organisations deal with trafficking in human beings directly or indirectly. We will start with the organisations which are directly concerned with the issue, in particular because they are in charge of monitoring the implementation of legal instruments dealing with trafficking in human beings (i). We will then proceed with the organisations which are concerned with security and migration issues and indirectly

---

[49] See for instance, the Convention on preventing and combating trafficking in women and children, signed in 2002 by the South Asian Regional Association for Regional Cooperation (SAARC), or the Convention against Trafficking in Persons, especially Women and Children, signed in 2015 by the Member States of the Association of Southeast Asian Nations (ASEAN).

with trafficking in human beings (ii). We will finish with the organisations whose mandate includes the protection of human rights (iii). For each of them, we will briefly present their history and their competences in relation to trafficking in human beings. The existence of monitoring mechanisms, which are of crucial importance for the enforcement of international standards, will be duly taken into account.

i. Organisations Directly Dealing with Trafficking in Human Beings

The organisations presented in this category share the common characteristic of being responsible for ensuring respect for and the correct implementation of legally binding (international or regional) instruments relating to trafficking in human beings or to one of its aspects. They also have in common the fact that they possess more or less advanced mechanisms to monitor the correct implementation of the norms enshrined in the different instruments. Four organisations are mentioned in this category, two active at regional level and two at international level, namely the EU, the Council of Europe, the United Nations Office on Drugs and Crime and the International Labour Organization.

The EU, and more particularly the EU institutions (Commission and the European Court of Justice) are responsible, by virtue of Articles 7 and 19 TEU,[50] for the correct transposition and implementation of EU law instruments. Their competences include the supervision of the implementation of key EU instruments symbolising the EU's approach, such as Directive 2011/36/EU or Directive 2004/81/EC.[51] For the former, Directive 2011/36/EU, adopted under the legal framework of the Lisbon Treaty, the Commission has had, since its adoption, full powers to supervise its correct transposition by the Member States. In April 2013, when the transposition period expired, it launched enforcement proceedings against several Member States, leading these States to adopt national transposing laws in relatively short time frames.[52] The latter, Directive 2004/81/EC, was adopted in the former First Pillar, under which the Commission and the Court already had extensive powers. The application of this instrument was evaluated in 2010 and 2014.[53] The evolution of the competences of the Commission and the Court, especially since the end of the transitional period on 1 December 2014,

---

[50] Art 7 provides that the Commission shall ensure the application of the Treaties, and of measures adopted pursuant to them. Art 19 provides that the Court of Justice shall ensure that in the interpretation and application of the Treaties the law is observed.

[51] See ch 1, II.B.ii 'Legislative Instruments'.

[52] European Migration Network Study, *Identification of victims of trafficking in human beings in international protection and forced return procedures* (2014) 10: 'The Commission has formally requested that Cyprus, Spain, Italy and Luxembourg, ensure their full compliance with their obligations under EU legislation on human trafficking'.

[53] Commission, 'Communication on the application of Directive 2004/81 on the residence permit issued to third-country nationals who are victims of trafficking in human beings or who have been the subject of an action to facilitate illegal immigration, who cooperate with the competent authorities', COM (2010) 493 final and COM (2014) 635 final.

reinforces their capacities to ensure the effective implementation of key EU instruments, especially those adopted in the field of police and judicial cooperation in criminal matters.

Since it was established in 1949, the Council of Europe has developed its actions in favour of human rights, the pre-eminence of law and pluralistic democracy. Membership of this organisation is broader than the membership of the EU. All European States, even those that are not yet members of the EU, participate in the Council of Europe's work, and more geographically remote countries, such as the US or Mexico, have obtained observer status.[54]

The main trafficking-related instrument adopted by the Council of Europe is the Convention on Action against Trafficking in Human Beings, signed in May 2005,[55] together with its Action Plan against human trafficking.[56] The Convention provides for 'a more victim-focused approach to the problem of human trafficking and is designed particularly for European implementation'.[57] It is often presented as the first instrument implementing a true human rights-based approach, emphasising victims' human rights and protection. The Convention provides for an innovative ad hoc monitoring mechanism: the Group of Experts on Action against Trafficking in Human Beings (GRETA), which is competent for evaluating the correct implementation of the Convention by its participating States. GRETA has already conducted its first and second rounds of evaluations, assessing the implementation of the Convention in EU and non-EU Member States and the third round of evaluations is currently ongoing. In each national report, GRETA addresses recommendations designed to improve the compliance of the national counter-trafficking legislation and policy with the Convention. There may also be follow-up meetings and discussions covering the issue of meeting the obligations in the Convention.[58] All the EU Member States have ratified the Convention, even though some were very slow to ratify it, postponing even further its entry into force in their national legal orders.[59] By contrast, all of the countries participating

---

[54] www.coe.int/en/web/about-us/our-member-states.

[55] Council of Europe, Convention on Action against Trafficking in Human Beings, Warsaw, 16 May 2005, CETS No 197. The Convention entered into force on 1 February 2008, after receiving 10 ratifications. The first States to ratify it were Albania, Austria, Bulgaria, Croatia, Cyprus, Denmark, Georgia, Moldova and Slovakia.

[56] Third Summit of Heads of State and Government, 'Action Plan', Warsaw, 16–17 May 2005, CM (2005) 80 final.

[57] H Cullen, 'The EU and Human Trafficking: Framing a Regional Response to a Global Emergency' in A Antoniadis, R Schütze and E Spaventa (eds), *The European Union and Global Emergencies: A Law and Policy Analysis* (Oxford, Hart Publishing, 2011) 225.

[58] Art 38, para 7: 'The Committee of the Parties may adopt recommendations addressed to this Party concerning for instance the measures to be taken to implement the conclusions of GRETA, and if necessary, setting a date for submitting information on their implementation'.

[59] Germany signed the Convention on 17 November 2005, but did not ratify it until 19 December 2012, postponing its entry into force to 1 April 2013. Some States were even slower (Hungary – ratification 4 April 2013, entry into force 1 August 2013; Greece – ratification 11 April 2014, entry into force 1 August 2014; or Estonia – ratification 5 February 2015, entry into force 1 June 2015).

in the Stabilisation and Association Process (SAP) have been prompt in ratifying the Convention[60] and their implementation of the Convention has already been evaluated for all of them. Some Western Balkans countries are already subject to their third round of evaluation,[61] and Kosovo has been subjected upon request to its government to an assessment of the compliance of the legislative, institutional and policy framework with the standards contained in the Convention.[62] Academics have recently reviewed the evaluation process conducted by GRETA, and they concluded that the 'importance of its task is reflected in the commitments of the States to contribute to GRETA's task, to provide GRETA with the requested information on time and the high level of representatives present at the dialogue with GRETA during country visits'.[63] Although several suggestions have been made to improve the qualities of GRETA's reports, the latter are praised as a very welcome additional source of information.

A second instrument has been adopted in the framework of the Council of Europe: the Convention against Trafficking in Human Organs, which was adopted in 2015.[64] Although trafficking in human organs must be distinguished from trafficking for the purposes of organ removal, this Convention seeks to supplement the existing international legal instruments in the field of trafficking in human beings.[65] The Convention has been welcomed as it identifies distinct activities that constitute 'trafficking in human organs' and obliges States parties to criminalise them. The implementation of this Convention will be monitored through a traditional method, ie, regular meetings and recommendations from the Committee of the parties. The recourse to traditional monitoring techniques, which have been criticised for their inefficiency, highlights the specific competences granted to GRETA.

It is interesting to refer briefly to a third instrument explained in the framework of the Council of Europe which is relevant, in particular to prevent trafficking in human beings for the purpose of sexual exploitation: the Convention on preventing and combating violence against women and domestic violence, known as the Istanbul Convention.[66] Whereas the text does not refer directly to human trafficking, it is considered to do so indirectly through its provisions

---

[60] The Convention has been ratified by and has entered into force in Albania (1 February 2008); Bosnia–Herzegovina (1 May 2008); Montenegro (1 November 2008); Serbia (1 August 2009); and FYROM (1 September 2009).

[61] This is the case for Albania and Montenegro.

[62] GRETA, *Report on the compliance of Kosovo with the standards of the CoE Convention on Action against Trafficking in Human Beings* (2015) 37.

[63] C Rijken, S Jansen-Wilhelm and E de Volder, 'Taking stock of GRETA's Monitoring Function' (unpublished). Findings of the study have been published in an Issue Paper by C Rijken, made available on the occasion of the 'Not For Sale' Conference organised in Vienna on 17 and 18 February 2014, available at: www.osce.org/secretariat/116662?download=true.

[64] Council of Europe, Convention against Trafficking in Human Organs, 25 March 2015, CETS No 216.

[65] Preamble, para 7.

[66] Council of Europe, Convention on preventing and combating violence against women and domestic violence, 11 May 2011, CETS No 210.

concerning physical, psychological and sexual violence, elements which form part of a continuum of violence against women that may eventually amount to a case of trafficking.[67] A specific monitoring body, the Group of Experts on Action against Violence against Women and Domestic Violence (GREVIO), also realises evaluation of national policies and legislations, in which trafficking in human beings may be addressed, in particular through the prohibition of the forced marriage of minors.[68]

At the international level, UNODC, which was established in 1997,[69] is mandated to assist Member States in their fight against crime, including trafficking in human beings.[70] The organisation deserves to be mentioned first as it has been appointed as the guardian of the UN Convention against Transnational Organised Crime[71] and the Protocol to Prevent, Suppress and Punish Trafficking in Persons.[72] The Office does not possess any power to monitor the implementation of the Protocol. The latter is considered to

> lose out on this front, operating under the very loose oversight of a working group of States Parties attached to the broader Conference of Parties to the UN Convention against Transnational Organized Crime that meets annually. The Working Group does not equate, in any respect, to a human rights treaty body or equivalent compliance body.[73]

The weakness in monitoring the implementation of the Protocol could have been remedied by the creation of a review mechanism.[74] After years of negotiations and controversies, States parties finally agreed, in October 2018, to create such a review mechanism, which is based on self-assessment questionnaires and desk-based reviews without the benefit of a country visit.[75] The Office has a limited role in such a mechanism, providing administrative support to its Secretariat,[76]

---

[67] European Institute for Gender Equality, *Gender-specific measures in anti-trafficking actions* (2018) 20.

[68] See, eg, GREVIO, *Baseline Evaluation Report for Albania*, 24 November 2017, GREVIO/inf(2017)13, para 145.

[69] UNODC was created through a merger between the UN Drug Control Programme and the Centre for International Crime Prevention.

[70] UNODC website: www.unodc.org/unodc/en/about-unodc/index.html?ref=menutop.

[71] UN General Assembly, United Nations Convention against Transnational Organized Crime, Resolution adopted by the General Assembly, 8 January 2001, A/RES/55/25.

[72] UN Trafficking Protocol (n 47).

[73] A Gallagher, 'Two Cheers for the Trafficking Protocol' (2015) 4 *Anti-trafficking Review* 21, 22.

[74] C Rose, 'The Creation of a Review Mechanism for the UN Convention against Transnational Organized Crime and Its Protocols' (2020) 114 *The American Journal of International Law* 51, 62.

[75] COP UNTOC, Resolution 9/1 Establishment of the Mechanism for the Review of the Implementation of the United Nations Convention against Transnational Organized Crime and the Protocols thereto and Annex Procedures and Rules for the Functioning of the Mechanism for the Review of the Implementation of the United Nations Convention Against Transnational Organized Crime and the Protocols Thereto.

[76] The Office will notably organise its own database SHERLOC as the main platform for collecting and disseminating information on the mechanism, ie, hosting questionnaires and responses (Procedures and Rules, paras 33–36).

but not being involved in the assessment. Although the review mechanism is still at an early stage in its existence,[77] its lack of transparency and inclusiveness has been pinpointed,[78] potentially due to States' resistance to the external scrutiny of their criminal justice systems, and the limited history of treaty monitoring in the field of transnational criminal law.[79] Beyond its function as guardian of the UN Trafficking Protocol, the Office has been implementing its own strategy to combat trafficking in human beings and migrant smuggling.[80] In this framework, UNODC carries out several actions. With regard to research and awareness raising, every two years UNODC publishes, on the basis of the information transferred by States, a Global Report on Trafficking in Persons[81] complemented by more specific Issue Papers. With regard to normative work, the Office promotes the adoption and implementation of the Protocol,[82] in particular through legislative assistance, strategic planning and policy development, as well as through technical assistance for criminal justice measures, prevention and victim protection. The work carried out by UNODC is itself monitored by the UN Commission on Crime Prevention and Criminal Justice, for whom the Office prepares an annual report,[83] and by the Conference of Parties to the UN Convention against Transnational Organized Crime (UNTOC), to which the Office reports every two years.[84] Finally, the Office also aims at strengthening partnerships and coordination, especially through its role as coordinator of the Inter-Agency Coordination Group against Trafficking in Persons.[85]

The ILO, an organisation that was established in 1919, has been the framework for the adoption of important conventions setting labour standards that are

---

[77] At the time of writing the latest development was the organisation in April 2020 of informal consultations on the harmonisation of self-assessment questionnaires, see: www.unodc.org/unodc/en/organized-crime/intro/revew-mechanism-untoc.html.

[78] Rose (n 74) 63; and Resolution 9/1, Annex: documentation used being by default inaccessible to the public unless the State party agrees to make them public (para 41), and civil society organisations only participating in constructive dialogues following the session of each working group (para 53).

[79] Rose (n 74) 63–66.

[80] UNODC, Comprehensive Strategy to Combat Trafficking in Persons and Smuggling of Migrants, (2012), available at: www.unodc.org/documents/humantrafficking/UNODC_Strategy_on_Human_Trafficking_and_Migrant_Smuggling.pdf.

[81] The latest and fourth *Global Report* was published in 2018.

[82] See the legislative guidelines published by UNODC, *Legislative Guides For The Implementation Of The United Nations Convention Against Transnational Organized Crime And The Protocols Thereto* (2004).

[83] Commission on Crime Prevention and Criminal Justice, Report of the Secretary General, *International cooperation in combating transnational organised crime and corruption*, 6 March 2019, E/CN.15/2019/4, paras 17–21.

[84] COP, *Activities of the UNODC to promote and support the implementation of the Protocol to Prevent, Suppress and Punish Trafficking in Persons, Especially Women and Children, supplementing the United Nations Convention against Transnational Organized Crime*, Report of the Secretariat, 23 July 2018, CTOC/COP/2018/2.

[85] UN General Assembly, Resolution 61/180 Improving the coordination of efforts against trafficking in persons, 20 December 2006, A/RES/61/180, para 13.

of particular relevance to prevent trafficking for the purpose of labour exploitation: the Forced Labour Convention,[86] and the Abolition of Forced Labour
Convention.[87] The first instrument addresses forced or compulsory labour in its
Article 2, defined as 'all work or service which is exacted from any person under
the menace of any penalty and for which the said person has not offered himself
voluntarily'. The second provides that State parties are bound to suppress and 'not
to make use of any form of forced or compulsory labour'[88] and to 'take effective
measures to secure the immediate and complete abolition of forced or compulsory labour'.[89] The involvement of the ILO in the fight against forced labour has
been given new impetus since the early 2000s. A special action programme was
launched in 2001, and since then has been the framework for carrying out activities such as research, training and capacity building.[90] More recently, new legal
instruments have been adopted in order to modernise the ILO's legal framework.
On the one hand, the Domestic Workers Convention, was adopted in 2011,[91] with
the aim of ensuring decent work conditions for domestic workers and of preventing abuses. On the other hand, a Protocol to the Forced Labour Convention was
adopted in June 2014,[92] and introduced measures on prevention, on the protection
of victims and on their compensation. These two instruments have not yet been
ratified by many States, including EU Member States and close partners,[93] but this
low rate of ratification is not an obstacle for the monitoring of state action in these
fields. States are all parties to the ILO's conventions, ie, the Convention on Forced
Labour and the Convention on the Abolition of Forced Labour, and the bodies in
charge of monitoring their implementation can interpret them in a dynamic way,
so as to integrate recent developments.

Two bodies are indeed tasked with the supervision of the implementation of these conventions. The Committee of Experts drafts reports, including

---

[86] ILO, Forced Labour Convention, C29, 28 June 1930, C29. The Convention has been ratified and is
in force in all EU Member States, as well as in the SAA and ENP countries.

[87] ILO, Abolition of Forced Labour Convention, C105, 25 June 1957, C105.

[88] ibid Art 1.

[89] ibid Art 2.

[90] More information of the forced labour programme is available at: www.ilo.org/global/topics/
forced-labour/WCMS_210827/lang--en/index.htm.

[91] ILO, Domestic Workers Convention, 16 June 2011, C 189. The Convention is in force in a limited
number of European countries (in Germany since September 2013; in Italy since January 2013; in
Ireland since August 2014; in Belgium since June 2015; in Portugal since July 2015; in Switzerland since
November 2015; and in Sweden since April 2019).

[92] ILO, Protocol of 2014 to the Forced Labour Convention, 11 June 2014, PO 29. The Commission
closely followed the process on the standard-setting item on supplementing the Forced Labour
Convention in the International Labour Conference (Commission, 'Mid-Term Implementation report'
(n 34) 15).

[93] The Protocol is in force in only 17 EU Member States (Austria*, Belgium*, Cyprus, Czechia,
Denmark, Estonia, Finland, France, Germany, Ireland, Latvia, Lithuania*, Malta, the Netherlands,
Poland, Spain and Sweden). By way of example, among Western Balkans countries, the Protocol is only
in force in Bosnia–Herzegovina. Source:www.ilo.org/dyn/normlex/en/f?p=NORMLEXPUB:11300:0::
NO:11300:P11300_INSTRUMENT_ID:3174672:NO.

observations and direct requests (requests for information).[94] The Conference Committee discusses and adopts conclusions addressing recommendations to governments and calling for ILO missions assistance.[95] The impact of these traditional monitoring mechanisms, taken together with other bodies in the system, has also been evaluated, and it is considered that 'the ILO has been able to counter the criticisms of inertia levelled on countless occasions at international organisations with the intention of reducing their action to mere declarations of principles without any real practical impact'.[96] The joint participation of representatives of governments, workers and employers in the Conference has been highlighted as one element of success.[97] The independence and the expertise of the members of the Committee of Experts have been highlighted as other elements of success.[98]

The organisations briefly presented in this section share a similar characteristic: they all have developed binding instruments on trafficking in human beings, not always limited to a purely criminal justice approach of the phenomenon. They are furthermore tasked with monitoring (or at least assisting in the monitoring) of their implementation by States. Although their competences and mandates vary, also reflecting the willingness of States to subject themselves to scrutiny at different levels of governance, they participate in creating an environment under which States are expected to develop and implement a response to trafficking in human beings. In addition, their other activities, notably in research, feed international, regional and local debates on the issue.

ii. Organisations Dealing with Security and/or Migration Issues

The organisations presented in this category all carry out activities in the areas of security and migration. Just as with the preceding organisations, they have developed programmes and actions to combat trafficking in human beings. Some are responsible for the implementation of legally enforceable international instruments that indirectly relate to trafficking in human beings. Five organisations are mentioned here: the Organisation for Security and Cooperation in Europe; the International Centre for Migration Policy Development (ICMPD); the International Organisation for Migrations; the UN High Commissioner for Refugees; and Interpol.

At the regional level, two organisations in particular are to be singled for their important counter-trafficking activities: the OSCE, which works on security issues; and the ICMPD, which focuses on migration issues.

---

[94] Source: www.ilo.org/global/standards/applying-and-promoting-international-labour-standards/committee-of-experts-on-the-application-of-conventions-and-recommendations/lang--en/index.htm.

[95] ibid.

[96] ILO, *The Committee on the Application of Standards of the International Labour Conference: A dynamic and impact build on decades of dialogue and persuasion* (2011) 145.

[97] Interview No 5.

[98] ILO, *The Committee on the Application of Standards of the International Labour Conference* (n 96) 146.

The OSCE is the institutionalised form of the Conference on Security and Cooperation in Europe. Between the 1970s and the 1990s, the Conference consisted of a series of meetings and conferences, during which politico-military, economic, environmental and human rights issues were addressed. In 1990, its members decided to give the newly created organisation permanent institution and operational capabilities. Several fields of competence of the OSCE are relevant to combating trafficking in human beings, ie, human rights and the rule of law, corruption and crime control, discrimination and inequality, and economic, labour and migration policies. The Office and post of Special Representative and Co-ordinator for Combating Trafficking in Human Beings was set up in 2003 to help participating States develop and implement effective national counter-trafficking policies. The OSCE Action Plan, adopted in 2003[99] and amended in 2005[100] and 2013,[101] provides for a multidimensional and comprehensive approach to the issue. It foresees actions to be taken at national level as well as by the OSCE institutions, bodies and field operations. In recent years, the OSCE has been further involved in preventing and combating trafficking in human beings, with the adoption of Ministerial Council Decisions on the matter, and in particular on child trafficking,[102] and the conduct of surveys to assess the implementation of OSCE's commitments by States.[103] In practice, the OSCE provides diverse forms of assistance to the participating States, ranging from awareness raising campaigns, training sessions and workshops for national authorities, to the publication of reports and conduct of research on specific aspects of counter trafficking.[104] Such activities are complemented by those undertaken by OSCE missions on the ground and by OSCE-associated bodies.[105] The efforts of participating States are subject to a light monitoring mechanism: the OSCE Special Representative regularly makes country visits and meets national actors (government, judiciary, NGOs etc), which lead to the drafting of a report containing concrete and focused recommendations.[106]

---

[99] OSCE Permanent Council, OSCE 'Action Plan to Combat Trafficking in Human Beings', Decision No 557, 24 July 2003.

[100] OSCE Permanent Council, Addendum to the OSCE 'Action Plan to Combat Trafficking in Human Beings', Decision No 557/Rev 1, 7 July 2005.

[101] OSCE, Permanent Council, Addendum to the OSCE 'Action Plan to Combat Trafficking in Human Beings: one decade later', Decision No 1107, 6 December 2013.

[102] OSCE, Office of the Special Representative, *Compendium of Ani-Trafficking Commitments adopted by the OSCE Ministerial Council*, 2019, available at: www.osce.org/files/f/documents/4/f/440786.pdf.

[103] OSCE, Survey Report 2016 of Efforts to Implemented OSCE Commitments and Recommended Actions to Combat Trafficking in Human Beings, 2016, available at: www.osce.org/files/f/documents/9/6/289951.pdf.

[104] See for instance, OSCE, *Handbook on the prevention of human trafficking for domestic servitude in diplomatic households* (2014); *Study on leveraging anti-money laundering regimes to combat trafficking in human beings* (2014); OSCE, *Study on enhancing cooperation to prevent trafficking in human beings in the Mediterranean region* (2013) etc.

[105] OSCE, *2018–19 Report of the Special Representative and Coordinator for Combating Trafficking in Human Beings*, 2019, available at: www.osce.org/files/f/documents/2/8/439712_1.pdf, 59–80.

[106] By way of example, Maria Grazia Giammarinaro, Special Representative between 2010 and 2014, has conducted in the course of her mandate 10 country visits and reviewed the national efforts of

Furthermore, it was under the auspices of the OSCE that the Alliance against Trafficking in Persons was established.[107]

The ICMPD, which was founded in 1993, was created to 'serve as a support mechanism for consultations, and to provide expertise and efficient services in … multilateral cooperation on migration and asylum issues'.[108] Fifteen Member States are part of this organisation, including a few EU Member States and almost all countries of the Western Balkans.[109] The organisation's work on human trafficking concerns, on the one hand, research activities, including for instance the annual publication of a yearbook on illegal migration, human smuggling and trafficking in central and Eastern Europe[110] and the conduct of specific research projects.[111] On the other hand, the organisation carries out capacity-building activities through its Competence Centre for Trafficking in Human Beings, such as support for the development and implementation of national anti-trafficking strategies and action plans or of transnational referral mechanisms for victims of trafficking.[112] The organisation started these activities in south-eastern Europe and in the EU and has gradually expanded them to other regions.

At the international level, more organisations are concerned, working either in the field of security, such as Interpol, or in the field of migration, such as the UNHCR or IOM.

In the field of security, Interpol, the largest police cooperation organisation, must be mentioned. Its goal is to facilitate international police cooperation even where diplomatic relations do not exist between particular countries. Originally established in 1923, the organisation is now organised through a constitution that has been in force since 13 June 1956. Tools such as criminal databases and secure communication exchange systems have been developed for the benefit of Interpol's parties.[113] With regard to human trafficking, the organisation offers its technical tools to enable information to be shared globally[114] and its support for operational activities (operations and projects) aim at dismantling human trafficking networks, especially those involved in forced child labour.[115]

---

the following States: United Kingdom (March 2011); Canada (August 2011); Moldova (October–November 2011); Ireland (January–February 2012); Bosnia–Herzegovina (June 2012); Azerbaijan (September 2012); Portugal (November 2012); Italy (June and July 2013); Romania (September 2013); and Uzbekistan (November 2013).

[107] See below V.B.i 'Multilateral Mechanisms of Coordination and Cooperation'.

[108] ICMPD website: www.icmpd.org/ABOUT-US.1513.0.html.

[109] The States parties are the following: EU Member States (Austria, Croatia, the Czech Republic, Hungary, Poland, Portugal, Romania, Slovakia, Slovenia and Sweden); countries from the Western Balkans (Bosnia–Herzegovina, Bulgaria, FYROM and Serbia) and Switzerland.

[110] The yearbooks published between 2000 and 2013 are available at: research.icmpd.org/1250.html.

[111] eg, the organisation is currently part of the FP7 project, entitled DemandAT (Addressing Demand in Anti-Trafficking Efforts and Policies). See: www.icmpd.org/Ongoing-Research.2014.0.html.

[112] Source: www.icmpd.org/Trafficking-in-Human-Beings.1565.0.html.

[113] See Interpol website: www.interpol.int/INTERPOL-expertise/Overview.

[114] Source: www.interpol.int/Crime-areas/Trafficking-in-human-beings/INTERPOL-tools.

[115] Source: www.interpol.int/Crime-areas/Trafficking-in-human-beings/Operations.

In the field of migration, two international organisations must be presented. First, the IOM, which was set up in the early 1950s as an operational logistics agency and mandated to help European governments identify resettlement countries for people uprooted by the ravages of war. Over a period of around 50 years, the organisation made the transition from being a logistics agency to being a migration agency. Today the IOM is in charge of advancing the understanding of migration issues, encouraging social and economic development through migration and upholding the human dignity and wellbeing of migrants.[116] The organisation has furthermore been appointed as coordinator and secretariat for the UN network on migration tasked to ensure effective and coherent system-wide support for the implementation of the Global Compact for Safe Orderly and Regular Migration.[117] On a more operational level, the organisation assists States in meeting the growing operational challenges of migration management. With regard to human trafficking, the IOM's activities are diverse. The organisation conducts information campaigns in source and destination countries, it carries out technical cooperation activities to build the capacities of both governmental and civil society institutions, and it regularly conducts research on the issue. The organisation distinguishes itself by the fact that it is the only one able to provide direct assistance to victims of trafficking (accommodation, training and assisted return to their countries of origin).[118]

Second, the UNHCR was established in 1950 and has been mandated by the UN General Assembly to lead and coordinate international action to protect refugees and resolve refugee problems worldwide. With regard to human trafficking, it carries out various activities, mostly relating to its prevention, often within the framework of its general activities addressing refugee protection and mixed migration. The organisation conducts for instance awareness raising activities to disseminate information and to incorporate trafficking in human beings as a variable when assessing the personal situation of a person; the development of informal referral mechanisms, training and capacity building on refugee status determination; and the development of a resettlement solution.[119] The organisation also plays a role in ensuring that potential international protection needs of trafficking victims are met, and that victims are afforded the corresponding right. It also assists States in cases where victims without identify documents need to establish their nationality status.[120]

---

[116] Source: www.iom.int/iom-history.

[117] UN General Assembly, Resolution 73/195, Global Compact for Safe, Orderly and Regular Migration, 19 December 2018, A/RES/73/195, para 44.

[118] IOM website: www.iom.int/counter-trafficking.

[119] For more details, see UNHCR, 'Considerations on the issue of human trafficking from the perspective of international refugee law and UNHCR's mandate', presented at the Second meeting of National Authorities on Human Trafficking (OAS), 25–27 March 2009, full text available at: www.unhcr. org/4ae6b66e9.html.

[120] UNHCR website: www.unhcr.org/unhcr-human-trafficking.html.

These organisations share the characteristic that their activities relate to specific aspects of the fight against trafficking in human beings: security and migration. Their work partially overlaps with the activities of the organisations directly tasked with overseeing the implementation of trafficking-related instruments. Their engagement in counter-trafficking efforts demonstrates the interest shared by a large number of actors, that are intervening in various geographical regions and with various mandates and expertise. While this may be perceived as a positive development, especially in light of the comprehensive approach to trafficking advocated internationally, it also presents risks of overlaps, duplications of work and may result in an increased need for coordination between partners.

iii. *Organisations Active in the Protection of Human Rights*

The third category of organisations is made up of those that have a general mandate to ensure the respect for and the protection of human rights. The offence of trafficking in human beings corresponds to a series of criminal activites which gravely violate the dignity of their victims. Forced prostitution of women, child sexual abuse and forced labour are some of the behaviours included in this 'umbrella' concept. Among the international human rights instruments, a number of them 'identify, define and describe different forms of exploitation, including those explicitly mentioned by the UN Trafficking Protocol – with the exception of the removal of organs'.[121] As a consequence, diverse intergovernmental organisations and/or bodies are in charge of ensuring respect for these instruments or supporting the bodies in charge of this mission.

Within the UN system, the role of the Office of the High Commissioner for Human Rights (OHCHR) must be highlighted as it provides support for the bodies in charge of monitoring respect for relevant instruments. Many instruments linked to the protection of human rights have been adopted at international level, and they contain binding obligations on States, that give substance to the human rights-based approach towards trafficking, conceptualised in the Recommended Principles and Guidelines on Human Rights and Human Trafficking.[122] Some conventions address sexual exploitation, such as the Convention on the Elimination of All Forms of Discrimination against Women,[123] and the Convention for the Suppression of the Traffic in Persons and of the Exploitation of the Prostitution of Others.[124] Slavery and practices similar to slavery are addressed in other

---

[121] Inter-Agency Coordination Group against Trafficking in Persons (ICAT), 'The International Legal Frameworks concerning Trafficking in Persons' (2012) ICAT Paper series – Issue 1, 4.

[122] OHCHR, text presented to the Economic and Social Council as an addendum to the report of the United Nations High Commissioner for Human Rights (E/2002/68/Add. 1).

[123] UN General Assembly, Convention on the Elimination of All Forms of Discrimination Against Women, 18 December 1979, 1249 UNTS 13. Its Art 6 requires States to take all appropriate measures to suppress all forms of trafficking in women and exploitation of prostitution of women.

[124] UN General Assembly, Convention for the Suppression of the Traffic in Persons and of the Exploitation of the Prostitution of Others, 2 December 1949, A/RES/317. For instance, its Art 17,

instruments, ie, the Slavery Convention[125] and its Supplementing Convention.[126] Child protection instruments are also relevant[127] and intend to guarantee children greater protection. Other human rights instruments prohibit practices linked to issues commonly experienced by trafficked persons. For instance, discrimination on ethnic, racial and gender-based grounds, one of the root causes of trafficking, is prohibited under at least six different instruments.[128] Some of these instruments served as a basis for the creation of UN bodies, such as the Committee on the Elimination of Discrimination against Women or the Committee on the Rights of the Child, which are mandated to monitor States parties' compliance with their treaty obligations.[129] The plentiful supply of monitoring bodies should not, however, nullify the criticisms that are often addressed against them: the lack of binding force of their conclusions and recommendations.

The OHCHR also provides its support to the UN Special Rapporteur on Trafficking in Persons, especially women and children, a position created in 2004.[130] Together with the other Special Rapporteurs, the Special Rapporteur on

para 1 provides that States undertake to adopt regulations 'necessary for the protection of immigrants or emigrants, and in particular, women and children, both at the place of arrival and departure and while *en route*'.

[125] League of Nations, Convention to Suppress the Slave Trade and Slavery, 25 September 1926, 60 LNTS 253, Registered No 1414. The Convention defines slavery as follows 'the status or condition of a person over whom any or all of the powers attaching to the right of ownership are exercised' (Art 1). It aims to prevent and suppress the slave trade and bring about, progressively and as soon as possible, the complete abolition of slavery in all its forms.

[126] UN General Assembly, Supplementary Convention on the Abolition of Slavery, the Slave Trade, and Institutions and Practices Similar to Slavery, Geneva, 7 September 1956, 266 UNTS 3. It extends the definition to practices similar to slavery, such as debt bondage, serfdom or any institution or practice that discriminate against woman in the context of marriage (Art 1).

[127] UN General Assembly, Convention on the Rights of the Child (CRC), 20 November 1989, 1577 UNTS 3; and UN General Assembly, Optional Protocol to the Convention on the Rights of the Child on the Sale of Children, Child Prostitution, and Child Pornography, 18 January 2002, 2171 UNTS 227. The latter prohibits trafficking in children for any purpose. See also ILO, Worst Forms of Child Labour Convention, C182, 17 June 1999, C182. The Convention prohibits, for all children under 18 years of age, all forms of slavery or practices similar to slavery. According to its Art 3(a)–(b), these practices include for instance 'the sale and trafficking of children, debt bondage and serfdom and forced or compulsory labour [as well as] the use, procuring or offering of a child for the purpose of prostitution'.

[128] United Nations General Assembly, Universal Declaration of Human Rights, 10 December 1948, 217 A (III); International Covenant on Civil and Political Rights, 16 December 1966, 999 UNTS 17; International Covenant on Economic, Social and Cultural Rights, 16 December 1966, 993 UNTS 3; Convention against Torture and Other Cruel, Inhuman or Degrading Treatment or Punishment, 10 December 1984, UNTS, vol 1465, 85; International Convention on the Protection of the Rights of all Migrant Workers and Members of their Families, 18 December 1990, 2220 UNTS 3, A/RES/45/158; International Convention on the Elimination of All Forms of Racial Discrimination, 21 December 1965, 660 UNTS 195; Convention on the Rights of Persons with Disabilities, 2515 UNTS 3. Selection operated in ICAT, 'The International Legal Frameworks concerning Trafficking in Persons' (n 121) 5, fn 12.

[129] For more details, see: www.ohchr.org/EN/HRBodies/Pages/HumanRightsBodies.aspx.

[130] Commission on Human Rights, Decision 2004/110, Special Rapporteur on Trafficking in Persons, especially women and children, 55th meeting, 19 April 2004. Mandate prolonged by Human Rights Council, Mandate of the Special Rapporteur on trafficking in persons, especially women and children, Resolution 26/8, 17 July 2014, A/HRC/RES/26/8.

Trafficking in Persons is part of what is known as the Special Procedures of the Human Rights Council, the largest body of independent experts in the UN human rights system.[131] The Special Rapporteur on Trafficking in Persons is entrusted with the mission of focusing on the human rights aspects of the victims of trafficking and can take actions in connection with violations committed against trafficked persons. The Rapporteur can also undertake country visits in order to study the situation in a given country and formulate recommendations.[132] Its work is complemented by the work of other Special Rapporteurs, such as the Special Rapporteur on contemporary forms of slavery,[133] the Special Rapporteur on the sale and sexual exploitation of children,[134] or the Special Rapporteur on violence against women.[135]

At the European level, in addition to the EU Charter of Fundamental Rights, which explicitly prohibits trafficking in human beings in its Article 5, the protection of human rights is ensured by a general convention: the European Convention for the Protection of Human Rights and Fundamental Freedoms (ECHR),[136] whose interpretation is entrusted in a specialised jurisdiction, the European Court of Human Rights (ECtHR). Although the ECtHR does not constitute a classic international intergovernmental organisation, it must be included in this section, since its judgments binding on the States parties to the ECHR, lead to the expansion of counter-trafficking standards.

The relevance of that Convention and of the case law of the ECtHR for preventing and combating trafficking in human beings was not initially self-evident. The text of the Convention does not refer to trafficking in human beings, as its Article 4 prohibits slavery, servitude and forced labour. The case law of the ECtHR did include trafficking in human beings within the scope of the prohibition enshrined in Article 4 ECHR, but not without hurdles. Without repeating the work of other authors, such as Vladislava Stoyanova, who have analysed in detail the case law of the ECtHR, the following paragraphs will retrace the main characteristics in order to identify to what extent the ECtHR counts among the relevant human rights actors active in preventing and combating trafficking in human beings.

---

[131] Acting in their individual capacity, the rapporteurs will carry out in the general name of the Human Rights Council independent fact-finding and monitoring mechanisms that address either specific country situations or thematic issues in all parts of the world.

[132] For an overview of the function, see M Grazia Giammarinaro, 'The Role of the UN Special Rapporteur on Trafficking in Persons, especially women and children' in R Piotrowicz, C Rijken and B Heide Uhl (eds), *Routledge Handbook of Human Trafficking* (New York, Routledge, 2018).

[133] Human Rights Council, Resolution 42/10 Special Rapporteur on contemporary forms of slavery, including its causes and consequences, 26 September 2019, A/HRC/RES/42/10.

[134] Human Rights Council, Resolution 34/16 Rights of the child: protection of the rights of the child in the implementation of the 2030 Agenda for Sustainable Development, 24 March 2017, A/HCR/RES/34/16.

[135] Human Rights Council, Resolution 41/17 Accelerating efforts to eliminate all forms of violence against women and girls, 12 July 2019, A/HRC/RES/41/17.

[136] Council of Europe, European Convention for the Protection of Human Rights and Fundamental Freedoms (ECHR), as amended by Protocols Nos 11 and 14 (ECHR), CETS No 5, 4 November 1950.

As a preliminary remark, it is worth stressing that cases concerning Article 4 ECHR, in which violations are committed by non-State actors, are not very frequent, and complaints may often be declared as inadmissible.[137] Situations of domestic servitude and slavery have, on several occasions, been judged to be contrary to Article 4 of the Convention and States have been punished for not imposing sanctions for the violation of an individual's rights by another.[138]

The case law of the Court can be analysed through two main perspectives. The first concerns the definition of human trafficking. The ECtHR made its entrance in the field of counter-trafficking[139] with its judgment in the *Rantsev* case.[140] For the very first time, the ECtHR acknowledged that even though Article 4 makes no mention of trafficking in persons, in view of its obligation to interpret the Convention in light of present day conditions, trafficking in human beings constitutes a vicious threat to human dignity, incompatible with the values of a democratic society and therefore falls within the scope of Article 4.[141] The legal reasoning of the Court has been criticised, especially for its assimilation of human trafficking to slavery,[142] and for muddying 'the waters as to where legal distinction should be made regarding various types of human exploitation'.[143] Two subsequent cases, *CN and V v France*[144] and *CN v the United Kingdom*,[145] reinforced this impression of a lack of a clear distinction between the different offences. The Court condemned France and the UK for violations, under Article 4, for servitude and forced labour, referring to human trafficking but without explaining the relationship between the different offences. Further cases did not bring any clarification. In the case *J and others v Austria*, the Court only added that it did not have to classify human trafficking as slavery, servitude or forced labour, since the identified elements of trafficking cut across these three categories.[146] And in the case of *Chowdury and others v Greece*, the Court maintained the confusion as it referred to human trafficking and forced labour as separate forms of violations, but also referred to forced labour as a form of exploitation within the

---

[137] V Stoyanova, 'European Court of Human Rights and the Right Not to Be Subjected to Slavery, Servitude, Forced Labor and Human Trafficking' in J Winterdyk and J Jones (eds), *The Palgrave International Handbook of Human Trafficking* (London, Palgrave Macmillan, 2020) 1394.

[138] See, inter alia, *Siliadin v France*, App No 73316/01 (ECtHR, 26 July 2005) paras 148–49; *CN and V v France*, App No 67724/09 (ECtHR, 11 October 2012); or *CN v the United Kingdom*, App No 4239/08 (ECtHR, 13 November 2012).

[139] V Stoyanova, 'Dancing on the borders of Article 4: Human trafficking and the European Court of Human Rights in the *Rantsev* case' (2012) 30 *Netherlands Quarterly of Human Rights* 163 164.

[140] *Rantsev v Cyprus and Russia*, App No 25965/04 (ECtHR, 7 January 2010).

[141] ibid para 281.

[142] J Allain, '*Rantsev v Cyprus and Russia*: The European Court of Human Rights and Trafficking as Slavery' (2010) 10 *Human Rights Law Review* 546.

[143] ibid.

[144] *CN and V v France* (n 138).

[145] *CN v the United Kingdom* (n 138).

[146] *J and others v Austria*, App No 58216/12 (ECtHR, 17 April 2017) para 108, referred to in Stoyanova, 'European Court of Human Rights and the Right Not to Be Subjected to Slavery' (n 137) 1402.

definition of human trafficking.[147] The judgment rendered in June 2020 by the Grand Chamber in the case of *SM v Croatia* was thus not unexpected, even though it only succeeded in resolving some of the conceptual confusions in the ECtHR case law. The judges notably clarified that a conduct or a situation could not be characterised as an issue of human trafficking unless the constitutive elements of the international definition of human trafficking are present.[148]

However, despite these definitional issues, the second main aspect of the case law of the ECtHR allows it to count among the relevant organisations active in combating trafficking in human beings. Indeed, since its judgment in the *Rantsev* case, the Court has identified strong positive obligations binding on States. They can be summarised as follows: (a) the obligation to adopt an appropriate legal and administrative framework; (b) the obligation to take protective operational measures; and (c) the obligation to conduct an effective criminal investigation and court proceedings.[149] These were examined in the case of *LE v Greece*,[150] in which the Court reviewed whether Greece had fulfilled such positive obligations, and found that there had been a violation of Article 4 ECHR, due notably to the shortcomings identified in the investigation.[151] In *J and others v Austria*, the Court further clarified the extent of such positive obligations, notably when the crimes allegedly committed took place abroad, and the relation between these obligations. The Court emphasised in particular how the identification and assistance of victims is independent from any criminal proceedings.[152] Such emphasis on the importance of victims' protection, even before the offence of human trafficking is established, echoes with other human rights-based instruments on trafficking.

These judgments of the ECtHR are thus particularly relevant for developing the regional legal framework governing the fight against trafficking in human beings. The new obligations imposed on States allow the Court to specify the content of the protection granted by Article 4 ECHR. Their implementation, both in the States condemned and others, is difficult to ascertain since it is monitored through a traditional and soft mechanism, the Committee of Ministers of the Council of Europe.[153] It nevertheless does not impede the ECtHR, a jurisdiction whose main

---

[147] *Chowdury and others v Greece*, App No 21884/15 (ECtHR, 30 March 2017) paras 93 and 99, analysed in Stoyanova, 'European Court of Human Rights and the Right Not to Be Subjected to Slavery' (n 137) 1404–05.

[148] *SM v Croatia*, App No 60561/14 (ECtHR, 25 June 2020) para 303. See V Stoyanova, 'The Grand Chamber Judgment in SM v Croatia: Human Trafficking, Prostitution and the Definitional Scope of Article 4 ECHR' (*Strasbourg Observers*, 3 July 2020), available at: strasbourgobservers.com/2020/07/03/the-grand-chamber-judgment-in-s-m-v-croatia-human-trafficking-prostitution-and-the-definitional-scope-of-article-4-echr/.

[149] Stoyanova, 'European Court of Human Rights and the Right Not to Be Subjected to Slavery' (n 137) 1401.

[150] *LE v Greece*, App No 71545/12 (ECtHR, 21 January 2016).

[151] ibid paras 83–84.

[152] *J and others v Austria* (n 146) para 115. See Stoyanova, 'European Court of Human Rights and the Right Not to Be Subjected to Slavery' (n 137) 1403.

[153] For more details, see Article 46 CEDH and the diagram, available at: www.echr.coe.int/Documents/Case_processing_ENG.pdf.

task is to protect human rights, to join the actors active in preventing and combating trafficking in human beings.

Despite the limits of their actions, the role of human rights organisations should not be underestimated. They contribute towards the promotion of a comprehensive approach to tackle trafficking in human beings and the measures aimed at ensuring the protection of the victims' human rights have demonstrated their importance and their complementarity with criminal justice measures. These organisations play a crucial role in the prevention of trafficking, notably by preventing human rights violations which may place a person in a vulnerable situation and at risk of being trafficked.

iv. Concluding Remarks

The presentation of the intergovernmental organisations active in combating trafficking in human beings is far from complete. Within the UN system, other organisations and offices are involved within their respective mandates in counter-trafficking efforts. This is notably the case for the UN Children's Fund (UNICEF), the UN Development Programme (UNDP) or the UN Entity for Gender Equality and the Empowerment of Women (UN Women).[154] Such diversity can be found outside the UN system. By way of example, a specialised organisation, such as the International Civil Aviation Association has engaged in counter-trafficking initiatives, and regional organisations, such as the Association of Southeast Asian Nations (ASEAN), have also developed a specific Convention[155] and programmes against trafficking in persons.[156] Due to the multidimensional nature of the trafficking issue, many intergovernmental organisations thus find within their mandate and competences the possibility to contribute directly or indirectly to counter-trafficking efforts. Cooperation and coordination between intergovernmental organisations thus becomes a necessity, especially where there are overlaps in their actions. The necessity for coordination is further reinforced by two elements. First, none of the intergovernmental organisations presented can claim a leadership role, and we will analyse later the importance taken by mechanisms and initiatives aimed at fostering inter-agency cooperation. Second, intergovernmental organisations are not the only actors involved in counter-trafficking. At each level of governance, ie, local, national, regional and international, private actors have also increasingly been involved in the fight against trafficking in human beings.

---

[154] For an illustration of their activities, see ICAT, 'ICAT expertise and experience in countering trafficking in persons, An overview of the mandate and activities of ICAT organizations' (2018), available at: icat.network/sites/default/files/publications/documents/ICAT%20expertise%20and%20experience%20in%20countering%20TIP.pdf.

[155] ASEAN Convention Against Trafficking in Persons, Especially Women and Children, signed on 22 November 2015.

[156] See, eg, the *ASEAN Handbook on International Legal Cooperation in Trafficking in Persons Cases*, edited twice in 2010 and 2018.

B. Non-Traditional Multilateral Actors: Private Actors

New actors have appeared and become more important on the international scene in recent decades. They may be designated by the general term of 'private actors'. These actors nowadays contribute to multilateral dialogues and actions in diverse global issues, such as environmental protection or the fight against terrorism. They have developed their own programmes of action against trafficking in human beings and thus contribute to the definition and implementation of international and European standards in this field. The subsequent paragraphs will give only a limited overview of these actors and their actions and will focus on two categories: NGOs, also referred to as civil society organisations, (i) and businesses (ii).

i. Involvement of Civil Society Organisations

Civil society organisations are not newcomers in the prevention and the combat of trafficking in human beings,[157] especially considering that some of its components (practices similar to slavery or forced labour) have a long history. Some civil society organisations, such as Anti-Slavery International, based in the UK, was founded almost 200 years ago by abolitionists protesting against the transatlantic slave trade.[158] In addition to organisations with a long history in addressing trafficking, other have integrated counter-trafficking into their activities in recent years, or were recently founded with counter-trafficking as a primary objective.[159] Their mandate, size and activities are diverse, ranging from large advocacy lobbying groups to international organisations and small local service providers providing assistance to identified victims of trafficking.[160]

Some act at local and/or national level, operating shelters for victims, or engaging in discussions on national counter-trafficking legislation and policy. In this regard, civil society organisations may carry out essential activities for the protection of victims of trafficking, as national authorities have often delegated and commissioned the implementation of their obligations in this regard to civil society organisations. Whereas these organisations may be in a privileged position to gain the trust of victims because of their independence from public authorities, they also face the risk of seeing their work limited to the missions requested

---

[157] For more details, see C Brière, 'Combatting trafficking in human beings: moving beyond labels with the EU's multidisciplinary, integrated and holistic approach' in F Galli and A Weyembergh (eds), *Do labels still matter? Blurring boundaries between administrative and criminal law: The influence of the EU* (Brussels, Editions de l'Université de Bruxelles, 2014).

[158] TE Do Carmo, 'Major International Counter-Trafficking Organizations: Addressing Human Trafficking from Multiple Directions' in J Winterdyk and J Jones (eds), *The Palgrave International Handbook of Human Trafficking* (London, Palgrave Macmillan, 2020) 1435.

[159] ibid 1434.

[160] M van Doorninck, 'Changing the system from within, The role of NGOs in the flawed anti-trafficking framework' in R Piotrowicz, C Rijken and B Heide Uhl, *Routledge Handbook of Human Trafficking* (New York, Routledge, 2018) 420.

by States. In other terms, their assistance might be restricted to the victims fulfilling the conditions defined in national legislation for being recognised as a victim of trafficking.[161] These civil society organisations can also play a key role in detecting victims, and in conducting awareness raising campaigns or training sessions in targeted sectors, which can help with the identification of victims of trafficking.[162] They may finally engage in policymaking and lobbying efforts in particular in the framework of national coordination mechanisms. This is for instance the case in Belgium, where one representative of the specialised reception centres for victims of trafficking is a member of the national coordinating body, the Interdepartmental Coordination Unit for Action against Trafficking in and Smuggling of Human Beings (*Cellule Interdépartementale de coordination de la lutte contre la traite des êtres humains*), in charge notably of the definition of the national multi-annual action plan.[163]

By contrast, other civil society organisations are more active at a transnational level,[164] where they engage in lobbying actions, and are involved in the development of public policies and/or legal instruments. They rely on their very specific experiences and expertise and their input is essential in the elaboration, adoption and implementation of policies that have an effective impact on the ground.[165] Their involvement was particularly noticeable in the negotiations of the UN Trafficking Protocol, in which the level of their participation was unprecedented and government delegations and the Secretariat were forced to deal with a growing group of well-organised civil society organisations. They came togther in two lobbying 'coalitions', the 'International Human Rights Network'[166] and the 'Human Rights Caucus',[167] reflecting the opposition to prostitution between abolitionists and regulationists.[168] Both coalitions attempted to influence the content of the

---

[161] ibid 426.

[162] Victims are traditionally identified by law enforcement authorities and other public authorities (border guards for instance). Professionals who may be in contact with potential victims in their professional activities (health, hotels) can identify victims and refer them to competent authorities. Persons working in sectors where exploitative situations amounting to trafficking are frequent can also help to identify victims.

[163] Royal Decree of 21 July 2014 modifying the Royal Decree of 16 May 2014 on the fight against human smuggling and trafficking, Moniteur Belge 1 September 2014.

[164] Most of the NGOs active at transnational level, such as, LA Strada, or Terre des Hommes, combine their transnational activities with local activities. These organisations are NGO networks, comprising member organisations located in different countries. La Strada International is for instance composed of member organisations in Belarus, Bulgaria, the Czech Republic, North Macedonia, Moldova, the Netherlands, Poland and Ukraine. An international secretariat, based in Amsterdam, maintains and expands the relations of the La Strada network with national and international organisations, national governments, European institutions and UN bodies. The secretariat supports capacity building of the members and provides a forum for civil society organisations on the issue of trafficking. Source: lastradainternational.org/about-lsi.

[165] van Doorninck (n 160) 428.

[166] Convened by the Coalition Against Trafficking in Women, regrouping 140 NGOs.

[167] Convened by the Global Alliance against Trafficking in Women, regrouping 90 NGOs.

[168] A Gallagher, 'Human Rights and the New UN Protocols on Trafficking and Migrant Smuggling: A Preliminary Analysis' (2001) 23 *Human Rights Quarterly* 975, 1002.

provisions of the future Protocol, in line with their respective political position on prostitution. Although evaluating the results of their lobbying actions is always a delicate task, academics managed, through a close analysis of the negotiations, to reveal that civil society organisations clearly influenced the decision of States, through their submissions and informal lobbying efforts. Their influence has been particularly highlighted concerning the inclusion of a coercion-based defintion of trafficking[169] or the recognition as one of the main objectives of the Protocol of the protection of victims of trafficking.[170] Their lobbying still continues today through their participation in UN dialogues, the publication of position papers or by initiating public campaigns.[171]

The involvement of civil society organisations in policymaking is also valid within regional organisations. In the EU, national authorities, and especially national rapporteurs or equivalent mechanisms,[172] are encouraged to and work closely with them.[173] In practice, such cooperation is effective and takes place through formal[174] and/or informal mechanisms. In order to reflect the involvement of civil society organisations in the development of national policies, and to involve them in the expansion of the EU's policy, in 2013 the Commission launched an EU Civil Society Platform, which aims in particular at enabling EU institutions to engage in constructive dialogue with civil society organisations.[175] Since its establishment, several meetings have been held and one may wonder about the added value of such a platform. The question had been raised whether civil society organisations attending these meetings really enjoy an opportunity to voice their opinions and potentially influence the EU's counter-trafficking policy. Yet the answer to such a question is by definition very difficult to give. It is not only very sensitive, but also very subjective. Each participant would have its own expectations and its own perception about the successes and/or shortcomings of the platform. Nevertheless, researchers have attempted to find an answer to this question. Kiril Shaparov conducted a critical analysis of the work of the EU Civil Society Platform.[176] On the basis of an online anonymous survey circulated to all platform members, and based on the 25 responses received, he attempted

---

[169] See below IV.C.i 'Definition of the Offence of Trafficking in Human Beings'.

[170] Gallagher, 'Human Rights and the New UN Protocols on Trafficking and Migrant Smuggling' (n 168) 1002.

[171] Do Carmo (n 158) 1438.

[172] Art 19 Directive 2011/36/EU. See also Commission, 'The EU Strategy towards the Eradication of Trafficking in Human Beings, 2012–2016' (n 33) 11.

[173] Preamble, Recital 6, Directive 2011/36/EU.

[174] See the example of the United Kingdom, where several NGOs are part of the National Referral Mechanism Oversight Group (Source: GRETA, *Report concerning the implementation of the Council of Europe Convention on Action against Trafficking in Human Beings by the United Kingdom* (2012) 6, 18, paras 38–39).

[175] 'Commission launches EU Civil Society Platform against trafficking in human beings', Press release IP/13/484, 31 May 2013.

[176] His current stage of research was presented in November 2015 during a conference, and the references are made to his PowerPoint presentation, available at: thbregionalimplementationinitiative.files. wordpress.com/2015/10/sharapov-eu-civil-society-platform-against-trafficking.pdf.

to draw preliminary conclusions. The results are mixed. Some participants have given positive feedback. In their opinion, their participation in the Platform's meetings allowed them to initiate partnership with other civil society organisations, as well as to contribute to the elaboration of the EU's counter-trafficking policy, or to discuss directly with Commission officials. In contrast, other participants expressed more negative feedback. They described the meetings of the Platform as being a formality, meaning that they did not offer to civil society organisations an opportunity to engage in open discussions with the Commission. These meetings were also criticised for having few concrete outcomes.[177]

Civil society organisations also cooperate with intergovernmental organisations other than the EU. For instance, they may assist the monitoring bodies in charge of evaluating the compliance of national legislation and policies with international and regional standards. For instance, during its country visits GRETA, the body in charge of monitoring the implementation of the Council of Europe Convention, systematically conducts separate meetings with national civil society organisations.[178] These meetings allow for open discussion about the involvement of civil society organisations in the national counter-trafficking efforts, or about what they perceive to be the weaknesses in national legislation and policy. Their feedback is often translated into recommendations to States parties, which provides them with additional tools for their lobbying efforts.[179]

Finally, civil society organisations are also involved in capacity-building and research projects. Within the former category, these organisations provide training for national authorities, support them in institution building, policy formulation and legal reform, data collection etc,[180] and facilitate international and inter-agency cooperation.[181] These activities are often carried out with the financial support of international and regional organisations,[182] or other sources of funding. The research activities of civil society organisations valuably complement those of national authorities and international and regional organisations, especially as civil society organisations have access to a wide range of data not available to other organisations.[183] In this regard, they participate in giving a more transparent account of the activities and projects carried out in target countries and regions,

---

[177] ibid slide 10.

[178] Rijken, Jansen-Wilhelm and de Volder (n 63).

[179] van Doorninck (n 160) 428.

[180] See for instance, the activities conducted by La Strada International: lastradainternational.org/ls-offices; or those reported in OSCE, *The Critical Role of Civil Society in Combating Trafficking in Human Beings* (2018) 50.

[181] For instance, the local office of the Geneva Centre for Security Sector Governance (DCAF) located in Ljubljana hosts and supports the Secretariat of the Police Cooperation Convention for South East Europe, which organises annual meetings, conferences on joint investigation teams, etc. For more information see: www.dcaf.ch/Region/Southeast-Europe/Projects/Police-Support-in-South-East-Europe.

[182] For an overview of EU-funded projects, see Commission, *Study on comprehensive policy review of anti-trafficking projects funded by the European Commission*, 2016, available at: ec.europa.eu/anti-trafficking/sites/antitrafficking/files/study_on_comprehensive_policy_review.pdf.

[183] van Doorninck (n 160) 428.

and whether anti-trafficking measures, when effectively implemented, achieve the objective they pursue.

Like intergovernmental organisations, the involvement of civil society organisations in the fight against trafficking in human beings varies depending on their status, competences and resources. While some only conduct activities relating to trafficking in human beings, others are involved in more general issues, such as the promotion of women's rights or the provision of counselling services to migrant workers. Their engagement is thus 'wide and diverse, inter-connected and multi-faceted'.[184] Another similarity with intergovernmental organisations lies in the absence of hierarchical organisations, which is largely explained by the abundance of civil society organisations active in this field. Signs of attempts to organise groups of civil society organisations have been identified both at international and regional level and some organisations are themselves composed of several local organisations. These signs demonstrate their willingness to engage in constructive dialogue not only with local and national actors, but also with those active at a transnational level. However, the actions of civil society organisations against trafficking in human beings face certain limits relating to the persistent perception of the phenomenon as a criminal justice issue. As an example of such limits, one can note that if civil society organisations can participate in broad debates and dialogues on trafficking-related topics, such as the annual International Dialogues on Migration,[185] they do not necessarily obtain a meaningful role in monitoring the implementation of States' obligations.[186] Finally, the response to trafficking in human beings evolves, including but not limited to, the increasing attention brought to trafficking for the purpose of labour exploitation, or to trafficking risks in mixed migration flows. This evolution calls for the involvement of new civil society organisations, such as migrant rights organisations, sex workers and labour unions etc, that have first-hand knowledge of these new trends, and should thus be consulted in the development of adequate responses.

ii. Involvement of the Business Sector

The business sector encompasses a diverse range of profit-oriented actors, including for instance travel or employment agencies, hotels and motorway restaurants. These actors can also be active transnationally or focus on more geographically restrained markers. Their contribution to counter-trafficking efforts is essential, since human trafficking may occur in legitimate businesses, or at least intersect with the private sector via supply chains, logistics or finance.[187]

---

[184] OSCE, *The Critical Role of Civil Society in Combating Trafficking in Human Beings* (n 180) 19.

[185] See, eg, IOM, International Dialogue on Migration 2018, List of Participants, available at: www. iom.int/sites/default/files/our_work/ICP/IDM/final_idm_spring_2018_list_of_participants.pdf.

[186] See above, the paragraph on UNODC and the Review Mechanism of the UNTOC.

[187] I de Vries MA Jose and A Farrell, 'It's Your Business: The Role of the Private Sector in Human Trafficking' in J Winterdyk and J Jones (eds), *The Palgrave International Handbook of Human Trafficking* (London, Palgrave Macmillan, 2020) 747.

Companies have to be distinguished from civil society organisations, as they can potentially be held liable and sanctioned if trafficking in human beings is committed for their benefit. National legislators are bound by virtue of international and European standards to adopt rules foreseeing the criminal or administrative liability of businesses and companies, also known as legal persons, if trafficking in human beings is committed for their benefit.[188] However, establishing their direct liability is extremely difficult in practice.[189] As pinpointed by the UN Special Rapporteur on Trafficking in Persons, legal frameworks are poorly prepared for the prosecution of cases of trafficking in the context of businesses' operations and there is a lack of understanding within law enforcement, the prosecution and the judiciary, of the indicators of trafficking in persons, especially in the field of labour exploitation.[190] Furthermore, there are no provisions in international or regional instruments criminalising their indirect contribution to the realisation of the offence, for example, when they fail to adequately supervise their sub-contractors.[191]

Efforts have nevertheless been undertaken at international and regional levels to support their involvement in counter-trafficking efforts, at least in an indirect way. Within the UN, actions have been undertaken to prevent the involvement of corporations in human rights infringements,[192] such as the adoption of the seven 'Athens Ethical Principles',[193] or of the UN Guiding Principles on Business and Human Rights (UNGPs).[194] In addition, the UN Human Rights Council has created a Working

---

[188] Art 10, UN Convention against Transnational Organised Crime; Art 22(3) Council of Europe Convention; and Art 5 Directive 2011/36/EU.

[189] S Schuman, 'Corporate Criminal Liability on Human Trafficking' in J Winterdyk and J Jones (eds), *The Palgrave International Handbook of Human Trafficking* (London, Palgrave Macmillan, 2020) 4–5.

[190] UN General Assembly, *Report of the Special Rapporteur on trafficking in persons, especially women and children*, A/74/189, 18 July 2019, para 18.

[191] Such condemnations may nevertheless be recognised by national courts. As an example, the *Carestel* case judged in Belgium, can be quoted. The Correctional Tribunal of Ghent convicted both the firm Carestel (the main contractor), which manages restaurants located in motorway service areas, and the firm Kronos (the sub-contractor) specialised in cleaning toilets. For the judges, the workers employed by the sub-contractor were victims of trafficking in human beings and the sub-contractor was found guilty of trafficking in human beings, with the aggravating circumstance of abusing the vulnerability of the workers. The originality of this case lies in the conviction of the main contractor as an accomplice. See Corr Division Gand, 19th Ch, 21 August 2014 (definitive).

[192] Adoption in 2008 of the 'Protect, Respect, Remedy' Framework; and adoption in 2011 of the UN Guiding Principles on Business and Human Rights, both resulting from the appointment and the work carried out by the UN Special Representative of the Secretary-General who was especially in charge of the issue of Human Rights and Transnational Corporations and Other Business Enterprises.

[193] The Athens Ethical Principles are the following: policy setting; public awareness raising; strategic planning; personnel policy enforcement; supply chain tracing; government advocacy and transparency. The Luxor Protocol, which includes implementation guidelines, has later complemented them. These principles have been criticised because of their focus on responsibilities down the supply chain and the absence of responsibility for the corporations' own activities. For a more detailed analysis of these principles, see N Jägers and C Rijken, 'Prevention of Human Trafficking for Labour Exploitation: The Role of Corporations' (2014) 12(1) *Northwestern Journal of International Human Rights* 47, 60.

[194] United Nations, Guiding Principles on Business and Human Rights Implementing the UN 'Protect, Respect and Remedy' Framework (2011).

Group tasked with the preparation of an international legally binding instrument,[195] which shall notably provide for the liability of natural and legal persons for violations of human rights undertaken in the context of business activities.[196] Regional actors also participate in such efforts. The EU has for instance discussed and promoted UNGPs within its human rights dialogues with third countries, and insisted on their importance also for its own Member States.[197] Although these efforts address human rights violations in a broad sense, they are relevant to prevent and combat trafficking in human beings, the latter being a potential form of human rights violations. These efforts further echo those developed on the issues of ethical or sustainable supply chains and the tools developed in this framework.[198]

Business actors have also launched their own initiatives and participate in private–public partnerships. As an example of a business-led initiative, the Global Business Coalition against Human Trafficking can be mentioned, which aims to improve the understanding of trafficking and to raise awareness in high-risk sectors, for instance the awareness of sex trafficking in travel and tourism.[199] It also promotes best practices and fosters connections between businesses and the other actors active in addressing human trafficking.[200] A European Business Coalition against trafficking in human beings, established in 2014, has been seen as a privileged framework to develop models and guidelines about reducing the demand for services provided by victims of trafficking in human beings, in particular in high-risk areas.[201] However, its concrete results are difficult to ascertain. Similarly, business associations, such as the International Organisation of Employers, develop their own guides and tools to promote the identification of exploitative situations and ways to address them.[202] Such initiatives are developed in the framework of public–private partnerships, such as the UN Global Compact supporting companies committed to uphold 10 principles, derived from international instruments and including the elimination of all forms of forced and compulsory labour.[203]

Finally, legitimate businesses may also be unwillingly involved in trafficking cases, for instance as a means to cover or launder the proceeds of trafficking. In such situations, credit and financial institutions can, on the basis of anti-money laundering legislation, contribute to the detection and identification of suspicious

---

[195] Resolution 26/9, Elaboration of an international legally binding instrument on transnational corporations and other business enterprises with respect to human rights, A/HRC/RES/26/9.

[196] Revised draft of 16 July 2019, Art 6.

[197] European Union, *Annual Report on Human Rights and Democracy in the World 2018*, Council Doc No 9024/19, 70–71.

[198] See eg, S Carpenter, 'Developing effective programmes to protect modern corporate supply chains against human trafficking and slavery' (2020) 2(3) *Journal of Supply Chain Management, Logistics and Procurement*, 233; or M O'Neil, 'International Business Encounters Organized Crime: The Case of Trafficking in Human Beings' (2018) 19 *German Law Journal* 1125.

[199] For more information see: gbcat.org/.

[200] Source: gbcat.org/#about.

[201] Commission, 'The EU Strategy towards the Eradication of Trafficking in Human Beings, 2012–2016' (n 33) 8.

[202] See as an example of the IOE's activities: IOE, *Employers' Guide to Forced Labour* (2010).

[203] UN Global Compact website: www.unglobalcompact.org/.

money flows, potentially linked to human trafficking cases. Their contribution is crucial to foster the development of financial investigations, promoted by most of the international and regional organisations as a key tool to diminish the financial attractiveness of human trafficking. Companies may also build on these obligations to develop actions specifically targeting trafficking in human beings. By way of example, the Bankers' Alliance against Human Trafficking, an initiative launched in the US, published a list of indicators enabling the identification of transactions potentially linked to trafficking in human beings.[204] A European Bankers Alliance was launched in June 2015, with the support of Europol, with the aim of developing 'red flag indicators' to scan banks' systems for suspicious transactions.[205] Banks can also cooperate closely with national authorities in charge of tracing the criminal assets earned by traffickers, and transferred to another country.[206] These initiatives are invaluable resources for criminal justice actors, and it is not limited to the financial sector. Other companies, such as those working in the hotel and tourism sector, may also be unwillingly involved in trafficking situations. Hotels are, for instance, particularly likely to be used for prostitution and hence sexual exploitation purposes. With the development of the 'secret prostitution sector', the modus operandi of the perpetrators change: they advertise sexual services online and arrange meetings in rented accommodation, directly at the clients' place or in more anonymous hotel rooms. In the latter case, hotel staff can detect suspicious situations and refer the case to law enforcement authorities.[207]

Although neither civil society organisations nor businesses are responsible for adopting or monitoring the implementation of standards, their involvement in counter-trafficking efforts at national, regional and global levels is essential. They are fully integrated in the multilevel and diverse governance framework aimed at addressing trafficking in human beings, and they can bring their own expertise, knowledge and practices to the preparation of policies that are best suited to address trafficking in human beings in all its complexities. However, their involvement and their collaboration could even be reinforced. Voluntary initiatives by businesses could for instance establish more effective mechanisms, not only to identify situations of trafficking, but also enable workers and their representative unions to access grievance mechanisms.[208] Furthermore, despite their numerous actions and contributions to countering trafficking in persons, they do not outshine the remaining importance of States.

---

[204] Presentation of B Koch, Senior Vice President, Chief Compliance Officer, on behalf of the Bankers' Alliance against Human Trafficking, 'White Paper Offers Guidance to Financial Institutions, Law Enforcement Agencies in Identifying Financial Transactions Linked to Human Trafficking', Vienna, February 2014, slides available at: www.osce.org/cthb/115618?download=true.

[205] Source: www.trust.org/item/20150609123650-dh91k/.

[206] Eurojust, *Strategic Project on Eurojust's Action against Trafficking in Human Beings – Final Report and Action Plan* (2012) 24.

[207] ibid 18. See for instance, the initiatives conducted in the Netherlands, or in the UK. (For a concrete example illustrating the impact of trainings: www.thisiswiltshire.co.uk/news/10927536. Gang_of_traffickers_used_town_hotel/?ref=rss.)

[208] UNGA, *Report of the Special Rapporteur on trafficking in persons* (n 190) paras 74–76.

C. A Tapestry Incomplete without Mentioning States

The analysis of the multilevel tapestry of actors involved in counter-trafficking efforts would not be complete without considering the importance of the actions undertaken by States.

The actions they conduct within their own territory are crucial for the transformation of international and European standards into well-established practices. States remain the primary players responsible for the implementation of these standards and they possess a certain margin of discretion to design their national counter-trafficking policy and legislation. It is for instance essential in this regard that their national actions extend beyond the mere copying of international and European obligations into their national legislation. To that end, they report to the diverse monitoring bodies that have been set up and receive recommendations whenever weak points and/or gaps are identified in their counter-trafficking efforts. The decisions taken by national authorities carry important weight. Political decisions taken at national level can influence the context in which counter-trafficking efforts will be conducted. For instance, the decision to grant to labour inspectorates the competence to inspect high-risk work locations can improve the detection of trafficking for the purpose of labour exploitation. Decisions of national authorities can also influence the success of counter-trafficking efforts in concrete cases. For instance, giving residence permits to trafficking victims may encourage them to collaborate with criminal proceedings, and thus lead to the conviction of suspected traffickers. Moreover, within their budgetary power national governments take decisions concerning the funding of public authorities, ie, law enforcement authorities, judicial authorities, social inspectorates etc, which are in charge of ensuring the effective implementation of and respect for counter-trafficking legislation, detecting and identifying victims and prosecuting traffickers. Some States also sometimes attribute funds to civil society organisations, especially when they delegate to them the tasks of assisting trafficking victims.

Their actions are also crucial when they develop their own external policy, and act on the international stage. As parties to major international and regional instruments, they are involved in their drafting, implementation and monitoring, and the content of these instruments often reflect their own views and priorities in addressing trafficking in human beings. More importantly, States play an essential role in the provision of adequate funding to counter-trafficking activities. Despite the evolution of the multilateral scene and the emergence of new actors, States remain in a dominant position when it comes to funding, starting with the financial support they provide to multilateral intergovernmental organisations.[209] Although some global companies contribute to the funding of counter-trafficking activities on an ad hoc basis, their contributions remain relatively modest when

---

[209] eg, budget of UNODC and the UN Voluntary Trust Fund.

compared with the contributions of States.[210] Furthermore, States possess distinct advantages when it comes to funding: they have their own resources, which they can use not only to fund counter-trafficking activities in their own territory, but also to fund such activities abroad or to fund international initiatives.

In relation to the funding of activities conducted abroad, certain States have an interest in funding counter-trafficking activities outside their national territory. Their ratification of international instruments or their support to the efforts of international and regional organisations do not prevent them from developing external actions on their own. They engage in bilateral and multilateral actions with other States[211] and some develop an ambitious external policy addressing trafficking in human beings outside their national borders. The US Department of State has, for instance, created an Office to Monitor and Combat Trafficking in Persons, which supervises the publication of the annual Trafficking in Persons Report, in which the efforts of each country to comply with the minimum standards for the elimination of trafficking[212] are evaluated.[213] This Office also manages the 'International Grants Programmes', a foreign assistance programme dedicated solely to combating human trafficking outside the US.[214] European States, whether EU Member States or not, have also developed similar counter-trafficking programmes in the framework of their external policy. These programmes are often foreseeing the long-term funding of specific counter-trafficking projects in third countries.[215] The Swiss Agency for Development and Cooperation is, for instance, particularly involved in tackling human trafficking in Eastern Europe and the South Caucasus, notably through the strengthening of regional networks,

---

[210] Contribution to some initiatives, such as the business coalition against trafficking in human beings or subscription to programmes to clear production chains from trafficking.

[211] See ch 2, III.C 'Agreements Concluded by the EU Member States'.

[212] These standards have been autonomously defined by the US legislator and consist of measures that national governments ought to have taken. Although no reference is made to international instruments, the measures contained therein correspond in substance to obligations stemming for instance from the UN Trafficking Protocol. A detailed version of the minimum standards is available at: www. state.gov/j/tip/rls/tiprpt/2011/164236.htm.

[213] The evaluation carried out determines the ranking of each country into one of the three tiers. A Tier 1 ranking indicates that a government has acknowledged the existence of human trafficking, made efforts to address the problem, and complies with the TVPA's minimum standards. Seventeen EU Member States are included in the Tier 1, but 10 are included in Tier 2 (BU, Croatia, Estonia, Greece, Hungary, Latvia, Lithuania, Malta, Portugal and Romania) and one in Tier 2 watch list (Cyprus). Armenia, Israel and FYROM are included in Tier 2, most of the SAA and ENP countries are in Tier 2, and Belarus, Bosnia–Herzegovina and Ukraine are in Tier 2 watch list.

[214] Additional funding is provided through the Programme 'Counter-trafficking in persons' of the US Agency for International Development (US Aid), under which $180 million has been attributed to more than 68 countries between 2001 and 2011. US Aid notably supported the development of transnational referral mechanism guidelines and standard operating procedures in Eastern Europe. (US Aid, *C-TIP Annual Review 2011–2012*, 6, available at: www.usaid.gov/sites/default/files/documents/1866/CTIP%20Annual%20Review%202012%209-11-13.pdf.

[215] They differ on that point from the actions of the EU Member States, mentioned in the previous chapter, which consist mainly of the conclusion of bilateral cooperation agreements and the conduct of occasional projects.

organisations and key players.[216] The Norwegian Ministry of Foreign Affairs has also developed a specific programme with the aim of supporting the fight against human trafficking,[217] in particular in the Western Balkans.[218]

Moreover, States play an essential role in financially supporting international and regional organisations active in the fight against trafficking in human beings. The Brussels Declaration of 2002 provided very explicitly that 'governments should ensure that all international organisations and intergovernmental organisations that play a significant role in the fight against trafficking have adequate resources to fulfil their mandate'.[219] For instance, States contribute voluntarily to certain global initiatives together with private companies, such the UN.GIFT[220] or the UN Voluntary Fund for Victims of Trafficking.[221] EU Member States can also fund certain activities to be carried out 'within the European Union's framework', meaning that they will rely on priorities and actions agreed upon between themselves and the EU institutions. France has for instance developed a specific strategic programme focusing on combating trafficking in human beings and related crime in south-east Europe, supported by a budget of around €350,000, and integrating coordinated initiatives with partner countries, civil society and international organisations.[222]

Funding from States thus appears crucial for supporting counter-trafficking activities, both within their own territories, and abroad. Nevertheless, countries benefiting from the financial assistance of other States should not rely too extensively on this support, and they must try to find within their own resources the budget for financing their own counter-trafficking activities in a sustainable way. They are indeed at risk of witnessing the suspension of the financial support they

---

[216] Source: www.eda.admin.ch/deza/en/home/themes-sdc/migration/human-trafficking.html.

[217] Norwegian Agency for Development, *Review of the Norwegian Ministry of Foreign Affairs Portfolio on Human Trafficking*, Norad rapport 9/2009 Discussion (2009) 5.

[218] 'Europe is by far the largest region in terms of funding and receives NOK 115.3 million (52%) of the total allocation for the period. Bosnia and Herzegovina is the largest single recipient country, and receives NOK 31.7 million (14%). Other major recipients are Albania and Macedonia. NOK 58.8 million (26.7%) has been allocated to Asia and NOK 47.9 million (21.7%) to Africa. The Southern African Counter-Trafficking Assistance Programme under the auspices of the IOM receives almost NOK 30 million of the total NOK 47.9 million to Africa', ibid 8.

[219] Brussels Declaration (n 36) 3–4.

[220] The UN.GIFT initiative is funded through 'a grant of the United Arab Emirates and has since received additional financial support from the Governments of Australia, Austria, Belgium, Canada, Switzerland as well as UNICEF, the United Nations Development Fund for Women (UNIFEM), the United Nations Development Programme (UNDP), the United Nations Fund for International Partnerships and public donations'. Source: www.ungift.org/knowledgehub/en/about/index.html.

[221] 'As of October 2013, the Fund received US$ 1.5 million in contributions from a wide range of supporters. These include 16 Member States, 12 private sector organisations and 12 individual donors. Orascom Telecom Holding, Qatar, Australia, France and the UAE are the five largest contributors to the Trust Fund'. Source: www.unodc.org/documents/human-trafficking/Human-Trafficking-Fund/UN_Victims_Trust_Fund_Basic_Facts_Oct2013.pdf.

[222] France, 2019 Programme for the French Strategic Cooperation in South-East Europe against Trafficking in Human Beings, and Activity Report for 2018, available at: onu-vienne.delegfrance.org/La-lutte-contre-la-traite-des-etres-humains-en-Europe-du-sud-est.

receive from abroad. The geographical focus of the national support programmes may shift to another region, or to other countries. This change can be explained by the fact that past support programmes achieved their objectives and led to the development of national counter-trafficking policies and/or the adoption of national legislation. Other actors may also have stepped in to strengthen and financially support counter-trafficking national activities. More pragmatically, budgetary constraints may push States to terminate their financial support to counter-trafficking initiatives or actors.

D. Conclusion

The identification of the relevant actors active in combating trafficking in human beings reveals a complex and multilevel tapestry, composed of traditional multilateral actors, such as States and intergovernmental organisations, and modern multilateral actors, such as private actors. These actors are often responsible for ensuring the implementation of the numerous instruments adopted at international and regional levels, with direct or indirect links with human trafficking. Many organisations have found within their mandates a basis to address human trafficking, either by focusing on one of its aspects, or on one type of measure, or by addressing it comprehensively. Close attention is paid to the implementation of the standards contained in international and regional binding instruments, as is clear from the existence of diverse monitoring mechanisms, whose power and binding force vary considerably. The instruments prepared by the different organisations within their own legal framework all coexist, and when States ratify more than one of them, they apply simultaneously within national legal orders. Legal pluralism is thus a reality in the field of the fight against trafficking in human beings.

However, despite these efforts at international, regional and national level, trafficking in human beings still affects hundreds and even thousands of victims worldwide. Given the multifaceted nature of trafficking in human beings and its scale, its victims are difficult to detect and identify. Moreover, shortcomings in terms of the prosecution and conviction of traffickers have meant that the attractiveness of the crime does not diminish, and victims are not being awarded fair compensation for the damages that they suffer. Given these remaining difficulties, increasing awareness about this phenomenon at all levels of governance is welcome as is the adoption of instruments addressing modern forms of trafficking. Furthermore, the involvement of a more diverse group of actors is essential to help address the issue in a comprehensive manner as they will contribute to the counter-trafficking effort with their specific competences and expertise. They are essential for the implementation of a comprehensive approach, which will be more likely to lead to the effective and long-term eradication of trafficking in human beings. The punishment of criminals involved in human trafficking helps reduce its attractiveness and its perception as a highly lucrative/low-risk activity. Protection and assistance given to victims are crucial to avoid future vulnerability and the risk of their ending up in trafficking situations again. Prevention, especially the initiatives tackling the root causes of trafficking, is also key for the long-term eradication of the phenomenon. Cross-border cooperation in all these matters is also of great importance as this enables trafficking chains in more than one country to be disrupted. In practice, the more the actors involved have different competences, the more trafficking in human beings can be combated in a comprehensive way and the more it can be eradicated in the long term.

Yet the complex and intertwined relations between the different actors and/or instruments are not exempt from risks of overlaps, first between instruments, which can potentially lead to conflicts of norms and/or incompatible obligations imposed on States, and second between the actions developed by each actor, on the basis of its competences and expertise, which may result in the duplication of counter-trafficking efforts. This would be for instance the case if more than one actor decided to financially support the same counter-trafficking activity, for example, the conduct of an awareness raising campaign towards vulnerable women, or the conduct of a study on national policy, in the same country.

However, the risks of overlaps are to be mitigated. The abundance of instruments does not constitute an obstacle to the establishment of a legal framework in the field of the fight against trafficking in human beings, in which compatible provisions can be found in the various instruments. Nor does the abundance of actors constitute an obstacle for the development of mechanisms aimed at providing insurance that unnecessary duplication of effort will be avoided to the maximum extent. Two elements are indeed essential to achieve these two aims: on the one hand through interactions, the relevant actors may develop a legal framework deprived of such conflicts of law, in which the instruments pursue compatible objectives, and provide for compatible obligations (III). On the other hand, the creation of 'coordination mechanisms' may allow for the development of synergies (IV).

IV. Normative Interactions:
The EU as a Norm-Taker or a Norm-Setter?

Faced with the challenge of dealing with a transnational phenomenon like trafficking in human beings, national governments soon realised that national measures would not be sufficient and recognised the importance of joint measures taken at international and regional levels. In the late 1990s, a consensus emerged about the need to develop and adopt common standards and objectives both at international and regional level. Policy recommendations and resolutions turned into the adoption of numerous legally binding instruments within the frameworks of the UN, the EU and the Council of Europe. Each of these instruments reflect the mandates of each organisation as well as the evolution over time of their approach towards trafficking in human beings. They are further complemented by the numerous action plans, global compacts and other soft law texts, determining the strategic objectives and priorities to be implemented. This abundance of norms and instruments should not be disregarded as it can play a major role in the development of comprehensive counter-trafficking efforts at all levels of governance. Nevertheless, the plethora of actors and the dynamism with which they adopt action plans and instruments potentially generate disorder. It is therefore crucial to avoid any contradiction or conflict between the objectives pursued by the relevant actors as well as between the obligations binding the States parties.

The following section will thus be devoted to the analysis of normative interactions in the field of trafficking in human beings. Our objective will be twofold. It will first consist of assessing the strength of these interactions and the extent to which they have led to the development of compatible, or even harmonised, objectives and standards. Our analysis focuses on the legal instruments adopted at international level and those adopted at regional level, more particularly on those adopted by the EU and the Council of Europe. When relevant, policy documents will also be analysed. Our second objective refers to the overall purpose of this book, which is to analyse the external dimension of the EU's policy against trafficking in human beings and the promotion of its policy. We will thus address the role played by the EU in this regard, as its interactions with its counterparts may lead to a two-way dialogue. The EU can build on standards adopted outside the EU framework to develop internal instruments and it can promote its own objectives and standards in other legal frameworks. Such reciprocal influence contributes towards the promotion of standards compatible, if not similar, to the EU acquis towards third countries and international organisations. Some countries indeed become parties to European and international instruments, while at the time they are being targeted by the EU's efforts to externally promote its own policy. In cases where reciprocal influences led to the adoption of 'harmonised standards', these countries will, in the framework of their implementation of European and international standards, have already implemented objectives and norms close to those promoted by the EU.

To answer to these two questions, our analysis will focus on two main elements: first, the presence of an approach and objectives shared by the relevant actors (A); and second, the degree of harmonisation between the standards contained in the relevant instruments (B).

A. Interactions Leading to a Common Approach and Objectives

The analysis of reciprocal influences between the EU, and other intergovernmental organisations active in combating trafficking in human beings in Europe, is particularly relevant in order to determine whether they can lead to a certain degree of harmonisation of their policies against trafficking in human beings.

Our analysis will start with an examination of the approach that these organisations consider best suited to address trafficking in human beings. Our analysis will then focus on the objectives they intend to pursue, as these objectives guide the content of their counter-trafficking activities. Only policy documents dealing directly with trafficking in human beings will be scrutinised.

i. Consensus in Favour of a Comprehensive Approach

Although each organisation possesses a specific mandate and specific competences, potentially limiting the activities that it can carry out to tackle human trafficking, our analysis reveals the existence of a consensus on the need to implement a comprehensive approach. The term 'comprehensive' can be defined as 'including or dealing with all or nearly all elements or aspects of something'.[223] In the context of counter-trafficking instruments, the use of this term can be perceived as indicating the will of these organisations to address all aspects of human trafficking at once, not limiting themselves to one of its dimensions only or to one type of counter-trafficking measure.

The origins of the 'comprehensive approach' to tackle trafficking in human beings cannot easily be attributed to one organisation or another. If the first instruments dealing with trafficking in human beings placed an emphasis on the prosecution of traffickers, policy documents adopted by the international community were stating the importance of a multidisciplinary and coordinated approach.[224] In the Brussels Declaration, the international community was called upon to 'provide an unambiguous and comprehensive response'.[225]

The importance of taking into account the protection of the human rights of victims of trafficking was also highlighted by the OHCHR its *Recommended Principles and Guidelines on Human Rights and Human Trafficking*.[226] Within the Council of Europe, a recommendation adopted by the Committee of Ministers also invited States to review their legislation and practice through the introduction of measures to prevent trafficking, to assist and protect the victims, to investigate and prosecute the traffickers as well as to coordinate and cooperate at national and international levels in the fight against trafficking.[227] In the OSCE's Action Plan of 2003, mention was also made of a comprehensive approach to trafficking in human beings, requiring 'a focus on bringing to justice those responsible

---

[223] *Oxford English Dictionary* (online version) para 1.

[224] See Conclusions of the European Commission Conference held in Vienna in June 1996, quoted in Commission, 'Communication on trafficking in women for the purpose of sexual exploitation', COM (1996) 567 final, 7.

[225] Brussels Declaration (n 36) 3.

[226] Text presented to the Economic and Social Council as an addendum to the report of the United Nations High Commissioner for Human Rights (E/2002/68/Add. 1).

[227] Committee of Ministers, Recommendation on action against trafficking in human beings for the purpose of sexual exploitation, 19 May 2000, Recommendation No R (2000) 11, Preamble.

for this crime, and on carrying out effective measures to prevent it, while maintaining a humanitarian and compassionate approach in rendering assistance to its victims'.[228] The EU joined the movement in the mid-2000s, and a comprehensive approach was first advocated by the EU Experts Group[229] and later by the EU institutions themselves.[230] These documents are of different political and legal value but they illustrate how a consensus emerged. This consensus can be evidenced, although these organisations do not replicate an identical formula in their respective documents. The consensus is subtler, as each organisation formulates similar ideas, yet in its own words.

Since then the consensus in favour of such a comprehensive approach has never disappeared. At international level, the UN General Assembly clearly proclaims, in its Global Action Plan, the need to 'promote comprehensive, coordinated and consistent responses, at national, regional and international levels, to counter trafficking in persons'.[231] Similarly, UNODC's Strategy on trafficking in human beings provides that 'a multi-faceted and comprehensive approach' is required.[232] At regional level, when the OSCE's Action Plan refers to the adoption of 'a multidimensional approach to combatting trafficking in human beings' and intends to address the problem 'comprehensively',[233] the Council of Europe Convention proclaims its intention to be 'a comprehensive international legal instrument'.[234] The EU institutions also support a similar approach, although it is labelled differently as a 'multidisciplinary, holistic and integrated approach'.[235] It thus appears that there is a certain degree of harmonisation in the approach to be implemented in order to tackle human trafficking.

B. Consensus About the Objectives to be Pursued

Each intergovernmental organisation also defines general objectives that it intends to pursue and, when comparing these objectives, a certain degree of harmonisation

---

[228] OSCE, Permanent Council, 'Action Plan to Combat Trafficking in Human Beings', Decision No 557, 24 July 2003, Doc PC.DEC/557, Annex, 1.

[229] Commission, *Report of the Experts Group on Trafficking in Human Beings*, 22 December 2004, 9.

[230] Commission, 'Fighting trafficking in human beings: an integrated approach and proposals for an action plan' (Communication), COM (2005) 514 final, Introduction. Council, 'EU Plan on best practices, standards and procedures for combating and preventing trafficking in human beings' [2005] OJ C311/1. European Parliament, Resolution on strategies to prevent the trafficking of women and children who are vulnerable to sexual exploitation [2006] OJ C287/75.

[231] UN General Assembly, *Global Action Plan to Combat Trafficking in Persons* (n 39) 4.

[232] UNODC, *A Comprehensive Strategy to Combat Trafficking in Persons and Smuggling of Migrants* (2012) 7.

[233] OSCE, Permanent Council, 'Action Plan to Combat Trafficking in Human Beings' (n 228) Annex, 1.

[234] Council of Europe, Convention on Action against Trafficking in Human Beings, CETS No197, 16 May 2005, Preamble, last paragraph.

[235] Reference to this approach can be found in the Preamble of the main EU internal instrument, Directive 2011/36/EU. Similar wording has been employed by the Council (see for instance, Council, 'EU Plan on best practices, standards and procedures for combating and preventing trafficking in human beings' [2005] OJ C311/1); the European Council (Council, 'The Stockholm Programme'

can be observed. The objectives proclaimed are often, if not always, the prevention of trafficking in human beings, the prosecution of the traffickers and the protection and assistance of victims of trafficking. Usually referred to as the 'Three Ps', these objectives are present in all policy documents selected, albeit with different wording.[236] The measures provided for in order to attain these consensual objectives can be summarised as follows:

- **Prevention of trafficking in human beings**: this objective aims at addressing varied and complex root causes, such as globalisation, poverty, lack of opportunities or demand for cheap labour or sexual services, which contribute to the creation and the persistence of a political, social and economic context that is favourable to trafficking in human beings. The pursuit of this objective encompasses different elements. Research is essential to obtain information on the scale of trafficking and its trends and to adapt, if necessary, national, regional and international responses. Awareness-raising activities are also important, for instance to inform vulnerable people about the risks and dangers of trafficking or to inform the general public about the importance of reporting suspicious situations. Training public authorities and capacity building complement these activities, for instance by ensuring that victims of trafficking are better detected and identified and that they receive a treatment respecting their fundamental rights.[237]

- **Prosecution of criminals**: this objective refers to criminal justice measures targeting the perpetrators of the crime of trafficking in human beings. It encompasses the conduct of investigations and prosecutions in accordance with modern investigative techniques, leading, when there is sufficient evidence of their guilt, to their conviction and to the confiscation, freezing and seizure of their criminal assets. To achieve that objective, the criminal legal framework ought to be developed at national, regional and international level, notably to facilitate cross-border cooperation between competent authorities. Furthermore, given the importance of victims' testimonies as evidence in trafficking cases, measures to improve their standing in criminal proceedings are to be adopted in the implementation of this objective.[238]

(n 25) s 4.4.2); or the European Parliament (European Parliament, Resolution on strategies to prevent the trafficking of women and children who are vulnerable to sexual exploitation (n 230)).

[236] The 'Three Ps' objectives are mentioned in Art 2(a) and (b) UN Trafficking Protocol; in para 3 of the OSCE Action Plan; in Art 1 para 1(a) and b) of the Council of Europe Convention; and in Art 1 of Directive 2011/36/EU.

[237] Prevention measures are provided for in Title III of the UN Trafficking Protocol (research, information and mass-media campaigns, border and documents safety measures); in Title IV of the OSCE's Action Plan (data collection and research, border measures, policies addressing root causes, awareness raising); in Chapter 2 of the Council of Europe Convention (research, information campaigns, measures to discourage demand, border measures, and documents safety); and in Art 18 Directive 2011/36/EU (education and training, awareness raising campaigns, criminalisation of the use of services which are the objects of exploitation).

[238] Prosecution measures are foreseen in Arts 5 and 10 of the UN trafficking Protocol, complemented by those provided for in the Convention against Transnational Organised Crime (criminalisation and

- **Protection and assistance to the victims**: this objective refers to the need to ensure the protection of the safety of the victims of trafficking as well as respect for their human rights. It encompasses measures such as assistance for their physical and psychological recovery, social and legal assistance and their right to obtain compensation for the damages suffered. These measures often correspond to the implementation of obligations that States have under international human rights law and they ought to be provided to trafficking victims regardless of their willingness or capacity to testify against their traffickers.[239]

Although it has been developed more recently and it is not always mentioned explicitly in the documents analysed, an additional objective, which could be designated as the 'Fourth P' standing for 'Partnership', deserves to be presented here as it reflects the parallel evolutions of each organisation's policy.[240] In substance, all these documents refer to the importance of developing measures favouring cooperation and coordination measures. This objective relates first to partnerships within a State, especially between public authorities and civil society organisations and/or businesses. Second, it encompasses cooperation among States, for instance in the prosecution of cross-border trafficking cases, the exchange of best practices or to ensure the safety of a victim who chooses to come back to his/her country of origin. Finally, it includes cooperation between international and regional organisations as well as cooperation with their partners (civil society organisations etc).[241]

---

exchange of information); in Title III of the OSCE's Action Plan (criminalisation, law enforcement response, law enforcement cooperation and information exchange, assistance and protection of witnesses and victims in criminal proceedings, training, etc); in Chapters IV and V of the Council of Europe Convention (criminalisation, sanctions, liability for moral persons, protection of victims, witnesses and persons collaborating with judicial authorities, etc); and in Arts 2–11 Directive 2011/36/EU (criminalisation, sanctions, jurisdiction, etc); and all measures adopted within the EU area of criminal justice.

[239] Protection measures are provided for in Title II of the UN Trafficking Protocol (legal assistance, measures for the physical, psychological and social recovery of victims, status and right to reside and repatriation); in Title V of the OSCE's Action Plan (data collection and research, national referral mechanisms, shelters, provision of documents and social assistance, repatriation, rehabilitation and reintegration, reflection delay and temporary or permanent residence, etc); in Chapter III of the Council of Europe Convention (identification, social, medical and legal assistance, recovery and reflection period, residence permit, compensation, repatriation); and in Arts 11–17 Directive 2011/36/EU (identification, assistance, special needs of child victims, compensation, etc); and in other EU instruments (Directive 2004/81/EC on residence permits, Directive on the rights of victims of crime, etc).

[240] The Fourth 'P' (Partnership, as a synonym for international cooperation) can be found in Art 2(c) UN Trafficking Protocol and in Art 1 para 1(c) of the Council of Europe Convention. The OSCE's Action Plan mentions it in VI point 8 (the tasks of OSCE institutions and bodies include 'engaging in more extensive regular exchange of information, data collection and research with the relevant international organisations'). The EU Directive several times mentions cooperation between law enforcement authorities (Preamble, para 5 and para 15); or between public authorities and civil society organisations (Art 18 for prevention activities, Art 19 cooperation with national rapporteurs). It refers to cooperation between organisations expressly in its Preamble (para 9), and in Art 11, para 4 on Assistance and Protection for Victims.

[241] Measures encouraging cooperation are present in Title of the UN Convention against transnational organised crime; in Title VI of the OSCE's Action Plan (national rapporteurs, bodies responsible for coordinating activities within a country, for OSCE institutions and bodies with engaging in more

The similarities in the objectives to be pursued as well as in the measures envisaged for their implementation constitute a first and solid indication of the existence of interactions between international and regional intergovernmental organisations. There is no doubt that these similarities facilitate the elaboration of coherent counter-trafficking policies at international and regional levels, and thus at national level. However, a shared understanding about the approach to be followed and the objectives to be pursued is a preliminary step towards the absence of conflicts of norms and it is necessary to analyse the obligations provided for in the legal instruments.

C. Interactions Leading to Consistent Standards

Many instruments relating to trafficking in human beings have been adopted at international and regional levels, and to favour their implementation, it is crucial that they contain norms that are compatible with each other. Given its scope, our study will only concern the interactions between intergovernmental organisations which have adopted binding instruments directly relating to trafficking in human beings. The following section will thus be devoted to the review of three instruments adopted in this field, binding on European States, being EU Member States and neighbouring countries.

The Protocol against Trafficking in Persons, attached to the UN Convention against Transnational Organised Crime (the UN Protocol),[242] is the first instrument on the list as it constitutes the framework for international action against trafficking in persons and has guided both the normative and policy responses to this crime.[243] The next is the Council of Europe Convention on Action against Trafficking in Human Beings. This Convention is important as it aims at being a comprehensive international legal instrument focusing on the human rights of victims of trafficking. It is of key importance as it has been ratified and implemented by many European States that are not yet members of the EU and often serves as a basis for their cooperation with EU Member States. Finally, Directive 2011/36/EU (EU Directive) must be included as it is the core instrument of the EU's counter-trafficking acquis, whose content is promoted externally to third countries.[244] When relevant, reference to the case law of the ECtHR will be integrated.

---

extensive regular exchange of information, data collection and research with relevant international organisations]; in Chapter VI of the Council of Europe Convention (international cooperation, cooperation with civil society); and in Arts 19 and 20 Directive 2011/36/EU (national rapporteurs, coordination of the Union Strategy); and in the EU strategy (Priority D Enhanced coordination and cooperation among key actors and policy coherence).

[242] UN Trafficking Protocol (n 47).

[243] UNODC, *A Comprehensive Strategy to Combat Trafficking in Persons and Smuggling of Migrants* (2012) 7.

[244] Other instruments belonging to the EU's counter-trafficking acquis, such as Directive 2004/81/EC, would also be mentioned but only incidentally.

While our analysis will highlight the similarities between these instruments, our intention is not to deny that they each have their own specific characteristics. First, the context of their adoption has influenced the content of their provisions. Whereas the UN Protocol was adopted in the early days of the international counter-trafficking response and foresees mostly criminal justice measures, the Council of Europe Convention and the EU Directive were adopted later. Human rights advocates were able to voice their concerns about the insufficient attention granted to prevention and protection of victims and to support a human rights-based approach.[245] New forms of exploitation have also emerged, requiring a change in the definition of the offence of trafficking in human beings to encompass these modern forms of trafficking. Second, these instruments have been adopted within different legal frameworks and these disparities influence the degree of detail and the content of the provisions they contain.[246] Nevertheless, these differences do not prevent normative interactions leading to compatible obligations in all three instruments.

To demonstrate the impact of these interactions, our analysis will focus on two representative examples. On the one hand, we will study the definition of trafficking in human beings since it constitutes the basis of counter-trafficking efforts and a common definition is a prerequisite for cooperation and coordination (i). On the other hand, we will examine the clause referring to the non-prosecution of victims who are compelled to take part in criminal activities (ii).[247] This clause is representative of a human rights-based approach. It is also representative of the modern approach in the fight against trafficking in human beings since its application often implies close cooperation with civil society organisations.

i. Definition of the Offence of Trafficking in Human Beings

The UN Protocol contains, in its Article 3, a definition of the offence of trafficking in persons constituted of three cumulative elements, which are the conduct of an action, the use of coercive means and the pursuit of a purpose of exploitation. It has been quickly recognised as the first universally agreed definition of this phenomenon,[248] and such definition was copied into the Council of Europe

---

[245] T Obokata, 'A Human Rights Framework to address Trafficking in Human Beings' (2006) 24 *Netherlands Quarterly of Human Rights* 379, 380.

[246] For instance, the possibility to fix the level of sanctions to be imposed in convictions does not exist for the United Nations or the Council of Europe.

[247] For a more detailed analysis of the interactions between the different instruments, see A Weyembergh and C Brière, 'The European Union and the fight against trafficking in human beings', realised in the framework of the CooptoFight project (HOME-2010-ISEC-AG-54); and see also A Weyembergh and C Brière, 'L'Union européenne et la traite des êtres humains' in D Bernard et al (eds), *Fondements et objectifs des incriminations et des peines en droit européen et international* (Limal, Anthémis, 2013).

[248] A Gallagher, *The International Law of Human Trafficking*, 1st edn, (Cambridge, Cambridge University Press, 2010) 241–42 'the adoption of the trafficking protocol … was widely considered to be the final word on the long-standing impasse over an international legal definition of trafficking'.

Convention without any difference.[249] The EU Directive also follows the internationally agreed definition, provided for in the UN Trafficking Protocol, and also confirmed the 'three-way definition' of the offence of trafficking in human beings.[250] Other soft law instruments, such as the OSCE Action Plan of 2005,[251] also consistently refers to the definition provided for in the UN Protocol as the reference for understanding the phenomenon, and the ECtHR ruled that it is impossible to characterise a conduct or situation as an issue of human trafficking under Article 4 ECHR unless these three elements are present.[252] Yet this widespread acceptance of the definition does not prevent the existence of inconsistencies between the different instruments, nor does it prevent the existence of definitional ambiguity.[253] Following the three constitutive elements of the offence as defined in the Protocol, our analysis will review the similarities as well as the differences in the definition of trafficking provided for in these three instruments.

Regarding the first element, whereas the UN Protocol and the Council of Europe Convention refer only to the 'recruitment, transportation, transfer, harbouring or receipt of persons', without further defining these terms, the EU texts developed the definition of the first element of trafficking. The 2002 Framework Decision provided for an extended definition of the action, which remains mostly unchanged in the 2011 Directive. It refers to the 'recruitment, transportation, transfer, harbouring and subsequent reception of persons, including the exchange or transfer of control over those persons'.[254] These last elements – 'the exchange or transfer of control over those persons' – are specific to the EU definition and they allow, for instance, for the scope of application of the offence to be extended to modern techniques of recruitment, such as the 'lover boy' method.[255] This broad definition means that it is not just recruiters, intermediaries and transporters who can be included in the scope of this definition but also owners, managers, supervisors and controllers of any place of exploitation.[256] It is interesting to stress that

'The majority of States have enacted comprehensive anti-trafficking laws that generally reflect the internationally agreed definition.'

[249] Art 4(a) of the Convention.

[250] These elements were already present in the Framework Decision of 2002, to which the Directive only made 'minor changes'.

[251] OSCE, Permanent Council, OSCE 'Action Plan to Combat Trafficking in Human Beings' (n 228).

[252] *SM v Croatia* (n 148) para 303.

[253] UNODC, 'The International Legal Definition of Trafficking in Persons, Consolidation of research findings and reflection on issue raised', Issue Paper (2018) 10, available at: www.unodc.org/documents/human-trafficking/2018/Issue_Paper_International_Definition_TIP.pdf.

[254] The definition provided for in the Directive remains almost identical to the one contained in the Framework Decision. The English version of the text does not change as it includes in both texts 'exchange or transfer of control over that person'.

[255] See TRACE Project, 'Report in the relevant aspects of the trafficking act (geographical routes and modus operandi) and on its possible evolutions in response to law enforcement', Deliverable D2.1 (2015) 36.

[256] Its potential broad scope of application has been criticised by academics, who consider that for instance a person involved unknowingly in the transport aspect of a trafficking can be held liable for the whole offence. See H Satzger, F Zimmerman and G Langheld, 'The Directive on Preventing and Combatting Trafficking in Human Beings and the Principles Governing European Criminal Policy: A Critical Evaluation' (2013) 3 *European Criminal Law Review* 107.

a person may be prosecuted for trafficking in human beings, even if he or she becomes a trafficker accidentally (or unintentionally).[257] There is a debate, both in practice and in the literature, as to whether the definition of the action in the UN Protocol restricts it to cases in which a transnational movement is present[258] and/or involving an organised criminal group.[259] However, several elements, notably listed by the ECtHR,[260] support a broad interpretation of the action, allowing its application to cases of domestic trafficking and/or cases not involving an organised criminal group. The limited definitional scope of the Palermo Protocol seems thus relative.[261]

The definition of the means used constitutes the second constitutive element of the offence and once more the UN Protocol is the text to refer to. The means it lists, namely the use of constraint, force or threats; the use of deceit or fraud; the abuse of authority or a situation of vulnerability; and the giving or receiving of payments or advantages to obtain the consent of a person having control over another, are mentioned in the EU instruments[262] as well as in the Council of Europe Convention.[263] The three instruments also provide that, when the acts in questions concerning a child, ie, being 'any person below 18 years of age',[264] the offence of trafficking then exists independently of the use of the coercive means targeted.[265] The only difference that can be identified lies in the definition of 'position of vulnerability'. The Explanatory Report to the Council of Europe Convention details what is to be understood by the notion,[266] and UNODC has published an Issue Paper dedicated to the notion.[267] Yet only the EU's instruments have integrated the definition into the text and have thus given it a binding definition.[268]

As for the third and final constitutive element of the offence, ie, the purposes of exploitation, further differences can be identified. The UN Protocol and the Council of Europe Convention provide for the exact same purposes: 'at a minimum, the exploitation of the prostitution of others or other forms of sexual exploitation,

---

[257] TRACE Project, 'Final Report', Deliverable D6.5 (2016) 42.

[258] For an overview of such debate, see S Scarpa, 'UN Palermo Trafficking Protocol Eighteen Years On: A Critique' in J Winterdyk and J Jones (eds), *The Palgrave International Handbook of Human Trafficking* (London, Palgrave Macmillan, 2020) 631.

[259] See, eg, Council of Europe, *Explanatory Report to the Convention on Action against Trafficking in Human Beings* (2005) para 61.

[260] See eg, UNODC, 'Model Law against Trafficking in Persons' (2009) 8, referred to in *SM v Croatia* (n 148) para 111.

[261] ibid para 295.

[262] They were first mentioned in the Framework Decision of 2002 (Art 1, para 1 Framework Decision 2002/629/JHA); and then in Art 2, para 1 Directive 2011/36/EU.

[263] Art 4(a) Council of Europe Convention.

[264] Art 3(d) UN Trafficking Protocol; Art 1, para 4 Framework Decision; Art 4(d) Council of Europe Convention; and Art 2, para 6 Directive 2011/36/EU.

[265] Art 3(c) UN Trafficking Protocol; Art 1, para 3 Framework Decision; Art 49(c) Council of Europe Convention; and Art 2, para 5 Directive 2011/36/EU.

[266] Council of Europe, *Explanatory Report to the Convention* (n 259) para 83.

[267] UNDOC, 'Abuse of a position of vulnerability and other "means" within the definition of trafficking in persons', Issue Paper (2013).

[268] Art 1, para 1(c) Framework Decision 2002/629/JHA; and Art 2, para 2 Directive 2011/36/EU.

forced labour or services, slavery or practices similar to slavery, servitude or the removal of organs', without defining them further. By comparison, the EU legal framework provides for an identical albeit slightly more detailed list of purposes. The purpose of sexual exploitation explicitly includes pornography.[269] Trafficking for the purpose of labour exploitation refers to exploiting the work or services of people[270] and, since 2011, to forced begging. This phenomenon, which is growing in the Member States,[271] is explicitly mentioned as an example of forced services. The third purpose of exploitation, ie, the removal of organs, is mentioned both in the UN Protocol and in the Council of Europe Convention. It was not mentioned in the EU Framework Decision, but this purpose of exploitation was introduced into the EU legal framework in 2011.[272] In that regard, Directive 2011/36/EU has also introduced new purposes of exploitation, notably in order to reflect evolutions of the phenomenon observed in practice and to adopt the most modern possible definition of the phenomenon. The exploitation of the criminal activities of others[273] or the situations of illegal adoption or forced marriage[274] have been inserted as new purposes.[275] These differences have limited consequences. The absence of certain forms of exploitation from the UN Protocol and the Council of Europe Convention is not problematic. The Protocol and the Convention are living instruments, which means that they can be interpreted in a dynamic way,[276] in order to reflect the evolution of the phenomenon and to allow the recognition of 'additional' purposes of exploitation.[277] This is supported in documents accompanying the implementation of these instruments,[278] referring also to other international instruments.

[269] This element was introduced in the EU legal order with the adoption of the Framework Decision of 2002.

[270] Art 1, para 1 of the Framework Decision provides that these forms of exploitation include at least forced or compulsory labour or services, slavery and practices similar to slavery or servitude.

[271] Eurostat, 'Trafficking in human beings, Statistical Working Paper' (2013) 46, Table 5. See also Project report, 'Report for the study on typology and policy responses to child begging in the EU', JLS/2009/ISEC/PR/008-F2 (2012) 31.

[272] Art 2(3) Directive 2011/36/EU.

[273] This form of exploitation covers for instance situations in which people are forced to steal or to practise fraud in relation to welfare benefits.

[274] Directive 2011/36/EU, Preamble, Recital: 'as well as, for instance, other behaviour such as illegal adoption or forced marriage in so far as they fulfil the constitutive elements of trafficking in human beings'.

[275] ibid.

[276] On the mandate of GRETA in relation to new developments (rulings by the ECtHR, new initiatives from other organisations and interpretation of provisions of the Convention, see Rijken, Jansen-Wilhelm and de Volder (n 63).

[277] See for instance, GRETA, *Fourth General Report on GRETA's activities covering the period from 1 August 2013 to 30 September 2014* (2015) 37: 'GRETA welcomes the attention paid to new forms of exploitation and stresses the importance of ensuring that legislation and practice take into account all forms of trafficking'. See also Council of Europe, *Explanatory Report to the Convention* (n 260) para 94. See for instance on illegal adoption, UNODC, *Travaux Préparatoires for the Organized Crime Convention and Protocols*, 342, note 13; 344, note 30; and 350, quoted in UNODC, 'The Concept of Exploitation in the Trafficking in Persons' Protocol', Issue Paper (2015) 38.

[278] UNODC, 'Model Law against Trafficking in Persons' (n 261) 13–19, including for instance the definition of forced or servile marriages, or Council of Europe, *Explanatory Report to the Convention* (n 259) paras 87–96.

The analysis of the definitions of the offence contained in the three instruments demonstrates their close similarities, which facilitates the compliance of States parties when they transpose these definitions into their national legal orders. As a consequence of the interactions between the different instruments, the adoption of a new instrument within the EU legal framework does not mean that States have to modify the definition that they adopted when transposing/implementing previous instruments. This is for instance illustrated in the case law of the ECtHR, which considered, in the case *Chowdury and others*, that Greece had satisfied the obligation under Article 4 ECHR to put in place an appropriate legal and regulatory framework since it had transposed into its national legal order the relevant EU law instruments.[279] In such context, the EU demonstrates its capacity to build on previously existing norms, in order to develop a definition of trafficking in human beings modernising the definitions provided in the UN Protocol and the Council of Europe Convention. This emergence and consolidation of a common definition of human trafficking has had, and continues to have, important consequences, because as stressed by Anne Gallagher, it provided the necessary prerequisite for the elaboration of a meaningful normative framework.[280] It did not prevent problems in practice, due in particular to tensions between the States which support a conservative and restrictive interpretation of the concept and those which advocate for its expansion.[281]

ii. Interactions Regarding Provisions on the Non-Punishment and Non-Prosecution of Victims of Trafficking

The non-prosecution or non-punishment clause with regard to victims of trafficking who have been compelled to commit illegal acts as a consequence of being trafficked constitutes a second example through which normative interactions can be analysed.

The clause was created to address the situation of victims of trafficking in human beings, who are routinely punished and prosecuted for crimes committed as a direct consequence of their being trafficked. These crimes may include, for instance, immigration offences, the use of false documents or drug cultivation.[282] The prosecution and punishment of trafficking victims is problematic since it

---

[279] *Chowdury and others v Greece* (n 147) paras 105–09.
[280] A Gallagher, 'Trafficking in Transnational Criminal Law' in R Piotrowicz, C Rijken and B Heide Uhl (eds), *Routledge Handbook of Human Trafficking* (New York, Routledge, 2018) 30.
[281] UNODC, 'The International Legal Definition of Trafficking in Persons' (n 253) 2–3.
[282] OSCE, Office of the Special Representative and Coordinator for Combating Trafficking in Human Beings, 'Policy and legislative recommendations towards the effective implementation of the non-punishment provision with regard to victims of trafficking' (2013) 7, available at: www.osce.org/secretariat/101002?download=true. See also S Rodriguez-López, 'Telling Victims from Criminals: Human Trafficking for the purposes of Criminal Exploitation' in J Winterdyk and J Jones (eds), *The Palgrave International Handbook of Human Trafficking* (London, Palgrave Macmillan, 2020) 305–10.

fails to take into account the serious crimes committed against them and it fails to ensure full respect for their human rights. It also dissuades trafficked victims from giving evidence against their traffickers and it enables traffickers to exert even further control over their victims by threatening exposure to punishment by the state.[283] Far from offering blanket immunity to victims, the principle of non-punishment aims at balancing the offences committed against them with those committed by victims. It also aims at enhancing their trust in the justice system, supporting in turn victims' ability and willingness to cooperate with criminal justice authorities in the prosecution of their traffickers.[284] This measure thus gives further substance to a human rights and victim-centred approach to trafficking, while also participating in the criminal justice objective of bringing the true perpetrators to justice.[285]

The principle of non-punishment first appeared in soft law instruments, enacted at regional[286] and international levels.[287] It became a legally binding obligation with the adoption of the Council of Europe Convention in 2005. The text contains an innovative clause providing for the non-punishment of trafficking victims for their involvement in unlawful activities that they have been compelled to carry out.[288] In the Explanatory Report, it is explained that States can comply with this provision 'by providing for a substantive criminal or procedural criminal law provision, or any other measure, allowing for the possibility of not punishing victims when the ... legal requirements are met'.[289] Parties to the Convention thus have a positive obligation to adopt measures dealing specifically with this issue.[290] A few years later, the EU legislator then drew inspiration from this provision to introduce a similar provision in Directive 2011/36/UE,[291] and complemented the

---

[283] ibid.

[284] R Piotrowicz and L Sorrentino, 'The non-punishment provision with regard to victims of trafficking: A human rights approach' in R Piotrowicz, C Rijken and B Heide Uhl (eds), *Routledge Handbook of Human Trafficking* (New York, Routledge, 2018) 172.

[285] ibid 174.

[286] Non-punishment of victims has been discussed since the early 2000s, for instance, in the OSCE Ministerial Council, Decision No 1 Enhancing the OSCE's Efforts to Combat Trafficking in Human Beings, 28 November 2000, MC (8).DEC/1, para 9: 'ensuring that victims of trafficking do not face prosecution solely because they have been trafficked'.

[287] UN High Commissioner for Human Rights, Recommended Principles and Guidelines on Human Rights and Human Trafficking, 2002, E/2002/68/Add.1, Principle 7 and Guideline 4.5. The High Commissioner expressly recommends that 'trafficked persons shall not be detained, charged or prosecuted for the illegality of their entry into or residence in countries of transit and destination, or for their involvement in unlawful activities to the extent that such involvement is a direct consequence of their situation as trafficked persons'.

[288] Art 26 Council of Europe Convention.

[289] Council of Europe, *Explanatory Report to the Convention* (n 260) para 274.

[290] Council of Europe, Committee of the Parties of the Council of Europe Convention on Action against Trafficking in Human Beings, Meeting Report of the 7th meeting of the Committee of the Parties (Strasbourg, 30 January 2011), THB-CP (2012) RAP7 (Strasbourg, 9 February 2012), Appendix II, para 7.

[291] Directive 2011/36/EU, Art 8: Member States 'shall, in accordance with the basic principles of their legal systems, take the necessary measures to ensure that competent national authorities are entitled not to prosecute or impose penalties on victims of trafficking in human beings for their involvement in criminal activities which they have been compelled to commit'.

non-imposition of penalties with an obligation of non-prosecution. Article 8 of the Directive mainly pursues the objectives of 'guaranteeing victims the benefit of human rights, avoiding fresh victimisation and encouraging them to come forward as witnesses in the context of criminal procedures entered into against the perpetrators of offences'.[292] This example may only reflect the proximity between the legislative work of the Council of Europe and the EU as the EU often transposes norms that have been set down by the Council into its legal order.[293] However, this would not take into account the dynamic interpretation of the UN Protocol. The Working Group on Trafficking in Persons[294] has, since 2009, recommended States parties to consider – in line with their domestic legislation – the non-punishment and non-prosecution of victims of trafficking.[295] Its recommendations encourage States parties to the Protocol 'to ensure, in line with their domestic legislation, that victims of trafficking are not penalised for unlawful acts committed by them in the course of, or in relation to, being trafficked'.[296] Through these recommendations, the Working Group introduces the possibility for States to introduce non-punishment clauses similar to those foreseen in the European instruments within the international legal order, and guidance is provided within the Model Law against Trafficking in Persons.[297] Finally, the 2014 ILO Forced Labour Protocol also introduced a non-punishment clause applying to victims of forced labour who may involuntarily commit a range of offences as a result of their forced labour.[298]

Whereas there is an abundance of soft and binding instruments providing for such a principle protecting victims forced to commit offences, inconsistencies are still present. Such differences concern the conduct covered by the principle, the threshold for applying the principle and the outcome of its application.[299] Such differences are also particularly noticeable in the States' implementation of the provision,[300] which varies greatly from country to country, with a very limited adoption of specific legal provisions and a restrictive interpretation of its scope

---

[292] Recital 14, Preamble, Directive 2011/36/EU.

[293] S Miettinen, *Criminal Law and Policy in the European Union* (Abingdon, Routledge, 2011) 80; and V Mitsilegas, 'The European Union and the Implementation of International Norms in Criminal Matters' in M Cremona, J Monar and S Poli (eds), *The External Dimension of the European Union's Area of Freedom, Security and Justice* (Brussels, Peter Lang, 2011) 268.

[294] This group has the function of advising and assisting the Conference of the Parties to the UN Convention against Transnational Organised Crime (COP-UNTOC), and it holds annual meetings during which it sets out recommendations to the Parties of the Convention.

[295] United Nations, Report on the meeting of the Working Group on Trafficking in Persons held in Vienna on 14 and 15 April 2009, CTOC/COP/WG.4/2009/2, 21 April 2009, 3, para 12. United Nations, Report on the meeting of the Working Group on Trafficking in Persons held in Vienna from 27 to 29 January 2010, CTOC/COP/WG.4/2010/6, 17 February 2010, 8, paras 50–51.

[296] United Nations, Report on the meeting of the Working Group on Trafficking in Persons held in Vienna from 6 to 8 November 2013, 26 November 2013, CTOC/COP/WG4/2013/5, 5, para 39.

[297] UNODC, 'Model Law against Trafficking in Persons' (n 261) 40–42.

[298] Piotrowicz and Sorrentino (n 284) 174.

[299] ICAT, Non punishment of victims of trafficking, Issue brief No 8 (2020) 3, available at: icat. network/sites/default/files/publications/documents/1910800 ICAT Issue Brief 8 Ebook0.pdf.

[300] See, eg, GRETA, *Second General Report on GRETA's activities covering the period from 1 August 2011 to 30 July 2012* (2012) 13, 16, paras 58–59: 'GRETA's first evaluation reports reveal a patchy pattern

of application.[301] In that regard, the EU does not necessarily distinguish itself, as it merely pinpoints the measures enacted by its Member States, without further initiatives on the matter.[302]

iii. Normative Cooperation rather than Normative Competition

The analysis of these two examples allows us to identify several interesting points. First, it seems that the definitions contained in the different instruments are harmonised and adhere to a certain hierarchy. The definition of the UN Protocol, the first to be adopted, appears to be a reference point for the adoption of definitions at regional and national level. Its three constitutive elements are always repeated. The differences identified seem to be motivated by the desire to adapt the definition to the most recent developments in the field, such as the emergence of new modus operandi or new purposes of exploitation. Second, such soft harmonisation and hierarchy are also present when considering the provision of the non-punishment and non-prosecution of trafficking victims compelled to commit criminal activities. In this situation, the UN Protocol is silent about this issue and cannot be considered as the instrument of reference, containing a standard that has acquired a universal value, and has then be repeated in regional instruments. This does not prevent the principle of non-punishment to be expressed in soft law international and regional instruments, before being translated into binding commitments in international and regional instruments, such as the Council of Europe Convention, the EU Directive or the ILO Protocol. Its absence from the UN Protocol further evidences the weakness of a human rights-based approach to trafficking, enshrined at international level mostly in soft law instruments,[303] prompting some to advocate in favour of a new UN treaty.[304]

The interactions are noticeable between the intergovernmental organisations responsible for the implementation of legally binding instruments at international and regional levels. Instead of a normative competition, each of them seeks to build on the instruments adopted in other legal frameworks when preparing a

---

as regards the implementation of Article 26 of the Convention. Some parties have adopted legislative measures specific to trafficking victims, while others rely on general duress provisions or provisions which allow prosecutors or judges to reduce sentences in the presence of mitigating circumstances'. See also GRETA, *Fourth General Report* (n 277) 52–54.

[301] Piotrowicz and Sorrentino (n 284) 177.

[302] Commission, 'Report assessing the extent to which Member States have taken the necessary measures in order to comply with Directive 2011/36/EU on preventing and combating trafficking in human beings and protecting its victims in accordance with Article 23 (1), COM (2016) 722 final, 6.

[303] This is notably evidenced by the fact that this measure is not included (so far) in the questionnaire prepared for the Review Mechanism of the UN Protocol, which only contains the limited provisions of the text on victims' protection. (Rolling text containing a draft self-assessment questionnaire for the Protocol to Prevent, Suppress and Punish Trafficking in Persons, Status as of 19 February 2020.)

[304] J Jones, 'Is It Time to Open a Conversation About a New United Nations Treaty to Fight Human Trafficking that Focuses on Victim Protection and Human Rights?' in J Winterdyk and J Jones (eds), *The Palgrave International Handbook of Human Trafficking* (London, Palgrave Macmillan, 2020) 1816.

new instrument. The implementation of previous instruments becomes a way to identify certain gaps, such as in the field of the protection of victims of trafficking. Moreover, previous instruments, and especially the UN Protocol, are not cast out. They remain standard setting, ie, of a specific and high-ranking value. Their extensive interpretation allows, within their legal framework, integration of the provisions and actions that form part of the most recent consensus on how to fight against trafficking in human beings. The differences in the mandate, the competences and the focus of each organisation influence the content of the instruments, but their result is often limited to inconsistencies in the degree of detail of their provisions or in the attention granted to each of the Three Ps.

The reality of their interactions is demonstrated by the instruments themselves, which contain cross-references as well as provisions dealing with their relationships. For instance, the Council of Europe Convention refers in its Preamble to the EU's internal instruments as well as to the UN Convention against transnational organised crime, the UN Protocol against trafficking in persons and other relevant international instruments. Its drafters consider that the Convention will participate in 'improving the protection they afford and developing the standards established by them'. Moreover, its Chapter VIII focuses on the relationship with other international instruments and the provisions contained therein stress that the Convention 'shall not affect the rights and obligations derived from them'.[305] Similarly, in the Preamble of Directive 2011/36/EU, the UN Protocol and the Council of Europe Convention are referred to as 'crucial steps in the process of enhancing international cooperation against trafficking in human beings',[306] and the ECtHR builds on the Council of Europe Convention to develop its own interpretation of trafficking in human beings within the meaning of Article 4 ECHR.[307]

D. Conclusion

The elements identified of soft harmonisation and hierarchy allow us to assess the strength of the normative interactions in the field of the fight against trafficking in human beings, and our analysis indicates that, in this field, the normative interactions between relevant organisations and instruments lead to compatible standards, preserving a margin of discretion and interpretation to States.

From the perspective of the EU, and its capacity to promote in multilateral settings key characteristics of its own policy, comparison between the EU instruments and those set out in other legal frameworks confirms the existence of a two-way dialogue.

---

[305] Arts 39 and 40 Council of Europe Convention.
[306] Preamble, para 9, Directive 2011/36/EU. The following paragraphs refer to the Geneva Convention relating to the Status of Refugees (para 10); and to ILO Convention No 29 concerning Forced and Compulsory Labour (para 11).
[307] See, eg, *SM v Croatia* (n 148) para 295.

The EU builds on these instruments, for instance with regard to the definition of the offence of trafficking in human beings. Internal developments, such as the introduction of new purposes of exploitation, are also promoted and taken into account outside its legal framework, as they influence the interpretation of previous instruments. The similarities between the instruments analysed facilitate their implementation by States parties, both EU Member States and third countries, as they may allow them to comply with all of them at once. Furthermore, although the Treaties do not address the question of agreements concluded by the EU Member States after their accession to the EU,[308] the EU Member States bound by their duty of loyal cooperation have to make sure that they respect EU norms when negotiating new agreements. The EU institutions are proactive and are quick to participate in the negotiations of new instruments in order to avoid conflicts of norms. The European Commission had, for instance, received a mandate to negotiate the Council of Europe Convention[309] and was an active member of the Ad Hoc Committee on Action against Trafficking in Human Beings set up for this purpose.[310]

The dialogue also encompasses the integration within the EU's legal order of norms and standards set out in other legal frameworks. The EU institutions follow the developments in other forums closely and the legislative instruments proposed and adopted are always compatible with the international and regional standards in force. The Commission has even proposed amending EU internal instruments whenever it was necessary to implement obligations stemming from other international instruments and thus to incorporate them into the EU's legal order. This was, for instance, the case after the adoption of the Council of Europe Convention, when the Commission proposed revising the 2002 Framework Decision and referred explicitly to the incorporation of certain provisions of the Convention.[311]

---

[308] Agreements concluded by States before their accession are addressed in Art 351 TFEU.

[309] See Commission, 'Proposal for a Council Decision authorising the Commission to negotiate a draft European Convention on the fight against trafficking in human beings', SEC (2004) 159 final; and Council, 'Proposal for a Common Position, on the basis of Article 34 of the Treaty on European Union, on negotiations relating to the draft European Convention on Action against Trafficking in Human Beings being undertaken in the Council of Europe, Council Doc 12314/04'. The final text has not been published since it is confidential.

[310] The Committee was set up by the Council of Europe, Committee of Ministers, 'Proposal to prepare a draft Council of Europe Convention on action against trafficking in human beings, adopted on 30 April 2003', CM/Del/Dec (2003) 838/4.4E/5 May 2003. Reference to the involvement of the Commission can be found in Council of Europe, Parliamentary Assembly, 'Report for debate on Draft Council of Europe Convention on action against trafficking in human beings', 15 March 2005, Doc No 10474, I. para 3: 'mostly at the initiative of the European Commission, which was negotiating on behalf of 22 member states of the European Community'.

[311] See in this regard the reference made to the Council of Europe Convention in the proposal for a new Framework Decision (Commission, 'Proposal for a Council on preventing and combating trafficking in human beings, and protecting victims', COM (2009) 136 final, 3 and 5); and in the Proposal for a new Directive (Commission, 'Proposal for a Directive of the European Parliament and of the Council on preventing and combating trafficking in human beings, and protecting victims' repealing Framework Decision 2002/629/JHA', COM (2010) 95 final, 5).

V. Multilateralism in Action: Coordination Mechanisms to Avoid Duplication of Efforts

Beyond normative interactions, the abundance of actors that are active in the fight against trafficking in human beings generates new challenges other than conflicts of norms. As stated in the EU Strategy, 'with such a wide range of legislative and policy measures there is a risk of overlapping and duplication of initiatives'.[312] This risk is valid for the actions launched by the EU institutions and its Member States as well as for the actions conducted at international, regional and local levels.

The idea that different organisations carry out similar actions does present some advantages. It may help to ensure the sustainability of certain counter-trafficking activities, for instance by providing new funding once one source of funding is terminated. It may also improve the promotion of certain standards and/or behaviour, especially towards national authorities. Indeed, if the incentives offered by one actor are not attractive enough, another actor may have different tools at its disposal. For instance, if the incentives offered by the EU, such as accession in the long term and visa-free travel in the short term, are not attractive enough, a more effective incentive may be the trade preferences granted by the US and which may be interrupted if the US Department of State judges national counter-trafficking efforts to be insufficient. Nevertheless, in a context in which limited resources are available to fund counter-trafficking actions both at national and transnational level, duplication of efforts should be avoided. Coordination mechanisms that bring together relevant actors should be developed. They foster exchange of information about each actor's counter-trafficking activities, which can help in reducing the risk of duplication of efforts, and strengthening cooperation.

The two notions of coordination and cooperation are closely linked given that it is hard to achieve coordination without close cooperation. Whereas cooperation refers to 'the action of working together with',[313] coordination can be defined as 'organising the activities of two or more groups so that they work efficiently and know what the others are doing'.[314] In other words, cooperation refers to the existence of exchanges between actors, sometimes formalised by the conclusion of cooperation agreements or memoranda of understanding, potentially leading to the conduct of joint actions. Coordination seems to refer to a more advanced stage of exchanges, in which these exchanges aim at organising the work carried out by each actor, potentially leading to a distribution of the tasks in order to avoid duplication of effort. However, the dividing line between the two terms is very thin and they are often used interchangeably.

---

[312] Commission, 'The EU Strategy towards the Eradication of Trafficking in Human Beings, 2012–2016' (n 33) 4.

[313] *Collins Dictionary* (online version).

[314] ibid.

In addition to preventing duplication of efforts, coordination among and cooperation between all relevant actors are a direct consequence of their general commitment in favour of a comprehensive approach to address human trafficking. Coordination should not only be ensured within each actor, which is particularly true for large intergovernmental organisations composed of affiliated organisations and sub-entities, such as the UN or the EU. Coordination may indeed ensure that diverse but complementary competences are mobilised in a coherent way to combat trafficking in human beings. Coordination is also essential among partners, whether they be intergovernmental organisations, civil society organisations or other bodies. To that end, ad hoc mechanisms have been set up to foster the exchange of information and/or to eventually agree on joint actions. These coordination mechanisms are relevant for all levels of action, ie, international, regional, national and even local levels.

The following paragraphs will present, on the one hand, the internal mechanisms of coordination (A) and on the other, the coordination mechanisms gathering two or more partners (B).

A. Internal Coordination Mechanisms in Large Organisations

The need for internal coordination mechanisms arises primarily within States. Public authorities have to coordinate their activities among themselves and to liaise with private actors. All relevant actors should be aware not only of the added value of their involvement in the fight against trafficking but also of the need for coordination and cooperation. International and European standards[315] often refer to the importance of establishing, at national level, an institutional framework favouring joint efforts and synergies, usually through the appointment of national coordinating bodies composed of representatives of all relevant actors. These bodies are often entrusted with the tasks of preparing a comprehensive national policy but also of following the (joint) actions carried out for its implementation.

---

[315] The EU's Strategy is not very precise in this regard and only stresses that 'there is a need for improved coordination and cooperation among key actors working in the field of trafficking in human beings' (Strategy, 11). But the EU plan on best practices, standards and procedures for combating and preventing trafficking in human beings, adopted by the Council in 2005 (n 230), was more explicit: 'Member States should work to develop, in line with national traditions, circumstances and practice, an appropriate governmental coordination structure to coordinate and evaluate national policies' (para 3(ii)). Although the Council of Europe Convention is silent on the organisation of such a mechanism, the GRETA discusses the existence of monitoring/multidisciplinary/inter-ministerial bodies in charge of coordination efforts when analysing the institutional framework of each State party (see GRETA reports on the UK, Cyprus and Spain). The OSCE Action Plan is more explicit, and it invites States to 'consider establishing ... bodies responsible for co-ordinating activities within a country' (17, VI, para 2). The UN Global Action Plan is also more precise since it promotes 'cooperation and coordination among governmental institutions, civil society and the private sector, as well as workers' and employers' organisations' (para 53).

The need to set up internal coordination mechanisms is equally valid for international and regional organisations and in particular for those that have a large mandate and/or are composed of sub-organisations/bodies/agencies.

Within the UN system, the diverse competences of UN-affiliated organisations, bodies and institutions led to the prompt recognition of the need for coordination. In response, a specific mechanism has been set up: the Inter-Agency Coordination Group against Trafficking in Persons (ICAT). This group held its first meeting in 2006, in response to Resolution 2006/27 of the Economic and Social Council, which called on UNODC to organise a meeting in order to coordinate the work against trafficking in persons of agencies and bodies within the UN system.[316] The UN General Assembly later called on the Secretary General to formalise its existence and role.[317] In its Global Plan of Action to Combat Trafficking in Persons, it invited all responsible UN entities to coordinate their efforts including by means of ICAT, which included coordination with human rights treaty bodies and mechanisms and other international organisations.[318] Over the last few years, the activities of ICAT have benefited from a new impetus, with new resolutions stressing its importance and mandating UNODC to organise its first meeting at principal level in May 2018, gathering the heads of the organisations belonging to the group.[319] As a consequence of this meeting, the group has been expanding its membership, and as of July 2020 counts 26 members,[320] including regional organisations outside the UN system, such as OSCE, the Organization of American States and the Council of the Baltic Sea States, and it established partnerships with the Council of Europe and the UN Special Rapporteur on Trafficking in Persons.[321] While UNODC acts as the secretariat of the group, a working group composed of 10 agencies is more actively involved in the preparation of ICAT outputs, being high-level events, joint contributions to intergovernmental processes or policy briefs seeking to provide a 'one UN' approach to selected trafficking issues.[322] Such a coordination mechanism allows for the smooth exchange of information between organisations active in preventing and combating trafficking in human beings, and it serves also as a framework for the establishment of joint initiatives, such as the co-chairmanship of the group

---

[316] UN, Economic and Social Council, Strengthening international cooperation in preventing and combating trafficking in persons and protecting victims of such trafficking, Resolution 2006/27, 27 July 2006, 5, para 16.

[317] UN, General Assembly, Improving the coordination of efforts against trafficking in human beings, Resolution 61/180, 8 March 2007, A/RES/61/180, 3, para 12.

[318] UN General Assembly, 'Global Action Plan to Combat Trafficking in Persons' (n 39) paras 11 and 56.

[319] UN General Assembly, Improving the coordination of efforts against trafficking in persons, Resolution 72/195, 19 December 2017, A/RES/72/195, para 10.

[320] For an overview of the activities of its members, see ICAT, 'ICAT expertise and experience in countering trafficking in persons: An overview of the mandate and activities of ICAT organisations' (2018), available at: icat.network/sites/default/files/publications/documents/ICAT%20expertise%20and%20 experience%20in%20countering%20TIP.pdf.

[321] List of ICAT members, available at: icat.network/about-us.

[322] ICAT, 'ICAT Factsheet', February 2020, available at: icat.network/sites/default/files/publications/ documents/FINAL%20published%20V1910798%20%281%29_Feb2020.pdf.

by UN Women and OSCE from 2019–20, and its efforts in adopting, harmonising and implementing sustainable procurement measures in UN supply chains.[323] The work of ICAT is further complemented by the work of another network, the UN Network on Migration, the successor to the Global Migration Group, which sought to promote the wider application of all relevant international and regional instruments and norms relating to migration and to encourage the adoption of more coherent, comprehensive and better coordinated approaches to the issue of international migration.[324] The new network has been established to support the implementation of the Global Compact for Safe, Orderly and Regular Migration, including the establishment of a capacity-building mechanism.[325] This new network is potentially relevant for the coordination of counter-trafficking efforts, since one of the objectives of the Global Compact is to prevent, combat and eradicate trafficking in persons in the context of international migration.[326] Duplication of activities may be avoided by the fact that almost all the organisations part of the UN's Network Executive Committee are also members of ICAT's Working Group.

At regional level, we have seen in the previous chapter how the EU has set up several coordination mechanisms, whose aim is to coordinate actions between the EU agencies active in Justice and Home Affairs issues and the different Directorates General of the Commission and has even appointed an Anti-Trafficking Coordinator,[327] with the objective of coordinating its internal and external actions.[328] Other organisations active at European level have set up similar mechanisms. The OSCE has, for instance, also engaged in internal coordination efforts by creating the position of OSCE Special Representative and Coordinator on Combating Trafficking in Human Beings in May 2004. The mandate of Special Representative and Coordinator explicitly includes the mission of coordinating the OSCE efforts in the fight against human trafficking, which are carried out by the organisation's institutions, structures and field operations,[329] in order to avoid duplication and to ensure their complementarity and coherence.

---

[323] ICAT, 'Chairs' Annual Report 2019', 5, available at: icat.network/sites/default/files/publications/documents/19-10797_ICAT%20Annual%20Report_Ebook.pdf.

[324] Global Migration Group website: globalmigrationgroup.org/.

[325] UN General Assembly, Resolution 73/195 Global Compact for Safe, Orderly and Regular Migration (n 117) para 45.

[326] ibid para 26.

[327] See ch 1, III.D.ii 'Institutional Dimension of the Quest for Coherence'.

[328] See for instance Commission, 'The EU Strategy towards the Eradication of Trafficking in Human Beings, 2012–2016' (n 33) Priority D. Enhanced coordination and cooperation among key actors and policy coherence; and Commission, 'Mid-Term Implementation report' (n 34) 5.

[329] The Office for Democratic Institutions and Human Rights (ODIHR) contributes to anti-trafficking efforts, especially through the strengthening of the protection of trafficked persons and vulnerable groups and preventing trafficking by focusing on a number of initiatives in the OSCE region. The Strategic Police Matters Unit (SPMU) also work on anti-trafficking issues and focuses on integrating the law enforcement perspective in OSCE anti-trafficking work and complementing the victim-centred approach with a strategic focus on offenders. Field operations are involved in project developments, providing advice on policy and exchange of information on good practices. They also provide strong support for activities such as country visits and assessments. For more details, see OSCE, *From Policy to Practice: Combating Trafficking in Human Beings in the OSCE region* (2006) 17–18.

Not all intergovernmental organisations need to develop mechanisms aimed at ensuring the internal coordination of their counter-trafficking activities. Such a need mainly concerns international and regional organisations with large and multidisciplinary mandates, such as the UN, the EU etc. In this section, we have seen that these organisations have been aware of the importance of internally coordinating their actions and have established internal coordination mechanisms. This helps to ensure that their actions are designed and implemented in a coherent way. Their coordination efforts are further extended to their external partners, with which they engage in bilateral and multilateral coordination and cooperation mechanisms.

B. Bilateral and Multilateral Mechanisms Among Partners

All the actors involved in combating trafficking in human beings are committed to the creation of multilateral solutions to this global problem. Their commitment, which is shared by the EU, forms the basis for modern forms of international relations, which are underpinned by the common belief that certain issues are better addressed on a multilateral basis. In the field of the combat against trafficking in human beings, just as in other policy fields, this commitment is demonstrated by the numerous interactions between relevant actors. One element may, however, distinguish this field: the plethora of coordination mechanisms. The large number of these mechanisms might be justified by the broad scope of activities necessary to address the issue comprehensively and by the broad range of actors involved. The EU as a regional actor is not necessarily involved in all these mechanisms, but it has as part of its external activities developed bilateral cooperation and coordination with key partners. Our analysis will start with the multilateral mechanisms of coordination (i), followed by bilateral mechanisms (ii). The latter are also crucial in developing coordination between close partners.

i. Multilateral Mechanisms of Coordination and Cooperation

Each actor involved in the fight against trafficking is aware of the abundance of actors active in the same field. Therefore, their commitment to coordination supports discussions and interactions at a multilateral level with all their partners. In 2002, in the Brussels Declaration, the international community stressed that

> all international bodies, governments and other actors … should intensify their co-operation and exchange of information with a view to achieving a better co-ordinated response, to avoid overlaps and duplications of work, and to maximise the impact of actions taken at international level.[330]

---

[330] Brussels Declaration (n 36) 3–4.

The support of multilateral cooperation and exchange of information has been repeated since then. The UN Global Action Plan was, for instance, presented as aiming to foster 'cooperation and coordination among all relevant stakeholders, including Member States, international organisations, civil society organisations and the private sector'.[331] The UN General Assembly insisted twice on the importance of encouraging and intensifying international and regional cooperation and coordination.[332] At European level, the OSCE Action Plan is also in favour of such efforts, as it tasks 'OSCE institutions and bodies with engaging in more extensive regular exchange of information, data collection and research with relevant international organizations'.[333] The European Commission has not been left behind since it announced its intention to 'work towards strengthening and formalising partnerships with international organisations active in the field of trafficking in human beings to improve the exchange of information, and ensure cooperation'.[334]

On the basis of this repeated consensus for stronger coordination, several mechanisms have been established, often composed of intergovernmental organisations, and non-governmental actors, such as civil society organisations/NGOs and business representatives.

The Alliance against Trafficking in Persons is the multilateral forum within which the actors active in this field within Europe can coordinate and cooperate.[335] The Alliance was launched in 2004 at the initiative of the first OSCE Special Representative, Mrs Helga Konrad, as an informal and voluntary platform for advocacy and cooperation among intergovernmental and NGOs. It provides a dynamic framework to develop synergies. The Alliance brings together intergovernmental organisations which are active at international level, such as the ICMPD, ILO, IOM, UNICEF, UNODC and UNHCR; or at regional level, such as the Council of Europe and the Council of Baltic Sea States. The European Commission and Europol represent the EU. The distinctive characteristics of the Alliance lie in the participation of numerous NGOs, which are active in the field of the protection of human rights, such as Amnesty International and Human Rights Watch, or focusing on (certain aspects of) human trafficking, such as La Strada International, Anti-Slavery International or ECPAT International. Organisations representing businesses are also present.[336] Every year a high level Alliance conference is

---

[331] UN General Assembly, 'Global Action Plan to Combat Trafficking in Persons' (n 39) para (f).
[332] ibid paras 51 and 55.
[333] OSCE Permanent Council, OSCE 'Action Plan to Combat Trafficking in Human Beings', Decision No 557/Rev. 1 (2005) 20, available at: www.osce.org/pc/15944?download=true.
[334] Commission, 'The EU Strategy towards the Eradication of Trafficking in Human Beings, 2012–2016' (n 33) 12. The privileged areas for such partnerships are the areas of policy planning, prioritisation, data collection, research and monitoring and evaluation. The importance of cooperation and coordination was already stressed in the EU Action Plan of 2005: 'Member States and EU institutions should continue to cooperate with relevant international organisations (eg, UN, OSCE and Council of Europe)' (point 5, iii); (Council, 'EU Plan on best practices, standard and procedures for combating and preventing trafficking in human beings', above n 235, 1).
[335] The full list of its participants can be found at: www.osce.org/secretariat/107221.
[336] The International Organisation of Employers describes itself as 'the recognised voice of business' (source: www.ioe-emp.org). The IOE is part of the Alliance against Trafficking in Persons. In 2008, the

organised and addresses recent issues in the field of the fight against trafficking, such as trafficking along migration routes (2015); ethical issues in preventing and combating human trafficking (2014); human trafficking as a form of modern day slavery (2013); and non-discrimination and empowerment in the context of human trafficking (2012).[337] The annual Alliance Conference facilitates a high-level dialogue between national authorities, civil society and other stakeholders in the OSCE region.[338] The issues discussed at the conference are sometimes later included in OSCE publications, giving them additional legitimacy.[339] In parallel with these conferences, the Alliance Expert Coordination Team (AECT)[340] holds meetings twice a year hosted by the OSCE Special Representative. These meetings have several purposes, and allow, for instance, for the discussion of problematic issues. In this regard, they have yielded common understandings on such issues as the protection and shelter for victims, national rapporteurs and the protection of migrant, unaccompanied and asylum-seeking children.[341] Their common views are sometimes expressed through their support for the publication of Issue Papers on specific issues, such as the non-punishment clause.[342] These meetings also play an important role in avoiding duplication of efforts and activities,[343] since they constitute the opportunity to update partners on activities carried out, share plans for the future and develop strategic networking, partnerships and projects among players active in the field.[344] The participants report them as being a very good

IOE produced an Employers' Guide to Forced Labour as a first attempt to clarify some of the questions surrounding the issue. The Guide draws the attention of employers and their members to the risks forced labour can represent within business operations. The publication gives guidance on how to identify and prevent situations of forced labour and provides some direction on what employers can do to address the issue (source: www.ioe-emp.org/policy-areas/forced-labour/).

[337] Source: www.osce.org/secretariat/152446?download=true.

[338] MP Lagon, 'Fighting Human Trafficking: Transformative versus "Cotton-Candy" Partnerships' in MP Lagon and AC Arend (eds), *Human Dignity and the Future of Global Institutions* (Washington, Georgetown University Press, 2014) 237.

[339] OSCE, *An Agenda for Prevention: Trafficking for Labour Exploitation* (2011). It has a special thematic focus on trafficking for labour exploitation and contains three experts' essays which build upon the 11th Alliance against Trafficking in Persons Conference on 'Preventing Trafficking in Human Beings for Labour Exploitation: Decent Work and Social Justice' (20–21 June 2011). Source: www.osce.org/secretariat/86293.

[340] The AECT includes representatives from the OSCE IWG on Gender Equality and Anti-Trafficking; OSCE Structures and institutions (SR, ATAU, SPMU, OCEEA, Senior Adviser on Gender Issues, ODIHR); UNHCHR, UNHCR, UNDP, UNICEF, UNICEF Innocenti Research Centre, UNIFEM, UNODC, ILO, WHO, NATO, IOM; International Federation of the Red Cross and Red Crescent Societies; Council of Europe; ICMPD; Europol; Interpol; European Commission; EC Expert Group; Dutch National Rapporteur; Nexus Institute; ACTA; Anti-Slavery International; Amnesty International; Caritas; ABA CEELI; ECPAT; La Strada International; International Federation of Terre des Hommes; Save the Children International Alliance. Source: OSCE, *From Policy to Practice* (n 330) 24, fn 7.

[341] Lagon (n 339) 236.

[342] eg, the OSCE's 'Paper on Policy and legislative recommendations towards the effective implementation of the non-punishment provision with regard to victims of trafficking' of June 2013 has been produced in consultation with the Alliance Expert Coordination Team (source: www.osce.org/secretariat/101002).

[343] Source: www.ohchr.org/Documents/Issues/Trafficking/Dakar_summary_structures_en.pdf.

[344] OSCE, *From Policy to Practice* (n 330) 24.

platform in which information is openly shared.[345] Nevertheless, the results of the Alliance's work are difficult to pin down. Its annual meetings and conferences do not always lead to the adoption of common policy documents or instruments. The diversity of the actors participating in these multilateral mechanisms may explain why these meetings do not seem to lead to joint projects being undertaken.

Smaller groups of partners might also establish specific coordination mechanisms, for example to work together on joint projects. The United Nations Global Initiative to Fight Human Trafficking (UN.GIFT), which was launched in March 2007 by five UN-affiliated organisations[346] and the OSCE, is an example of this trend. UN.GIFT was an initiative that ran until 31 December 2014. It offered access to expertise, knowledge and innovative partnerships to combat human trafficking. The UN.GIFT.HUB provided an online space, not only to collect information but where users could participate in the creation and dissemination of knowledge on human trafficking. The aim of the dissemination of information was to provide more transparency about the counter-trafficking activities carried out by each actor and to favour the emergence of regional and thematic networks involving civil society, intergovernmental organisations and the private sector.[347] The UN.GIFT organisations emphasised the results achieved, such as the development of 'a wealth of technical tools and influential publications' and the implementation of joint programmes designed to support the efforts of Member States.[348]

Multilateral activities seem to be the exception while meetings and discussions within multilateral mechanisms of coordination are the norm. The importance of these meetings should not be underestimated as they play a crucial role in the exchange of information on the activities of each actor active in the field. Furthermore, they offer formal and informal forums for discussions, which contribute towards the creation of more direct relations between experts.[349] This is essential for a mutual understanding of each actor's competences and mandate. The relations developed through these regular meetings, in which all key stakeholders participate, may further stimulate deeper and more concrete coordination and cooperation on a bilateral basis. Most of the organisations/actors participating in these multilateral platforms of exchange have also engaged in bilateral relations with each other. This situation has led to the development of a complex array of bilateral relations/interactions, which can remain informal or be formalised through the conclusion of cooperation agreements, memoranda of understanding or the exchange of letters.

---

[345] Interview No 4.
[346] ILO, OHCHR, UNICEF, UNODC and IOM.
[347] UNODC, *The Global Initiative to Fight Human Trafficking* (2007) 5, available at: www.unodc.org/pdf/gift%20brochure.pdf.
[348] Joint Statement by the Member Organisations of the UN.GIFT Steering Committee (2015), available at: www.ungift.org/knowledgehub/en/stories/March2015/joint-statement.html.
[349] Interviews Nos 23 and 24.

ii. *The EU's Bilateral Cooperation with its Partners*

The EU has developed bilateral relations with most of the other intergovernmental organisations active in the fight against trafficking in human beings. Such a situation illustrates once more its commitment to effective multilateralism and the consideration given to its external partners,[350] who are taken into account in the external promotion of its policy against trafficking in human beings. Coordination and cooperation on a bilateral basis between the EU and other intergovernmental organisations varies substantially from one organisation to another. Whereas with some organisations the EU has developed close cooperation in the fight against trafficking in human beings, in other cases the cooperation is looser and/or concerns fields indirectly relating to human trafficking. During the presentation of the various bilateral relationships between the EU and its partners, two elements will be highlighted: the degree of their cooperation and how formal it is.

a. Bilateral Cooperation with the Council of Europe

From a general perspective, the EU and the Council of Europe have always had a close relationship since they were set up in the aftermath of the Second World War. Whereas the Council of Europe intends to build a common European home based on human rights, the pre-eminence of law and pluralistic democracy within an intergovernmental framework, the EU has evolved from a common economic area to a sui generis supranational organisation with broad competences in various fields. Despite their different vocations and development methods, the two organisations 'were the products of the same idea, the same spirit, the same ambition' and are complementary.[351] The desire to develop mutual relations has been very clear and consisted until 2001 in the exchange of letters, providing for the exchange of reports, regular contact and attendance at meetings.[352] The formalisation of their relationship started in 2001 with the signing of a Joint Declaration of Cooperation and Partnership,[353] building upon the success of their joint programmes. The Juncker Report reflected on the creation of a new framework of enhanced cooperation and interaction in areas of common concern, proposing without success the accession of the EU to the Council of Europe by 2010.[354] Instead, the two

---

[350] Commission, 'The EU Strategy towards the Eradication of Trafficking in Human Beings, 2012–2016' (n 33) 12.

[351] Council of Europe, *Council of Europe – European Union, 'A sole ambition for the European continent'*, Report by J-C Juncker, Prime Minister of the Grand Duchy of Luxembourg to the attention of the Heads of State and Governments of the Member States of the Council of Europe, 11 April 2006, 1 and 3, available at: www.coe.int/t/der/docs/RapJuncker_E.pdf.

[352] T Streinz, 'Fraternal Twins: The European Union and the Council of Europe' in H de Waele and JJ Kuipers (eds), *The European Union's Emerging International Identity* (Leiden, Martinus Nijhoff Publishers, 2013) 107.

[353] Full text available at: www.jp.coe.int/Upload/110_Joint_Declaration_EF.pdf.

[354] Council of Europe, *Council of Europe – European Union, 'A sole ambition for the European continent'* (n 352).

organisations signed, in 2007, a Memorandum of Understanding[355] which produced certain effects, such as the reinforcement of the institutional presence of each organisation.[356] The Memorandum of Understanding identifies shared priorities and focal points for cooperation, including the fight against trafficking in human beings. The Council of the EU plays an important role from an EU perspective as it sets out directions for the cooperation with the Council of Europe. These directions can be found in texts directly relating to trafficking in human beings, in which the EU is invited to 'encourage the signature and ratification of the Council of Europe Convention'[357] and GRETA is recognised as having 'the potential to cater for concrete recommendations for further action in this context'.[358] The Commission is also invited to 'make full use of the monitoring reports of international organisations, especially of the (GRETA)'.[359]

In addition, every two years the Council of the EU adopts priorities for cooperation with the Council of Europe, with increased ambitions. Beyond the possible accession of the EU to the ECHR, the priorities adopted in December 2015 were particularly detailed regarding their cooperation in countering trafficking in human beings.[360] Their cooperation aimed at improving the implementation of the Council of Europe Convention and the EU's accession to this Convention was mentioned as the long-term objective. The priorities added that the two organisations would continue their regular dialogue, especially between the EU Anti-Trafficking Coordinator and the Council of Europe, and that they would promote the Council of Europe Convention outside the EU. These priorities were repeated in 2018,[361] and more recently, the priorities for 2020–22 referred more generally to their cooperation in strengthening and promoting the protection and promotion of human rights, and stressed how action against trafficking in human beings requires joint efforts and a coordinated and coherent approach in all relevant policy areas in EU internal and external policies.[362]

In practice, the EU's enlargement policy and the development of the European Neighbourhood Policy (ENP) gave fresh impetus to their cooperation in this field

---

[355] Full text available at: ec.europa.eu/justice/international-relations/files/mou_2007_en.pdf.

[356] The EU created an EU delegation to the Council of Europe, and the Council of Europe opened a Liaison Office in Brussels.

[357] Council, 'Council conclusions on the new EU Strategy towards the Eradication of Trafficking in Human Beings 2012–2016', 25 October 2012, Council Doc No 11838/6/12 Rev. 6, 3.

[358] Council, 'Implementing the Strategy for the External Dimension of Justice and Home Affairs: Global Freedom, Security and Justice – Action-Oriented Paper on Strengthening the EU External Dimension on Action against Trafficking in Human Beings: Towards Global EU Action against Trafficking in Human Beings', Council Doc No 6865/10, 15, point 3, vi).

[359] Council, 'Council conclusions on the new EU Strategy towards the Eradication of Trafficking in Human Beings 2012–2016' (n 358) 5.

[360] Council, 'EU priorities for cooperation with the Council of Europe in 2016–2017', Council Doc No 14919/15, 7.

[361] Council, 'EU priorities for cooperation with the Council of Europe in 2018–2019', Council Doc No 5553/18, 9.

[362] Council, 'EU priorities for cooperation with the Council of Europe in 2020–2022', Council Doc No 9283/20, 9, para 19.

since the EU emphasises the ratification and implementation of the instruments set out by the Council of Europe.[363] For some authors, the ratification of these instruments can be considered as a test for EU membership and as a first step towards the assumption of full EU obligations.[364] Cooperation with the EU is also illustrated in GRETA's annual general reports through the mention of exchange of views and information with EU institutions and agencies and the participation of GRETA members and Secretariat in consultations, round tables and conferences.[365] Moreover, in its country evaluations, GRETA takes note of the simultaneous application of EU standards in EU Member States.[366]

b. Bilateral Cooperation with Other European Organisations

Bilateral cooperation between the EU and OSCE has been constantly developing without being formalised. In the 1990s, their cooperation remained exceptional and took place on an ad hoc basis, but the early 2000s saw a decisive shift towards greater intensification and the formalisation of their relations.[367] Regular dialogue now takes place between different entities of the two organisations. The EU delegation to international organisations in Vienna, which coordinate the EU policies in the OSCE,[368] represents the EU in the OSCE. Its members thus have regular contact and discussions with the OSCE officials.[369] Close and regular contacts have also been established between the persons working in OSCE field missions and those working in the EU delegations, notably in the countries of south-east Europe.

In the field of the fight against human trafficking, the EU has expressed its commitment to work with the OSCE and its Special Representative 'in order to accomplish the aims of the new EU strategy and to respond to the challenges of this threat ..., in particular by strengthening cooperation with OSCE participating States that are not members of the EU'. The EU considers the OSCE as 'a credible

---

[363] Adam, et al (n 10) 150, para 306.

[364] Mitsilegas (n 294) 268.

[365] See for instance, GRETA, *Fourth General Report* (n 277) 25–26.

[366] See as examples the reports on France (GRETA (2012) 16, 11, para 16); and Romania (GRETA (2012) 2, 10, para 14).

[367] With the entry into force of the Amsterdam Treaty, the EU obtained new competences to play a comprehensive role in the area of crisis management. Furthermore, with the development of the SAP and the ENP, the EU's actions concerned countries traditionally covered by OSCE actions. These developments 'have led to accusations that (the EU) has breached the OSCE's area of jurisdiction, which has resulted in a geographical and functional overlap' (source: E Stewart, 'Restoring EU–OSCE Cooperation for Pan-European Conflict Prevention (2008) 29 *Contemporary Security Policy* 266, 267, quoted in D Paunov, 'Assessing the success of EU-OSCE cooperation: a case of mutualism?' (2013) 24 *Security and Human Rights* 373, 386). As a consequence, it was necessary to develop cooperation in order to avoid duplication of efforts.

[368] The Delegation in Vienna developed close contacts with all OSCE institutions, notably the OSCE Secretariat in Vienna as well as the OSCE Office for Democratic Institutions and Human Rights (ODIHR) in Warsaw.

[369] Source: eeas.europa.eu/delegations/vienna/eu_osce/index_en.htm.

partner' and notes with satisfaction the 'existing, effective cooperation between the OSCE and EU'.[370] The EU Anti-Trafficking Coordinator regularly attends and participates, in person or through a representative, in the OSCE conferences.[371] Similarly the OSCE Special Representative regularly meets all relevant EU institutions and structures, including the EU Anti-Trafficking Coordinator[372] and has, for instance, attended the meeting of the EU's informal network of national rapporteurs.[373] Their cooperation also takes a more substantial form with the provision of funding to carry out counter-trafficking activities. The OSCE acknowledges that the EU and its Member States are a major source of extra-budgetary funding of OSCE activities in the field.[374]

The EU also cooperates closely with the ICMPD although no cooperation agreement has been signed between the two organisations. The European Commission provides the largest part of the funding attributed to the organisation: 36 per cent in 2012, 41 per cent in 2013 and 55 per cent in 2014.[375] In addition to funding coming from a commitment to occasional/one-off medium-term projects, the organisation has also concluded a Delegation Agreement in the framework of the Internal Security Fund, an instrument established for financial support for police cooperation, preventing and combating crime, and crisis management.[376] The ICMPD is entrusted with the indirect management of the Mobility Partnership Facility with a budget of €1.5 million. This facility will be used to fund actions whose main focus will be the provision of support to partner countries to fight and neutralise criminal networks and organisations active in migrant smuggling into the EU as well as to ensure effective law enforcement cooperation in that regard.[377] Given the blurred boundaries between the smuggling of migrants and trafficking in human beings, the implementation of these actions may have an important impact in fostering capacities in third countries and in strengthening their cooperation with EU Member States.

---

[370] European Union, 'EU Statement – session 8, Combating trafficking in human beings', at the occasion of the OSCE Human Dimension Implementation Meeting 2012, 28 September 2012, HDIM. DEL/0193/12, 2, available at: www.osce.org/odihr/94417?download=true.

[371] As examples, see the Agenda of the 2013 Conference of the Alliance against Trafficking in Persons, available at: www.osce.org/secretariat/102415?download=true; and the Agenda of the 2020 Conference, available at: www.osce.org/files/f/documents/9/d/447718_2.pdf, at which the Acting Coordinator gave a keynote address and the former coordinator intervened as a panellist.

[372] OSE/CTHB, *Combating Trafficking and Exploitation: Human Rights, Social Justice and the Rule of Law, 2013 Annual Report* (2013) 55.

[373] ibid 56.

[374] Source: www.osce.org/networks/111481.

[375] Source: www.icmpd.org/fileadmin/ICMPD-Website/ICMPD-website_2011/ICMPD_General/ICMPD_funding_info_2012-2014.pdf.

[376] Regulation (EU) No 513/2014 of the European Parliament and of the Council of 16 April 2014 establishing, as part of the Internal Security Fund, the instrument for financial support for police cooperation, preventing and combating crime, and crisis management and repealing Council Decision 2007/125/JHA [2014] OJ L150/93.

[377] Commission, Annex to the Commission Implementing Decision concerning the adoption of the work programme for 2014 and the financing for Union actions within the framework of the Internal Security Fund, C (2014) 5651, Annex 1, 14.

c. Bilateral Cooperation with International Organisations

The EU develops its bilateral cooperation with international organisations and especially with UN-affiliated organisations. These organisations are funded through yearly contributions and, as evidence of their close cooperation, the EU ranks among the biggest contributors.[378]

Some UN-affiliated organisations cooperate only indirectly with the EU in the fight against trafficking in human beings. For instance, the EU signed two Strategic Partnership Agreements with the UNHCR in 2005.[379] The second Agreement, signed with the Commissioner for Justice, Freedom and Security through an exchange of letters, aimed at facilitating stronger cooperation on asylum and refugee protection issues.[380] Similarly, little can be said about the cooperation between the EU and the ILO in the combat against trafficking in human beings. The two organisations signed cooperation agreements in 1953 and 1958, and the Community, represented by the Commission, has since 1989[381] obtained official observer status at the ILO Conference and in the ILO Governing Body. In practice, high-level meetings are organised every year with the European Commission, and on a day-to-day basis, both formal and informal meetings are held between the EU institutions and the ILO Brussels Office.[382] Interestingly, the EU has made 'Trade and Sustainable Development Chapters' a standard component of its new generation comprehensive free trade agreements,[383] in which the parties notably undertake to make continued and sustained efforts towards ratifying and effectively implementing the fundamental ILO Conventions, including the ILO Forced Labour Convention.[384]

Cooperation with other UN-affiliated organisations has been more intense, especially in the fight against trafficking in human beings. The EU has, for instance,

---

[378] 'The EU is the single largest financial contributor to the UN system. The EU funds 38% of the UN's regular budget, … and about one-half of all UN Member States' contributions to UN funds and programmes'. Source: ec.europa.eu/europeaid/node/13864.

[379] The first one has been signed with the then External Relations and ENP Commissioner, in order to develop and better structure existing cooperation on protection and assistance for refugees and other people of concern outside EU borders. Trafficking in human beings is not directly mentioned in this Agreement; however the EU and UNHCR commit themselves to encourage a close cooperation notably in the fields of Repatriation, and Reintegration of refugees and other persons in need. Agreement, 5, full text available at: www.refworld.org/docid/42135e6c4.html.

[380] UNHCR, News Stories, 'UNHCR signs cooperation agreements with European Commission', Press release of 15 February 2005, available at: www.unhcr.org/4212384f4.html.

[381] With the entry into force of the Amsterdam Treaty, and the new competences conferred on the EU in the areas of employment and social policy, the Commission and the ILO renewed the exchange of letters in May 2001. See R Delarue, 'The EU–ILO Partnership and the Global Identify of the Union's Social Model' in H de Waele and JJ Kuipers (eds), *The European Union's Emerging International Identity* (Leiden, Martinus Nijhoff Publishers, 2013) 137–38.

[382] Interview No 5.

[383] G Marín Durán, 'Sustainable Development Chapters in EU Free Trade Agreements: Emerging Compliance Issues' (2020) 57 *Common Market Law Review* 1031, 1032.

[384] See, eg, Free trade Agreement between the European Union and the Republic of Singapore [2019] OJ L294/99. The references to the ILO Conventions can be found in Art 12.3(4).

concluded a Framework Agreement with the IOM for streamlining financial and administrative procedures. An EU–IOM Strategic Partnership, which was signed in 2012, foresees regular meetings between senior officials as well as the regular exchange of views on comprehensive migration policies and related operational matters.[385] The IOM is notably called on to cooperate with the EU in the implementation of the Global Approach to Migration and Mobility.[386] The organisation has even received preferential treatment in the receipt of EU funding because of its expertise and its long-standing cooperation with the EU. It has, for instance, received a direct grant for a project on 'safe and sustainable return and reintegration of victims of trafficking in human beings', to be conducted in Albania, Morocco and Ukraine,[387] which was justified by 'the specific characteristic of the actions requiring a high degree of specialisation on trafficking in human beings and return issues'.[388]

Cooperation with UNODC is also more developed. The two organisations have signed letters of intent on cooperation,[389] which have resulted in different activities being carried out. Europol and UNODC have concluded a Strategic Cooperation Agreement foreseeing mutual consultation, exchange of information and technical cooperation between them.[390] The two organisations in 2015 launched the Global Action to Prevent and Address Trafficking in Persons and the Smuggling of Migrants, renewed in 2018. Implemented in partnership with the IOM and UNICEF, the first phase of the programme assisted 13 selected countries in the development and implementation of comprehensive national counter-trafficking and smuggling responses, including regional and transregional cooperation, and the protection of victims of trafficking and smuggled migrants.[391] Notably, activities under this framework supported the strengthening of countries' capacities to tackle trafficking and smuggling and the inter-linkages between them efficiently. A second phase launched in 2018 focused on four countries (Afghanistan, Iran, Iraq and Pakistan) and anticipated similar activities. This initiative is worth mentioning, first, because of the important budget allocated by the EU, respectively €11 million and €12 million for each phase, and second, because it illustrates how the EU may through such large-scale programmes support the work of

---

[385] Source: ec.europa.eu/dgs/home-affairs/what-is-new/news/news/2013/docs/20130502_eu_iom_faq_en.pdf. See also Commission, 'Mid-Term Implementation report' (n 34) 15: 'In 2012, DGs HOME, DEVCO and ECHO, together with EEAS, established a framework for strategic cooperation with IOM which serves as a basis for interaction and outlines the structure and development of their relationship'.

[386] Source: eeas.europa.eu/delegations/un_geneva/eu_un_geneva/migration_asylum/iom/index_en.htm.

[387] Commission, 'Annex to the Commission Implementing Decision concerning the adoption of the work programme for 2014 and the financing for Union actions and emergency assistance within the framework of the Asylum, Migration and Integration Fund (AMIF)', COM (2014) 5652 final, 7–8.

[388] ibid 8.

[389] Commission, 'Mid-Term Implementation report' (n 34) 15.

[390] For more details about Europol's cooperation agreements, see ch 2, III.B.i 'Cooperation with Europol'.

[391] Egypt, Morocco, Mali, Niger, South Africa; Nepal, Lao PDR, Kyrgyzstan, Pakistan, Belarus, Ukraine, Brazil and Colombia.

international organisations, implementing objectives compatible with its own external priorities.

The EU has thus developed its bilateral cooperation with most of the other intergovernmental organisations active in combating trafficking in human beings. It is no surprise that its closest cooperation has been identified with those in charge of monitoring the implementation of binding instruments in this field: the Council of Europe and UNODC, thus complementing the normative interactions between instruments and the ongoing dialogue on the interpretation to be given to them.

iii. Other Bilateral Cooperation Initiatives

Other intergovernmental organisations have been keen to develop their bilateral cooperation, independently of the EU, illustrating the widespread commitment in favour of cooperation.

The Council of Europe deserves special attention in this section, especially considering the importance of its counter-trafficking efforts in south-east Europe, where it monitors the correct implementation of the Convention. As a consequence, the organisation has developed strong bilateral relations with the other organisations active in this field and in this geographic area. The overlapping mandates and membership of the OSCE and Council of Europe, as well as their complementary structures, provide ample room for cooperation. The two organisations started their cooperation in 2000 with the setting out of a Common Catalogue of Cooperation Modalities. A few years later in decisions made in parallel with the Council of Europe Committee of Ministers[392] and the OSCE Permanent Council, the two organisations established a Coordination group,[393] whose first mission was to establish and review the list of priority areas for their cooperation.[394] A Joint Statement, with a Declaration on Cooperation, was signed in May 2005, calling on the Coordination Group to give priority to the formulation of concrete recommendations on how to foster coordination and cooperation in areas of common concern, such as combating trafficking in human beings.[395] The Council of Europe has also opened a Liaison Office in Vienna. Their cooperation

---

[392] The Committee of Ministers is the Council of Europe's statutory decision-making body, that acts on behalf of the organisation. It is composed of the Ministers for Foreign Affairs of the Council of Europe Member States.

[393] OSCE, Permanent Council, Enhanced cooperation between the OSCE and the Council of Europe, Decision No 637, PC.DEC/637, 2 December 2004, available at: www.osce.org/pc/14732?download=true; and Council of Europe, Committee of Ministers, Enhanced cooperation between the OSCE and the Council of Europe, 1–2 December 2004, Decision No CM/865/01122204, available at: wcd.coe.int/ViewDoc.jsp?id=798905&Site=COE&BackColorInternet=C3C3C3&BackColorIntranet=EDB021&BackColorLogged=F5D383.

[394] Source: wcd.coe.int/ViewDoc.jsp?id=790665&Site=COE&BackColorInternet=C3C3C3&BackColorIntranet=EDB021&BackColorLogged=F5D383.

[395] Declaration, quoted in G Ulfstein, 'The Council of Europe and the OSCE: enhancing cooperation and complementarity through greater coherence' (Report), DPP (2012) 1, 5 and 6.

takes different forms: for instance, the two organisations participate in each other's events, and the OSCE Special Representative has obtained the status of observer with the Committee of Parties of the Council of Europe Anti-Trafficking Convention. In 2012, an expert noted that it was 'difficult to find many joint activities', but their cooperation has found a new impetus since then.[396] The respective secretariats of GRETA and the OSCE Special Representative regularly exchange information, 'in particular in the context of the preparation of evaluation visits by GRETA and country visits by the OSCE SR/CTHB'. The Country Evaluation Reports produced by GRETA reveal that, where appropriate, GRETA meets the OSCE's mission.[397] New forms of cooperation have been introduced, such as joint events[398] and joint activities, such as the organisation of workshops for judges and prosecutors, which will help States implement the GRETA and OSCE recommendations.[399] The Coordination Group regularly examines cooperation in the area of the fight against trafficking in human beings.[400] The Council of Europe has also engaged in bilateral relations with UN-affiliated organisations. With the IOM, it engages in discussions on migration issues[401] and the Parliamentary Commission draws up regular reports on the IOM's activities,[402] insisting on the existence of a 'clear convergence between the Council of Europe's and the IOM's activities in the field of trafficking'.[403] Besides the organisation of joint events, cooperation between the Council of Europe and international organisations includes cooperation in the monitoring of the implementation of international and European standards by States parties to the Convention. GRETA reports its meetings with representatives working in local offices of UN agencies (IOM, ILO,

---

[396] For a detailed account of the activities undertaken, Council of Europe and OSCE, 18th meeting of the Coordination Group between the Council of Europe and the OSCE, Vienna, 25 October 2013, CM/Inf (2013) 35, Appendix 2, para 5(o).

[397] See for instance, GRETA, *Report on Bosnia–Herzegovina* (2013) 7, 45; and GRETA, *Report on Montenegro* (2012) 9, 52.

[398] Joint Council of Europe–OSCE 'Not for Sale' Conference held in Vienna in February 2014.

[399] The second workshop was organised in April 2015 and focused on the implementation of the non-punishment principle. Further information at: www.coe.int/t/dghl/monitoring/trafficking/docs/seminarsconf/workshop2_press_release_EN.asp.

[400] See Council of Europe and OSCE, 20th meeting of the Co-ordination Group between the Council of Europe and the OSCE, held in October 2014 (CM/Inf (2014) 29 not publicly available). The next examination took place in the second half of 2015 (see CM/Inf(2015)10, 24 April 2015, available at: wcd.coe.int/ViewDoc.jsp?Ref=CM/Inf(2015)10&Language=lanEnglish&Ver=original&Site=COE&BackColorInternet=C3C3C3&BackColorIntranet=EDB021&BackColorLogged=F5D383, Appendix 2, para 13).

[401] Secretariat General, *Framework for Council of Europe work on migration issues 2011–2013*, 10 June 2011, SG/Inf (2011) 10 rev, para 9, available at: wcd.coe.int/ViewDoc.jsp?id=1777209&Site=CM. The text reads as follows: 'A coordination unit could ensure the coordination of the Council of Europe work in the field and … secure cooperation and joint action within the Council of Europe with other international organisations (EU, UNHCR, IOM, OSCE)'.

[402] Parliamentary Assembly, *Activities of the IOM*, Report, 9 July 2007, Doc No 11351, paras 33–39, available at: assembly.coe.int/ASP/Doc/XrefViewHTML.asp?FileID=11595&Language=EN.

[403] Parliamentary Assembly, *Activities of the IOM*, Report, 9 July 2007, Doc No 11351, para 38, available at: assembly.coe.int/ASP/Doc/XrefViewHTML.asp?FileID=11595&Language=EN.

UNHCR, UNICEF) during its country evaluation visits[404] and includes references to the country-specific work of UN human rights bodies.[405]

Other international organisations active in the field of the fight against trafficking in human beings develop bilateral (or even tripartite) relations in order to enhance their cooperation and coordination. Their cooperation can lead to the publication of joint reports/studies, such as the study on Strengthening Migration Governance, published by the OSCE and the ILO in December 2010,[406] or the Handbook on Establishing Effective Labour Migration Policies in Countries of Origin and Destination, published by the OSCE, the IOM and the ILO in 2006.[407] International organisations may also conclude cooperation agreements. UNODC and the IOM, for instance, signed a Memorandum of Understanding in April 2012, in order 'to enhance coordination, to further exchange information and to extend joint activities between both agencies, especially in the combat of trafficking in persons'.[408] Meetings are also regularly organised, such as staff level meetings between the UN, the Council of Europe and the OSCE for the exchange of information and coordination of activities,[409] or between the Brussels offices of UN-affiliated organisations.[410]

C. Importance of the Coordination and Cooperation Efforts

It is no surprise that the degree of coordination and cooperation reached in bilateral settings is higher than in multilateral settings. Bilateral cooperation presents the advantages of allowing the conclusion of binding instruments and facilitates the organisation and conduct of joint activities. The commitment of actors involved in the field of the fight against trafficking in human beings in favour of multilateral, comprehensive and coordinated activities is clear from the abundance and diversity of bilateral cooperation initiatives that have been developed. This results in a tangled web of relations, which are more or less formalised.

---

[404] See for instance, GRETA, *Report on Bosnia–Herzegovina* (2013) 7, 45; and GRETA, *Report on Montenegro* (2012) 9, 52; GRETA, *Fourth General Report* (n 277) 23.

[405] GRETA, *Third General Report on GRETA's activities covering the period from 1 August 2012 to 31 July 2013* (2013) 27. GRETA also meets representatives of NGOs active in each country, being either part of large transnational NGOs (La Strada, Terre des Hommes, etc – GRETA, *Report on Moldova* (2011) 25, 41); or part of local networks of NGOs (GRETA, *Report on Croatia* (2011) 20, 35).

[406] ILO, 'OSCE, ILO launch new study 'Strengthening Migration Governance', Press release of 16 December 2010, available at: www.ilo.org/global/about-the-ilo/media-centre/press-releases/WCMS_150031/lang--en/index.htm.

[407] Full text of the Handbook is available at: www.osce.org/eea/19242.

[408] UNODC, 'UNODC and IOM sign agreement for closer cooperation to combat human trafficking, migrant smuggling and to improve border management', Press release of 17 April 2012, availableat:www.unodc.org/unodc/en/press/releases/2012/April/unodc-and-iom-sign-agreement-for-closer-cooperation-to-combat-human-trafficking-migrant-smuggling-and-to-improve-border-management.html.

[409] Source: www.osce.org/networks/111477.

[410] Interview No 5.

In this landscape, the EU appears as a crucial partner, seeking to formalise its relations with its partners and keen on providing funding opportunities to them. Its competences in a large scope of fields relevant for the implementation of a comprehensive approach against human trafficking might explain why the EU has developed relations with almost all members of the Alliance against Trafficking in Human Beings.[411] Nevertheless, the EU is not the only organisation seeking to establish bilateral relations with its partners. Many organisations engage in bilateral relations with partners other than the EU. The Council of Europe and the OSCE have, for instance, developed a strong bilateral relationship leading to more advanced cooperation in the field of the fight against human trafficking than the one they have with the EU.

The rationale behind the increase in the number of these mechanisms of coordination and cooperation, established in multilateral or bilateral forms, lies in the wish to avoid duplication of effort and the waste of resources of relevant actors. International and regional organisations, especially those depending on States parties' contributions to their budget, do not have unlimited resources at their disposal. The development of large-scale projects, such as Glo.Act between the EU and UNODC thus gives a certain place to the EU, which becomes through its funding programmes a key partner for international organisations, and gains the capacity to shape their activities in line with its own strategic priorities. Coordination and cooperation with their partners allows them to concentrate on the tasks and activities for which they have the most expertise and experience. Even though they limit themselves to one aspect of the counter-trafficking response, this solution leads to a certain extent to an allocation of tasks between relevant actors. This idea of allocation of tasks is further reinforced by the fact that certain organisations, such as the EU, even delegate certain tasks to these specialised organisations and provide them with specific funding opportunities to carry them out. The funding of the ICMPD's activities[412] reflect for instance the tendency of the EU to delegate certain tasks to its partners, especially to those with an expertise in certain policy fields.

Coordination and cooperation efforts are also noticeable in the efforts to monitor the implementation of international and European standards by States parties. The abundance of monitoring mechanisms may generate a certain 'fatigue' for national authorities, which are called on to answer questionnaires, to welcome experts carrying out country visits and to report in numerous forums on their counter-trafficking actions. Although the recognition of a single monitoring mechanism is neither feasible nor desirable, the frequency of cross-references to other instruments and monitoring bodies' work is to be welcomed and encouraged.

---

[411] UNHCR, ILO, Council of Europe, OSCE, UNODC, IOM, Interpol, etc.

[412] For instance, in 2014 while contributions from the ICMPD Member States represented 31% of the budget, contributions from its partners represented 61% of the budget. Source: www.icmpd. org/fileadmin/ICMPD-Website/ICMPD-website_2011/ICMPD_General/ICMPD_funding_info_ 2012-2014.pdf.

GRETA's reports constitute a best practice to be praised and imitated because they include references to instruments set out in other frameworks (EU or UN) and because they are partially based on the information gathered during meetings with other relevant actors (local offices/missions of other organisations or of NGOs). The European Commission, which is fully aware of the importance of 'monitoring and evaluation procedures that do not create repetitive reporting mechanisms', intends to 'exploit as far as possible existing reporting mechanisms, such as … the reports of the GRETA'.[413]

VI. Conclusion

With trafficking in human beings being an issue of concern for many actors, it is no surprise that the EU is not the only actor on the international scene that decided to develop its own policy to address this issue and is willing to cooperate with other relevant stakeholders. Since the 1990s, actors belonging to all levels of governance have developed initiatives, instruments and activities aimed at reducing trafficking in human beings and in the long-term at eradicating it. At each level, interactions exist between all actors active in this field, such as intergovernmental organisations, States, civil society organisations and businesses. Their interactions were based on their commitment to multilateralism and the belief that common challenges require common solutions. Their interactions have, for instance, led to the shared belief that a comprehensive approach to human trafficking is essential. This comprehensive approach is traditionally referred to as the 'Three Ps', ie, 'Prevention, Prosecution and Protection', and one might consider that it has now gained an additional objective: a fourth P standing for 'Partnership'. Recent policy documents adopted by lawmakers, such as the intergovernmental organisations active at international and regional level, repeatedly stress the importance of building partnerships among themselves and with all other relevant actors. As a consequence, there is a real openness towards the work carried out by others, and their mutual interactions are particularly interesting to analyse. Mutual cooperation is often present too and leads to joint initiatives being carried out. Although it cannot be said that all relevant actors coordinate their actions, it must be stressed that they are willing to cooperate, and this helps to avoid duplication of their efforts.

The field of the fight against trafficking in human beings is thus marked by the abundance of actors, whose constant interactions contribute towards shaping a common and comprehensive approach to addressing the phenomenon. In this context, it is complicated (if not impossible) to assess the exact influence of the efforts of the EU to externally promote its counter-trafficking policy on the

---

[413] Commission, 'Mid-Term Implementation report' (n 34) 15–16.

development of a global response to trafficking, as well as on the national policies and legislation of its Member States and of targeted third countries. The potential influence of intergovernmental organisations and other external actors on policies and legislation adopted and implemented at national level cannot be attributed to a single organisation or actor. In contrast, the EU's external activities integrate themselves in the joint efforts of the wide range of actors active in the fight against trafficking in human beings at all levels of governance. This presents an additional challenge for the EU, which must carry out its efforts to externally promote the EU's policy against trafficking in human beings, not only in a coherent way across diverse EU policy areas, but also in full awareness of the activities designed and implemented by other actors. By way of example, and as a demonstration of such awareness, the EU has been fully engaged in the negotiations and adoption of the Global Compact for a Safe, Orderly and Regular Migration, which contains key recommendations on how best to address trafficking in human beings in the context of international migration.[414] The EU has taken its own position on the text, and supports its adoption, despite the decision of some EU Member States not to sign it.[415] This situation lets us to make two remarks concerning the challenges met in the course of the external promotion of the EU's counter-trafficking policy.

First, it is impossible to identify precise elements, norms or an approach which would be specific to the EU and which could have been successfully promoted and incorporated into other legal frameworks. In the course of our analysis, we were unable to find one example where the EU has been the standard-setter for the rest of the actors active in this field. For instance, the authorship of the comprehensive approach to address trafficking in human beings cannot be attributed to the EU or to a specific actor. Such a situation results from the transformations of traditional law-making at international level. In the current context, the EU has limited power to influence the preparation of international and regional standards alone, and it is thus integrated into all relevant frameworks at international and regional levels, addressing its own priorities, including in human rights forums. However, the fact that the EU appears as a key partner for all the other actors active at international level in combating trafficking in human beings should not be underestimated. The EU has earned the competence and capacity to become a fully-fledged member on the international scene in a field encompassing security and migration issues. This constitutes an achievement considering that these areas have traditionally been reserved for EU Member States alone. The latter remain eager to preserve their competences. Consequently, they have only accepted sharing their competences

---

[414] For a short overview of the EU's involvement, see: eeas.europa.eu/delegations/un-new-york_en/39335/Towards%20a%20Global%20Compact%20on%20Migration.

[415] As of 5 November 2018, Hungary and Austria have announced their decision not to participate in the adoption of the instrument, and other EU Member States might follow. For an overview, see, 'EU criticises Austria for not signing UN global migration pact', *The Guardian* (1 November 2018), available at: www.theguardian.com/world/2018/nov/01/austria-criticised-not-signing-un-global-migration-compact-european-commission.

with the EU, and they remain active on the international scene in the field of the combat against trafficking in human beings. Notwithstanding these elements, the added value of the external action of the EU in this sensitive field has been recognised as, for instance, when the Council granted the Commission the mandate to negotiate the Council of Europe Convention against trafficking in human beings, or when EU delegations delivered coordinated statements in the negotiations of the Global Compact on Migration.[416] Such practice has shown that the EU institutions manage to defend common positions and intervene in multilateral processes, either through the intermediary of the Member States or through the participation of its institutions as observers.

Second, the influence of the Union's promotion efforts is equally difficult to assess with regard to the evolution of national legislation and policies in its Member States and in third countries targeted by these efforts. The evolution of national policies and laws seems to result from a diversity of factors, which are complex to identify and to isolate. Some can be internal, such as the pressure on national governments and legislators from local civil society organisations, or the feedback received from national law enforcement and judicial authorities. Other factors can be external, and may lie, for instance, in their obligation to report frequently to monitoring bodies about the actions engaged in placing national laws and practices in line with international and regional standards. In this regard, an additional and fundamental factor of complexity should not be overlooked. All the legal instruments we have analysed recognise a margin of discretion that is left to the national authorities when they transpose into their national legal orders the standards contained therein and implement them. Many monitoring bodies have stressed the diversity of national norms, supposedly transposing and implementing the same provisions, and their recommendations seem insufficient to address such diversity. This finding is also valid for the instruments set out by the EU and their implementation by EU Member States.[417] Combating and preventing trafficking in human beings is addressed through a directive, a legislative instrument that binds Member States only with regard to the objectives to be achieved and leaves them with a margin of discretion. The existence of normative interactions between key international and European instruments does not guarantee a uniform, or at least coherent, transposition and implementation of the norms contained therein. Furthermore, the implementation of a comprehensive approach towards the prevention of and the fight against trafficking in human beings goes beyond the transposition of international and European standards. Practical elements defined through the preparation of national action plans and priorities, albeit highly sensitive and political, play an essential role, as well as the decision to fund specific

---

[416] Commission, 'Proposal for a Council Decision authorising the Commission to approve on behalf of the Union the Global Compact for Safe, Orderly and Regular Migration in the area of immigration policy' (Communication), COM (2018) 168 final, 1.

[417] See, eg, Commission, 'Report assessing the extent to which Member States have taken the necessary measures in order to comply with Directive 2011/36/EU' (n 303).

counter-trafficking activities. For instance, developing financial investigations enabling law enforcement authorities to trace and follow cash flows originating from trafficking activities means having qualified teams who are regularly trained in new methods developed by traffickers, and who are able to cooperate with their counterparts located in other countries. The allocation of stable and continuous public funding is thus necessary to develop such financial investigations and, more broadly, to develop counter-trafficking initiatives in line with international and European recommendations. Similarly prosecuting traffickers and securing their convictions is a key aspect of the counter-trafficking response, which lies solely in the hands of States, being called upon to address the negative trend of decreasing prosecution and convictions in Europe.[418] Further limits can be identified in the external promotion of the EU's counter-trafficking policy.

---

[418] Closing remarks by OSCE Special Representative at the occasion of the 20th Alliance Conference against Trafficking in Persons, SEC.GAL/104/20, 23 July 2020, available at: www.osce.org/files/f/documents/0/3/460222.pdf.

4

Limits of the EU's Actions and Future Avenues for Research

The external activities of the EU to strengthen the prevention and combat of trafficking in human beings are multifaceted and integrate themselves in multiple interactions with external partners, through which norms and policies tend to align. Nevertheless, fragmentation and complexity remain present, and they are further reinforced by the way migration, including human trafficking and migrant smuggling, has been increasingly perceived and addressed at global and regional levels. This evolution is reflected in the external counter-trafficking activities of the EU, and the present part will be devoted to the analysis of two new aspects of its activities that introduce new challenges in the development of the external dimension of the EU's policy against trafficking. The first aspect relates to the emergence of mixed migration flows, in which the persons on the move may fall under different legal regimes, being economic migrants, refugees and asylum seekers, smuggled migrants or victims of trafficking, with the possibility of overlaps and changes of 'status' throughout their journey. Such a phenomenon, coupled with the perceived increasing migratory pressure on the EU's external borders, in particular since 2015, has led to a new impetus in the EU's activities addressing migration. We will analyse how human trafficking is more and more addressed together with the smuggling of migrants, and how a response focusing again on criminal justice and border management measures seem to be preferred (I). As a side note, it is important to stress that in the 'EU jargon', the expression 'smuggling of migrants' is often replaced by other expressions such as irregular and/or illegal immigration, unauthorised entry etc. The second aspect derives from the same context, which led to changes in the policies and competences mobilised to address migration, including trafficking and smuggling. Both at international and regional level, counter-trafficking measures have been introduced in activities belonging to the field of defence and military activities. Within the EU, this resulted in resorting to competences and tools belonging to the Common Foreign Security Policy, in order to address trafficking and smuggling in particular in the Mediterranean (II). Further analysis of these two aspects is required. They potentially influence the coherence of the external dimension of the EU's counter-trafficking policy, and they also potentially further endanger the pursuit of a comprehensive policy including human rights-based measures fostering the protection of fundamental rights.

I. Addressing Trafficking in the Framework of a Renewed EU Migration Policy

The EU's activities in countering the smuggling of migrants have been developed in parallel with those concerning trafficking in human beings, and this reflects in part the approach followed at international level. Before analysing the recent process through which human trafficking and smuggling are increasingly addressed simultaneously, it is necessary to take a step back to briefly discuss the distinction between the two notions, which are subject to separate legal definitions and a separate set of instruments.

Such distinction was not self-evident. When the European legislator adopted the Joint Action of 1997, its definition of trafficking in human beings confused the two phenomena. Some elements, such as the criminalisation of any behaviour which facilitates the entry into, transit through, residence in or exit from the territory of a Member State for gainful purposes reflected the stereotype in force at that time. Victims of trafficking were seen as third-country nationals, entering and/or residing illegally within Europe, and the distinction between victims of exploitation and irregular migrants was not always very clear. The adoption of the UN Convention against Transnational Organised Crime marked a first step in the distinction between the two phenomena as two separate Protocols were drafted to address them: the Protocol against Trafficking in Persons, especially Women and Children, and the Protocol against Smuggling of Migrants by Land, Sea and Air.[1] Such a distinction was also introduced in the EU legal order, with the adoption in 2002 of two sets of instruments: on the one hand the 2002 Council Framework Decision on the fight against trafficking in human beings,[2] since then replaced by the 2011 Directive; and on the other, a directive defining the facilitation of unauthorised entry, transit and residence,[3] and a Framework Decision on the strengthening of the penal framework to prevent the facilitation of unauthorised entry, transit and residence.[4] These instruments were adopted on various legal bases granting competences to the EU for approximating national criminal legislations (current Article 83 of the Treaty on the Functioning of the European Union (TFEU)) and for developing a common migration policy (current Article 79(1) TFEU).

---

[1] UN General Assembly, Protocol against the Smuggling of Migrants by Land, Sea and Air, Supplementing the United Nations Convention against Transnational Organized Crime, 15 November 2000, 2241 UNTS 507, Doc A/55/383.

[2] Council Framework Decision 2002/629/JHA of 19 July 2002 on combating trafficking in human beings [2002] OJ L203/1.

[3] Council Directive 2002/90/EC of 28 November 2002 defining the facilitation of unauthorised entry, transit and residence [2002] OJ L328/17.

[4] Council Framework Decision 2002/946/JHA of 28 November 2002 on the strengthening of the penal framework to prevent the facilitation of unauthorised entry, transit and residence [2002] OJ L328/1.

From a legal perspective, the following elements allow for a distinction between the two phenomena. First, one of the three constitutive elements of the offence of trafficking in human beings (the means) implies that the offence is carried out with the use of certain means, including coercion and/or deception. Such a definition suggests that traffickers use coercion or deception when they are recruiting and transporting people from one place to another.[5] On the contrary, the offence of smuggling does not imply that these means, for example, coercion and/or deception are used. Second, trafficking in human beings entails an element of subsequent exploitation from which traffickers profit, while smugglers derive profit through payments for smuggling services, which end when people reach their destination. Third, trafficking in human beings can take place both within States and across national frontiers, and in the latter case, the entry into a State can be achieved legally, especially when traffickers arrange authentic travel documents and visas. In cases of smuggling of migrants, international movement is always required, and the offence is characterised by illegal entry of a person into a State of which the person is not a national or a permanent resident. Finally, whereas for smuggling the consent of the migrant is deemed present, in trafficking situations the person has often been coerced into exploitation. Even if the person has consented, for instance to work as a prostitute abroad, his or her consent becomes irrelevant as soon as coercive means have been used against him or her. Tom Obokata summarises this theoretical distinction as follows: 'trafficking can be summarized as a migratory process in which people are transported involuntarily within or across national borders for the purpose of subsequent exploitation, while smuggling is about facilitation, for profit, of illegal entry with consent of individuals'.[6] The distinction in their legal regime is also noticeable regarding the rights granted to the persons concerned. Whereas persons deemed to be trafficking victims are entitled to certain rights and benefits due to their status, persons branded as having been smuggled may be stigmatised for the role that they have willingly played in attempting to breach international borders and may face detention and deportation.[7] Very few measures of protection and assistance are foreseen for smuggled migrants. They can benefit from the measures provided in Directive 2004/81/EC, which foresees the deliverance of residence permits to those who cooperate with the competent national authorities.[8] However, whereas Member

[5] T Obokata, 'Trafficking of Human Beings as a Crime Against Humanity: Some Implications for the International Legal System' (2005) 54 *International & Comparative Law Quarterly* 445, 447.

[6] ibid 448. See also in this respect V Roth, *Defining Human Trafficking and Identifying its Victims: A Study on the Impact and Future Challenges of International, European and Finnish Legal Responses to Prostitution-related Trafficking in Human Beings* (Leiden, Martinus Nijhoof Publishers, 2011) 77–154.

[7] M McAdam, 'Who's Who at the Border? A rights-based approach to identifying human trafficking at international borders' (2013) 2 *Anti-Trafficking Review* 33, 35.

[8] Council Directive 2004/81/EC of 29 April 2004 on the residence permit issued to third-country nationals who are victims of trafficking in human beings or who have been the subject of an action to facilitate illegal immigration, who cooperate with the competent authorities [2004] OJ L261/19.

States are obliged to transpose the text for victims of trafficking in human beings, they have discretion to decide whether or not they wish to extend it to smuggled migrants.[9] In 2014, only 10 Member States had made use of this possibility and some had added additional conditions.[10]

Yet separate legal definitions of the phenomena do not exclude overlaps and complexity in distinguishing them. Overlap and confusion are favoured by the presence of the concept of exploitation in both offences. Article 6(3)(b) of the Smuggling Protocol foresees smuggling with aggravating circumstance when it entails 'inhuman or degrading treatment, including for exploitation', which does not amount to the type of exploitation foreseen in the Trafficking Protocol. Exploitation in the framework of smuggling may for instance happen when a smuggler exploits a person's imminent migration needs by charging exorbitant smuggling fees or when landlords take advantage of migrants' irregular status to charge excessive fees.[11] However, in other cases the two criminal activities are very entangled and the distinction is more difficult, especially because migrants who place themselves at the mercy of smugglers are highly vulnerable to more severe forms of exploitation. For instance, a migrant paying the smuggling fees by providing a sexual service can be considered in a situation involving the grooming of a trafficked victim for sexual exploitation. Similarly, a migrant undertaking criminal activity, such as drug smuggling in lieu of payment for smuggling services, may be either considered as a person trafficked for exploitation in criminal activities or as a drug smuggler.[12]

Such porosity between trafficking and smuggling is further reinforced by the mixed nature of current migration flows, which include economic migrants, refugees and asylum seekers in need of international protection, victims of trafficking, stateless persons or unaccompanied minors,[13] who use the same routes and rely on the same smugglers to reach Europe.[14] Persons on the move may fall into one of these categories at the point when they reach a border, but they can belong to another category when they reach their destination.[15] This change happens frequently as persons who start their journeys in a voluntary manner

---

[9] Art 3, para 2 of the Directive provides that 'Member States may apply this Directive to the third country nationals who have been the subject of an action to facilitate illegal immigration'.

[10] Commission, 'Communication on the application of Directive 2004/81 on the residence permit issued to third-country nationals who are victims of trafficking in human beings or who have been the subject of an action to facilitate illegal immigration, who cooperate with the competent authorities', COM (2014) 635 final, 3.

[11] McAdam (n 7) 37–38.

[12] ibid 38.

[13] 'Regional Mixed Migration Secretariat, going West: contemporary mixed migration trends from the Horn of Africa to Libya and Europe' (2014) 15, available at: www.mixedmigration.org/wp-content/uploads/2018/05/008_going-west.pdf.

[14] M Ventrella, 'Identifying Victims of Human Trafficking at Hotspots by Focusing on People Smuggled to Europe' (2017) 5 *Social Inclusion* 69, 71.

[15] McAdam (n 7) 35.

are also vulnerable to networks of labour or sexual exploitation.[16] In practice, it is often unclear and difficult to determine whether someone is being trafficked or smuggled, and frequent overlaps are noticed, reducing the distinction between the two phenomena into a strange legal fiction.[17] Moreover, migrant smuggling has become an increasingly violent form of crime, often involving serious physical or psychological violence and human rights abuses, exposing women and children to particular risk.[18] It has for instance been reported that criminal networks are increasingly forcing irregular migrants to pay for smuggling services by illegal labour,[19] or through the exchange of sexual services.[20] Unaccompanied children are particularly vulnerable to these forms of exploitation. Among the large numbers of unaccompanied minors arriving in the EU (85,482 in 2015), up to 60 per cent of them have gone missing from asylum and reception centres and there is a serious risk that they fell prey to trafficking networks.[21]

Such a blur between human trafficking and smuggling is further evidenced when analysing policy and legal documents. The latter contain frequent occurrences in which both phenomena are referred to simultaneously. This is for instance the case within the TFEU, in which Article 79, paragraph 1 provides that 'the Union shall develop a common immigration policy aimed at ensuring, at all stages, ... the prevention of, and enhanced measures to combat, illegal immigration and trafficking in human beings'. Both phenomena are also subject to very similar, if not identical, approaches. The EU Action Plan against migrant smuggling[22] further highlights such blurring of the boundaries between the two phenomena. This text, which aims at countering and preventing migrant smuggling while ensuring the protection of the human rights of migrants, is explicitly 'based on a multidisciplinary approach, involving actors and institutions at local, regional, national and international levels'.[23] The EU's answer is based on four pillars, in which criminal justice remains a strong and essential component of the first two pillars. Enhanced police and judicial response, encompassing criminal justice measures, such as enhancing financial investigations or operational cooperation between national authorities, is supported, and shall be accompanied by improved gathering and sharing of information, which aims at obtaining a better picture of the modus

---

[16] Commission, 'EU Action Plan against migrant smuggling (2015–2020)' (Communication), COM (2015) 285 final, 8.

[17] Y Dandurand and J Jahn, 'The Failing International Legal Framework on Migrant Smuggling and Human Trafficking' in J Winterdyk and J Jones (eds), *The Palgrave International Handbook of Human Trafficking*, (London, Palgrave Macmillan, 2020) 787.

[18] Council, 'Conclusions on migrant smuggling', 10 March 2016, Council Doc No 6995/16, 2. See also Commission, 'Communication on the State of Play of Implementation of the Priority Actions under the European Agenda on Migration', COM (2016) 85 final, 16.

[19] Europol, *Migrant smuggling in the European Union* (2016) 2.

[20] UNICEF, *Neither Safe nor Sound: Unaccompanied children on the coastline of the English Channel and the North Sea* (2016) 79–81.

[21] Europol (n 19) 11–12.

[22] Commission, 'EU Action Plan against migrant smuggling (2015–2020)' (n 16).

[23] ibid 3.

operandi, routes and economic models of smuggling networks in order to target the crime more effectively. The third pillar refers to enhanced prevention of smuggling, but even though it refers to the assistance to vulnerable migrants, it follows a strong border control rationale, focussing on preventing migrants from reaching the territory of the EU. This translates for instance in measures aimed at deterring migrants from undertaking their journey, raising awareness about the risks of smuggling among prospective migrants, or in measures supporting cooperation with business operators, especially in the sectors most at risk: transport and shipping. This echoes with a series of legislative measures imposing liability on carriers who fail to comply with immigration control-related obligations.[24] Finally, stronger cooperation with third countries constitutes the fourth pillar of this Action Plan and it concerns a wide variety of policy areas. Besides continuing with its efforts to address the root causes of migration, the EU pledges to also encourage partner countries to become Parties to the UN Protocol on Smuggling of Migrants, and provide them with capacity-building support, especially to promote the exchange of information and to strengthen investigations into and the prosecution of smuggling offences in their territories.[25]

Many of the measures envisaged present similarities and connections with those implemented to combat trafficking in human beings, especially concerning the need for extended cooperation with third countries. Such a trend continues in later documents, including for the envisaged EU's external activities.[26] For the European Commission, 'external migratory pressure is the "new normal" both for the EU and for partners countries', and formal or informal agreements should be concluded in order to tackle migration upstream.[27] In order to give substance to this objective, the EU has developed countless initiatives,[28] funds and frameworks, mixing various objectives relating to migration, security or development cooperation and relying on various incentives. The Commission for instance proposed a change in approach with the expansion of compacts aimed at ensuring a coherent and tailored engagement of the EU and its Member States, acting in a coordinated manner putting together instruments, tools and leverage to reach comprehensive partnerships with third countries. Such compacts should reflect a differentiated content, taking into account the acute pressure faced by transit and host countries to provide assistance to migrants and refugees, and to

---

[24] V Mitsilegas, *The Criminalisation of Migration in Europe: Challenges for Human Rights and the Rule of Law* (Berne, Springer International Publishing, 2015) 23–24.

[25] Commission, 'EU Action Plan against migrant smuggling (2015–2020)' (n 16) 9.

[26] Commission, 'Communication on establishing a new Partnership Framework with countries under the European Agenda on Migration', COM (2016) 385 final.

[27] S Poli, 'The Integration of Migration Concerns into EU External Policies: Instruments, Techniques and Legal Problems' (2020) 5 *European Papers* 71, 72.

[28] Commission, 'EU Action Plan against migrant smuggling (2015–2020)' (n 16) 9: cooperation to address smuggling of migrants including 'through the Rabat, Khartoum, Budapest and Prague Processes, the ACP-EU Dialogue, the EU–Africa Migration and Mobility Dialogues and the Malta Summit devoted to migration'.

target criminal networks involved in smuggling and trafficking.[29] Close attention has been paid to these new cooperation mechanisms, with authors taking stock of the diversity of the external measures implemented, among which compacts are just one of the many mechanisms developed.[30] This preference for informal arrangements has also been pinpointed, notably for their consequences on the institutional balance within the EU legal order,[31] and many authors uncovered the 'burden-shifting' or containment strategy behind such instruments, introducing a clear conditionality rewarding the countries that cooperate in managing the flows of irregular migrants and refugees, while penalising others.[32] This approach does not simply result from the external pressures of migration, but it also constitutes to a certain extent a policy alternative to 'escape' several policy failures, relating for instance to relocation and readmission of migrants within and outside the EU.[33] Its implementation involves a wide range of actors: the EU institutions and agencies[34] are in the frontline, together with the EU Member States,[35] but measures are also implemented in cooperation with other stakeholders. Third countries located along the key migratory routes to the EU are called upon to assist the EU in managing its external borders. Such a form of extraterritorial border control is accompanied by financial support destined to cover the basic needs of refugees and migrants, such as access to food and basic services, and to help the countries to strengthen their migration management capacity, including supporting temporary reception centres.[36] International and regional organisations also collaborate with the EU and receive funding[37] to develop activities supporting increased prosecution of traffickers and smugglers, or which aim to improve assistance to trafficking victims and migrants in their countries of origin. The large multi-year funding attributed to the United Nations Office on Drugs

---

[29] Commission, 'Communication on establishing a new Partnership Framework with countries under the European Agenda on Migration' (n 26) 6.

[30] P Garcia Andrade, I Martin and S Mananashvili, *EU cooperation with third countries in the field of migration*, Study for the European Parliament, PE 536.469 (2015).

[31] Poli (n 27) 79–80; or P Garcia Andrade, 'The Distribution of Powers between EU Institutions for Conducting External Affairs through Non-Binding Instruments' (2016) 1 *European Papers* 115.

[32] eg, R Cortinovis, 'Forced Displacement and EU External Action: Exogenous Shocks, Policy Frames and Institutional Dynamics' (2017) 22 *European Foreign Affairs Review* 473, 487–88.

[33] L Marin, 'The Cooperation Between Frontex and Third Countries in Information Sharing: Practices, Law and Challenges in Externalizing Border Control Functions' (2020) 26 *European Public Law* 157, 158.

[34] See for instance the increased mandate given to Frontex for cooperation with third countries, detailed in Marin, ibid 157.

[35] N Reslow, 'Making and Implementing Multi-Actor EU External Migration Policy: The Mobility Partnerships' in S Carrera, L den Hertog, M Panizzon and D Kostakopoulou (eds), *EU External Migration Policies in an Era of Global Mobilities: Intersecting Policy Universes* (Leiden, Brill Nijhoff, 2019) 282–83.

[36] Commission, 'Progress Report on the Implementation of the European Agenda on Migration' (Communication), COM (2019) 481 final, 8.

[37] L den Hertog, 'Implementers? The Role of International Organisations in EU Funding for External Migration Policy' (2017) 12(1) *Journal of Regional Security* 5.

and Crime (UNODC) by the EU to set up and implement the Global Action to Prevent and Address Trafficking in Persons and the Smuggling of Migrants is representative of such trend whereby the EU tasks one of its partners to develop the capacity of third countries to tackle trafficking and smuggling on their territory, supposedly in a comprehensive manner.[38]

From the perspective of our analysis of the external dimension of the EU's policy against trafficking in human beings, these developments are important as they signal the intention of the EU to continue to outsource as much as possible certain missions and tasks to third countries. Beyond the necessity for third countries to conform with international and European standards on trafficking in order to facilitate cross-border police and judicial cooperation in criminal matters, the current approach of the EU also implies that third countries should themselves be involved in preventing trafficking flows from reaching the EU through the implementation of comprehensive measures. These include not only those belonging to the criminal justice approach to the phenomenon, such as the prosecution of traffickers, or to a border management perspective, through the reinforcement of the capacities of border guards to detect trafficking victims, but also those participating in a human rights-based approach to trafficking, directly detecting and identifying victims of trafficking and/or vulnerable persons who may fall into exploitation and providing them with assistance and protection.

This raise several questions that cannot unfortunately be addressed here, such as the lack of accountability of EU institutions for such externalisation of the EU migration's policy[39] and the attempts undertaken to remedy it through the lens of EU public procurement and budgetary rules,[40] or the challenge imposed on third countries with limited financial and administrative capacity to uphold migrants' rights.[41] The latter concern finds an echo at international level, with the adoption and the implementation of the Global Compact on Safe, Orderly and Regular Migration, which contains clear commitments regarding the provision of financial and technical assistance and the establishment of a capacity-building mechanism in the United Nations.[42]

---

[38] For an illustration of the interplay between this programme and other sources of funding, as well as the objectives pursued, see Vice-President Mogherini, Answer to the Parliamentary question on organ harvesting and trafficking in Egypt, E-006224/2017(ASW).

[39] S Carrera et al, *Oversight and Management of the EU Trust Funds, Democratic Accountability, Challenges and Promising Practices*, Study for the European Parliament, PE 603.821 (2018).

[40] See T Spijkerboer and E Steyger, 'European External Migration Funds and Public Procurement Law' (2019) 4 *European Papers* 493; and the audits realised by the European Court of Auditors, eg, *Special Report No 9 /2016 EU external migration spending in Southern Mediterranean and Eastern Neighbourhood countries until 2014*, available at: www.eca.europa.eu/en/Pages/DocItem. aspx?did=35674.

[41] M Barslund, M Lücke and M Ruhs, *Rethinking EU migration and asylum policies: Managing immigration jointly with countries of origin and transit*, 2019 MEDAM Assessment Report on Asylum and Migration Policies in Europe (Kiel, IfW, 2019) 28.

[42] UN General Assembly, Global Compact on Safe, Orderly and Regular Migration, A/RES/73/195, paras 39(b) and 43.

Last but not least, the evolution of the EU's migration policy, including addressing trafficking and smuggling jointly/concomitantly, raises several questions concerning the coherence of the EU's external activities, and their coherence with the activities of other stakeholders. Many authors have analysed this aspect, including defending a certain policy incoherence as long as checks and balances are in place to check that compliance with the rule of law and human rights are in place.[43] However, further pressure is placed on such coherence with the mobilisation of new tools to address trafficking and smuggling: the resort to defence and military missions.

II. Militarisation of the Response to Trafficking in Human Beings

The comprehensive approach developed by the EU to address trafficking in human beings, as well as the smuggling of migrants, includes activities from various policy fields. In the external dimension of its policy against human trafficking, our analysis highlighted the importance of the criminal justice measures, addressing trafficking as a criminal threat to be fought through increased cooperation in criminal matters with third countries. It also highlighted the combined attention paid to the response to trafficking in human beings and the smuggling of migrants. The two phenomena share another characteristic that has already received substantial attention from academics: the introduction of a militarised approach to address these phenomena.[44]

A. The Mobilisation of CFSP Competences

The intention of the EU and its Member States was clearly stated from an early stage with the presentation of the EU Action Plan against Smuggling, which was then to be seen in connection with ongoing work to establish a Common Security and Defence Policy operation to systematically identify, capture and dispose of vessels used by smugglers.[45]

Such an idea was not a novelty. The use of Common Foreign and Security Policy (CFSP) competences to pursue objectives linked to internal security objectives, such as the fight against unauthorised entry, transit and residence, or trafficking

---

[43] L den Hertog, 'In Defence of Policy Incoherence – Illustrations from EU External Migration Policy' in S Carrera, L den Hertog, M Panizzon and D Kostakopoulou (eds), *EU External Migration Policies in an ERA of Global Mobilities: Intersecting Policy Universes* (Leiden, Brill Nijhoff, 2019) 379.

[44] A Gomez Arana and S McArdle, 'The EU and the migration crisis: reinforcing a security-based approach to migration?' in S Carrera, J Santos Vara, M Strik and A Hermina (eds), *Constitutionalising the External Dimensions of EU Migration Policies in Times of Crisis* (Cheltenham, Edward Elgar Publishing, 2019) 276.

[45] Commission, 'EU Action Plan against migrant smuggling (2015–2020)' (n 16) 9.

in human beings, had been raised previously. Since the early 2000s, the external objectives of the Area of Freedom, Security and Justice (AFSJ) have to a considerable extent entered other external fields, such as the CFSP, and there is evidence of an instrumentalisation of these fields for AFSJ purposes. This movement coincides with the dynamics driving the externalisation of the AFSJ and more particularly the growing realisation amongst Justice and Home Affairs policymakers that external action is essential and the increasing attention given to security matters in the framework of the EU's CFSP.[46] The notion of security indeed covers various understandings, and the distinction between the internal security, relying on AFSJ internal and external measures, and the international security of the EU, relying more on foreign and CFSP measures, did not hold facing certain realities.[47] This is particularly true regarding counter-terrorism, an activity concerned with both EU internal security and international security. Such complexity is for instance illustrated by the coexistence of two legal bases (Articles 75 and 215 TFEU) attached to AFSJ and CFSP competences for imposing restrictive measures on those suspected of being associated with terrorist activities.[48] On that matter, the Court of Justice had the opportunity to stress that while

> admittedly the combating of terrorism and its financing may well be among the objectives of the AFSJ …, the objective of combating international terrorism and its financing in order to preserve international peace and security corresponds, nevertheless, to the objectives of the Treaty provisions on external action by the Union.

The Court ruled in favour of the CFSP legal basis for the adoption of a blacklisting measure.[49] However, whereas the question of using CFSP measures to combat terrorism had been raised and discussed for some time, the use of such measures to address human trafficking and migrant smuggling did not materialise until 2015, when the EU responded to the situation at its external borders.

While still pursuing their objective to block criminal threats at the external borders of the EU, the EU Member States chose to rely on instruments provided for under the CFSP to address human trafficking and migrant smuggling. The EU Naval Force Mediterranean (EUNAVFOR MED), later renamed Operation Sophia, has been launched as a crisis management operation to provide surveillance, intelligence gathering and potential operational engagement against smuggling activity in the southern central Mediterranean.[50] Its actions are complemented by the

---

[46] J Monar, 'The integration of police and judicial cooperation in criminal matters into the EU external relations: Achievements and problems' in C Fijnaut and J Ouwerkerk (eds), *The Future of Police and Judicial Cooperation in the EU* (Leiden, Martinus Nijhoff Publishers, 2010).

[47] M Cremona, 'External Unity, Institutional Complexity and Structural Fragmentation: The evolution of EU external competence in the AFSJ' in M Telò and A Weyembergh (eds), *Supranational Governance at Stake: The EU's External Competences caught between Complexity and Fragmentation* (New York, Routledge, 2020) 74.

[48] See, eg, Case C-130/10, *European Parliament v Council of the EU* [2012] EU:C:2012:472.

[49] ibid, paras 61 and 72.

[50] Council Decision (CFSP) 2015/778 of 18 May 2015 on a European Union military operation in the Southern Central Mediterranean (EUNAVFOR MED) [2015] OJ L122/31.

operations carried out by other EU agencies, such as Frontex, Europol, Eurojust or the European Asylum Support Office, and other actors like the United Nations High Commissioner for Refugees (UNHCR), UNODC or the International Organization for Migration (IOM), with whom it concluded memorandums of understanding and/or cooperation arrangements.

This mission is the first operation to engage in the intersection between CFSP and AFSJ so directly. Premises of such engagement can be reported in previously launched Common Security and Defence Policy (CSDP) missions, such as the EUFOR Mission Althea[51] in Bosnia–Herzegovina, active since 2004 whose mandate is to maintain a safe and secure environment in the country indirectly and restrictively integrate supporting tasks in addressing organised crime;[52] or the EULEX mission[53] in Kosovo and its intended role in tackling organised crime.[54] However, the activities of these missions indirectly contribute to the internal security of the EU. When establishing Operation Sophia, the EU Member States, through the Council of the EU, did not only decide to use one CFSP legal basis and measure for the purpose of achieving an AFSJ objective, but they also foresaw cooperation and coordination between actors belonging to these two policy fields, ie, between this crisis management operation and EU AFSJ agencies.[55] This is for instance evidenced by the conclusion in 2018 of a Working Arrangement between the EU NAVFOR MED and Europol, foreseeing exchange of information and coordination of activities.[56] This misuse of legal bases integrates itself in an undisputed, yet heavily criticised, trend towards the militarisation of border control, and the fight against migrant smuggling is presented as the key justification for such a move.[57] The Council Decision establishing Operation Sophia also illustrates some weaknesses previously identified. First, although EU policy documents contain a rhetoric of a comprehensive approach, the mission, one of its most direct actions to address the situation in the Mediterranean, follows a heavily securitised approach.[58] The presentation of the mission as part of a strong commitment to prevent human tragedies and people dying at sea does not contradict such an approach. Second, the Decision refers indistinctly to the 'smuggling of people',

---

[51] Council Joint Action 2004/570/CFSP of 12 July 2004 on the European Union military operation in Bosnia and Herzegovina [2004] OJ L252/10.

[52] J Knauer, 'EUFOR Althea: Appraisal and Future Perspectives of the EU's Former Flagship Operation in Bosnia–Herzegovina' (2011) EU Diplomacy Papers 7/2011, College of Europe, 9.

[53] Council Joint Action 2008/124/CFSP of 4 February 2008 on the European Union Rule of Law Mission in Kosovo, EULEX KOSOVO [2008] OJ L42/92.

[54] JJ Proksik, 'EULEX and the fight against organised crime in Kosovo: what's the record?' (2018) 21 *Trends in Organized Crime* 401.

[55] Gomez Arana and McArdle (n 44) 277.

[56] See: www.europol.europa.eu/partners-agreements/working-arrangements.

[57] Council Decision (CFSP) 2015/778 (n 50) Preamble, para 2. V Mitsilegas, 'Extraterritorial immigration control, preventive justice and the rule of law in turbulent times: lessons from the anti-smuggling crusade' in S Carrera, J Santos Vara, M Strik and A Hermina (eds), *Constitutionalising the External Dimensions of EU Migration Policies in Times of Crisis* (Cheltenham, Edward Elgar Publishing, 2019) 297.

[58] Gomez Arana and McArdle (n 44) 273.

the EU's commitment 'to fighting the traffickers' or the 'concept of a CSDP operation to disrupt the business model of smugglers'.[59] Rather than neglecting the legal distinction of the two phenomena, acknowledged through a reference to the two UN relevant protocols, it illustrates the indistinct approach of both phenomena subject this time not to distinct but similar measures, but to a single and unique measure. Third, the AFSJ dimension of the mission is never far away, since States are invited to take appropriate measures against persons suspected of smuggling or trafficking 'with a view of their possible arrest and prosecution'.[60]

Although the mission has been closed as of 31 March 2020,[61] its mandate has evolved in the course of its operations, notably to integrate further AFSJ supporting tasks. The mission was for instance granted the competence to collect information during its surveillance activities which may be released not only to relevant authorities of Member States and competent Union bodies, but also to 'the legitimate Libyan authorities'.[62] The mission also hosted a Crime Information Cell, composed of staff from relevant law enforcement authorities of Member States and of Union agencies, receiving, collecting and transmitting information on human smuggling and trafficking.[63] It also participated in capacity building and training activities on law enforcement tasks at sea for the Libyan coastguard and navy,[64] further better enabling third countries' authorities to enforce their national borders and consequently the EU's borders.[65] This support for the externalisation of border control is further evidenced by the launch in 2013 of a civilian CSDP mission, referred to as EU BAM Libya, supporting the Libyan authorities in developing border management and security at the country's land, sea and air borders.[66] The blur between AFSJ and CFSP objectives is not corrected by the EU's decision to launch a new CSDP mission, EUNAVFOR MED IRINI, in the Mediterranean which will succeed Operation Sophia.[67] While its main objective would be to contribute to enforcing the arms embargo on Libya, it would through its supporting tasks continue efforts to disrupt the human smugglers' business model.[68] The substance of its tasks replicate those conferred on

---

[59] Council Decision (CFSP) 2015/778 (n 50) Preamble, paras 1–5.

[60] ibid para 9.

[61] Council Decision (CFSP) 2020/471 of 31 March 2020 repealing Decision (CFSP) 2015/778 on a European Union military operation in the Southern Central Mediterranean [2020] OJ L101/3.

[62] Council Decision (CFSP) 2017/1385 of 25 July 2017 amending Decision (CFSP) 2015/778 on a European Union military operation in the Southern Central Mediterranean [2017] OJ L194/61.

[63] Council Decision (CFSP) 2018/717 of 14 May 2018 amending Decision (CFSP) 2015/778 on a European Union military operation in the Southern Central Mediterranean [2018] OJ L 120/10.

[64] Council Decision (CFSP) 2016/993 of 20 June 2016 amending Decision (CFSP) 2015/778 on a European Union military operation in the Southern Central Mediterranean [2016] OJ L162/18.

[65] Gomez Arana and McArdle (n 44) 281.

[66] Council Decision (CFSP) 2013/233 of 22 May 2013 on the European Union Integrated Border Management Assistance Mission in Libya (EUBAM Libya) [2013] OJ L138/15.

[67] Council Decision (CFSP) 2020/472 of 31 March 2020 on a European Union military operation in the Mediterranean (EUNAVFOR MED IRINI) [2020] OJ L101/4.

[68] UN, 'Report of the Secretary General on Implementation of Resolution 2437 (2018), Smuggling of migrants and trafficking in persons in the Mediterranean Sea off the coast of Libya', S/2019/7, para 7.

Operation Sophia. They include the detection and monitoring of trafficking and smuggling networks through information gathering and patrolling by air above the high seas, as well as the collection and storage of relevant data, which it may then transmit to the relevant law enforcement authorities of Member States and to competent Union bodies.[69]

Interestingly the activities of the EU in the Mediterranean further reflect a broader evolution under which trafficking in persons and smuggling of migrants are seen as 'hard security issues', falling under the mandate of organisations and institutions traditionally more concerned with international security and the maintenance of peace. The UN Security Council (UNSC) and its increasing activities in relation to trafficking and smuggling constitute a first illustration of such a phenomenon. The UNSC adopted a series of resolutions focusing on the situation in Libya and more particularly on human trafficking and migrant smuggling. The first UNSC Resolution 2240 (2015)[70] on the matter refers explicitly to the EU's mission EUNAVFOR MED launched a few months before and calls on Member States acting nationally or through regional organisations to take various measures against migrant smuggling or human trafficking from Libya. The Resolution covers only partially the activities of the EU's CSDP Mission, namely the search, seizure and disposal of vessels suspected of being used for smuggling or trafficking from Libya,[71] but it nevertheless provided the EU with some authority for action,[72] and a legal basis for further developing Operation Sophia.[73] The following resolutions adopted in 2016, 2017, 2018 and 2019 renewed the authorisations to States and regional organisations to tackle all acts of migrant smuggling and human trafficking into, through and from Libya.[74] The approach of migrant smuggling and human trafficking like another threat to international peace and security was further emphasised by the decision of the UN Security Council to impose sanctions on six individuals accused of leading smuggling and trafficking networks in Libya.[75] These decisions imply that these persons would be submitted to specific sanctions, such as freezing of assets and travel bans, most often applied to persons suspected of endangering peace through violations of arms embargoes or support for terrorism. The militarisation of the response to smuggling and trafficking is also reflected in the involvement of new actors, such as the North Atlantic Treaty Organisation (NATO). Whereas the organisation has, since

---

[69] Council Decision (CFSP) 2020/472 (n 67) Art 5.

[70] UNSC, Resolution 2240 (2015) of 9 October 2015, S/RES/2240 (2015).

[71] ibid, paras 7–9.

[72] Gomez Arana and McArdle (n 44) 280.

[73] Mitsilegas, 'Extraterritorial immigration control, preventive justice and the rule of law in turbulent times' (n 57) 299.

[74] UNSC, Resolution 2312 (2016) of 6 October 2016, S/RES/2312 (2016); Resolution 2380 (2017) of 5 October 2017, S/RES/2380 (2017); Resolution 2437 (2018) of 3 October 2018, S/RES/2437 (2018); and Resolution 2491 (2019) of 3 October 2019, S/RES/2491 (2019).

[75] UN Security Council, 'Decisions LYi.021–LYi.026, adding to the Sanctions List individuals identified as leaders of human trafficking and migrant smuggling networks', Press release SC/13371 of 7 June 2018, available at: www.un.org/press/en/2018/sc13371.doc.htm.

the early 2000s, marked its commitment in combating trafficking in human beings, in the late 2010s it developed peacekeeping operations specifically devoted to halting migrant smuggling and human trafficking, such as Operation Sea Guardian in the Mediterranean, or its presence in the Aegean Sea and at the Turkish–Syrian border.[76] The involvement of new actors offers new avenues for cooperation and creates new coordination needs. The EU thus for instance engaged in further cooperation and coordination with NATO in the course of its activities in the Mediterranean, the two sea operations benefiting from information sharing and logistical support.[77]

B. Trafficking in Armed Conflicts

The militarisation of the response to trafficking in human beings echoes the increasing attention paid to trafficking in human beings in the context of armed conflicts. Such attention results from raising awareness of the consequences of armed conflicts, which increase the social and economic vulnerabilities of the persons living in the conflict areas and those fleeing them.[78] The disruption of state structures and the lack of respect for the rule of law also offers a certain impunity to those willing to exploit vulnerable persons. Trafficking in armed conflicts refers for instance to the abduction of women and girls for forced marriages, the recruitment of children into armed groups or forced labour.[79] It has for instance received media attention at the occasion of events such as when around 200 girls from a school in northern Nigeria were abducted in 2014 by the armed group Boko Haram, or when fighters of the Islamic State in Iraq and al-Sham abducted more than 6,000 women and girls from the Yazidi community.[80]

Such behaviours are sometimes difficult to qualify, as a range of crimes, including trafficking in persons, include elements of persons being transported, recruited or transferred with some form of coercive, deceptive or abusive means for the purpose of being exploited.[81] Elements falling under the definition of trafficking in persons may also fall within the definitions of other crimes that can take place in situations of armed conflicts, including the smuggling of migrants.[82]

---

[76] LJ Ruiz-Díaz, 'The Role of Regional Organizations in Addressing Human Trafficking in Conflict: The Cases of NATO and the EU' in J Muraszkiewicz, T Fenton and H Watson (eds), *Human Trafficking in Conflict: Context, Causes and the Military* (London, Palgrave Macmillan, 2020) 285.

[77] BMJ Szewczyk, 'Operational Cooperation' in G Lindstrom and T Tardy (eds), *The EU and NATO: The Essential Partners* (Paris, EU Institute for Security Studies, 2019) 23.

[78] ICMPD, *Targeting Vulnerabilities, The Impact of the Syrian War and Refugee Situation on Trafficking in Persons, A Study of Syria, Turkey, Lebanon, Jordan and Iraq* (2015).

[79] UNODC, *Global Report on Trafficking in Persons in the context of armed conflict* (2018) 9.

[80] S El-Masri, 'Prosecuting ISIS for the sexual slavery of the Yazidi women and girls' (2018) 22 *The International Journal of Human Rights* 1047, 1052.

[81] UNODC, *Global Report on Trafficking in Persons* (n 79).

[82] UNODC, 'Countering Trafficking in Persons in Conflict Situations', Thematic Paper (2018), available at: www.unodc.org/documents/human-trafficking/2018/17-08776_ebook-Countering_Trafficking_in_Persons_in_Conflict_Situations.pdf, 21–33.

Forms of sexual exploitation can be qualified as conflict-related sexual violence, which can for instance fall within the definition of international crimes defined in international humanitarian law or international criminal law. Sexual slavery, enforced prostitution or any other form of sexual violence constitute serious violations of Article 3 common to the four Geneva Conventions, and fall under the jurisdiction of the International Criminal Court (ICC) as a war crime[83] and/or a crime against humanity.[84] As another example, the recruitment of child soldiers is also prohibited in international humanitarian law, in the Convention on the Rights of the Child and in the Statute of the ICC.[85] Such crimes have received long-standing attention and several cases before international criminal courts have convicted perpetrators of such international crimes. As such, these definitional overlaps do not constitute hurdles in addressing trafficking in armed conflicts, as trafficking is only retained when the three constitutive elements provided for in the UN Protocol against Trafficking in Persons are present.

A difference might reside in the fact that trafficking in the context of armed conflicts currently benefits from a new impetus subject to increasing international attention. Awareness of the phenomenon, ie, the prevalence of trafficking in conflict and post-conflict contexts, dates from the 1990s. For instance, regarding the situation in Bosnia–Herzegovina, the signing of the Dayton Peace Agreement did not put an end to violence against women and girls and international sources reported that trafficked women and girls from Moldova, Romania and Ukraine were held in debt bondage and forced to provide sexual services to clients (including international peacekeepers present in the country).[86] Further research analysed how international peacekeeping operations may fuel the demand for sexual trafficking and incentivise the creation of criminal networks,[87] promoting the adoption of specific measures to address the issue.[88] First signs of renewed attention to the issue can be traced back to a Presidential Statement from the UN Security Council issued in 2015, in which it condemned reported instances of trafficking in persons in areas affected by armed conflict.[89] Since then the UN Security Council has adopted several resolutions concerning trafficking in persons in areas affected by armed conflicts,[90] inviting UN-affiliated organisations and States to integrate,

---

[83] ICC Statute, Art 8(2)(b)(xxii) and (e)(vi).

[84] ICC Statute, Art 7(1)(g).

[85] ICRC, Customary IHL Database, *Rule 136 Recruitment of Child Soldiers*, available at: ihl-databases. icrc.org/customary-ihl/eng/docs/v1_rul_rule136.

[86] Human Rights Watch, 'Hopes betrayed: Trafficking of Women and Girls to Post-Conflict Bosnia and Herzegovina for Forced Prostitution' Vol 14, No 9 (D) (2002) 4. See also OSCE Mission to BiH, *Trafficking in Human Beings and Responses of the Domestic Criminal Justice System, A Critical Review of Law and Emerging Practice in Bosnia and Herzegovina in Light of Core International Standards* (2009) 7.

[87] CA Smith and B Miller-de la Cuesta, 'Human Trafficking in Conflict Zones: The Role of Peacekeepers in the Formation of Networks' (2011) 12 *Human Rights Review* 287.

[88] DPKO, 'Policy Paper Human Trafficking and United Nations Peacekeeping', March 2004, available at: www.un.org/womenwatch/news/documents/DPKOHumanTraffickingPolicy03-2004.pdf.

[89] UNSC, Statement by the President of the Security Council, S/PRST/2015/25 (2015).

[90] UNSC, Resolution 2331 (2016) of 20 December 2016, S/RES/2331 (2016); and Resolution 2388 (2017) of 21 November 2017, S/RES.2388(2017).

when relevant, the issue in their activities, to assess and respond to situations of trafficking in armed conflicts. The Secretary General was in particular tasked with reporting on a yearly basis on the activities developed by Member States and UN bodies, as well as other international and regional organisations.[91] The inclusion of new actors and new fields of action in counter-trafficking efforts, notably resulting from the nexus between terrorism, conflict-related sexual violence and trafficking, has been increasingly explored and recognised by both practitioners and academics.[92]

The EU's involvement in the activities relating to trafficking in persons in armed conflicts is somewhat difficult to outline. Many of its external counter-trafficking activities, including those developed under its CFSP competences, can be seen as part of the response to the situation,[93] as well as actions targeting specific countries, carried out in cooperation with other international actors.[94] In addition, existing areas of the EU's external activities may now be further mobilised to address specific forms of trafficking in armed conflicts. It was for instance the case in the EU's external activities relating to the rights of children, as evidenced by the references to trafficking in the EU Action Plan on Children's Rights in External Action adopted in 2008;[95] or its activities on gender equality and women's empowerment in the EU's external relations.[96] As a consequence, the EU is called upon to rely on an even broader range of external competences to address new forms of trafficking and promote its counter-trafficking policy.[97]

The duty of coherence in the EU's external actions, provided for in Article 21(3) of the Treaty on European Union (TEU), becomes of even more crucial importance. Furthermore, Member States obtain a much stronger role in shaping the European and international response to new trends in human trafficking, especially in light of the militarisation of the approach to these incidents. These developments are to be followed closely, especially as they are representative of a shift in the way

---

[91] See, eg, UNSC, 'Report of the Secretary General on trafficking in persons in armed conflict pursuant to Security Council resolution 2388' (2017), S/2018/1042.

[92] UN CTED, 'Identifying and Exploring the Nexus between Human Trafficking, Terrorism, and Terrorism Financing' (2019), available at: www.un.org/sc/ctc/resources/publications; or A-M de Brouwer, E de Volder and C Paulussen, 'Prosecuting the Nexus between Terrorism, Conflict-related Sexual Violence and Trafficking in Human Beings before National Legal Mechanisms: Case Studies of Boko Haram and Al-Shabaab' (2020) 18 *Journal of International Criminal Justice* 499.

[93] See, eg, Statement on behalf of the EU and its Member States at the Security Council Debate on Trafficking in Persons in Conflict Situations, 21 November 2017, ID 171128_13.

[94] See, eg, Task force on the situation of stranded migrants in Libya, launched by the African Union, the EU and the UN, referred to in UNSC, 'Report of the Secretary General' (n 91) para 6.

[95] Commission, 'A Special Place for Children in EU External Action' (Communication), COM (2008) 55 final.

[96] Commission and High Representative, 'Gender Equality and Women's Empowerment: Transforming Lives of Girls and Women through EU External Relations 2016–2020', 2020' (Joint Staff Working Document), SWD (2015) 182 final.

[97] European Parliament Resolution of 5 July 2016 on the fight against trafficking in human beings in the EU's external relations, P8_TA(2016)0300.

migration, and particularly human trafficking and smuggling, is approached, and the importance granted to national interests and policies in addressing specific migration crimes. The importance of a comprehensive approach with regard to all external activities relating to security issues also becomes stronger. The adoption of an EU Global Strategy on Foreign and Security Policy, can be welcomed and further reflects the commitment to a comprehensive approach in the EU's external policies, which deserves to be fully appraised to determine whether it reflects a truly comprehensive approach which also protects the rights of the persons at risk of being exploited.

III. Conclusion

What does the EU do to address trafficking in human beings, a global phenomenon that requires a comprehensive response based on prevention, protection, prosecution and partnerships? How does it implement such an approach in the external dimension of its policy against human trafficking? Answering these apparently simple questions is like opening a Pandora's box, as the EU's external activities relevant to counter trafficking in human beings seem to be found in most policy fields, and to develop almost on their own without any coherence or planning. The main aim of this book was to investigate the mechanisms though which the EU has been engaged in promoting its own policy in this field towards its external partners, third countries and international organisations alike. Its ambition was rather modest, and choices were necessary to restrict the scope of the examination. The analysis of specific bilateral relations with third countries was excluded, and only marginally addressed through the examination of the EU's cooperation with a group of countries through a regional framework of cooperation. Similarly, the activities of individual Member States, both in their relations with individual countries or in their activities within international organisations, were not addressed. The heart of this book consists in answering a legal question concerning the capacity of the EU to deliver an external response to trafficking in human beings in line with its own constitutional principles and the comprehensive approach it advocates.

A. Is the EU's Response Coherent?

The search for coherence for the sake of coherence is not necessarily in itself a worthy objective, but faced with a multifaceted phenomenon, requiring a response spanning through extremely various and diverse policy fields, the EU has developed a response to trafficking in human beings relying on various external competences and activities. This gives rise to the first question we sought to analyse, whether the EU's response is developed in compliance with its own constitutional objectives and more particularly the duty of coherence, enshrined in Article 21 TEU.

As identified in the first chapter, retracing the main characteristics of the EU's policy against trafficking in human beings, the EU has developed a policy aimed at addressing trafficking in human beings, both internally within the AFSJ and relying externally on the external competences at its disposal. The following chapters of the book have shown how the EU has been engaged in externally promoting its own standards, without hesitation in instrumentalising its external competences for attaining internal security objectives. For such promotion, the EU relied on unilateral mechanisms, such as the framework of the Stabilisation and Association Process with the Western Balkans countries, where it used the perspective of accession as well as other incentives, such as visa-free travel agreements, as incentives for the transposition and implementation of counter-trafficking standards. The EU also relied on multilateral mechanisms, especially through its support to activities carried out by other key counter-trafficking actors and its support for coordination efforts, thus promoting synergies rather than a duplication of efforts. The EU made particular use of its financial resources to fund and thus delegate the implementation of capacity-building activities in strategic third countries, integrating itself into an intricate network of inter-governmental organisations, NGOs and States particularly concerned with the eradication of trafficking in human beings.

In its bilateral and multilateral engagements, the EU has relied upon various external competences in fields as diverse as EU criminal law, development coop-eration, social policy or migration. This diversity was justified by the necessity of promoting the multifaceted measures deemed relevant to address trafficking in human beings, not only to combat and redress existing situations of trafficking, but also to prevent, possibly permanently, the emergence of new flows and/or new patterns of trafficking. Whereas such diversity is praiseworthy with regard to the complexity of trafficking and its multiple forms, it also leads to the identification of a first challenge, namely the risk of incoherence in the external dimension of the EU's policy. Such a risk is fully acknowledged by the EU, and in particular by the main EU institutions, which have notably supported the establishment of an EU Anti-Trafficking Coordinator tasked with the strategic oversight and manage-ment of the Commission's counter-trafficking activities, including the activities of the European External Action Service (EEAS). The preparation and publication of EU strategies to eradicate trafficking in human beings, which fully integrate the external counter-trafficking activities conducted or envisaged, further participate in the ambition to comply with the constitutional duty of coherence. The recent militarisation of the response to trafficking and other migration issues further aggravates the risk of inconsistencies, as it has notably led to an increasing recourse to CFSP measures to address human trafficking and migrant smuggling, and the EU institutions have attempted to remedy it, notably by an increasing coopera-tion between the Commission and the High Representative, which publish joint documents defining common priorities. Finally, the recent reforms of the legal frameworks governing the external activities of the EU agencies have attempted to streamline their cooperation with external partners, requiring them to conclude their cooperation agreements under the general legal frameworks of Article 218 TFEU. This ambition has been since been somehow contradicted by the practice, yet unchallenged before the Court of justice of the EU, of some agencies, which prefer to resort to the conclusion of working arrangements, in which they retain flexibility and discretion.

The book has further highlighted another, potentially stronger limit, to the quest for coherence in the EU's response to trafficking: the nature of the EU's competences in most of the fields relevant for developing the external dimension of its counter-trafficking policy. The EU's external competences in the areas of police and judicial cooperation in criminal matters, migration or development cooperation, share the same characteristic: their shared nature and the role Member States retain externally in preventing and combating trafficking in human beings. Although this aspect has only been touched upon briefly, Member States remain important actors in supporting and building cooperation and partnerships with third countries and other intergovernmental organisations. They possibly possess stronger incentives, such as the capacity to conclude bilateral agreements in operational matters, or additional resources to support counter-trafficking activities better designed to target specific flows or groups, or to protect trafficking victims. Their role further seems to increase in the context of the militarisation of the international and European responses to trafficking in human beings, especially since they can within the UN Security Council participate in blurring the lines between internal and international security, between crime prevention and the maintenance of international peace and security.

As a consequence, the answer to this first question is rather nuanced, even though some elements can mitigate the risk of inconsistencies. The duty of sincere cooperation, also enshrined in EU primary law, and interpreted by the Court of Justice, constitutes a possible limit to Member States' autonomous ambitions. Coherence is also reinforced by the standards promoted by the EU – mostly standards themselves deriving from, or at least substantially influenced by – international standards. The normative interactions between the EU's norms and norms set out in other regional and international frameworks, which are complemented by mirroring policy objectives, lead to synergies in the approach promoted and implemented by the relevant stakeholders.

B. Is the EU's Response Comprehensive?

The EU, like all actors involved in eradicating trafficking in human beings, upholds a comprehensive approach to the phenomenon. Such an approach relies on the understanding of trafficking in human beings as a multifaceted phenomenon, which can equally be addressed as a severe violation of human rights, as a criminal offence and as a threat to international security. It translates into the equal attention supposedly granted to the three main policy objectives, which are complementary to eradicate trafficking, namely the prevention of trafficking, the prosecution of traffickers and the protection of and assistance for trafficking victims. The implementation of a comprehensive approach thus supposes that counter-trafficking measures expand beyond measures aimed at bringing traffickers to justice and/or at managing migration flows.

The EU has in its policy and legally binding documents repeatedly stressed its attachment and commitment in favour of such a comprehensive approach. Addressing trafficking from a human rights-based approach, although defended since the early 2000s, has been granted even stronger political and legal weight with its explicit prohibition in the EU Charter of Fundamental Rights, which has formed part of EU primary law since the entry into force of the Lisbon Treaty. It is thus unsurprising that it is reflected in Directive 2001/36/EU, one of the main EU counter-trafficking instruments, which includes in its title and substance the protection of victims of trafficking. However, this book, in particular the chapter dissecting the main characteristics of the EU's policy against trafficking, has shown the gap between the objectives proclaimed and the content of the legally binding provisions. Human rights-based measures remain limited, as demonstrated for instance by the substance of the Residence Permit Directive which conditions the assistance to victims on their cooperation with the law enforcement authorities and their participation in criminal proceedings, despite the risks of re-victimisation it entails. Similarly, the provision on the non-prosecution or non-punishment of trafficking victims who are forced to commit crimes as a result of their exploitation remains relatively vague and has not, despite few positive examples,[98] been widely implemented. The current deadend concerning the reform of the EU asylum policy, which plays an essential part in detecting foreign victims of trafficking and in preventing vulnerable persons from falling under exploitation, is also an element that illustrates the difficulty in the current context in developing and implementing EU standards in favour of the protection of migrants' rights.

This gap between the proclaimed comprehensive approach and the implementation of more security-focused measures can also be found in the EU's external counter-trafficking activities. The references to a human rights-based approach are multiple and translate into the support of activities and cooperation with organisations competent in the promotion of human rights. The book has shown how the EU has been following, accompanying and where possible supporting the counter-trafficking activities developed by human rights organisations. The EU has for instance been involved in the promotion of transnational referral mechanisms, favouring the safe repatriation of trafficking victims to their country, and the continuous benefit of protection and assistance measures aimed at preventing situations of re-trafficking. It has also followed the activities of UN-affiliated organisations whose mandates cover only human rights and the EU Anti-Trafficking Coordinator has liaised with UN Special Rapporteurs on Trafficking in Persons or

---

[98] See, eg, a case reported in the UNODC Case Law Database: Germany, Landgericht Berlin, 25 June 2019 (513 Kls) 255 Js 637/18 (38/18), UNODC No DEUx022.

on contemporary forms of slavery. However, the book also demonstrated how the external dimension of the EU's policy against trafficking merges more and more with the external dimension of its policy against smuggling, and for both, external activities are increasingly focusing on externalising, even outsourcing, counter-trafficking measures to third countries. Under such evolution, even though the EU States support an externalisation of all measures, including the protection of victims and vulnerable persons, the focus remains very much on border control and criminal justice measures.[99] The launch of measures on the legal basis belonging to the CFSP supports such an evaluation, and the constant renewal of CSDP operations, mandated to disrupt smugglers and trafficking networks with the support of the UN Security Council, does nothing to mitigate it.

C. The Accountability Gaps

A last and transverse aspect deserves our attention in answering whether the EU has delivered a comprehensive and coherent external response to trafficking in human beings. Throughout the book, the important and ever-increasing number of actors involved in countering trafficking in human beings has been stressed. This is further reinforced by the attention granted to situations qualified as new forms of trafficking, such as trafficking in the context of armed conflicts, or the discussions concerning the definition of human trafficking, which are still subject to debate and advocacy efforts to include new forms of exploitation.[100] It results in an abundance of actors, whether States, public authorities, intergovernmental organisations, NGOs, private foundations etc, all being involved in multifaceted actions to address trafficking in human beings. Such an abundance presents clear benefits: it provides diverse incentives for competent actors, especially States, to fully implement their international commitments, notably regarding the protection of victims. It further exposes them to various mechanisms designed to supervise, monitor and evaluate their national policies and legislation and determine whether they address all dimensions of the comprehensive approach they developed. In a context of scarce public resources, revealed by the budgetary challenges faced by well-established international organisations, the development of joint projects and activities, and funding by partner organisations or private foundations is also to be welcomed. In addition to granting them further independence from States, it further contributes to the mutualisation of efforts and synergies between the various but essential expertise and experiences acquired by different stakeholders. The joint and frequent collaboration between the EU

---

[99] Mitsilegas, 'Extraterritorial immigration control, preventive justice and the rule of law in turbulent times' (n 57) 303.

[100] See, eg, JA Chuang, 'Exploitation Creep and the Unmaking of Human Trafficking Law' (2014) 108 *American Journal of International Law* 609; or M van Reisen and C Rijken, 'Sinai Traffikcing: Origin and Definition of a New Form of Human Trafficking' (2015) 3 *Perspectives on Human Trafficking and Modern Forms of Slavery* 113.

and UN-affiliated organisations like the IOM, UNHCR or UNICEF, demonstrates the added value of such synergies, especially to address more complex forms of trafficking.

Nevertheless, the abundance of stakeholders and initiatives also presents constraints. First, it renders it difficult to understand who does what in addressing trafficking in human beings. This book has been, in this regard, envisaged as a modest contribution to this issue by providing a panorama of some of the organisations and actors involved in countering trafficking, even though its focus on the EU has led to the exclusion of other key actors particularly active in other regions of the world. Second, the abundance of actors leads to an expansion of initiatives aimed at addressing trafficking in human beings. Legally binding instruments, such as the UN Protocol against Trafficking in Persons or the ILO conventions at international level, are more and more complemented by soft law instruments, such as the Global Compact for a Safe and Orderly Migration, or the 2030 Agenda for Sustainable Development, which prompt the creation of new platforms, new coordination mechanisms, involved in very similar activities. Whereas their ambition of streamlining various activities and policy objectives is laudable, they also participate in the dilution of responsibilities.

The EU is also concerned by such evolution, as reflected in the development of various processes and forums, and new soft law instruments, named partnerships, compacts or frameworks, in which measures against trafficking are provided for. This book has shown how the recourse to such soft law instruments, as well as the reliance on CFSP measures, is problematic, especially from the perspective of institutional balance within the EU, as the role of the European Parliament, the institution representing the EU citizens and directly accountable before them, decreases. Such a gap in political accountability is also mirrored with efforts at the international level. These efforts to address new forms of trafficking do not result from the adoption of a new multilateral treaty or the revision of the UN Protocol, but from an executive action of the UNSC.[101] Further accountability gaps can also be pinpointed. The Court of Justice of the EU, the institution before which EU institutions in the frontline of the EU's external counter-trafficking activities are judicially accountable for their respect of EU law, has proven to be very restrained in reviewing new forms of EU instruments and activities. Its judgment on its lack of competence for reviewing the EU–Turkey deal represents a negative precedent, in a context of an increasing reliance on soft law arrangements in the EU's cooperation with third countries in sensitive matters.[102] It seems to

---

[101] Mitsilegas, 'Extraterritorial immigration control, preventive justice and the rule of law in turbulent times' (n 57) 297.

[102] Case T-192/16, *NF v European Council* [2017] EU:T:2017:128; Case T-193/16, *NG v European Council* [2017] EUT:2017:129; and Case T-257/16, *NM v European Council* [2017] EU:T:2017:130. See M Gatti and A Ott, 'The EU–Turkey statement: legal nature and compatibility with EU institutional law' in S Carrera, J Santos Vara, M Strik and A Hermina (eds), *Constitutionalising the External Dimensions of EU Migration Policies in Times of Crisis* (Cheltenham, Edward Elgar Publishing, 2019).

indicate a worrying trend towards shielding EU and Member States' cooperation with third States from European rule of law and human rights accountability
mechanisms.[103] Finally, and probably most importantly, the application of human
rights standards and respect for the rule of law seem to be set aside in favour of
migration control and crime prevention. The EU's ambition to confer upon third
countries the responsibilities of prosecuting traffickers and protecting victims of
trafficking seems to fail to acknowledge that not all countries are equipped for
such tasks. Weaknesses in the respect for the rule of law or the prevalence of
corruption of public officials, including judges, may favour the impunity of traffickers all the more when trafficking occurs in failed States, where armed conflicts
have taken down state structures. Even in countries with functioning administrations, the lack of public resources may endanger the protection of human
rights and, in particular, those of the victims. The jurisdiction of the European
Convention for the Protection of Human Rights and Fundamental Freedoms may
in some countries neighbouring the EU mitigate the risk of violation of human
rights occurring within their territories, as well as its jurisdiction over actions of
EU Member States occurring on the territory of third States. It is not however
sufficient to remedy severe violations that may occur in countries considered as
strategic partners of the EU.

---

[103] Mitsilegas, 'Extraterritorial immigration control, preventive justice and the rule of law in turbulent
times' (n 57) 307.

BIBLIOGRAPHY

Adam, S et al, *L'Union européenne comme acteur international*, Commentaire Mégret, 3rd edn (Brussels, Editions de l'Université de Bruxelles, 2015).
—— 'Chronique de la jurisprudence de l'Union, Les relations extérieures (1er Janvier 2013–31 décembre 2016)' (2017) 3 *Cahiers de droit européen* 737.
Allain, J, '*Rantsev v Cyprus and Russia*: The European Court of Human Rights and Trafficking as Slavery' (2010) 10 *Human Rights Law Review* 546.
Audeoud, O, 'L'acquis communautaire, du mythe à la pratique' (2002) 33(3) *Revue d'études comparatives Est-Ouest* 67.
Barslund, M, Lücke, M and Ruhs, M, *Rethinking EU migration and asylum policies: Managing immigration jointly with countries of origin and transit*, 2019 MEDAM Assessment Report on Asylum and Migration Policies in Europe (Kiel, IfW, 2019).
Bartels, L, *Human Rights Conditionality in the EU's International Agreements* (Oxford, Oxford University Press, 2005).
Benlolo Carabot, M, 'L'influence extérieure de l'Union Européenne' in M Benlolo-Carabot, U Candas and E Cujo, *Union Européenne et Droit International* (Paris, Editions Pedone, 2013).
Betts, A (ed), *Global Migration Governance* (Oxford, Oxford University Press, 2011).
Betts, A and Kainz, L, 'The history of global migration governance' (2017) Refugee Studies Centre Working Paper Series No 122.
Borchardt, GM and Wellens, KC, 'Soft Law in European Community Law' (1989) 14 *European Law Review* 267.
Bosma, A and Rijken, C, 'Key Challenges in the Combat of Human Trafficking' (2016) 7 *New Journal of European Criminal Law* 315.
Boswell, C, 'The "external dimension" of EU immigration and asylum policy' (2003) 79 *International Affairs* 619.
Bradford, A, *The Brussels Effect: How the European Union Rules the World* (Oxford, Oxford University Press, 2020).
Brière, C, 'Combatting trafficking in human beings: moving beyond labels with the EU's multidisciplinary, integrated and holistic approach' in F Galli and A Weyembergh (eds), *Do labels still matter? Blurring boundaries between administrative and criminal law: The influence of the EU* (Brussels, Editions de l'Université de Bruxelles, 2014).
—— 'Protecting the EU's financial interests together: cooperation between EU actors' in I Sammut and J Agranovska, *Implementing and Enforcing EU Criminal Law: Theory and Practice* (The Hague, Eleven International Publishing 2019).
—— 'The Future of Judicial Cooperation in Criminal Matters between the European Union and the United Kingdom' in J Santos Vara, RA Wessel and PR Pollak (eds), *Routledge Handbook on the International Dimension of Brexit* (London, Routledge, 2020).
Brière, C and Weatherburn, A, 'Regulating Desire: The Impact of Law and Policy on Demand for Sexual Exploitation in Europe' (2017) 1 *Ex-Ante* 56.
Brodowski, D, 'Judicial Cooperation between the EU and Non-Member States' (2011) 2 *New Journal of European Criminal Law* 21.
Brsakoska, J, 'The legal personality of the European Union' (2011) 2 Iustianius Primus Law Review 1.
Calderoni, F, 'A definition that does not work: the impact of the EU Framework Decision on the Fight against Organized Crime' (2012) 49 *Common Market Law Review* 1365.

Carrera, S et al, *Oversight and Management of the EU Trust Funds, Democratic Accountability, Challenges and Promising Practices*, Study for the European Parliament, PE 603.821 (2018).

Carrera, S, Santos Vara, J and Stirk, T (eds), *Constitutionalising the External Dimensions of EU Migration Policies in Times of Crisis: Legality, Rule of Law and Fundamental Rights Reconsidered* (Cheltenham, Edward Elgar Publishing, 2019).

Carrera, S, den Hertog, L, Panizzon, M and Kostakopoulou, D (eds), *EU External Migration Policies in an Era of Global Mobilities: Intersecting Policy Universes* (Leiden, Brill Nijhoff, 2019).

Carpenter, S, 'Developing effective programmes to protect modern corporate supply chains against human trafficking and slavery' (2020) 2(3) *Journal of Supply Chain Management, Logistics and Procurement* 233.

Casolari, F, 'EU Member States' international engagements in AFSJ domain: Between subordination, complementarity and incorporation' in C Flaesch-Mougin and L Rossi (eds), *La dimension extérieure de l'Espace de Liberté, Sécurité et Justice de l'Union Européenne après le Traité de Lisbonne* (Brussels, Bruylant, 2013).

Chamon, M, 'Implied Exclusive Powers in the ECJ's Post-Lisbon Jurisprudence: The Continued Development of the ERTA Doctrine' (2018) 55 *Common Market Law Review* 1101.

Chamon, M and Demedts, V, 'Constitutional limits to the EU agencies' external relations' in M Chamon, HCH Hofmann and E Vos (eds), *The External Dimension of EU Agencies and Bodies: Law and Policy* (Cheltenham, Edward Elgar Publishing, 2019).

Chetail, V, 'The Common European Asylum System: *Bric-à-brac* or System?' in V Chetail, P de Bruycker and F Maiani, *Reforming the Common European Asylum System: The New European Refugee Law* (Leiden, Brill Nijhoff, 2016).

Chuang, JA, 'Exploitation Creep and the Unmaking of Human Trafficking Law' (2014) 108 *American Journal of International Law* 609.

Clesse, C-E, *La traite des êtres humains: un cadre légal perfectible pour une meilleure protection des victimes? Etude de la législation belge, éclairée des normes internationales et de législations française, luxembourgeoise et suisse* (Brussels, Larcier, 2013).

Coninsx, M, 'The fight against terrorism and the role of Eurojust: cooperation with third countries' in E Herlin-Karnell and C Matera (eds), 'External Dimension of the EU Counter-Terrorism Policy' (2014) CLEER Working Paper 2014/2.

Coman-Kund, F, 'The cooperation between the European Border and Coast Guard Agency and third countries according to the new Frontex Regulation: legal and practical implications' in M Chamon, HCH Hofmann and E Vos (eds), *The External Dimension of EU Agencies and Bodies: Law and Policy* (Cheltenham, Edward Elgar Publishing, 2019).

Corten, O, *Méthodologie du droit international public* (Brussels, Editions de l'Université de Bruxelles, 2009).

Cortinovis, R, 'Forced Displacement and EU External Action: Exogenous Shocks, Policy Frames and Institutional Dynamics' (2017) 22 *European Foreign Affairs Review* 473.

Cremona, M, 'Coherence through law: what difference will the Treaty of Lisbon make?' (2008) 3 *Hamburg Review of Social Sciences* 11.

—— 'Defending the Community Interest: the Duties of Cooperation and Compliance' in M Cremona and B de Witte (eds), *EU Foreign Relations Law: Constitutional Fundamentals* (Oxford, Hart Publishing 2008).

—— 'EU External Action in the JHA Domain: A Legal Perspective' in M Cremona, J Monar and S Poli (eds), *The External Dimension of the European Union's Area of Freedom, Security and Justice* (Brussels, Peter Lang, 2011).

—— 'Structural Principles and their Role in EU External Relations Law' in M Cremona (ed), *Structural Principles in EU External Relations Law* (Oxford, Hart Publishing, 2018).

—— 'Extending the Reach of EU Law: The EU as an International Legal Actor' in M Cremona and J Scott (eds), *EU Law Beyond EU Borders: The Extraterritorial Reach of EU Law* (Oxford, Oxford University Press, 2019).

—— 'External Unity, Institutional Complexity and Structural Fragmentation' in M Telò and A Weyembergh, *Supranational Governance at Stake: The EU's External Competences caught between Complexity and Fragmentation* (New York, Routledge, 2020).

Cremona, M and Hillion, C, 'L'Union fait-elle la force? Potential and Limitations of the European Neighbourhood Policy as an Integrated EU Foreign and Security Policy' (2006) EUI Working Paper Law 2006/39.

Cremona, M, Monar, J and Poli, S (eds), *The External Dimension of the European Union's Area of Freedom, Security and Justice* (Brussels, Peter Lang, 2011).

Cremona, M and Scott, J (eds), *EU Law Beyond Borders: The Extraterritorial Reach of EU Law* (Oxford, Oxford University Press, 2019).

Cullen, H, 'The EU and Human Trafficking: Framing a Regional Response to a Global Emergency' in A Antoniadis, R Schütze and E Spaventa (eds), *The European Union and Global Emergencies: A Law and Policy Analysis* (Oxford, Hart Publishing, 2011).

Dandurand, Y and Jahn, J, 'The Failing International Legal Framework on Migrant Smuggling and Human Trafficking' in J Winterdyk and J Jones (eds), *The Palgrave International Handbook of Human Trafficking* (London, Palgrave Macmillan, 2020).

De Baere, G, *Constitutional Principles of EU External Relations* (Oxford, Oxford University Press, 2008).

De Biolley, S, 'Panorama du droit pénal de l'Union' in G de Kerchove and A Weyembergh, *Sécurité et justice: enjeu de la politique extérieure de l'Union* (Brussels, Editions de l'Université de Bruxelles, 2003).

De Brouwer, A-M, de Volder, E and Paulussen, C, 'Prosecuting the Nexus between Terrorism, Conflict-related Sexual Violence and Trafficking in Human Beings before National Legal Mechanisms: Case Studies of Boko Haram and Al-Shabaab' (2020) 18 *Journal of International Criminal Justice* 499.

De Bruycker, P and Weyembergh, A, 'The external dimension of the European Area of Freedom, Security and Freedom' in M Telo, *The European Union and Global Governance* (Abingdon, Routledge, 2009).

De Vido, S, 'The ratification of the Council of Europe Istanbul Convention by the EU: a step forward in the protection of women from violence in the European legal system' (2017) 9(2) *European Journal of Legal Studies* 69.

De Vries, I, Jose, MA and Farrell, A, 'It's Your Business: The Role of the Private Sector in Human Trafficking' in J Winterdyk and J Jones (eds), *The Palgrave International Handbook of Human Trafficking* (London, Palgrave Macmillan, 2020).

De Witte, B, 'Too Much Constitutional Law in the European Union's Foreign Relations?' in M Cremona and B de Witte, *EU Foreign Relations Law: Constitutional Fundamentals* (Oxford, Hart Publishing, 2008).

Den Hertog, L, 'Implementers? The Role of International Organisations in EU Funding for External Migration Policy' (2017) 12(1) *Journal of Regional Security* 5.

—— 'In Defence of Policy Incoherence – Illustrations from EU External Migration Policy' in S Carrera, L den Hertog, M Panizzon and D Kostakopoulou (eds), *EU External Migration Policies in an ERA of Global Mobilities: Intersecting Policy Universes* (Leiden, Brill Nijhoff, 2019).

Do Carmo, TE, 'Major International Counter-Trafficking Organizations: Addressing Human Trafficking from Multiple Directions' in J Winterdyk and J Jones (eds), *The Palgrave International Handbook of Human Trafficking* (London, Palgrave Macmillan, 2020).

Dashwood, A and Maresceau, M (eds), *Law and Practice of EU External Relations: Salient Features of a Changing Landscape* (Cambridge, Cambridge University Press, 2011).

Delarue, R, 'The EU–ILO Partnership and the Global Identify of the Union's Social Model' in H de Waele and JJ Kuipers (eds), *The European Union's Emerging International Identity* (Leiden, Martinus Nijhoff Publishers, 2013).

Delcourt, C, 'The *Acquis Communautaire*: Has the concept had its day?' (2001) 38 *Common Market Law Review* 829.

Delmas-Marty, M, *Le pluralisme ordonné, Les forces imaginantes du droit (2)* (Paris, Editions du Seuil, 2006).

Dony, M, 'Retour sur les compétences externes implicites de l'Union' (2018) 1 *Cahiers de droit européen* 109.

Eckes, C, 'How the EP's Participation in International Relations Affects the Deep Tissue of the EU's Power Structures' (2014) Jean Monnet Working Paper 12/2014.

Eeckhout, P, *EU External Relations Law*, 2nd edn (Oxford, Oxford University Press, 2012).

El-Masri, S, 'Prosecuting ISIS for the sexual slavery of the Yazidi women and girls' (2018) 22 *The International Journal of Human Rights* 1047.

Estrada Coñamares, M, '"Building Coherent EU Responses": Coherence as a Structural Principle' in M Cremona (ed), *Structural Principles in EU External Relations Law* (Oxford, Hart Publishing, 2018).

Fahey, E, *The Global Reach of EU Law* (Abingdon, Routledge, 2016).

Fakiolas, ET and Tzifakis, N, 'Transformation or Accession? Reflecting on the EU's Strategy Towards the Western Balkans' (2008) 13 *European Foreign Affairs Review* 377.

Fallon, N, 'New Moves: Opening up EU Prospects for North Macedonia and Albania' (2020) IIEA Briefing Paper.

Gallagher, A, 'Human Rights and the New UN Protocols on Trafficking and Migrant Smuggling: A Preliminary Analysis' (2001) 23 *Human Rights Quarterly* 975.

—— 'Recent Legal Developments in the Field of Human Trafficking: A Critical Review of the 2005 European Convention and Related Instruments' (2006) 8 European Journal of Migration and Law 163.

—— *The International Law of Human Trafficking*, 1st edn (Cambridge, Cambridge University Press, 2010).

—— 'Two Cheers for the Trafficking Protocol' (2015) 4 *Anti-trafficking Review* 21.

—— 'Trafficking in Transnational Criminal Law' in R Piotrowicz, C Rijken and B Heide Uhl (eds), *Routledge Handbook of Human Trafficking* (New York, Routledge, 2018).

Galli, F and Weyembergh, A (eds), *Approximation of Substantive Criminal Law in the EU: The Way Forward* (Brussels, Editions de l'Université de Bruxelles, 2013).

Garcia Andrade, P, 'The Distribution of Powers between EU Institutions for Conducting External Affairs through Non-Binding Instruments' (2016) 1 *European Papers* 115.

—— 'EU External Competences in the Field of Migration: How to Act Externally When Thinking Internally' (2018) 55 *Common Market Law Review* 157.

—— 'EU external competences on migration: which role for mixed agreements?' in S Carrera, J Santos Vara, M Strik and A Hermina (eds), *Constitutionalising the External Dimensions of EU Migration Policies in Times of Crisis* (Cheltenham, Edward Elgar Pubishing, 2019).

Garcia Andrade, P, Martin, I and Mananashvili, S, *EU cooperation with third countries in the field of migration*, Study for the European Parliament, PE 536.469 (2015).

Gatti, M and Ott, A, 'The EU–Turkey statement: legal nature and compatibility with EU institutional law' in S Carrera, J Santos Vara, M Strik and A Hermina (eds), *Constitutionalising the External Dimensions of EU Migration Policies in Times of Crisis* (Cheltenham, Edward Elgar Publishing, 2019).

Gialdino, CC, 'Some Reflections on the *Acquis Communautaire*' (1995) 32 *Common Market Law Review* 1089.

Gomez Arana, M and McArdle, S, 'The EU and the migration crisis: reinforcing a security-based approach to migration?' in S Carrera, J Santos Vara, M Strik and A Hermina (eds), *Constitutionalising the External Dimensions of EU Migration Policies in Times of Crisis* (Cheltenham, Edward Elgar Publishing, 2019).

Govaere, I, 'External Competence: What's in a Name? The Difficult Conciliation between Dynamism of the ECJ and Dynamics of European Integration' in P Demaret, I Govaere and D Hanf (eds), *European Legal Dynamics/Dynamiques juridiques européennes* (Brussels, Peter Lang, 2007).

—— '"Setting the International Scene": EU External Competence and Procedures Post-Lisbon Revisited in the Light of ECJ Opinion 1/13' (2015) 52 *Common Market Law Review* 1036.

Grazia Giammarinaro, M, 'The Role of the UN Special Rapporteur on Trafficking in Persons, especially women and children' in R Piotrowicz, C Rijken and B Heide Uhl (eds), *Routledge Handbook of Human Trafficking* (New York, Routledge, 2018).

Guild E and Minderhoud, P (eds), *Immigration and Criminal Law in the EU: The Legal Measures and Social Consequences of Criminal Law in Member States on Human Trafficking and Smuggling in Human Beings* (Leiden, Martinus Nijhoff Publishers, 2006).

Hanf, D and Dengler, P, 'Accords d'association' (2004) College of Europe Research Papers in Law 1/2004.

Heimans, D, 'The External Relations of Europol – Political, Legal and Operational Considerations' in B Martenczuck and S van Thiel (eds), *Justice, Liberty and Security: New Challenges for EU External Relations* (Brussels, VUB Press, 2008).

Hillion, C, 'Tous pour un, un pour tous! Coherence in the External Relations of the European Union' in M Cremona (ed), *Developments in EU External Relations Law* (Oxford, Oxford University Press, 2008).

—— 'EU Enlargement' in P Craig and G de Burca (eds), *The Evolution of EU Law* (Oxford, Oxford University Press, 2011).

Jägers, N and Rijken, C, 'Prevention of Human Trafficking for Labour Exploitation: The Role of Corporations' (2014) 12(1) *Northwestern Journal of International Human Rights* 47.

Jones, J, 'Is It Time to Open a Conversation About a New United Nations Treaty to Fight Human Trafficking that Focuses on Victim Protection and Human Rights?' in J Winterdyk and J Jones (eds), *The Palgrave International Handbook of Human Trafficking* (London, Palgrave Macmillan, 2020).

Kaddous, C, 'Un nouveau cadre pour la dimension externe de l'espace de liberté, de sécurité et de justice' in C Kaddous and M Dony (eds), *D'Amsterdam à Lisbonne, Dix ans d'espace de liberté, de sécurité et de justice* (Basel, Helbing Lichtenhahn, 2010).

Kaddous, C (ed), *The European Union in International Organisations and Global Governance* (Oxford, Hart Publishing, 2015).

Kelsen, H, *Théorie pure du droit*, 1934 puis 1960 (traduction française, Paris, LGDJ, 1999).

Knauer, J, 'EUFOR Althea: Appraisal and Future Perspectives of the EU's Former Flagship Operation in Bosnia–Herzegovina' (2011) EU Diplomacy Papers 7/2011, College of Europe.

Koutrakos, P, 'The External Dimension of the AFSJ and Other EU External Policies' in M Cremona, J Monar and S Poli (eds), *The External Dimension of the European Union's Area of Freedom, Security and Justice* (Brussels, Peter Lang, 2011).

Labayle, H, 'L'espace pénal européen et le monde: instrument ou objectif?' in G de Kerchove and A Weyembergh (eds), *Sécurité et justice: enjeu de la politique extérieure de l'Union européenne* (Brussels, Editions de l'Université de Bruxelles, 2003).

Lagon, MP, 'Fighting Human Trafficking: Transformative versus "Cotton-Candy" Partnerships' in MP Lagon and AC Arend (eds), *Human Dignity and the Future of Global Institutions* (Washington, DC, Georgetown University Press, 2014).

Larik, J, 'Entrenching Global Governance: The EU's Constitutional Objectives Caught Between a Sanguine World View and a Daunting Reality' in B Van Vooren, S Blockmans and J Wouters, *The EU's Role in Global Governance: The Legal Dimension* (Oxford, Oxford University Press, 2013).

—— 'The Substance of Constitutional Foreign Policy Objectives' in J Larik, *Foreign Policy Objectives in European Constitutional Law* (Oxford, Oxford University Press, 2016).

Larik, J and Wessel, RA, 'Instruments of EU External Action' in RA Wessel and J Larik (eds), *EU External Relations Law: Text, Cases and Materials*, 2nd edn (Oxford, Hart Publishing, 2020).

Lavenex, S, 'EU external governance in "wider Europe"' (2004) 11 Journal of European Public Policy 680.

—— 'Channels of Externalisation of EU Justice and Home Affairs' in M Cremona, J Monar and S Poli (eds), *The External Dimension of the European Union's Area of Freedom, Security and Justice* (Brussels, Peter Lang, 2011).

Lenaerts, K and Van Nuffel, P, *European Union Law*, 3rd edn (London, Sweet & Maxwell, 2011).

Levrat, N, 'Legal Studies and Global Governance' in M Telo, Globalisation, Multilateralism, Europe: Towards a Better Global Governance? (Farnham, Ashgate Publishing, 2013).

Maes, M, Vanheule D, Wouters J and Foblets M-C, 'The International Dimension of EU Asylum and Migration Policy: Framing The Issues' in P de Bruycker, M-C Foblets and M Maes (eds), *External Dimensions of European Migration and Asylum Law and Policy* (Brussels, Larcier, 2011).

Manners, I, 'Normative Power Europe: A Contradiction in Terms?' (2002) 40 *Journal of Common Market Studies* 235.

Marin, L, 'The Cooperation Between Frontex and Third Countries in Information Sharing: Practices, Law and Challenges in Externalizing Border Control Functions' (2020) 26 *European Public Law* 157.

Marín Durán, G, 'Sustainable Development Chapters in EU Free Trade Agreements: Emerging Compliance Issues' (2020) 57 *Common Market Law Review* 1031.

Martin, S and Callaway, A, 'Human Trafficking and Smuggling' in A Betts (ed), *Global Migration Governance* (Oxford, Oxford University Press, 2011).

Matera, C, 'The Influence of International Organisations on the EU's Area of Freedom, Security and Justice: A First Inquiry' in RA Wessel and S Blockmans (eds), *Between Autonomy and Dependence: The EU Legal Order Under the Influence of International Organisations* (The Hague, TMC Asser Press, 2013).

—— 'Much ado about opt-outs? The impact of variable geometry in the AFSJ on the EU as a Global Security Actor' in S Blockmans (ed), *Differentiated Integration in the EU: From the Inside Looking Out* (CEPS, 2014).

—— 'The External Dimension of EU Counter-Terrorism Policy: An Overview of Existing Agreements and Initiatives' in E Herlin-Karnell and C Matera (eds), 'External Dimension of the EU Counter-Terrorism Policy' (2014) CLEER Working Paper 2014/2.

—— 'The External Dimension of the Area of Freedom, Security and Justice' in RA Wessel and J Larik (eds), *EU External Relations Law: Text, Cases and Materials*, 2nd edn (Oxford, Hart Publishing, 2020).

McAdam, M, 'Who's Who at the Border? A rights-based approach to identifying human trafficking at international borders' (2013) 2 *Anti-Trafficking Review* 33.

Middelburg, A and Rijken, C, 'The EU legal framework on combating THB for labour exploitation' in C Rijken (ed), *Combating Trafficking in Human Beings for Labour Exploitation* (Nijmegen, Wolf Legal Publishers, 2011).

Miettinen, S, *Criminal Law and Policy in the European Union* (Abingdon, Routledge, 2011).

Mitsilegas, V, 'The New EU–USA Cooperation on Extradition, Mutual Legal Assistance and the Exchange of Police Data' (2003) 8 *European Foreign Affairs Review* 515.

—— 'The European Union and the Implementation of International Norms in Criminal Matters' in M Cremona, J Monar and S Poli (eds), *The External Dimension of the European Union's Area of Freedom, Security and Justice* (Brussels, Peter Lang, 2011).

—— *The Criminalisation of Migration in Europe: Challenges for Human Rights and the Rule of Law* (Berne, Springer International Publishing, 2015).

—— 'Extraterritorial immigration control, preventive justice and the rule of law in turbulent times: lessons from the anti-smuggling crusade' in S Carrera, J Santos Vara, M Strik and A Hermina (eds), *Constitutionalising the External Dimensions of EU Migration Policies in Times of Crisis* (Cheltenham, Edward Elgar Publishing, 2019).

Monar, J, 'EU Justice and Home Affairs in the Eastward Enlargement: The Challenge of Diversity and EU Instruments and Strategies', Zentrum für Europäische Integrationsforschung (2001) Universität Bonn, Discussion paper C 91.

—— 'The EU as an International Actor in the Domain of Justice and Home Affairs' (2004) 4 *European Foreign Affairs Review* 395.

—— 'The integration of police and judicial cooperation in criminal matters into the EU external relations: Achievements and problems' in C Fijnaut and J Ouwerkerk (eds), *The Future of Police and Judicial Cooperation in the EU* (Leiden, Martinus Nijhoff Publishers, 2010).

—— *The External Dimension of the EU's Area of Freedom, Security and Justice: Progress, Potential and Limitations after the Treaty of Lisbon* (Swedish Institute for European Policy Studies, 2012).

Muraszkiewicz, J, *Protecting Victims of Human Trafficking from Liability: The European Approach* (London, Palgrave Macmillan, 2019).

Navasartian, A, 'EU–Vietnam Free Trade Agreement: Insights on the Substantial and Procedural Guarantees for Labour Protection in Vietnam' (2020) 5 *European Papers* 561.

Novak-Irons, F, 'Unable to Return? The Protection of Victims of Trafficking in Need of International Protection' in R Piotrowicz, C Rijken and B Heide Uhl (eds), *Routledge Handbook of Human Trafficking* (New York, Routledge, 2018).

O'Neil, M, International Business Encounters Organized Crime: The Case of Trafficking in Human Beings (2018) 19 *German Law Journal* 1125.

Öberg, M-L, 'Expanding the EU Internal Market without Enlarging the Union: Constitutional Limitations' (PhD thesis, EUI, 2015).

Obokata, T, 'EU Council Framework Decision on combating trafficking in human beings: a critical appraisal' (2003) 40 *Common Market Law Review* 917.

—— 'Trafficking of Human Beings as a Crime Against Humanity: Some Implications for the International Legal System' (2005) 54 International & Comparative Law Quarterly 445.

—— 'A Human Rights Framework to address Trafficking in Human Beings' (2006) 24 Netherlands Quarterly of Human Right 379.

—— 'EU Action against Trafficking of Human Beings: Past, Present and the Future' in E Guild and P Minderhoud (eds), *Immigration and Criminal law in the European Union: The Legal Measures and Social Consequences of Criminal Law in Member States on Human Trafficking and Smuggling in Human Beings* (Leiden, Martinus Nijhoff Publishers, 2006).

Obokata, T and Payne, P, 'Implementing Action against trafficking of Human Beings under the TFEU: A Preliminary Analysis' (2012) 3 *New Journal of European Criminal Law* 298.

Orsini, A (ed), *The European Union with(in) International Organisations* (Farnham, Ashgate Publishing, 2014).

Ott, A, 'The Legal Bases for International Agreements Post-Lisbon: Of Pirates and the Philippines' (2014) 21 *Maastricht Journal of European and Comparative Law* 739.

—— 'EU External Competence' in RA Wessel and J Larik (eds), *EU External Relations Law: Text, Cases and Materials*, 2nd edn (Oxford, Hart Publishing, 2020).

Pech, L and Grogan, J, 'EU External Human Rights Policy' in RA Wessel and J Larik (eds), *EU External Relations Law: Text, Cases and Materials*, 2nd edn (Oxford, Hart Publishing, 2020).

Peers, S, *EU Justice and Home Affairs Law*, 3rd edn (Oxford, Oxford University Press, 2011).

—— *Trends in differentiation of EU Law and lessons for the future*, In-Depth Analysis for the AFCO Committee of the European Parliament (2015).

Pescatore, P, 'Aspects juridiques de l'acquis communautaire' [1981] *Revue Trimestrielle de Droit Européen* 617.

Petrov, R, 'The External Dimension of the Acquis Communautaire' (2002) EUI Working Paper 2002/07.

—— 'The Dynamic Nature of the acquis communautaire in European Union External Relations' (2006) 18 *European Review of Public Law* 741.

—— 'Exporting the Acquis Communautaire into the Legal Systems of Third Countries' (2008) 13 *European Foreign Affairs Review* 33.

Piotrowicz, R and Sorrentino, L, 'The non-punishment provision with regard to victims of trafficking: A human rights approach' in R Piotrowicz, C Rijken and B Heide Uhl (eds), *Routledge Handbook of Human Trafficking* (New York, Routledge, 2018).

Pirjatanniemi, E, 'Victims of Trafficking in the Migration Discourse' in R Haverkamp, E Herlin-Karnell and C Lernestedt (eds), *What is Wrong with Human Trafficking? Critical Perspectives on the Law* (Oxford, Hart Publishing, 2019).

Plouffe-Malette, K, *Protection des victimes de traite des êtres humains, Approches internationales et européennes* (Brussels, Larcier, 2013).

Poli, S, 'The Integration of Migration Concerns into EU External Policies: Instruments, Techniques and Legal Problems' (2020) 5 *European Papers* 71.

Prifti, E, 'Introduction: from stabilisation to integration' in E Prifti (ed), *The European Future of the Western Balkans: Thessaloniki @10 (2003–2013)* (EU Institute for Security Studies, 2013).

Proksik, JJ, 'EULEX and the fight against organised crime in Kosovo: what's the record?' (2018) 21 *Trends in Organized Crime* 401.

Rees, W, 'Inside Out: The External Face of EU Internal Security Policy' (2008) 30 *Journal of European Integration* 97.

Reslow, N, 'Making and Implementing Multi-Actor EU External Migration Policy: The Mobility Partnerships' in S Carrera, L den Hertog, M Panizzon and D Kostakopoulou (eds), *EU External Migration Policies in an Era of Global Mobilities: Intersecting Policy Universes* (Leiden, Brill Nijhoff, 2019).

Rijken, C, *Trafficking in Persons: Prosecution from a European Perspective* (The Hague, TMC Asser Press, 2003).

—— 'The External Dimension of EU Policy on Trafficking in Human Beings' in M Cremona, J Monar and S Poli (eds), *The External Dimension of the European Union's Area of Freedom, Security and Justice* (Brussels, Peter Lang, 2011).

Rijken, C and de Volder, E, 'The EU's Struggle to Realize a Human Rights-Based Approach to Trafficking in Human Beings. A Call on the EU to take THB-Sensitive Action in the Relevant Areas of Law' (2009) 45 *Connecticut Journal of International Law* 49.

Rijken, C (ed), *Combating Trafficking in Human Beings for Labour Exploitation* (Nijmegen, Wolf Legal Publishers, 2011).

Rodriguez-López, S, 'Telling Victims from Criminals: Human Trafficking for the purposes of Criminal Exploitation' in J Winterdyk and J Jones (eds), *The Palgrave International Handbook of Human Trafficking* (London, Palgrave Macmillan, 2020).

Rosas, A, 'EU External Relations: Exclusive Competence Revisited' (2015) 38 *Fordham International Law Journal* 1073.

Rose, C, 'The Creation of a Review Mechanism for the UN Convention against Transnational Organized Crime and Its Protocols' (2020) 114 *The American Journal of International Law* 51.

Rossi, LS, 'From EU Pillar to Area: The Impact of the Lisbon Treaty' in C Flaesch-Mougin and LS Rossi, *La dimension extérieure de l'Espace de Liberté, Sécurité et Justice de l'Union Européenne après le Traité de Lisbonne* (Brussels, Bruylant, 2013).

Roth, V, *Defining Human Trafficking and Identifying its Victims: A Study on the Impact and Future Challenges of International, European and Finnish Legal Responses to Prostitution-related Trafficking in Human Beings* (Nijmegen, Martinus Nijhoff Publishers, 2011).

Ruiz-Díaz, LJ, 'The Role of Regional Organizations in Addressing Human Trafficking in Conflict: The Cases of NATO and the EU' in J Muraszkiewicz, T Fenton and H Watson (eds), *Human Trafficking in Conflict: Context, Causes and the Military* (London, Palgrave Macmillan, 2020).

Rousselin, M, 'The EU as a Multilateral Rule Exporter. The Global Transfer of European Rules via International Organizations' (2012) KFG Working Paper Series No 48.

Ryan, B, 'The Migration Crisis and the European Union Border Regime' in M Cremona and J Scott (eds), *EU Law Beyond EU Borders: The Extraterritorial Reach of EU Law* (Oxford, Oxford University Press, 2019).

Sakelliadou, Z, 'EU Anti-trafficking Coordinator: Trajectory of a Unique Mandate' in J Winterdyk and J Jones (eds), *The Palgrave International Handbook of Human Trafficking* (Basingstoke, Palgrave Macmillan, 2020).

Santos Vara, J and Fahey, E, 'Transatlantic relations and the operation of AFSJ flexibility' in S Blockmans (ed), *Differentiated Integration in the EU: From the Inside Looking Out* (CEPS, 2014).

Satzger, H, Zimmerman, F and Langheld, G, 'The Directive on Preventing and Combatting Trafficking in Human Beings and the Principles Governing European Criminal Policy: A Critical Evaluation' (2013) 3 *European Criminal Law Review* 107.

Scarpa, S, 'UN Palermo Trafficking Protocol Eighteen Years On: A Critique' in J Winterdyk and J Jones (eds), *The Palgrave International Handbook of Human Trafficking* (London, Palgrave Macmillan, 2020).

Schuman, S, 'Corporate Criminal Liability on Human Trafficking' in J Winterdyk and J Jones (eds), *The Palgrave International Handbook of Human Trafficking* (London, Palgrave Macmillan, 2020).

Scott, J, 'The new EU "extra-territoriality"' (2014) 51 *Common Market Law Review* 1343.

Senden, L, *Soft Law in European Community Law* (Oxford, Hart Publishing, 2004).

Smith, CA and Miller-de la Cuesta, B, 'Human Trafficking in Conflict Zones: The Role of Peacekeepers in the Formation of Networks' (2011) 12 *Human Rights Review* 287.

Spijkerboer, T and Steyger, E, 'European External Migration Funds and Public Procurement Law' (2019) 4 *European Papers* 493.

Stoyanova, V, 'Dancing on the borders of Article 4: Human trafficking and the European Court of Human Rights in the *Rantsev* case' (2012) 30 Netherlands Quarterly of Human Rights 163.

—— 'European Court of Human Rights and the Right Not to Be Subjected to Slavery, Servitude, Forced Labor and Human Trafficking' in J Winterdyk and J Jones (eds), *The Palgrave International Handbook of Human Trafficking* (London, Palgrave Macmillan, 2020).

Stewart, E, 'Restoring EU–OSCE Cooperation for Pan-European Conflict Prevention (2008) 29 *Contemporary Security Policy* 266.

Streinz, T, 'Fraternal Twins: The European Union and the Council of Europe' in H de Waele and JJ Kuipers (eds), *The European Union's Emerging International Identity* (Leiden, Martinus Nijhoff Publishers, 2013).

Surano, L, 'L'action extérieure d'Eurojust' in M Dony (ed), *La dimension externe de l'espace de liberté, de sécurité et de justice au lendemain de Lisbonne et de Stockholm: un bilan à mi-parcours* (Brussels, Editions de l'Université de Bruxelles, 2012).

Szewczyk, BMJ, 'Operational Cooperation' in G Lindstrom and T Tardy (eds), *The EU and NATO: The Essential Partners* (Paris, EU Institute for Security Studies, 2019).

Symeonidou-Kastanidou, E, 'Directive 2011/36/EU on Combating Trafficking in Human Beings: Fundamental Choices and Problems of Implementation' (2016) 7 *New Journal of European Criminal Law* 465.

Toom, V, Granja, R and Ludwig, A, 'The Prüm Decisions as an Aspirational regime: Reviewing a Decade of Cross-Border Exchange and Comparison of Forensic DNA Data' (2019) 41 *Forensic Science International Genetics* 50.

Topic, L, 'Regional cooperation' in E Prifti (ed), *The European Future of the Western Balkans: Thessaloniki @ 10 (2003–2013)* (EU Institute for Security Studies, 2013).

Trauner, F, 'Deconstructing the EU's Routes of Influence in Justice and Home Affairs in the Western Balkans' (2009) 31 *Journal of European Integration* 65.

Van Doorninck, M, 'Changing the system from within, The role of NGOs in the flawed anti-trafficking framework' in R Piotrowicz, C Rijken and B Heide Uhl (eds), *Routledge Handbook of Human Trafficking* (New York, Routledge, 2018).

Van Elsuwege, P, 'EU External Action after the Collapse of the Pillar Structure: in search of a new balance between delimitation and consistency' (2010) 47 *Common Market Law Review* 987.

—— 'Legal Creativity in EU External Relations: The Stabilisation and Association Agreement between the EU and Kosovo' (2017) 22 *European Foreign Affairs Review* 393.

Van Reisen, M, and Rijken, C, 'Sinai Trafficking: Origin and Definition of a New Form of Human Trafficking' (2015) 3 *Perspectives on Human Trafficking and Modern Forms of Slavery* 113.

Van Vooren, B 'The Principle of Pre-emption after Opinion 1/03 and coherence in EU readmission policy' in M Cremona, J Monar and S Poli (eds), *The External Dimension of the European Union's Area of Freedom, Security and Justice* (Brussels, Peter Lang, 2011).

—— *EU External Relations Law and the European Neighbourhood Policy: A Paradigm for Coherence* (Abingdon, Routledge, 2012).

Ventrella, M, 'Identifying Victims of Human Trafficking at Hotspots by Focusing on People Smuggled to Europe' (2017) 5 *Social Inclusion* 69.

Walker, N, 'In search of the Area of Freedom, Security and Justice: A Constitutional Odyssey' in N Walker (ed), *Europe's Area of Freedom, Security and Justice* (Oxford, Oxford University Press, 2004).

Weatherburn, A 'Clarifying the scope of labour exploitation in human trafficking law: Towards a legal conceptualisation of exploitation' (PhD thesis, Tilburg University, 2019).

Weyembergh, A and Brière, C, 'L'Union européenne et la traite des êtres humains' in D Bernard, Y Cartuyvels, C Guillain, D Scalia and M van de Kerchove (eds), *Fondements et objectifs des incriminations et des peines en droit européen et international* (Limal, Anthémis, 2013).

Weyembergh, A and Santamaria, V (eds), *The Evaluation of European Criminal Law: The Example of the Framework Decision on Combatting Trafficking in Human Beings* (Brussels, Editions de l'Université de Bruxelles, 2009).

Wouters, J, 'The United Nations and the European Union: Partners in Multilateralism' (2007) Working Paper No 1, Leuven Centre for Global Governance Studies.

Wouters, J and de Meester, B, *The World Trade Organisation: A Legal and Institutional Analysis* (Antwerp, Intersentia, 2010).

Commission

Commission, '2019 Communication on EU Enlargement Policy', COM (2019) 260.

—— 'A credible enlargement perspective for and enhanced EU engagement with the Western Balkans' (Communication), COM (2018) 65 final.

—— 'A European Agenda on Migration' (Communication), COM (2015) 240 final.

—— 'A Special Place for Children in EU External Action' (Communication), COM (2008) 55 final.

—— 'A Strategy on the External Dimension of the Area of Freedom, Security and Justice' (Communication), COM (2005) 491 final.

—— 'A Union of Equality: Gender Equality Strategy 2020–2025' (Communication), COM (2020) 152 final.

—— 'Adjusted Commission Work Programme 2020' (Communication), COM (2020) 440 final.

—— 'Amended proposal for a Council Decision on the conclusion, on behalf of the European Community, of the Protocol to Prevent, Suppress and Punish Trafficking in Persons', COM (2005) 503 final.

—— 'Annex to the Commission Implementing Decision concerning the adoption of the work programme for 2014 and the financing for Union actions and emergency assistance within the framework of the Asylum, Migration and Integration Fund (AMIF)', COM (2014) 5652 final.

—— 'Combating trafficking in human beings and combating the sexual exploitation of children and child pornography' (Communication), COM (2000) 854 final.

—— 'Communication on circular migration and mobility partnership between the European Union and third countries', COM (2007) 248 final.

—— 'Communication on establishing a new Partnership Framework with countries under the European Agenda on Migration', COM (2016) 385 final.

—— 'Communication on mutual recognition of final decisions in criminal matters', COM (2000) 495 final.

—— 'Communication on the application of Directive 2004/81 on the residence permit issued to third-country nationals who are victims of trafficking in human beings or who have been the subject of an action to facilitate illegal immigration, who cooperate with the competent authorities', COM (2010) 493 final and COM (2014) 635 final.

—— 'Communication on the Stabilisation and Association Process for countries of South East Europe', COM (1999) 235 final.

—— 'Communication on the State of Play of Implementation of the Priority Actions under the European Agenda on Migration', COM (2016) 85 final.

—— 'Communication on trafficking in women for the purpose of sexual exploitation', COM (1996) 567 final.

—— 'Delivering an area of freedom, security and justice for Europe's citizens, Action Plan Implementing the Stockholm Programme' (Communication), COM (2010) 171 final.

—— 'Delivering on the European Agenda on Security to fight against terrorism and pace the way towards an effective and genuine Security Union' (Communication), COM (2016) 230 final.

—— 'Eastern Partnership' (Communication), COM (2008) 823 final.

—— 'Enhancing the accession process – A credible EU perspective for the Western Balkans' (Communication), COM (2020) 57 final.

—— 'Evaluation and monitoring of the implementation of the EU Plan on best practices, standards and procedures for combating and preventing trafficking in human beings' (Communication), COM (2008) 657 final.

—— 'EU Action Plan against migrant smuggling (2015–2020)' (Communication), COM (2015) 285 final.

—— 'Enlargement Strategy and Main Challenges 2006–2007' (Communication), COM (2006) 649.

—— 'EU Enlargement Strategy', COM (2015) 611 final.

—— 'EU Strategy on victims' rights (2020–2025)' (Communication), COM (2020) 258 final.

—— Experts Group on Human Trafficking, 'Opinion No 1/2008 on the revision of the Council Framework Decision of 19 July 2002 on combating Trafficking in human beings', 17 October 2008.

—— Experts Group on Human Trafficking, 'Opinion No 4/2009 on a possible revision of Council Directive 2004/81/EC on the residence permit issued to third-country nationals who are victims of trafficking in human beings or who have been the subject of an action to facilitate illegal immigration, who cooperate with the competent authorities', 16 June 2009.

—— 'Fighting trafficking in human beings: an integrated approach and proposals for an action plan' (Communication), COM (2005) 514 final.

—— 'Guidelines for the identification of victims of trafficking in human beings, especially for consular services and border guards' (2013).

—— 'Helping national authorities to fight abused of the right to free movement: Handbook on addressing the issue of alleged marriages of convenience between EU citizens and non-EU nationals in the context of EU law on free movement of EU Citizens', COM (2014) 604 final.

—— 'Mid-Term Implementation report of the EU Strategy towards the Eradication of Trafficking in Human Beings', SWD (2014) 318 final.

—— 'Mobility partnership as a tool of the Global Approach to Migration', SEC (2009) 1240 final.

—— 'Model Status Agreement as referred to in Article 54(4) of Regulation (EU) 2016/1624' (Communication), COM(2016) 747 final.

—— 'Montenegro 2019 Report', SWD (2019) 217 final.

—— 'North Macedonia 2019 Report', SWD (2019) 218 final.

—— 'Progress Report on the Implementation of the European Agenda on Migration' (Communication), COM (2019) 481 final.

—— 'Proposal for a Council Decision authorising the Commission to approve on behalf of the Union the Global Compact for Safe, Orderly and Regular Migration in the area of immigration policy' (Communication), COM (2018) 168 final.

—— 'Proposal for a Council Decision authorising the Commission to negotiate a draft European Convention on the fight against trafficking in human beings', SEC (2004) 159 final.

—— 'Proposal for a Council Decision on the conclusion of the Agreement between the European Union and Iceland and Norway on the application of certain provisions of Council Decision 2008/615/JHA on the stepping up of cross-border cooperation, particularly in combatting terrorism and cross-border crime and Council Decision 2008/616/JHA on the implementation of Decision 2008/615/JHA on the stepping up of cross-border cooperation, particularly in combatting terrorism and cross-border crime, and the Annex thereto', COM (2009) 707.

—— 'Proposal for a Council Decision on the conclusion on behalf of the European Community of the Protocol to Prevent, Suppress and Punish Trafficking in Persons, Especially Women and Children, supplementing the United Nations Convention Against Transnational Organised Crime', COM (2003) 512 final.

—— 'Proposal for a Council Directive on the short-term residence permit issued to victims of action to facilitate illegal immigration or trafficking in human beings who cooperate with the competent authorities', COM (2002) 71 final.

—— 'Proposal for a Council Framework Decision on preventing and combating trafficking in human beings, and protecting victims, repealing Framework Decision 2002/629/JHA', COM (2009) 136 final.

—— 'Proposal for a Directive of the European Parliament and of the Council on preventing and combating trafficking in human beings, and protecting victims, repealing Framework Decision 2002/629/JHA', COM (2010) 95 final.

—— 'Proposal for a Regulation of the European Parliament and of the Council on standards for the qualification of third-country nationals or stateless persons as beneficiaries of international protection', COM (2016) 466 final.

—— 'Proposal for a Regulation of the European Parliament and of the Council on the European Union Agency for Criminal Justice Cooperation (Eurojust)', COM (2013) 535 final.

—— REFIT 'Evaluation of the EU legal framework against facilitation of unauthorised entry, transit and residence: The Facilitators Package (Directive 2002/90/EC and Framework Decision 2002/946/JHA)', SWD (2017) 117 final.

—— 'Regional cooperation in the Western Balkans: A policy priority for the European Union' (leaflet) 2005.

—— 'Report assessing the extent to which Member States have taken the necessary measures in order to comply with Directive 2011/36/EU on preventing and combating trafficking in human beings and protecting its victims in accordance with Article 23 (1), COM (2016) 722 final.

—— 'Report based on Article 10 of the Council Framework Decision of 19 July 2002 on combating trafficking in human beings', COM (2006) 187 final.

—— 'Report of the Experts Group on Trafficking in Human Beings', 22 December 2004.

—— 'Report on the implementation of the Global Approach to Migration and Mobility (2010–2012)'.

—— 'Report on the implementation of the Global Approach to Migration and Mobility 2012–2013', COM (2014) 96 final.

—— 'Report on the progress made in the fight against trafficking in human beings', Commission Report to the Council and European Parliament, COM (2016) 267 final.

—— 'Reporting on the follow-up to the EU Strategy towards the Eradication of trafficking in human beings and identifying further concrete actions' (Communication), COM (2017) 728 final.

—— 'Second activity report following the joint statement of the Heads of the EU JHA agencies, Annex to the Mid-term report on the implementation of the EU strategy towards the eradication of trafficking in human beings', SWD (2014) 318 final.

—— 'Serbia 2019 Report', SWD (2019) 219 final.

—— 'Staff Working Document accompanying the Second report on the progress made in the fight against trafficking in human beings (2018) as required under Article 20 of Directive 2011/36/EU on preventing and combating trafficking in human beings and protecting its victims', SWD (2018) 473 final.

—— 'The EU Internal Security Strategy in Action: Five steps towards a more secure Europe' (Communication), COM (2010) 673 final.

—— 'The EU rights of victims of trafficking in human beings' (2013).

—— 'The EU Security Union Strategy' (Communication), COM (2020) 605 final.

—— 'The EU Strategy towards the Eradication of Trafficking in Human Beings 2012–2016' (Communication), COM (2012) 286 final.

—— 'The European Agenda on Security' (Communication), COM (2015) 185 final.

—— 'The Global Approach to Migration and Mobility' (Communication), COM (2011) 743 final.

—— 'Towards an EU Criminal Policy: Ensuring the effective implementation of EU policies through criminal law' (Communication), COM (2011) 573 final.

—— 'Wider Europe – Neighbourhood: A new framework for relations with our Eastern and Southern Neighbours' (Communication), COM (2003) 104 final.

—— 'Work Programme 2020. A Union that strives for more' (Communication), COM (2020) 37 final.

Commission and High Representative for Foreign Affairs and Security Policy, 'A new response to a changing Neighbourhood' (Communication), COM (2011) 303 final.

—— 'A Partnership for Democracy and Shared Prosperity with the Southern Mediterranean' (Joint Communication), COM (2011) 200.

—— 'EU Action Plan for Human Rights and Democracy 2020–2024' (Joint Communication), JOIN (2020) 5 final.

—— 'Gender Equality and Women's Empowerment: Transforming the Lives of Girls and Women through EU External Relations 2016–2020' (Joint Staff Working Document), SWD (2015) 182 final.

—— 'Review of the European Neighbourhood Policy' (Joint Communication), JOIN (2015) 50 final.
Commission, Council of the EU and European Parliament, 'Joint Statement and Common Approach on decentralised agencies', 19 July 2012.

Council

Council, 'A secure Europe in a better world, European Security Strategy' (2003).
—— 'Action-Oriented Paper on Improving Cooperation on Organised Crime, Corruption, Illegal Immigration and Counter-terrorism between the EU, Western Balkans and relevant ENP countries', 12 May 2006, Council Doc No 9272/06.
—— 'Action-Oriented Paper on strengthening the EU external dimension on action against trafficking in human beings – First implementation report/update of information on Member States' external action', 31 May 2011, Council Doc No 9501/3/11.
—— 'Action-Oriented Paper on strengthening the EU external dimension on action against trafficking in human beings – Second implementation report/update of information on Member States' external action', 3 December 2012, Council Doc No 13661/3/12.
—— 'Action-Oriented Paper on strengthening the EU external dimension on action against trafficking in human beings – Towards Global EU action against THB', Council Doc No 11450/5/09.
—— 'Annual Report on Human Rights and Democracy in the World 2018', Council Doc No 9024/19.
—— Conclusions, 'A Strategy for the External Dimension of JHA: Global Freedom, Security and Justice', Council Doc No 14366/3/05.
—— 'Conclusions on readmission agreements and the consequences of the entry into force of the Amsterdam Treaty', Council Doc No 8654/99.
—— Conclusions and Annex, 'The Thessaloniki Agenda for the Western Balkans: moving towards European Integration', Council Doc No 10369/03.
—— Conclusions, 'Internal Security Strategy for the European Union: Towards a European Security Model', Council Doc No 5842/2/10.
—— 'Conclusions on Enlargement and Stabilisation and Association Process', 25 March 2020, Council Doc No 7002/20.
—— 'Conclusions on the new EU Strategy towards the Eradication of Trafficking in Human Beings 2012–2016', Council Doc No 11838/6/12.
—— 'Council conclusions on enhancing cooperation with Western Balkans partners in the field of migration and security', 5 June 2020, Council Doc No 8622/20.
—— 'Council Conclusions on EU External Action on Preventing and Countering Terrorism and Violent Extremism, 15 June 2020', Council Doc No 8868/20.
—— 'Conclusions on migrant smuggling', 10 March 2016, Council Doc No 6995/16, 2.
—— 'Enlargement and Stabilisation and Association Process – Conclusions', 15 December 2015, Council Doc No 15356/15.
—— 'EU priorities for cooperation with the Council of Europe in 2016–2017', Council Doc No 14919/15.
—— 'EU priorities for cooperation with the Council of Europe in 2018–2019', Council Doc No 5553/18.
—— 'EU priorities for cooperation with the Council of Europe in 2020–2022', Council Doc No 9283/20.
—— 'EU Priorities in UN Human Rights Fora in 2019 (Conclusions)', Council Doc No 6339/19.
—— 'Implementing the Strategy for the External Dimension of Justice and Home Affairs: Global Freedom, Security and Justice – Action-Oriented Paper on Strengthening the EU External Dimension on Action against Trafficking in Human Beings; Towards Global EU Action against Trafficking in Human Beings', Council Doc 6865/10.
—— 'Internal Security Strategy for the European Union' (2010).
—— 'Outcome of the Council meeting JHA on 13 March 2020', Council Doc No 6582/20.

—— Presidency Conclusions of 14–15 December 2006, Council Doc No 16879/1/06.
—— Presidency Conclusions – Thessaloniki, 19 and 20 June 2003, Council Doc No 11638/03.
—— 'Report on the state of implementation by Member States and EU bodies of Action-Oriented Paper on Improving Cooperation on Organised Crime, Corruption, Illegal Immigration and Counter-terrorism, between the EU, Western Balkans and relevant ENP countries', Council Doc No 15013/1/06.
—— 'Strengthening migration management capacities in the Western Balkan region' (Presidency discussion paper), 12 May 2010, Council Doc No 7896/20.
—— 'The European Union Counter-Terrorism Strategy', 30 November 2005, Council Doc No 14469/4/05.
—— 'The Hague Programme, strengthening freedom, security and justice' (2004).

European Council

European Council, Conclusions of 16–17 December 2010, EUCO 30/1/10.
—— Conclusions of 1–2 March 2012, EUCO 4/3/12.
—— Conclusions of 26–27 June 2014, EUCO 79/14.
—— EU Strategic Agenda for 2019–2024, Conclusions of 20 June 2019, EUCO 9/19.

European Union

EU, 'Brussels Declaration on Preventing and Combating Trafficking in Human Beings', 29 November 2002, Council Doc No 14981/02.
—— Statement on behalf of the EU and its Member States at the Security Council Debate on Trafficking in Persons in Conflict Situations, 21 November 2017, ID 171128_13.

Eurojust

Eurojust, *Annual Report 2018*.
—— *Implementation of the Eurojust Action Plan against THB 2012–2016*, Final evaluation report, January 2017.
—— *Strategic meeting on trafficking in human beings, Outcome report* (2015).
—— *Strategic Project on Eurojust's action against Trafficking in Human Beings – Final Report and Action Plan* (2012).

Europol

Europol, *Europol in brief* (2018).
—— *Migrant smuggling in the European Union* (2016).
—— *Serious Organised Crime Threat Assessment* (2013).
—— *Situation Report, Trafficking in human beings in the EU* (2016).
—— *Trafficking in Human Beings in the EU* (2011).

Eurostat

Eurostat, 'Trafficking in Human beings, Statistical Working Papers' (2013).
—— 'Trafficking in Human beings, Statistical Working Papers' (2014).

GRETA

GRETA, *Fourth General Report on GRETA's activities covering the period from 1 August 2013 to 30 September 2014* (2015).
—— *Report concerning the implementation of the Council of Europe Convention on Action against Trafficking in Human Beings by Bosnia–Herzegovina* (2013).
—— *Report concerning the implementation of the Council of Europe Convention on Action against Trafficking in Human Beings by Croatia* (2011).
—— *Report concerning the implementation of the Council of Europe Convention on Action against Trafficking in Human Beings by Moldova* (2011).
—— *Report concerning the implementation of the Council of Europe Convention on Action against Trafficking in Human Beings by Montenegro* (2012).
—— *Report concerning the implementation of the Council of Europe Convention on Action against Trafficking in Human Beings by Switzerland* (2015).
—— *Report concerning the implementation of the Council of Europe Convention on Action against Trafficking in Human Beings by the United Kingdom* (2012).
—— *Report on the compliance of Kosovo with the standards of the CoE Convention on Action against Trafficking in Human Beings* (2016).
—— *Second General Report on GRETA's activities covering the period from 1 August 2011 to 30 July 2012* (2012).
—— *Third General Report on GRETA's activities covering the period from 1 August 2012 to 31 July 2013* (2013).

ILO

ILO, *The Committee on the Application of Standards of the International Labour Conference: A dynamic and impact build on decades of dialogue and persuasion* (2011).
ILO (with Walk Free Foundation and IOM), *Global Estimates of Modern Slavery: Forced labour and forced marriage* (2017).

OSCE

OSCE, 2018–19 'Report of the SR/CTHB' (2019).
—— *An Agenda for Prevention: Trafficking for Labour Exploitation* (2011).
—— *From Policy to Practice: Combating Trafficking in Human Beings in the OSCE region* (2006).
—— *Handbook on the prevention of human trafficking for domestic servitude in diplomatic households* (2014); *Study on leveraging anti-money laundering regimes to combat trafficking in human beings* (2014).
—— Mission to BiH, *Trafficking in Human Beings and Responses of the Domestic Criminal Justice System, A Critical Review of Law and Emerging Practice in Bosnia and Herzegovina in Light of Core International Standards* (2009).

—— Office of the Special Representative and Coordinator for Combating Trafficking in Human Beings, *Combating Trafficking and Exploitation: Human Rights, Social Justice and the Rule of Law, 2013 Annual Report* (2013).

—— Office of the Special Representative and Coordinator for Combating Trafficking in Human Beings, *Policy and legislative recommendations towards the effective implementation of the non-punishment provision with regard to victims of trafficking* (2013).

—— Permanent Council, 'Action Plan to Combat Trafficking in Human Beings', Doc PC.DEC/557, 24 July 2003.

—— Permanent Council, 'Action Plan to Combat Trafficking in Human Beings', Decision No 557, 24 July 2003, Doc PC.DEC/557, Annex.

—— Permanent Council, 'Action Plan to Combat Trafficking in Human Beings', Decision No 557/Rev. 1, Preamble, 7 July 2005.

—— Permanent Council, Addendum to the OSCE 'Action Plan to Combat Trafficking in Human Beings', Decision No 557/Rev 1.

—— Permanent Council, Addendum to the OSCE 'Action Plan to Combat Trafficking in Human Beings: one decade later', Decision No 1107, 6 December 2013.

—— *Study on enhancing cooperation to prevent trafficking in human beings in the Mediterranean region* (2013).

—— *The Critical Role of Civil Society in Combating Trafficking in Human Beings* (2018).

United Nations

United Nations, Guiding Principles on Business and Human Rights Implementing the UN 'Protect, Respect and Remedy' Framework (2011).

UN General Assembly, *Report of the Special Rapporteur on trafficking in persons, especially women and children*, A/74/189, 18 July 2019.

Conference of the Parties to the UNTOC, *Activities of the UNODC to promote and support the implementation of the Protocol to Prevent, Suppress and Punish Trafficking in Persons, Especially Women and Children, supplementing the United Nations Convention against Transnational Organized Crime*, Report of the Secretariat, 23 July 2018, CTOC/COP/2018/2.

—— Report on the meeting of the Working Group on Trafficking in Persons held in Vienna on 14 and 15 April 2009, CTOC/COP/WG.4/2009/2, 21 April 2009.

—— Report on the meeting of the Working Group on Trafficking in Persons held in Vienna from 27 to 29 January 2010, CTOC/COP/WG.4/2010/6, 17 February 2010.

—— Report on the meeting of the Working Group on Trafficking in Persons held in Vienna from 6 to 8 November 2013, CTOC/COP/WG4/2013/5, 26 November 2013.

Security Council, 'Report of the Secretary General on trafficking in persons in armed conflict pursuant to Security Council resolution 2388' (2017), S/2018/1042.

UNODC

UNODC, *A Comprehensive Strategy to Combat Trafficking in Persons and Smuggling of Migrants* (2012).

—— 'Abuse of a position of vulnerability and other "means" within the definition of trafficking in persons', Issue Paper (2013).

—— 'Countering Trafficking in Persons in Conflict Situations', Thematic Paper (2018).

—— *Crime and its Impact on the Balkans and affected countries* (2008).

—— *Global Report on Trafficking in Persons – Europe* (2009).

—— *Global Report on Trafficking in Persons* (2014).

—— *Global Report on Trafficking in Persons* (2018).
—— *Global Report on Trafficking in Persons in the context of armed conflict* (2018).
—— *Legislative Guides For The Implementation Of The United Nations Convention Against Transnational Organized Crime And The Protocols Thereto* (2004).
—— 'The Concept of Exploitation in the Trafficking in Persons' Protocol', Issue Paper (2015).
—— *Travaux préparatoires for the Organized Crime Convention and its Protocols* (United Nations Publications, 2006).

Press Releases

'Commission launches EU Civil Society Platform against trafficking in human beings', Press release IP/13/484, 31 May 2013.
Council, 'Recommendations on Trade in human beings', Press release 10550/93 of 29–30 November 1993, Annex 2.
Europol, 'Operational centre at Europol: 30 countries team up to combat crime in the Western Balkans', Press release of 9 September 2019.

Other

ASEAN Handbook on International Legal Cooperation in Trafficking in Persons Cases (2010) (2018).
Commission on Crime Prevention and Criminal Justice, Report of the Secretary General, *International cooperation in combating transnational organised crime and corruption*, 6 March 2019, E/CN.15/2019/4.
Council of Europe, Committee of the Parties of the Council of Europe Convention on Action against Trafficking in Human Beings, Meeting Report of the 7th meeting of the Committee of the Parties (Strasbourg, 30 January 2011), THB-CP (2012) RAP7 (Strasbourg, 9 February 2012).
—— *Explanatory Report to the Convention on Action against Trafficking in Human Beings* (2005).
—— Parliamentary Assembly, 'Report for debate on Draft Council of Europe Convention on action against trafficking in human beings', 15 March 2005, Doc No 10474.
—— Support to the Prosecutors' Network in South Eastern Europe Regional PROSECO Project, Assessment of existing cooperation networks, contact points and legal frameworks for their operating, 28 May 2009, PC-TC (2009).
Council of Europe and OSCE, 18th meeting of the Coordination Group between the Council of Europe and the OSCE, Vienna, 25 October 2013, CM/Inf (2013).
European Conference on Trafficking in Women, which was held in Vienna on 10 and 11 June 1996 on the initiative of the European Commission.
Foreign Affairs Committee, *UK–Turkey relations and Turkey's regional role* (HC 2010–12, 1567).
Fundamental Rights Agency, *Severe labour exploitation: workers moving within or into the European Union* (2015).
Frontex, *Risk Analysis for 2020* (2020).
GREVIO, *Baseline Evaluation Report for Albania*, 24 November 2017, GREVIO/inf(2017)13.
Human Rights Watch, 'Hopes betrayed: Trafficking of Women and Girls to Post-Conflict Bosnia and Herzegovina for Forced Prostitution' Vol 14, No 9 (D) (2002).
ICMPD, Guidelines for the development of a Transnational Referral Mechanism for Trafficked Persons (2009).
—— *Targeting Vulnerabilities, The Impact of the Syrian War and Refugee Situation on Trafficking in Persons, A Study of Syria, Turkey, Lebanon, Jordan and Iraq* (2015).

Inter-Agency Coordination Group against Trafficking in Persons (ICAT), 'The International Legal Frameworks concerning Trafficking in Persons' (2012) ICAT Paper series – Issue 1.

IOE, *Employers' Guide to Forced Labour* (2010).

Norwegian Agency for Development, *Review of the Norwegian Ministry of Foreign Affairs Portfolio on Human Trafficking*, Norad rapport 9/2009 Discussion (2009).

OHCHR, text presented to the Economic and Social Council as an addendum to the report of the United Nations High Commissioner for Human Rights (E/2002/68/Add. 1).

—— 'Ouagadougou Action Plan to combat Trafficking in Human Beings, Especially Women and Children', as adopted by the Ministerial Conference on Migration and Development of the European Union and the African Union, Tripoli, 22–23 November 2006.

TRACE Project, 'Report in the relevant aspects of the trafficking act (geographical routes and modus operandi) and on its possible evolutions in response to law enforcement', Deliverable D2.1 (2015).

UNICEF, *Neither Safe nor Sound: Unaccompanied children on the coastline of the English Channel and the North Sea* (2016).

Vice-President Mogherini, Answer to the Parliamentary question on organ harvesting and trafficking in Egypt, E-006224/2017(ASW).

World Congress against the Sexual Exploitation of Children, Stockholm 27–31 August 1996.

INDEX

312   *Index*

Lightning Source UK Ltd.
Milton Keynes UK
UKHW020156150921
390607UK00002B/49